THE INTERNATIONAL HEYER SOCIETY ANNUAL 2021

Nonpareil #7 - #18
The Weekly Post Vol. II

EDITED BY RACHEL HYLAND

Overlord Publishing

overlordpublishing.com

Copyright Declaration

For all the Heyerites everywhere

Georgette Heyer (1902 - 1974)

ABOUT THE INTERNATIONAL HEYER SOCIETY

Unlike receiving a voucher for Almack's or an invitation to box with Gentleman Jackson, becoming a member of the International Heyer Society is easy! As the name suggests, we welcome members from all over the world, and offer an abundance of perks along with our monthly circular, *Nonpareil,* and the aptly named *Weekly Post*.

Officially launched on July 1, 2020, the Society aims to promote the works of Georgette Heyer throughout the world. Come join us!

HEYERSOCIETY.COM

CONTENTS

THE WEEKLY POST, VOL II. 100

2021 MEMBERSHIP ROLL

Belinda Aitken	Sally Dale	Joanna Henwood	Jane McCaffrey	Joan Sheedy
Peta Allen	Kirsten Davis	Heather Higgs	Tam McKenzie-Smith	Kathy Skok
Amelia Autin	Elisabeth Daszkowski	Sam Hirst	Elizabeth McKittrick	Joanne Smith
Sue Baillie	Annette Dent	Sally Houghton	Megan McMillan	Miranda Spatchurst
Josephine Bayne	Lisa Derfler	Mary Hounslow	Jacqueline	Gillian Steel
Diane Beck	Lisa DeRome	Eileen Hunter	Meintzinger	Christine Stinson
Paul Bethel	Anne Dunn	Philippa Hutton	Megan	Vanessa Stockford
Marie Biddle	Kitty Estopinal	Ruth Hyland	Brigitta Merchant	Margaret Sullivan
Laura Boon	Mary Fagan	Jennifer Jaco	Kirsten Merchant	Fleur Taylor
Lorraine Brock	Carrie Feron	Pat Jefferson	Margo Moore	Nola Thacker
Roberta Brody	Cath Garrett	Sharman Jeffries	Maryanne Moore	Nelly Theresia
Charlotte Brothers	Beryl Gale	Jane James	Margaret Morgan	Barbara Thiele
Rachel Brown	Laura George	Leonie Jennings	Cathy Nelson	Jacks Thomas
Chris Browne	Marguerite Gibson	Amanda Jones	Jacinta Okeefe	Frances Turner
Anne Burns	Donna Gilbert	Harriet Jordan	Megan Osmond	Elizabeth Webb
Anne Carpenter	Kathleen Glancy	Gabrielle Keating	Catherine Parker	Selina Walker
Mercia Chapman	Cynthia Glenney	Patricia Keith	Lynne Parrott	Kim Wilkins
Stella Clark	Alison Goodman	Julia Kelly	Charlotte Pettigrew	Ruth Williamson
Elizabeth Collins	Suzanne Gotro	Vicki Liberman	Rachel Piercey	Janice Wilson
Elizabeth Collison	Anne Gracie	Jill Livingstone	Vicky Price	Sara Wisnia
Angela Connell	Rachel Grant	Rachel Loryman	Jacob Proffitt	Malvina Yock
Geraldine Connor	Heather Gray	Christine Ludlum	Zorica Rapaich	Megan Yucel
Patricia Costello	Wendy Gray	Megan Kemmis	Samantha Rayner	Joanna Zantuck
Samuel Costello	Kerrie Gribble	Susan Mackenzie	Colleen Reed	Katherine Zimmerman
Holly Cotterell	Gillian Hanhart	Judith Magee	Collen Reid	A Lady (x 8)
Elizabeth Cowan	Anne Hurst Hardock	Rebekah Manson	Elda Ribeiro	A Gentleman (x 4)
Sarah Crowley	Sarah Harvey	Julie Mapp	Sharon Roberts	
Sonia Cruikshank	Lori Helms	Kathryn Matthews	Esther Scotton	

Patronesses: Rachel Hyland
               Jennifer Kloester
               Susannah Fullerton

INTRODUCTION

When Georgette Heyer sat down to write her inimitable novels, she first used a fountain pen, and later a typewriter. If she wished to discuss those novels with friends, or her publisher, she picked up a pen and wrote a letter. How amazed she would be, were she to know that today her novels sell as on-line copies or as recorded audio versions, that there are internet groups in her name, zoom conferences are held in which aspects of her fictional world are discussed and that an International Heyer Society exists which brings members together, via the internet, from around the world. I am honoured to be one of the Lady Patronesses of that society and to be introducing to you our second *International Heyer Society Annual*.

Throughout 2021 members of the society received fascinating newsletters, posts and articles. From animals in her novels, to the homes in which Georgette Heyer lived, from Belinda's purple dress to the extraordinary covers that have graced her books, we have been informed, entertained and delighted.

Sometimes people ask me why I join literary societies. I always respond by stressing what a huge amount I get from my membership of such groups. Talks which teach me more, a deeper appreciation of the writings of an author, intriguing knowledge about their world, and further reading suggestions. But what I especially love is that such groups make me feel wonderfully normal! I am constantly made aware, as a member of the International Heyer Society, that others share my passion for her books. We might have our different favourites, and have come to the novels in very different ways, or even in different languages, but we are united in an appreciation of a master storyteller, humour that never fails to raise a laugh, memorable characters and, of course, utterly glorious heroes and heroines. We can revisit the novels of Georgette Heyer again and again, and at different times in our lives (I have found her books especially therapeutic during the pandemic), and we can do so in good company with other members of this group.

I hope you enjoy all the fabulous reading that our editor, Rachel Hyland, has brought together in this annual, and I hope that we can all unite in future conferences and events and share our admiration for this wonderful novelist.

– Susannah Fullerton, OAM FRSN
Sydney, 2022

JOIN THE INTERNATIONAL HEYER SOCIETY AT
HEYERSOCIETY.COM

FROM THE PATRONESSES

Welcome once again to the monthly circular of the International Heyer Society!

Here we go in-depth into *Helen*, Georgette Heyer's second contemporary novel and the one considered in many quarters to be her most autobiographical. Don't miss Ruth Williamson's incisive exploration of the book's themes, or the comprehensive listing of the many notable figures from the world of arts and literature referenced throughout. And, as always, there are reviews, locations, character bios and more.

> "I don't want her to be able to pass senseless examinations, or to waste her time over subjects that won't do her a bit of good."
>
> — *Helen*, Part I, Chapter VI, I

> "Oh, loud and sustained cheers!" she said. "You're just in time for tea, Helen, and I was going to eat it dismally alone."
>
> — *Helen*, Part III, Chapter VII, VI

HELEN

THERE is a point in *Helen* in which our titular young woman is called a "reactionary" by the self-described "modern" artist, Ralph Lorne. It is in the midst of WWI, he has just been shipped home from the Front due to injury, and he speaks fervently of how the War has been a great leveller, and how the country can never return to its previous class-driven society. Helen refuses to believe it. She is "County" and, as a major beneficiary of the status quo, is incredibly resistant to see it changing.

In the very next chapter, she goes on a tirade about Woman not being the equal of Man; women, says Helen, are "unbalanced" and "hysterical." Never can they hope to achieve the dignities of men. She believes that strong women are, in short, the worst.

What is remarkable about this particular piece of out-dated thinking is just how reflective it is of the attitudes prevalent at the time. There is no doubt that Helen is an anti-suffragist (she finds a friend's interest in the movement tiresome), and let us not forget that women were not accorded the vote in the UK until 1918, around the same time this portion of the story is set. To the modern reader (especially, the modern female reader) Helen's claims are farcical, false, and utterly enraging. But to a reader at the time, they would simply have been commonplace attitudes heard everywhere, and while some disagreement persisted (in *Helen*, by women who are not as "good" as our heroine), it was often taken as fact that women were simply lesser creatures.

Fascinatingly, Georgette Heyer maintained a similar stance to her Helen (believed to be her most autobiographical creation) throughout her life, and yet she lived in a manner that was completely opposite to this avowed belief. For this insight alone, *Helen* is a must-read.

— Maura Tan

~ | ~

THE CHARACTERS

HELEN MARCHANT
Privileged, pretty, popular and quite prissy, the straight-forward Helen grows from child to woman and learns much about life, and love, all while being very much devoted to her charming, indulgent father.

JAMES "JIM" MARCHANT
Her charming, indulgent father, a landholder and avid sportsman left widowed upon Helen's birth.

KATHLEEN "KITTY" MARCHANT
Helen's deceased mother, silently mourned.

MILDRED BEAZLEY
Helen's aunt, Kitty's sister, an easily scandalized mother of three, who hopes her indolent son will marry Helen, an heiress. **HARRY BEAZLEY** Her gruff, often absent, husband.

MARION BEAZLEY
Helen's cousin, a kind and earnest girl at odds with most of her family, but very dutiful.

ROSE DANE, NÉE BEAZLEY
Marion's sister, much spoiled due to her beauty, and given to saintly airs.

THOMAS DANE
Rose's husband, who makes no appearance.

THOMAS HILARY JAMES DANE
Their infant son.

LEONARD BEAZLEY
An easily-led young man who fancies himself in love with his cousin Helen, until he meets her friend, the redoubtable Angela.

ANGELA BEAZLEY, NEE LORNE
A close friend of Helen's, whom she met while they volunteered as nurses during WWI. An artist and Bohemian, she is very clever indeed.

RALPH LORNE
A talented modern artist, he is an outspoken non-conformist who does not believe in marriage—until he falls for Helen.

JANE PILBURY
Helen's outspoken and unhappily married one-time governess, who has a great affection for her pupil. And her pupil's father.

NANNY BARTON
Kitty Marchant's old nurse who also cared for the child Helen. Fat and jolly.

CARTER
Butler at Uplands (in Collett) the Marchants' home. Stoic and stately, but very fond.

MRS SIMS
Housekeeper at Uplands.

SNOWDEN
Cheerful nurse to the infant Helen.

THEODORE JEROME
The Rector at Uplands, a learned and kindly man, and a good friend of James Marchant.

RICHARD "DICKY" CARMICHAEL
Helen's neighbour and childhood playmate who conceives a love for her when they reach adulthood. Sometimes possessive but always patient. Her "sort," according to everyone.

CHARLES SANCROFT
Another neighbour and suitor at Uplands; has known Helen from her cradle.

PEGGY MUNROE
His sister, a fellow student of Jane Pilbury's.

VICTORIA "VIC" CARMICHAEL
Dubbed "Auntie Vic," she is affectionate, understanding, and one of Helen's strongest supporters and most trusted confidantes.

FRANK CARMICHAEL
Her very nice husband.

BEATRICE JEROME
Her far more filial sister.

MAURICE VERE-CRAWLEY
A great friend of Helen's, big and blundering but clever, and the suitor she looked upon most favourably. If only he had known...

LUCILLA JEROME
His lovely wife, very fond of Helen.

CELIA JEROME
Their eldest daughter, a "modern girl" who drives trucks during the War and opens a hat shop against her parents' wishes. Most unconventional in many ways; a close friend of Helen. Until...

LADY CHILDE
His somewhat oppressive mother.

PETER CHILDE
Another local suitor of Helen's who later moves to London and becomes a very languid pleasure-seeking man about town.

BOBBIE MUNROE
Their son, another childhood friend, and later suitor, of Helen's. Much missed.

SIR BASIL MUNROE
A neighbour at Collett, friend to Marchant.

JOHN STANDISH
Another Collett local.

MRS FFOLLIOT
Mother of Elizabeth, Rhoda and Ursula, all students of Jane Pilbury alongside Helen.

GERALD FERRIER
A friend of Sir Basil's, avid hunter.

MONICA DARE
His sister, very enthusiastic about Girl Guides.

BILLY DARE
An "effeminate" young man of much sensibility, who professes to adore Helen.

MRS POMP
The charwoman for the nurse volunteers. Has opinions.

BILL JOHNSON
A friend of Richard's.

PEGGY COMYNS
Another volunteer, not always tactful.

MOLLY
The Beazleys' parlour maid.

HARRY VAUGHAN
A cigar merchant, wants to take Helen out.

EDWARD "TEDDY" HAZLITT
Another London gadabout; Helen likes him.

BARBARA "BABS" MERRIDEW
Celia's partner in her hat shop, a very modern woman who disgusts Helen enormously.

CECIL HERRINGTON
Studying for the Bar; makes Helen laugh.

CHARLES HOPE-SHAW
An acquaintance of Angela's.

BERYL COCKBURN
A social climbing fellow-volunteer alongside Helen; the unfortunate Angela's roommate.

JOAN FINCH
Another volunteer; sentimental.

IVOR COLLINS
A pacifist; persuades Leonard of his beliefs.

MRS MOORE
A friend of Mrs Jerome.

FLETCHER
A servant at Uplands.

JACKSON
A servant at Uplands.

LORD CHARLES BLANDISON
In love with Babs. Always in debt.

LUCY
The Marchants' parlour maid.

FAY CRUICKSHANK
A widow, early object of Richard's affection.

JARDINE
A stockbroker, thinks Helen standoffish.

CHARLES HOPE-SHAW
An acquaintance of Angela's.

TOM
Ralph Lorne's servant.

MAJOR HARRIS
An acquaintance of James Marchant.

"I'm a bit scared of these modern girls," said Richard. "They take my breath away."
— *Helen*, Part III, Chapter V, IV

"Don't think that life's sordid and cruel just because we're going through a sort of horrible nightmare. It'll pass."
— *Helen*, Part II, Chapter V, VI

CELEBRITY SIGHTINGS

AUSTEN, JANE
1775 - 1817. Daughter of a clergyman, who always encouraged her in her writing, her first novel, the witty and often caustic yet very romantic *Sense and Sensibility* was printed anonymously in 1811. Five more novels followed, all of them now considered classics; Jane Austen has become one of the most famous authors in the English language, celebrated throughout the world, and her early death mourned anew on each anniversary. Hundreds of adaptations have been made of her works, including film, television, theatre, radio, graphic novels and artworks. There are now also thousands of novels

and stories featuring either her characters, or Jane Austen herself.

BRONTË, ANNE, CHARLOTTE AND EMILY
1820 - 1849; 1816 - 1855; 1818 - 1848. Often known collectively as the Brontë Sisters, these three daughters of a parson went on to become renowned poets and acclaimed authors of much-loved Victorian melodrama. Charlotte's *Jane Eyre*, Emily's *Wuthering Heights* and Anne's *Tenant of Wildfell Hall* are the most famous and enduring of their works. All three died young, as did their brother Branwell, as a result of tuberculosis.

DICKENS, CHARLES

1812 - 1870. English writer, publisher, editor and social critic. Despite his lack of formal education, Dickens is one of the most famous and revered of all English-language novelists. His fifteen novels include some of the most beloved in all literature.

DRYDEN, JOHN
1631 - 1700. A poet and playwright, many of his works reflect the political tumult of his day, especially during the time of Oliver Cromwell, and the Restoration of Charles II. An astute courtier, he was adept at finding favour with those in power through his verse; in 1668 he was appointed the first Poet Laureate of England. His writings were so

plentiful and ubiquitous that the time period is often referred to by scholars as the Age of Dryden.

DÖRPFIELD, WILHELM
1753- 1940. A German archaeologist and architect, he is famed for unearthing Bronze Age sites across Europe, and especially for his efforts at the city of Troy. He was convinced that the works of Homer held geographical truths, and could prove the basis for archaeological excavation; this conviction led to several important discoveries, and influenced the field to this day.

EPSTEIN, SIR JACOB
1880 - 1959. Born in New York, he emigrated to the UK in 1902. There he found success as a sculptor, as well as controversy, as he often pushed the bounds of what was considered appropriate in public artwork, especially with his many nudes. His sculpture for Oscar Wilde's tomb in Paris was considered obscene.

GILBERT, SIR WILLIAM SCHWENK
1836 - 1911. Son of William Gilbert, a writer, he began his artistic career by illustrating his father's works, but he soon turned his attention to poetry, plays and song lyrics. Already something of a success, his career hit new heights when he teamed up with composer Arthur Sullivan, Their fourteen comic operas, including the popular *Pirates of Penzance, The Mikado*, and *H. M. S. Pinafore*, continue to be performed worldwide.

GRAHAME, KENNETH
1859 - 1932. A Scottish writer, mostly of children's fiction, who is most famous for *The Wind and the Willows*, which began as bedtime tales he told his sickly son, Alistair. Tragically, Alistair committed suicide on a railway track while only nineteen, in 1920, though the death was ruled accidental.

GREUZE, JEAN-BAPTISTE
1725 - 1805. A French portraitist and ambitious painter of historical scenes, he is renowned for his "genre painting," depicting scenes from French life. He died in great poverty due to bad management and embezzlement from his wife.

GORSKY, ALEXANDER ALEXEYEVICH
1871 - 1924. A Russian ballet choreographer, his work is notable for its relative realism and use of drama rather than excessive athleticism. He is known for having restaged classic ballets with a more modern twist, not always to acclaim.

KANT, IMMANUEL
1724 - 804. A German philosopher, and chief among Enlightenment thinkers, he pioneered "transcendental realism" and is still an influential figure in the field. His skull was larger than most people's. His dying words were "It is good."

KAUFFMAN, MARIA ANNA ANGELIKA
1741 - 1807. A Swiss historical painter and portraitist who was one of two founding female members of the Royal Academy of Art in London.

A friend of Sir Joshua Reynolds, she travelled throughout Europe painting commissions for much of her life. There is a museum in Austria dedicated to her work.

KEATS, JOHN
1795 - 1821. An English poet and leader of the Romantic school, He did not achieve great fame in life, but his legacy grew after his death, and he is even now considered one of the country's best, and is remembered chiefly for his *Odes*.

KIPLING, RUDYARD
1865 - 1936. Indian-born English writer known for his works set in Colonial-era India. He won the 1907 Nobel Prize for Literature, the first English-language and still youngest to do so. Notable works include *Kim, Gunga Din* and *Mandalay*, but he is perhaps best remembered as the author of *The Jungle Book*.

LE BRUN, ÉLIZABETH LOUISE VIGÉE
1755 - 1842. A French portraitist who made a name for herself under the patronage of Marie Antoinette, of whom she painted dozens of pictures. She fled France during the Revolution, living in Italy for the next 11 years. She painted over 800 works in her lifetime, and in her 80s she published her memoirs, in three volumes.

MEREDITH, GEORGE
11828 - 1909. English novelist and poet best remembered for his bleak work *The Egoist*. He was nominated for the Nobel Prize seven times.

PETRONIUS
27 - 66. Gaius Petronius Arbiter was a Roman courtier under Nero, and is credited with the Satyricon, a novel which broke then-literary conventions with its focus on characterization.

PLATO
C. 428 - 348 BC. An Athenian philosopher whose ideas are still prevalent in the field today, as well as in the wider community, especially his concept of non-romantic love, which we now call "platonic," after him.

ROSSETTI, CHRISTINA
1830 - 1894. An English poet, and sister to the artist, she is perhaps best remembered for her devotional and children's writing.

ROSSETTI, GABRIEL CHARLES DANTE
1828 - 1882. An English painter who frequently wrote poems to go with his works. He is well known for his historical works, many of them religious, which he painted using models who became his muses–one of whom he married.

SAVAGE, ETHEL MAY DELL
1881 - 1939. Under the name Ethel M. Dell, she was a very private writer of romance novels, and a huge best-seller in her day. Her first novel, *The Way of the Eagle*, saw thirty printings in just four years.

SCHOPENHAUER, ARTHUR

1788 - 1860. A German thinker who is considered the father of "philosophical pessimism." He promoted atheism, and incorporated Indian teachings into his work.

SCHUBERT, FRANZ PETER
1797 - 1828. An Austrian composer and pianist, he initially studied education before enrolling in a prestigious music school. In his short life he produced hundreds of works, and while then little known, he has since been recognized as one of the greats of classical music. His official cause of death was typhoid, but historians believe it may have been syphilis.

SITWELL, DAME EDITH LOUISA
1887 - 1964. A British poet who played with abstract form, she also wrote historical works and was an avid critic of... well, everything.

STOPES, MARIE CHARLOTTE CARMICHAEL
1880 - 1958. A paleobotanist by training, Stopes infamously campaigned for the right to birth control, and her book *Married Life* created a scandal with its frank depiction of sex and its advocacy for a woman's right to choose. Sadly, she was also a eugenicist, tarnishing her legacy.

THACKERAY, WILLIAM MAKEPEACE
1811 - 1863. Indian-born English author and illustrator best remembered for *Vanity Fair* and *The History of Henry Esmond*, in which he attempted to write in a 17th-century style.

VELÁZQUEZ, DIEGO RODRIGUEZ DE SILVA Y
1599 - 1660. Spanish painter in the court of Philip IV, he was a leading figure in the Spanish Golden Age. He was a major influence on the Realist, Impressionist and Cubist schools, and lived a life of comfort and acclaim, unlike many of his peers, who only found fame in death.

VIRGIL
70 - 19 BC. Publius Vergilius Maro was a Roman epic poet whose major works include the *Aenid*, which follows on from Homer's *Iliad* and recounts myths of the foundation of Rome. His style was revolutionary, and he was immediately acclaimed as the greatest Latin poet, even in his own lifetime.

WELLS, HERBERT GEORGE
1866 - 1946. An English pioneer of modern science fiction, his novels *The War of the Worlds, The Time Machine* and *The Island of Doctor Moreau* still influence the genre to this day. He was nominated for the Nobel Prize in Literature four times; his works have been adapted dozens of times; and he has been written as a character into many films and television shows. His *War of the Worlds* was famously broadcast on American radio by Orson Welles in 1938, and was so realistic that many believed aliens really were invading.

~ | ~

"Do you ever write in the impassioned night-hours?"

Her long fingers closed on the arm of the chair. "Yes, I've done that," she said. "When it's so still your thoughts seem to crowd round you, and your pen won't move fast enough to keep up with them."

— *Helen*, Part III, Chapter III, II

"I hate marriage and most other man-made rules, too. But they don't amount to a row of beans, my hatred or my beliefs [...] I hate marriage," he repeated. "I hate all Forms and Rules and Restrictions. But I believe in Love. And I love you."

— *Helen*, Part III, Chapter IV, V

~ | ~

THE LOCATIONS

COLLETT
Location estimated: close to London; "down" to the country; good hunting.
- Uplands, home of the Marchants
- The Carmichaels'
- The Rectory
- The White House, home to Maurice Vere-Crawley
- Four Ways, home to Cecil Herrington

LONDON
- The Grosvenor
- The Cecil
- V.A.D Hospital
- The Strand Corner House
- Claridge's
- Rotten Row
- Jermyn Street
- Hans Place
- Eaton Place
- Wimbledon, home of the Beazleys
- Richmond Park

SCOTLAND
Locations estimated: good hunting.
- The Marchants' hired hunting lodge
- The Munroes' hunting lodge

PARIS
MARSEILLE
GENOA
ROME
SEVILLE

WHAT A QUIZ!

Think you know your Heyer? These questions will test your knowledge...

1. In which year was *Helen* first published?
2. How does Helen's mother die?
3. Name Helen's three cousins?
4. Where do the Beazleys live?
5. Who is Helen's governess?
6. What work does Helen do during World War I?
7. How does Helen persuade her cousin Leonard, a pacifist, to enlist in the Army?
8. Who is Ralph Lorne, and what is his relationship to Helen?
9. What makes Helen realize she doesn't love Ralph?
10. Who does Helen end up marrying, and why?

ANSWERS: 1. 1928; 2. In childbirth; 3 Leonard, Marion and Rose Beazley; 4 Wimbledon; 5. Jane Pilbury; 6. Volunteer nursing; 7. She tells him she is ashamed to be seen with him; 8. A talented painter in love with Helen. 9. Discovering he had an affair with her friend Celia; 10. Her childhood friend Richard Carmichael, mainly because her father has died and she misses male companionship.

SELECTED COVER GALLERY

Longmans, UK
(1928)

Longmans, UK
(1931)

Longmans, UK
(1936)

WHAT THEY SAID

Contemporary Reviews of *Helen*

The Springfield Republican, May 11, 1928

YOUNG WOMAN OF POISE AMID PEOPLE IN A WHIRL

Helen was a 20th century girl in England and the story of her experiences is told by Georgette Heyer in *Helen*. Helen's absorbing love for her father is presented as a father complex. Her mother dying at her birth, and Helen being the only child, she grows up under her father's tutelage on their country estate. She develops along lines that relieve her from many feminine foibles. She is accustomed to thinking matters out straight from the shoulder, is alarmingly pretty and not easily side-tracked.

Helen Marchant, like her father, is not talkative. As she tells one young man, she is not a "petter." Participation in outdoor sports is the sure way to her favor. Through the stress of growing up into a very popular and likable young lady, Helen never loses her father complex.

Then along comes the war, taking most of her friends away and plunging herself into war work in London. While she runs around with a rather hilarious set in London for a time after the war, she assures her father she is not "of it," merely carrying on for the adventure. Marchant is content to let her sow her wild oats, for her trusts her good sense and honesty, and stands by to lend a hand should there be need.

The author shows this girl realizing the attraction of sex and refusing it as unsatisfactory. Companionship and friendship mean more to her than do the blandishments that pass for romance. However, there is an affair with an artist which is on the point of involving her deeply when she brings it to an end. All this time there has been one impatient young man waiting for her to realize that he is in the running. He is a neighbour with whom she has grown up and about whom she cherished no romantic feelings, but who always interested her more than anyone else and who knew how not to talk.

After Marchant's sudden death, Helen realizes the value of this disinterested friend. Running through the book is the admiration of Helen's chaperon governess for Marchant, which he never suspects, but of which Helen is aware. This situation brings about a queer friendship between the young woman and the older. One of the best bits of character sketching in the book is that of Mrs Beazley, Helen's Aunt Mildred, tiresome, conventional and constant. Apart from this, the story is rather artificial.

~ | ~

The Times Literary Supplement, May 17, 1928

This story is described somewhat misleadingly on the paper cover as the study of a girl who had a "father-complex" which for considerable time prevented her marrying. The natural affection and companionship that existed between Helen, a motherless only child, and her father did not for one moment keep away young men; nor was Helen's interest in them in the least perfunctory. She did not marry the first one that asked her, nor yet the second, but what proof is that that she differed in any way from the daughter of a widow? Indeed, her relationship with her father is treated with such coolness and care—if anything, underemotionalized—that the reader can have no psychological qualms. In due time Helen is bound to marry an exceptionally agreeable young man; all her training indicates such an end. This being his inner conviction, the reader can take his time over this leisurely tale, which takes an even course through pleasant English scenes and shows us the growth and development of a thoroughly "nice" girl, candid, athletic, and affectionate. Contrasted with Helen, who is perhaps just a trifle too worthy for deep interest, there is Miss Pilbury, a fantastically slangy and abrupt governess, whose abilities as a teacher and intellectual qualities we are obliged to take on trust, and a diverse lot of young men and maidens whose activities are sufficiently amusing to hold the attention. Marchant himself, Helen's father, is very well drawn, with quiet sincerity. The War comes, and by the time it is over and Helen's hunters are back in the stables, the field of her admirers has been notably thinned. Marchant remains, and so does Mis Pilbury—now a companion—and so does Richard Carmichael. Then Miss Heyer remembers the "father-complex" theme, and ruthlessly sacrifices a normal and unselfish parent. Marchant is given a day and a half of pneumonia; enters Richard the consoler. The argument that while her father lived he would have satisfied Helen completely and prevented her marriage fails to carry conviction; otherwise this is a story which contains some good work.

~ | ~

The New York Times Book Review, May 27, 1928

The theme of this novel might be pounced upon eagerly by a psychologist of the Freudian school; yet the author shows little sign of being influenced by the doctrines of Freud. The theme is that of a father and daughter who become bound together with so close an attachment that the girl comes to regard her parent as all-in-all and appears incapable of adopting a normal attitude toward her various suitors. From childhood she has been her father's companion; and her devotion to him, arising in part from the fact that each had only the other to care for, is accentuated and fortified by their similarity of character and of inherent interests. Neither she nor her father seems to perceive the possible harm of their relationship; but the result is that, although she grows up to charming and vivacious womanhood, she still esteems her father almost to the exclusion of other men. She does enjoy masculine companionship, it is true, and on one occasion does find herself on the point of yielding to passion; but, on the whole, she regards her male friends as good pals rather than as possible lovers, and they find it impossible to batter down the barriers she has erected. Only after the death of her father, when she finds herself suddenly desolate, does she yield to the call of her more normal impulses and cry welcome to the advances of the man who has been waiting for her for years. There are excellent possibilities, obviously, in this theme of a paternal complex; and some, but not all, of those possibilities have been utilised by Miss Heyer. She makes an arresting beginning and has depicted the childhood of her heroine interestingly and well; but, having reached midchannel, she does not progress with equal effectiveness, but conducts the reader with about the average degree of success through the mazes of her protagonist's social life. Here one will find stretches of the trivial and the tedious, though no more than in three novels out of every four; but one reads on in the hope that the author will yet redeem herself. This hope, however, is disappointed by a cheap and easy device: instead of travelling to the end of the path she was following and showing the logical effect of the paternal attachment upon the girl's life, the author summons in the pneumonia germ to assist her at a crucial moment; and, having thus removed the father with bacterial aid, it is able to proceed without the embarrassment of the situation which gives the book its sole reason for being. And thus she is able to reach an end not unlike that of the average romantic novel.

HELEN: DADDY'S GIRL BY RUTH WILLIAMSON

GEORGETTE HEYER condemned all four of her contemporary novels, including *Helen*. 'They aren't thrillers and they stink, and I want them to be buried in decent oblivion', she wrote.[i] Why did she wish them to vanish without trace? Does *Helen* have redeeming features, or does it lack the hallmarks of Heyer's successful work?

James Marchant is the first character to appear and he shares some traits with Heyeroes. He is reserved in the face of personal tragedy, and regards his sister-in-law Mildred with the kind of wry indifference Lord Rule applies to Horry's sisters. Marchant takes a close interest in the upbringing and education of his only child, Helen. She, like many a Heyer heroine (Hero Wantage, Pen Creed, Judith Taverner, Serena Carlow), grows up without a mother. The influence of her father, a powerful figure not unlike Justin Alastair, is paramount. So far, so good.

Marchant affronts Mildred by announcing he will 'keep' Helen, as 'an experiment'. He arranges her education as he wishes, not according to the rules of 'flinty-eyed ramrods' because he does not wish Helen's head to be filled with subjects that won't 'do her a bit of good'. He makes provocative quips, such as when he claims that 'the whole point of our language is that it has no grammar'. Heyer probably heard many such witticisms from her own charming, amusing father.

Helen's young mind is moulded just as Marchant intends: she shows little outward emotion, attaches scant importance to family connections, but does worship her father. Dislike is mutual between Helen and Aunt Mildred, a woman who makes respectability her by-rule.

As Helen grows into a good-looking young lady, she attracts a circle of local admirers to her country home, Uplands, including the 'boy next door', Richard Carmichael. Richard was a name Heyer liked; characters favoured with it play major roles in her novels. This incarnation is a good looking, athletic young man, but Helen rejects his advances. Will anyone match up to Daddy?

Just as World War I breaks out, Helen begins to mature. Georgette also grew up in this period, and was familiar with the slow build-up of the nightmare, when early predictions of a three-month campaign gave way to the reality of a prolonged conflict. One by one Helen's admirers leave for military duty, but she appears unperturbed, until her father decides to 'do his bit' through military service. He explains he must be involved, rather than a mere spectator. Heyer would have understood this response to the call to arms: her father volunteered for military service in France during the Great War.

Outwardly Helen bears the parting stoically, burying her sorrow inside. She elects to join the VAD (Voluntary Aid Detachment), undertaking nursing care. But when her cousin Leonard Beazley 'fails' to join up, Helen applies some remarkable psychology. She convinces him to abandon pacifism and rush to the recruitment office. This is no minor commitment because Leonard's enlistment could prove fatal. Yet Helen shows no compunction; instead, she reflects that the army will do him a great deal of good. Even Sophy made sure not to kill before taking aim. Helen has a substantial sense of entitlement.

During her war service in London, her social life is occupied by a new set of friends. They debate traditional conventions versus rising ideas, but Helen is not one to adopt radical values, including feminism. Helen dislikes women 'who suffer from a magnified sense of their own importance' and extols the way a man in authority 'conducts himself like an ordinary human being' unlike women who have 'an essential irrationalism'. Helen's opinions are reactionary, but consistent with Heyer's views about electoral emancipation and suffragettes. She consistently rejected them.

Like Heyer, Helen is unrepentant: 'You don't really think that if [woman] were Man's equal instead of his complement she'd have remained in the background? No, no... woman is all right in her own sphere, and quite as good in it, I agree, as man is in his. But don't mix them up. You'd scoff loudly if I drew a picture of Man giving the cook her orders for the day.' She expresses Heyer's personal views at length.

Helen's immediate success as a novelist is identical to Heyer's [ii]. Both publish at first attempt, and back the conservative ideas of the 'landed proprietor'. When she wrote this novel, Heyer was the family breadwinner and soon to be a working mother, but she advocated traditional roles, which suit her historical novels. While Helen inhabits the early 20th century, her attitudes reflect the past.

Other elements used in Heyer's Regency novels appear in contemporary form. One character, Babs Merridew, leads the latest fashion trends and has a monkey as a trophy pet. Cue Sophy Stanton-Lacy. Both *Helen* and *The Grand Sophy* treat Jewish elements in a manner sure to raise eyebrows. In *Helen*, there is a 'wealthy young cigar merchant of Jewish origin' of whom a friend says, 'I'll swear he was born Isaacs [...] Brooded a lot over your refusal to lunch with him', to which Helen replies she has refused five times, yet he still persists, while 'oozing wealth and being amorous'. This reflects a disquieting, but common contemporary outlook.

Other arcane attitudes may provoke a snort from today's reader. Back at Uplands, the Rector claims 'if the young man of today is effete or lax, I lay it at woman's door.' How convenient. In *Helen*, discussions about social and personal values are frequent, but are rarely talked about in Heyer's Regency novels.

Fortunately, Helen's challenges as a writer, including problems like distractions and blocks, remain current. One day, she produces only 'half a dozen disjointed sentences to her credit, and a great deal of uncomfortable speculation.' Later, she speaks of having just cleared 'a very beast of a fence' in her writing, just as Heyer might have described resolving similar problems.

Does *Helen* display the humour of Heyer's Regency fiction? The focus is on a serious heroine's maturing process, rather than the entertainment value of characters, so humour is relegated to the background. There is occasional comic relief when Helen meets Billy and Monica Dare, who hold their own against amusing characters in other Heyer novels. Think of Claud Darracott as an heir to Billy Dare, or Monica reincarnated as hearty Miss Plymstock in *Cotillion*. Many of *Helen*'s witty asides and minor characters are vintage Heyer.

What might Helen, still Daddy's Girl, lack as a professional novelist? It is strong, steady Richard Carmichael who insists that she have 'some scheme' for her writing, but while she is creative, she cannot produce one. In Heyer's case, it took Ronald Rougier, her husband, to apply his legally trained mind to the task of coming up with whodunit twists for her detective novels.

Just as Heyer did, Helen faces a devastating loss. The fictional heroine takes longer to acquire a husband after bereavement than did her creator, but the outcome is the same. In this novel, Heyer presents a range of male/female relationships, but Helen chooses what has always been in front of her. Those preferences are conservative and as such, may either irritate or engage readers.

Its conclusion is positive. Helen resumes writing after her personal loss. She works through what she could not finish before. Her relish for writing returns: 'a different pleasure she had in it now…but…there still was pleasure in her work.'

She, like Heyer, persists with a writing career. Helen may not be a great contemporary novel, but some elements are successful. Because they supply rare insights into the author and her craft, *Helen* deserves attention

— *Ruth Williamson*

[i] J Kloester, *Georgette Heyer: Biography of a Bestseller*, UK: Random House, 2011, p.106
[ii] J Kloester, op cit, page 134-135.

NONPAREIL

International Heyer Society Circular #8, February 2021

FROM THE PATRONESSES

Welcome once again to the monthly circular of the International Heyer Society!

Here we go in-depth into *The Masqueraders*, Heyer's second Georgian romp in a row involving secret identities and cross-dressing, not to mention romance. Indeed, *two* romances. Don't miss Rachel Hyland's adoration of the novel's (main) heroine, or the comprehensive listing of the many notables referenced throughout. And, as always, there are reviews, locations, character bios and more.

~ | ~

Robin folded pious hands. "'I believe my sense of propriety is offended'," he quoted maliciously.

The shot glanced off her armour. "You've none, child, rest assured." — *The Masqueraders*, Chapter III

"I have never met the man who had vision large enough to appreciate my genius," he said simply. "Perhaps it was not to be expected." — *The Masqueraders*, Chapter XIX

~ | ~

THE MASQUERADERS

I WELL remember my confusion upon my first reading of this novel. I was all of fourteen, and subtext was not yet something I always understood. (Not that it always is now.) So when, in the first chapter, Miss Kate Merriot bemoaned her role in a "lost cause" and spoke of "the Butcher" (a quick Google gave me some clue as to what that was all about), I didn't get it. What had Miss Merriot possibly done in that rebellion? Why did she seem so much more upset about its failure than her brother, who must surely have been the one to take part? I did not understand what was happening there, and as I read on, became only more confused. Why did Peter grimace at Kate becoming friendly with Letty Grayson, and holding her hand? Why did he suggest that his sister might be "jealous" of Sir Anthony Fanshawe's impressive inches?

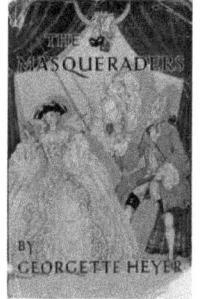

WHY?

Of course, it doesn't take very long for Georgette Heyer to establish that Miss Merriot is, in fact, Master Robin, and that Mr. Merriot is Mistress Prudence, and at last, all became clear. Or, at least, clearer. I remember speaking aloud a long "Ahhhh!" when I belatedly figured out what was going on, and I remember stopping reading and clutching the book to my chest in a hug, I was just so happy about the turn the story had taken. To this day, every time I reread *The Masqueraders* I have the same feeling; a feeling mingling pride and pleasure and awe. Every. Time. Of this book, Georgette Heyer once wrote, in a letter to her agent, that she wanted to change "all the awful inversions" in it, and just the thought of that makes my insides hurt. *The Masqueraders* is perfect exactly as it is. Even more so when you understand subtext. (Kind of.)

— *Clara Shipman*

THE CHARACTERS

PRUDENCE TREMAINE, AKA PETER MERRIOT
Clever, accomplished and eminently sensible, her life as an adventuress has prepared her well for infiltrating London society dressed as a man. But when she meets Sir Anthony Fanshawe, she comes to regret her disguise...

ROBIN TREMAINE, AKA ROBIN LACEY, KATE MERRIOT; L'ICONNU
Utterly captivating, whether in skirts or in pants, the daring, mischievous Robin fears nothing except losing the heart of Letty Grayson, and perhaps the hangman's noose.

ROBERT TREMAINE, VISCOUNT BARHAM, AKA THE OLD GENTLEMAN; MR. COLNEY; MR DAUGHTREY; PRINCE VANILOV; MR CHALLONER
A magnificent conman of grandiose aspect, his supreme egoism is matched only by his superior intellect. Father to Prudence and Robin, even they can't tell when he is telling the truth and when he is running a scam.

MARIA TREMAINE, NÉE BANSTEAD
A beautiful farmer's daughter who eloped with Robert Tremaine in his youth; mother to Prudence and Robin.

DOROTHEA TREMAINE
Late sister of Robert Tremaine.

JOHANNA TREMAINE
Robert Tremaine's late aunt.

SUSANNA TREMAINE
Another late aunt of Robert Tremaine's.

JOHN BURTON
A trusted servant of the Tremaines, he is devoted to them and enters into many of their escapades, though not always with approval.

SAMUEL BURTON
His brother, lodgekeeper at the estate of Lord Barham.

MRS MAGGIE STAINES, NÉE BURTON
Their sister.

RENSLEY
Claimant to the title of Viscount Barham, as the supposed nearest male relative. Known for shady dealings, especially at cards.

THÉRÈSE, LADY LOWESTOFT, NÉE DE BRUTON
An old and dear friend of the Tremaines, a Frenchwoman they met on the Continent, before she settled down to respectability in England.

SIR ROGER LOWESTOFT
Her wealthy, deceased, husband.

SIR ANTHONY FANSHAWE
Deceptively slow-witted, his large person and sleepy demeanour hide a cunning wit and unequalled perception. Begins to question whether things are as they seem as he starts to find his new protege Peter Merriot very intriguing indeed. Handy with a sword.

LETITIA "LETTY" GRAYSON
Spoiled and spirited, in love with the idea of romance, the teenage heiress is at the mercy of fortune hunters until her new best friend Kate Merriot leads her into the arms of the mysterious *L'Iconnu...*

SIR HUMPHREY GRAYSON
Her (mostly) indulgent father.

CORDELIA GRAYSON
An elderly relative who acts as her chaperone.

BEATRICE, LADY ENDERBY, NEE FANSHAWE
Sir Anthony's unconventional sister, large and indolent.

SIR THOMAS ENDERBY
Her husband, thin as a rake, fond of roses.

GREGORY MARKHAM
A fortune hunter determined to wed Letty Grayson, despite her every objection. A friend of Rensley's, but only due to his newly-inherited wealth. Rensley's second.

THE HONOURABLE CHARLES BELFORT
A kind-hearted young man who quickly befriends Peter Merriot, and is seemingly on good terms with everyone in town. Loves to play dice; never wins. Peter's second in his proposed duel against Rensley.

DEVEREAUX
Takes a drunken liking to Peter; acts as his other second against Rensley.

JESSUP
Acts as Rensley's second in his duel with Peter.**MR. LORD KESTREL**
Rensley's second in his duel with Sir Anthony, a gossip.

SIR RAYMOND ORTON
Rensley's other second against Sir Anthony.

TROUBRIDGE
Sir Anthony's second in his duel with Rensley.

MOLYNEUX
Sir Anthony's other second.

FARADAY
Tells Sir Anthony about Rensley's fencing lesson, in preparation for his duel with Peter.

DENDY
An acquaintance of Peter Merriot's.

THOMAS, LORD CLEVEDALE
An old friend of Robert Tremaine.

FONTENOY
Another old friend of Robert Tremaine, unconvinced he has returned.

LADY ELTON
Holds a rout party.

LADY DORLING
Gives a masked ball at which Letty Grayson meets her mysterious swain L'Iconnu. It is Lady Dorling who makes the introduction.

SIR FRANCIS JOLLYOT
Invites Peter to play piquet at Lady Lowestoft's rout, sure that he can take advantage of his youth. This does not work out for Jollyot at all.

GIROLAMO GALLIANO
A renowned fencing master of Italian extraction.

TINO
His servant.

MR CLAPPERLY
A retired lawyer who previously dealt with the estate of the Viscount Barham.

MR CLAPPERLY, THE YOUNGER
His son, now having joined the firm.

MR BRENT
He is called upon to decide on the identity of Robert Tremaine, Viscount Barham, as representative of Clapperly and Brent, the family's lawyers.

FAWLEY
His clerk.

MATTHEW
One of the officers sent to arrest Peter Merriot for the murder of Gregory Markham.

HENRY
Servant to Robert Tremaine.

LAWTON
Captain of the Pride o' Rye. Probably a smuggler.

GASTON
France-based servant of Robert Tremaine.

MARTHE
French maid of Lady Lowestoft; a colossus.

STEPHEN
Servant to Lady Lowestoft, at Richmond.

POMPEY
Lady Lowestoft's page.

TOM
Works at an inn near Norman Cross.

POLLY
Trim maid at the inn near Norman Cross.

~ | ~

CELEBRITY SIGHTINGS

DE SAXE, MAURICE, COUNT OF SAXONY
1696 – 1750. Illegitimate son of Polish King Augustus II, he became famed as a soldier, initially serving the Holy Roman Empire before entering French service, where he attained the rank of Marshal General of France. His most famous descendent is Amandine Dupin, better known by her pseudonym, George Sand.

CHARLES "III" OF ENGLAND
1720 – 1788. Charles Edward Louis John Casimir Sylvester Severino Maria Stuart was the great-grandson of James II and claimant to the throne of England. Also known as "the Young Pretender" and "Bonnie Prince Charlie," his various rebellions all failed and he died in exile.

COVENTRY, MARIA, COUNTESS OF

COVENTRY (NÉE GUNNING)
1732 - 1760. Sister to Elizabeth, the beautiful Maria Gunning wed the Earl of Coventry in 1752. It was not a happy marriage, with the Earl taking up a mistress in the form of courtesan Kitty Fisher, much to Maria's distress. Maria, then already mother of three, died of lead poisoning (caused by makeup) at the age of 27. She was known as a "victim of cosmetics."

DOUGLAS, CATHERINE "KITTY," DUCHESS OF QUEENSBURY
1701 – 1777. Wife to the 3rd Duke, the couple had two sons, both of whom predeceased them. She was Queen Anne's Lady of the Bedchamber, but was banned from Court by George II for being too "forward" when asking for help for a dramatist

under her wing. She was a patron of the arts known for her balls and masquerades, as well as her personal style and beauty. In her later years she was notable for retaining the fashion of her youth, as well as for often wearing an apron, unusual in a noblewoman.

DOUGLAS, WILLIAM, 4TH DUKE OF QUEENSBURY, AKA LORD MARCH *
1724 - 1810. Cousin to the 3rd Duke, he had previously inherited the Earldoms of March and Ruglen from his parents. March, later fondly known as "Old Q", was famous for his love of gaming and was a great favourite of the Prince of Wales (George IV). He never married but had a daughter, Maria, who wed the Marquess of Hertford in 1798. and was the Duke's principal heir.

HAMILTON, ELIZABETH CAMPBELL, DUCHESS OF ARGYLL AND 1ST BARONESS HAMILTON OF HAMELDON (NÉE GUNNING)

1733 - 1790. An Irish beauty of no fortune, she and her sister Maria took London by storm in 1750. She wed the Duke of Hamilton on Valentine's Day, 1752, in a secret wedding only the month after they first met. The couple had three children. Upon widowhood she wed the Marquis of Lorne (later Duke of Argyll), with whom she had a further five children. Created a Baroness in her own right in 1776.

MURRAY, LORD GEORGE

1694 - 1760. Sixth son of the Scottish Duke of Atholl, Lord George fought for Charles Stuart in the rebellions of 1715 and 1719. Pardoned in 1725, he swore allegiance to George II, but rescinded this when he again fought for Charles in the fateful 1745 campaign. He escaped Culloden with his life in 1746, and lived in exile until his death. His son became the 3rd Duke of Atholl.

MURRAY, SIR JOHN OF BROUGHTON, 7TH BARONET OF STANHOPE

1715 - 1777. Staunch supporter of the Jacobite cause, upon his capture he revealed other co-conspirators, leading to several executions. Branded a traitor, he was in fact a true believer, and only gave the names of those who had failed to support the '45 Rising, despite their promises. He remained a friend of "Charles III."

SELWYN, GEORGE AUGUSTUS

1719 - 1791. Wit, politician, and great friend of Horace Walpole, with whom he shared a frequent correspondence. Despite his reputed intellect, he spent 44 years in the House of Commons without making a speech. An avid member of the Hellfire Club, he had a keen interest in the macabre and loved executions.

STUART, JOHN, 3RD EARL OF BUTE

1713 - 1793. Lawyer, Scottish nobleman and statesman, he was a close friend of Frederick, Prince of Wales and acted as tutor to his son, later George III. Bute's parliamentary career was chequered, but eventually he attained the office of Prime Minister in 1762, the first Scot and the first Tory to do so. He oversaw the Treaty of Paris, ending the Seven Years War, but his policy of heavy taxation led to the American Revolution. He resigned after only a year in office, following a falling out with George III. The two were never reconciled.

WALPOLE, HORACE

1717 - 1797. Noted wit, gamester, epistolarian and author of The Castle of Otranto, generally regarded as the first Gothic novel. Youngest son of the first British Prime Minister, the 1st Earl, he succeeded to the title in 1791, upon the death of his nephew. His house at Twickenham, Strawberry Hill House, was an early example of Gothic revival architecture and kickstarted a trend that lasted over a century But it is his Letters – he wrote thousands, many of which have been preserved – that remain his lasting legacy, as they form the basis of much of the sociological history that now exists of the time

WILLIAM AUGUSTUS, PRINCE, DUKE OF CUMBERLAND

1721 - 1765. Youngest son of George II, he quelled the Jacobite rebellion in 1745, in which Charles Edward Stuart attempted to reclaim the throne. Cumberland ordered his troops to give "no quarter", personally oversaw the murder of the wounded, and then set upon a campaign of ruthless extermination of all suspected Jacobite sympathizers, including women and children. He was then gifted with the monikers His later military career was unsuccessful, but he retained much political influence, especially early in the reign of his nephew, George III. Several counties and landmarks in the US are named after him, but in 2005 he was selected by History Magazine as the 18th century's "Worst Briton" (for which title there is fierce competition), due to his lasting reputation as the "Butcher of Culloden."

WILLIAMS, GEORGE JAMES "GILLY"

1719 - 1805. Wit, epistolarian, friend to Horace Walpole, and Receiver-General of Excise for more than twenty-five years.

---

* NOTE: * Here, with the specific inclusion of Lord March, Heyer made a rare mistake. Lord March was a distant cousin of the Douglas family who inherited the Dukedom due to the untimely death of both of the 3rd Duke's sons – the eldest son of the house was given the courtesy title Earl of Drumlanrig, and both received it. Neither Henry Douglas (1722 - 1754) nor Charles Douglas (1726–1756) are especially remembered by history, unlike Lord March, which is doubtless how the error occurred, but at the time this novel was set, in 1746, both of the Queensberry heirs were still alive, though neither appear in the story, even at their mother's own ball; and a reference to Lord March as the Duchess's "son," as seen in Chapter 10, is patently incorrect.

~ | ~

"Oh, cursed bad news, my boy. That old aunt of his from whom he has expectations has rallied, and they say she'll last another ten years. Poor old Devereux, y'know! Must try and raise his spirits."

— *The Masqueraders*, Chapter XIII

"I have made up my mind that my son must inherit an Earldom at the least. I shall once more contrive. Do not doubt that I shall contrive! I am a great man, Thérèse: I realise it at last. I am a very great man."

— *The Masqueraders*, Chapter XXXII

~ | ~

THE LOCATIONS

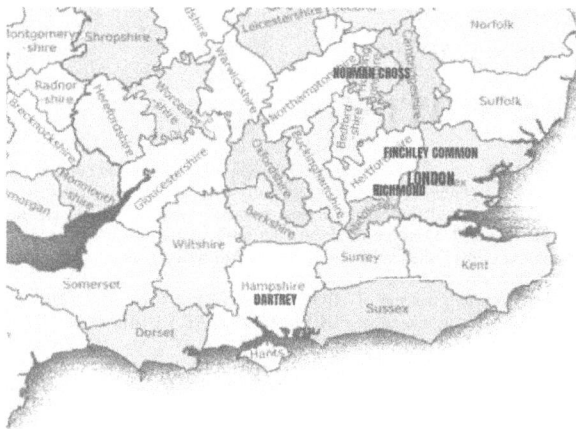

LONDON
- Arlington Street, home to Lady Lowestoft
- Clarges Street, home to Sir Anthony Fanshawe
- Half-Moon Street, temporary home to Robert Tremaine
- Grosvenor Square, home to Viscount Barham
- White's
- Signor Galliano's, in the Haymarket
- Kensington Gardens
- Vauxhall Gardens

NORMAN CROSS
In Huntingdonshire, north of London

FINCHLEY COMMON
In Middlesex, north of London

DARTREY
In Hampshire, home to Sir Thomas and Lady Enderby

BARHAM COURT
Location unknown

WHAT THEY SAID

Contemporary Reviews of *The Masqueraders*

The Spectator, September 1, 1928

In *The Masqueraders* we find a certain confusion of sex; but a gay and superficial confusion arranged as a disguise. A sister takes her brother's sword, and the brother uses her fan. The time is the eighteenth century, just after the '45, and the masqueraders are the children of an adventurous father who has been implicated in the rising. They are charming young people; and the elegant life of the period sets them off very prettily, though sometimes embarrassingly. The figures point appearance in monstrous fine clothes like those in Aubrey Beardsley's illustrations to The Rape of the Lock. What with elopements, rescues, duels, and cards, the story goes excitingly; and finally the magnificent and dubious father proves himself a Viscount. It is a picturesque and engaging story.

~ | ~

The Times Literary Supplement, September 20, 1928

The scene of this amusing story is London in 1746. Its amusing quality is due to "the old gentleman," as his son and daughter always call him. Tremaine, by birth an aristocrat, was by nature a clever, shifty, restless, boastful vagabond, a Cyrano de Bergerac grown elderly. Having made a runaway match with a farmer's daughter, wandered far, kept gaming-houses, and served in various armies, including the Pretender's in 1745, he found it convenient to hide his history while claiming his viscountcy, inherited at the death of his brother. So we find his madcap son Robin disguised as Kate and his staid daughter Prudence disguised as Peter carrying out the circuitous plans of their bewildering father, and slipping into embarrassing love-affairs of their own. There is much club life, dancing, duelling, and one rascal killed; for in novels miraculous swordsmanship always belongs to the virtuous party. The author works ingeniously up to her curtain, with the two young "masqueraders" restored to orthodox clothes and happily wedded, and the old gentleman planning to become at least an earl.

~ | ~

The New Statesman, September 29, 1928

If you admit the truth to yourself about your reading, you will confess that stories like *Graustark, The Three Musketeers, If I Were King* and *Alice in Wonderland* have stayed with you longer than any problem novel that was ever written. When you are sitting by yourself thinking over all the stories you like best, those four really ought to stand out. Not one of them points to a moral—except perhaps on the subject of courage; not one of them has the underlying purpose of righting wrongs existing in the world. They appeal to your imagination rather than your reason; to your fun loving, adventurous side rather than to your sedate, conventional self. And they are a secret source of constant satisfaction to you whenever you need the companionship of characters who are lively and brave and vivid.

With such a preamble, you will certainly read *The Masqueraders*, by Georgette Heyer, published by Longmans Green and Company. And that is exactly what we are trying to convince you to do. Miss Heyer's story is a romance of the eighteenth century. The Merriots, brother and sister, are implicated in the Stewart [sic] rebellion, and masquerade as each other. And though they were in the shadow of Tyburn tree, they enjoyed it enough. After all, what was danger to the Merriots. They were the children of "the old gentleman" who had so many disguises that, when he at last decided to be himself, none either recognised him or believed him.

There are no Dr. Jekylls or Mr. Hydes in the many masquerades which appear on the pages of *The Masqueraders*. No evil influences the destinies of these young people. They fall in love, get into one scrape after another, voluntarily, and get out of them all gracefully. The love affairs are happy ones, without sordidness or problem, and if those latter characteristics are absent from all but fairy stories, we are willing to admit that *The Masqueraders* is a fairy story. The style is deft and witty, and the characters are bubbling over with life and ideas. We particularly like the ideas!

Political intrigue, the story of the Stuarts, and the danger of those days form the background for the story, but are not discussed with any longwindedness. In fact the story moves too rapidly for one to grow bored at any moment.

We particularly recommend *The Masqueraders* to you. It is now the intellectual nor informatory, but we guarantee you a lively two hours. The book is selling very well, although it has just been published this month. Miss Heyer is blessed with a happy faculty of popping surprises at you from the pages of her novel, and of not allowing you to grow sleepy at any time. She has not picked types for her characters. They're just people with a good sense of humour and in agility in getting out of troubles. Read the book, and pass it on to the next fellow. You will be glad to have read it and so will he.

~ | ~

WHAT A QUIZ!

Think you know your Heyer? These questions will test your knowledge...

1. In which year was *The Masqueraders* first published?
2. What threat is Robin hoping to escape with his female disguise?
3. Where is Lady Lowestoft from?
4. Where does she live now?
5. Who forces a duel on Prudence, as Peter Merriot?
6. Who does Robin kill?
7. Name two of the old gentleman's aliases?
8. How does Sir Anthony let Prudence know he has seen through her disguise?
9. What is the name of his sister?
10. In what guise does Robin woo Letty Grayson?

ANSWERS: 1. 1928; 2. Being hanged as a traitor; 3. France; 4. In London and Richmond; 5. Rensley; 6. Gregory Markham; 7. Mr Colney, Mr Daughtrey, Prince Vanilov, Mr Challoner, Robert Tremaine, Viscount Barham; 8. He catches her arm when she is hiding wine; 9. Beatrice; 10. As L'Iconnu (the Unknown).

~ | ~

"I'll see the colour of your money, my lord."

My lord folded the paper. He was still smiling. "It would disappoint you, my friend. It is just the same colour as everyone else's."

— *The Masqueraders*, Chapter XX

"Have you limitations, my lord?" asked Sir Anthony.

My lord looked at him seriously. "I do not know," he said, with a revealing simplicity. "I have never yet discovered them."

— *The Masqueraders*, Chapter XXIII

~ | ~

"But where is my son? Where is the beautiful Miss Merriot?"

— *The Masqueraders*, Chapter XIV

"Not twice in five hundred years is my like seen."

"The world has still something to be thankful for."

— *The Masqueraders*, Chapter XI

SELECTED COVER GALLERY

Heinemann, UK
(1928)

Heinemann, UK
(1955)

Pan, UK1
(1960)

Dutton, US
(1967)

Pan, UK
(1968)

Mandarin, US
(1986)

Pan, UK
(1973)

Fawcett, US
(1976)

Pan, UK
(1981)

Amereon, US
(1983)

Arrow, UK
(1991)

Harlequin, Canada
(2004)

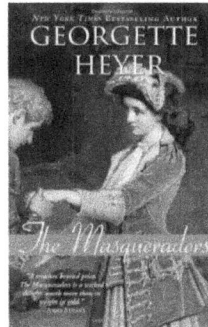

Sourcebooks, US
(2009)

CreateSpace, US
(2012)

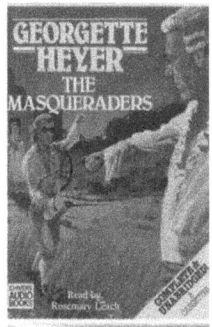

Chivers Audio, UK
(1989)

SELECTED TRANSLATED EDITIONS

GERMAN: Rowohlt
(1974)

POLISH: Da Capo
(1995)

GERMAN: Dtv
(1999)

ITALIAN: Mondadori
(2005)

JAPAN: ハーレクイン
(2012)

PRUDENCE TREMAINE: ROLE MODEL BY RACHEL HYLAND

THERE are many Heyer heroines whom I love and admire. From the crusading Arabella Tallant to the amusing Sarah Thane; from the determined Frederica Merriville to the delightful Venetia Lanyon; from the innocent Kitty Charing to the independent Ancilla Trent; these are women of spirit, intelligence, wit and charm (though not always all four of those things, and certainly not always in that order) who enliven their narratives as fully-realized human beings with flaws and foibles, yes, but also with great courage, and kindness, and even cunning.

But no Heyer heroine, to my mind, embodies the essence of what it is to be a "Heyeroine" so convincingly, so enchantingly, and so compellingly as does the reluctant confidence woman that is Prudence Tremaine of *The Masqueraders*.

Let us take a look at what we know of our Prudence's young life pre-book.

Eldest child of the endlessly inventive "old gentleman," she and her younger brother Robin lost their mother when they were still children. Taken throughout Europe by their father as he assumed personas from royal to rebellious, she became the caretaker of the family, the steady centre when all about them was chaos, all while uncomplainingly taking on prescribed personas of her own. It is clear that Prudence was never completely sold on the adventuring life, and there must have been times when she despaired of its uncertainty, but still she took it all in her stride, no matter what was asked of her, as shown in this passage from Chapter III:

> "The truth was she was too well used to a precarious position to be easily disturbed, and certainly too used to an exchange of personality with Robin to boggle over her present situation. She had faith in her own wits; these failing her she had a rueful dependence on the ingenuity of her sire."

That early mention of frequent "exchange[s] of personality" with Robin tells us much. We learn that this is far from the first time Prudence has been called upon to don a man's garb, and guise, and she has clearly proven herself adept in the role. She remembers a gaming house with dubious clientele in which her safety depended on her pretending to be a boy with a "dice box in one pocket, and a pistol in the other", and for all that she laments that it was hardly "proper training for a girl just coming out of her teens!", she is philosophical about it, and even seems grateful for all that she learned throughout her peripatetic, impersonation-filled life.

It is clear that, despite her own inclination towards the more conventional, she has always done all she could to ensure that her slippery parent's schemes succeeded, even down to giving up her skirts and apparent femininity whenever the situation called for it. But Prudence's role model status lies in more than just her ability to take on different personas and to cross-dress at will. Even Pen Creed managed that, after all. It is the reason she does so here that is so appealing: to ensure the life of her swashbuckling brother, after his part in the ill-fated rebellion of Charles Stuart against George II, for which many have already been slaughtered out of hand, or hanged as traitors. Among her many, many sterling qualities, it has to be said that Prudence Tremaine is a very good sister. Indeed, one of the most engaging aspects of *The Masqueraders* is the trust, love and easy camaraderie that exists between siblings Prudence and Robin, who begin the story as Peter and Kate. Their shared language and humour, and the way they just get each other, almost wordlessly, is at the core of the novel's appeal, and it is their relationship, far more than either of their romances, that propels the reader forward.

> "That's a very pretty pair, Tony. I don't deny it. You must know you've to embrace the brother if you would embrace the sister."
>
> "My dear Beatrice, do you suppose I did not know it? It's a devoted couple. I wouldn't have it otherwise." - Chapter XXXII

In every way that counts, Prudence is Robin's equal, and is accorded an equal role in almost all of their undertakings by their Machiavellian father, despite her sex. (Though she was not sent to war, and had no part in the Rebellion, obviously.) Perhaps it is the frequency with which she has found herself acting the male part, or the way in which she is at home in masculine company and surroundings, but in a very real way, Prudence is treated as such even by those who know she is female. From their faithful retainer John Burton to co-conspirator Lady Lowestoft to the old gentleman himself, there is little care given to Prudence's gender throughout their dangerous game (except when her father plans for her a great marriage, in which it is assumed she will have little say), and indeed, while Robin wishes to take care of her, he also trusts her to take care of herself:

> "As a family, sir, we stand by each other. It's for Prue to decide, and for me to support her decision." – Chapter XIX

Certainly, Prudence's competence in the face of embarrassment and adversity, and her almost complete sangfroid, set her apart from all other Heyer heroines—or all other heroines, period. Whether unexpectedly confronted with seeming footpads, the prospect of a duel, or her own father, she thinks and acts quickly to carry off even the most outlandish of situations with perfect aplomb. Even Sir Anthony's discovery of her true identity she could surely have explained away, had she wanted to; had she not leapt at the chance to be honest with him.

Because above all, it is her innate honesty that makes her such a compelling enigma, given the dishonest life she has led, and continues to lead throughout our narrative.

There is no getting around the fact that she lies, again and again, throughout the time we know her, and of course much of her life has been a constant fiction. (As well as, well, a literal one.) But at her core, she is someone who is honest with herself and with those she loves, and at least Prudence doesn't deliberately use her position as Sir Anthony's friend to trick him into falling for her alter ego, which is absolutely what Robin does to Letty Grayson, and he should be ashamed of himself.

Prudence might be as accomplished a liar as Robin, but she is one with a conscience, and she is not malicious nor untrustworthy, for all of her lifetime spent outwitting unsuspecting others. Even if there had been some way for her to inveigle her way into Sir Anthony's good graces as Peter, while putting forward the case for Prudence, we know that she wouldn't have done it. She is too good for that. So good that when Tony reveals that he knows his new friend Peter is actually a woman — which he mostly worked out due to "the affection for her I discovered in myself" — and one with whom he is in love and wishes to marry, without knowing her name, her antecedents or her life story, Prudence will not allow him to make such a sacrifice out of hand. It would solve all of her problems, but she is determined that she should be worthy of him, and that her "birth" should be proven to match his before she will consent to it. Misguided this might be (and another example of Georgette Heyer's nature-vs-nurture campaign, most pointedly made in *These Old Shades*), but it speaks to her selflessness, which is another aspect of her personality that permeates the book.

In all, Prudence Tremaine is a woman of heart, courage, self-sacrifice and cleverness. Add in her ready wit, grace, beauty and charm, as well as her can-do attitude and ability to take life as it comes, and she really is a role model for us to emulate, or at least aspire to.

Let's not go too far and waste all that good wine down our arms, though.

— *Rachel Hyland*

~ | ~

NONPAREIL

International Heyer Society Circular #9, March 2021

FROM THE PATRONESSES

Welcome once again to the monthly circular of the International Heyer Society!

Here we go in-depth into *Pastel*, Heyer's third contemporary novel, one she firmly suppressed, and one that is very often considered to be quite revealing about her family life and marriage. Don't miss Ruth Williamson's insightful examination of the novel, or the comprehensive listing of the notables referenced throughout. And, as always, there are reviews, locations, character bios and more.

~ | ~

She had never had Oliver, never could have had him, and she shut a door in her mind on that disastrous episode. But though she might resolutely refuse to dwell on this last miserable year, she could not altogether banish the hurt, or be unaffected by its results. For her Oliver spelled Romance, very fleeting but very sweet. That was over: there could be no more Romance, and never another hero from Asgard. There remained the second best things – the dull, and the satisfactory.

— *Pastel*, Chapter XII

~ | ~

PASTEL

OF the themes found in *Pastel*, Georgette Heyer's third contemporary novel, perhaps the most obvious is sibling rivalry, as our sedate heroine Frances feels perpetually overshadowed by her sparkling younger sister, Evelyn. Another main theme is the idea of settling for second-best – in this case, in marriage – when the object of your desire is out of reach. And yet another is how marriage changes people, and relationships, and (at least in the 1920s, when *Pastel* is set) shifts the power dynamic between a couple to give the man, once so tender and devoted, a kind of absolute authority over the household, and his wife, so that he can act towards her as horribly as he wishes, and it is she who is left trying to placate him, in wifely submission.

So far, so infuriating to the modern reader. But another, far more important, theme of the novel is how easy it is to romanticize people, to fall in love with an idea of them, our own vision of them, and not see them for what they really are while we are in the depths of our own infatuation. In the case of Frances, she fell for the blonde handsomeness of her "hero from Asgard," Oliver Fayre, and his easy charm, and was certain he was the man for her. But as she learns more about him, long after she has, fortunately, not married him (and we have come to feel quite sorry for his wife), she discovers that, far from her Ideal Husband (Frances likes to label things in Capital Letters), he is a human being with flaws, no better and possibly much worse than anyone else. At the same time, the reader too falls out of love with Oliver, especially when he delivers a misogynist rant so egregious as to set our blood boiling. All of this makes *Pastel* a clever, and salient, if uncomfortable, novel, enlivened by some few flashes of true humour, and even satire, here and there.

— *Maura Tan*

THE CHARACTERS

FRANCES STORNAWAY
Twenty-five and attractive, but in a quiet way, Frances is a rather serious, even shy, young woman who wishes she could be more like her younger sister, the enchanting Evelyn.

EVELYN STORNAWAY
Popular, effervescent and very, very pretty, with effortless style and boundless charm, the carefree Evelyn is as self-involved as she is successful at, apparently, everything.

MARGARET STORNAWAY
Their kind, sensible, affectionate mother who wants only what is best for them, and is sure she knows what that is.

VICTOR STORNAWAY
Their father, fond of teasing them. And gardening at their home: Bray Lodge, Meldon.

PARKS
Butler at Bray Lodge.

MISS JENKINS
Seamstress to the Stornaways.

MISS GALERTY
Evelyn's elocution teacher.

NORMAN ACRE
A large and stolid young man, a Meldon local, who has long been in love with Frances, but whom she considers dull and unromantic. Works at his father's brokerage firm.

MRS ACRE
Norman's very sweet, if involved, mother.

COLONEL HARPINGTON
A Meldon local, with a booming voice.

ALTHEA DOVE
A theatre critic and local "Clever Woman" who pulls no punches.

LADY BROWNLOW
Another Meldon local; lover of Shakespeare.

MRS HERIOT
A Meldon local, not blessed with tact.

MR HERIOT
Her husband, equally unblessed.

MRS MINTY
A Meldon local, and lover of bangles.

MISS MITTON
A Meldon local; admires Evelyn's acting.

MR BEALBY
Another Meldon local.

MRS DANGERFIELD
Organizer of Meldon's hospital fundraiser.

MRS INCH
A new arrival into Meldon.

MRS DENTON
A neighbour of Mrs Inch and perpetrator of domestic violence.

OLIVER FAYRE
Handsome and charismatic, he is a barrister from a wealthy family who seems like the ideal romantic hero. But...

GEOFFREY MILDMAY
His best-friend. And best man. Unremarkable.

AGNES, LADY FAYRE
Oliver's mother, a curiously detached woman.

SIR SAMUEL FAYRE
Her husband, rather a dear.

AGNES GREGSON, NEE FAYRE
Oliver's sister, a mother of three, has "Let Herself Go."

MALCOLM GREGSON
Her husband, not always discreet.

MICHAEL GREGSON
Their eldest son, will do anything for an ice.

ANNE FARRADAY, NEE FAYRE
Oliver's favourite sister, newly returned from India.

MR FARRADAY
Her husband, and lively and jovial man,.

JOHN HARDING
Her childhood friend, won over by Evelyn.

GILBERT FAYRE
Sir Samuel's brother.

MRS FAYRE
His wife.

BETRAM FAYRE
Their son, nice but clumsy.

JENNINGS
The butler at Oliver and Evelyn's house.

MRS JENNINGS
His wife, their cook.

PAMELA GRAY
A school friend of Evelyn's, a lover of avant-garde theatre.

MURIEL
Another school friend.

ZOE BANKS
An actress, currently an understudy.

ALICE MARTIN
A very good actress.

BERYL MARSH
Not a good actress.

GEORGE CREWE
An actor who often plays himself.

LOTTIE VANDERMERING
A theatre producer and director.

LADY ARTHUR FONT
Her friend, fond of heavy jewellery.

JOHN ANSON
Playwright. Apparently a genius.

MARY, LADY TWYFORD
A good friend of Margaret Stornaway's, she is a generous hostess who is sure she has found just the right match for her goddaughter, Frances.

SIR JAMES TWYFORD
Her sweet, rather absent-minded husband.

BEATRICE ANDERLEY
An avid sportsperson and colonialist, and a spinster with a very decided personality. A good friend of Lady Twyford.

MAJOR RICHARD "DICK" FAWCETT
A good friend of the Twyfords.

ELEANOR PASSEY
Lady Twyford's friend, a determined invalid.

LIONEL PASSEY
Her very sympathetic husband.

CONNIE DAVENTRY
A newlywed acquaintance of Lady Twyford's.

PTER DAVENTRY
Her newly wedded husband.

FALKINER
Butler at Blessings, the Twyfords' home.

BRENT
Chauffeur at Blessings.

JARVIS
Groom at Blessings.

JOHN
Acted opposite Evelyn in As You Like It.

BASIL KENT
Aspirant to Evelyn's hand.

THOMAS
Ditto.

ANDREW
Ditto.

ROSE
Sullen maid working for Frances and Norman.

MRS FORD
Rose's replacement, garrulous but kindly.

MRS PETERS
Charwoman for Frances and Norman.

DR BENTLEY
Frances's doctor.

BRIGGS
The Gregsons' chauffer.

NIBS
Frances's dog, a Sealyham.

PETER
Beatrice Anderley's dog, a fox-terrier.

SUSAN
Sir James' dog, a cocker-spaniel.

~ | ~

"The Man speaks," said Anne ironically. "So naturally Woman is held responsible for all the evils of the present time."
— *Pastel*, Chapter XXIII

She might desire spasmodically not to be ordinary but there were times when she took pride in it.
— *Pastel*, Chapter XXI

~ | ~

""You aren't anyone much if you are a spinster."
— *Pastel*, Chapter XII

~ | ~

CELEBRITY SIGHTINGS

AUSTEN, JANE
1775 - 1817. Daughter of a clergyman, who always encouraged her in her writing, her first novel, the witty and often caustic yet very romantic Sense and Sensibility was printed anonymously in 1811. Five more novels followed, all of them now considered classics; Jane Austen has become one of the most famous authors in the English language, celebrated throughout the world, and her early death mourned anew on each anniversary. Hundreds of adaptations have been made of her works, including film, television, theatre, radio, graphic novels and artworks. There are now also thousands of novels and stories featuring either her characters, or Jane Austen herself.

BROOKE, RUPERT
1877 – 1915. An English poet and soldier, he was famed for his idealistic verses dealing with war, published during World War I, over just one year. He died at 27 from septicaemia caused by a mosquito bite before the war's end.

DICKENS, CHARLES
1812 - 1870. English writer, publisher, editor and social critic. Despite his lack of formal education, Dickens is one of the most famous and revered of all English-language novelists. His fifteen novels include some of the most beloved in all literature.

ELIZABETH I OF ENGLAND
1533 - 1603. Daughter of Henry VIII and Anne Boleyn, she was declared illegitimate when her parents' marriage was annulled following Anne's beheading, when Elizabeth was just two years old. She nevertheless succeeded to the throne in 1558, ruling with quiet good sense (aside from a few notable lapses in judgement, especially in regard to Mary, Queen of Scots) for 44 years and bringing some stability to a country plagued by infighting and religious schism. Known for or vanity, and as the Virgin Queen, she never married or produced and heir, but she did expand England's influence greatly at home and abroad, and the Elizabethan era is remembered as a time of exploration, innovation and creativity.

KEATS, JOHN
1795 - 1821. An English poet and leader of the Romantic school, He did not achieve great fame in life, but his legacy grew after his death, and he is even now considered one of the country's best, and is remembered chiefly for his Odes.

HUXLEY, ALDOUS
1894 - 1963. An English author, poet and playwright, he was nominated for the Nobel Prize in Literature seven times, and accounted one of the foremost intellectuals of his time. His most famous work, the dystopian novel Brave New World, is nothing short of a masterpiece.

FRANCOIS VI, DUC DE LA ROCHEFOUCAULD, PRINCE DE MARCILLAC
1613 - 1680. A French moralist best remembered for his Maxims, he was also a soldier who participated in several rebellions. His ethical pronouncements had a profound effect on later philosophers, particularly Nietzsche, and he was greatly respected in his lifetime.

MENDELSSOHN, FELIX
1809 - 1847. Born into a wealthy German family, Jakob Ludwig Felix Mendelssohn-Bartholdy gave his first public concert at the age of 9, and by 15 had composed his first full symphony. At 16 he began work on music for A Midsummer Night's Dream, and almost 20 years later he would compose the "Wedding March" for the same play, which would go on to become standard at weddings throughout the world. In his later life, and while married, he fell in love with famed soprano Jenny Lind. The extent of their relationship is not known, but Lind, in her grief at his death, founded a scholarship on Mendelssohn's behalf.

ROSSETTI, CHRISTINA
1830 - 1894. An English poet, and sister to the artist, she is perhaps best remembered for her devotional and children's writing.

SCOTT, SIR WALTER
1771 - 1832. Famed Scottish historical novelist, playwright and historian best remembered for the sweeping epics Waverley, Rob Roy and Ivanhoe. By profession a lawyer and judge, he was made baronet in 1820. He is often considered English's first historical novelist.

SHAKESPEARE, WILLIAM
1564 - 1616. Considered the greatest playwright in the English language, Shakespeare's origins were humble. Son of a glove-maker in the hamlet of Stratford-upon-Avon, he married at 18, but 10 years later he had left his wife at home to pursue an acting career in London. It is not known when he began to write, but over the decades he produced dozens of plays, from histories to comedies to tragedies, and was so prolific and brilliant that much debate still rages over the true authorship of his works. He also wrote poetry, and his Sonnets are considered some of the most romantic, and are certainly the most famous, in all literature.

STOPES, MARIE
1880 - 1958. A paleobotanist by training, Stopes infamously campaigned for the right to birth control, and her book Married Life created a scandal with its frank depiction of sex and its advocacy for a woman's right to choose. Sadly, she was also a eugenicist, tarnishing her legacy.

THACKERAY, WILLIAM MAKEPEACE
1811 - 1863. Indian-born English author and illustrator best remembered for Vanity Fair.

WAGNER, WILHELM RICHARD
1813 - 1883. German composer known for his operas, he is famed for Der Ring des Nibelungen, which takes 15 hours to perform a. Often exiled, penurious and involved in scandal, he was also an antisemite whose music was a favourite of Adolf Hitler.

WILDE, OSCAR FINGAL O'FLAHERTIE WILLS
1854 - 1900. An Irish dramatist and wit who dazzled with his plays, poems and epigrams, as well as his acclaimed novel The Portrait of Dorian Gray. Following an ill-advised lawsuit for libel regarding his sexuality, Wilde was convicted of "gross indecency with men" in 1895 and sentenced to two years hard labour. When released he fled England, and soon died impoverished, of meningitis, in a French hotel.

YONGE, CHARLOTTE
1823 - 1901. English author of children's literature of a moralistic tone founded in her ardent Christianity. Strong advocate for public health, public works and proper sanitation.

THE LOCATIONS

LONDON
- Claridge's
- Victoria Station
- Hans Place, home of Sir Samuel and Lady Fayre
- Smith Square, Westminster, home of Oliver and Evelyn
- Belgrade Mansions, South Kensington, home to Frances and Norman

MELDON
Location approximate: just ten miles from London; on the District Railway.

- Bray Lodge, home of the Stornaways

BLESSINGS
In Hertfordshire, not far from St Albans

THE TWYFORDS' HUNTING BOX
In Scotland, not far from Aboyne

WHAT THEY SAID

Contemporary Reviews of *Pastel*

The Times Literary Supplement, June 13, 1929

Pastel, by Georgette Heyer, is a very readable, pleasant novel, which keeps to the surface of things and introduces us to some friendly and agreeable people. Its subject is the rivalry between two sisters. Frances, the heroine, is outdone in every way by her brilliant younger sister Evelyn. Evelyn is like a black-and-white drawing, while Frances is a pastel; but the sisters are all the same very fond of each other. A crisis comes for Frances with Evelyn's marriage to a handsome young man with whom Frances had been in love herself and who, until he met Evelyn, had seemed to like Frances. The marriage leaves her not really heartbroken but extremely disconsolate, and in this mood she agrees to marry Norman, the dull but excellent young man who has been in love with her for years. Up to this point the ups and downs of Frances's career have been very well described, and our interest in her has never been allowed to waver; but after Frances's marriage we begin to notice that Miss Heyer has a moral in mind and is writing with a purpose. Frances married Norman with many doubts and fears; and after her marriage she finds that the old rivalry with Evelyn still remains, for Evelyn's husband is much richer than Norman, and Evelyn's dinner parties are much more successful than Frances's. But, on the other hand, Oliver is moody and bad-tempered, while Norman has all the solid virtues. So Frances settles down and decides not to envy Evelyn anymore. The book remains readable to the end, but as soon as we begin to suspect the author's disinterestedness our belief in the story wavers.

~ | ~

Boston Evening Transcript, May 15, 1929

In *Pastel* may be found a thoughtful and realistic portrayal of the dreams and longings of a romantic girl who all her life has had to take second place. We sympathize with and love Frances because, whether we admit it or not, many of us have had similar longings and have had the same discouragements. The restful conclusion is a comfort, because it epitomizes the desire in the hearts of many, to be able to face life, undaunted and serene.

~ | ~

The Spectator, May 11, 1929

Miss Heyer proves once again that the oldest theme can yield new charm in the hands of a competent artist. *Pastel* is a simple tale of two sisters, the younger of whom outshines the older in fascination and threatens to monopolize the prizes. In the end, of course, Miss Heyer shows us that all that glitters is not happiness. Within her prescribed limits, she introduces us to real people and real scenes, all characteristically English; and, thought she attempts no heights or depths, her plain is pleasantly fertile with humour and sympathy.

~ | ~

It was a mistake to think that the thing of which one dreamed was better than the thing which one had. You could always find points in the dream that excelled corresponding points in the reality.

— *Pastel*, Chapter XXI

SELECTED COVER GALLERY

Longmans, UK
(1929)

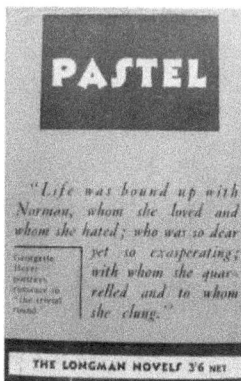

Longmans, UK
(1931)

Longmans, UK
(1934)

NO KNOWN TRANSLATED EDITIONS EXIST

~ | ~

WHAT A QUIZ!

Think you know your Heyer? These questions will test your knowledge...

1. In which year was *Pastel* first published?
2. On what real train line is the fictional town of Meldon said to be situated?
3. In what play do Evelyn and Frances act?
4. Why doesn't Lady Twyford invite Evelyn to Blessings?
5. What is Miss Anderley's favourite sport?
6. Who is Mrs Inch?
7. What colour does Evelyn think will not suit Frances?
8. What is the name of Frances's dog?
9. Where do Frances and Norman make their home?
10. Why is the novel called *Pastel*?

ANSWERS: 1. 1929; 2. The District Railway 3. *As You Like It*; 4. She is trying to set up Frances with Oliver Fayre; 5. Shooting; 6. A new neighbour at Meldon; 7. Grey; 8. Nibs; 9. South Kensington; 10. Frances says her sister is like a line drawing, but that she is a muted pastel.

~ | ~

The truth was, Life was a giant practical joke played on humanity by some malign genius, and all that vague talk of expiation, preparation, was man's pathetic attempt to find an answer to the riddle that had none.
— *Pastel*, Chapter IX

"When people get married they expect too much of each other, and they get most frightfully peeved when things don't pan out according to the beautiful plans they made."
— *Pastel*, Chapter XIX

~ | ~

AN EXPERIMENT IN PASTEL BY RUTH WILLIAMSON

GEORGE HEYER loved the theatre. His daughter inherited this passion, and appeared onstage with him at the age of eleven. Several scenes in her third contemporary novel, *Pastel* (1929), take place at London theatres. As the book opens, Margaret Stornaway is fielding compliments on the performance of her younger daughter, Evelyn, as Rosalind from Shakespeare's *As You Like It*. Margaret's elder daughter, Frances, has played Celia, but praise for her is merely polite. She is 'just a foil' for Evelyn. Only steady Norman Acre has preferred to watch Frances, because he always does. For everyone else, Evelyn's vivacious presence puts her older sister in the shade. Both Stornaway sisters may enjoy the theatre, but it is Evelyn who shines brightly on and offstage.

Despite her lack of magnetic beauty or sparkling personality, Frances is the novel's focal point. While Elizabeth, the naïve heroine of Heyer's first contemporary novel (*Instead of the Thorn*) was also diffident, her beauty attracted attention. She had no siblings, let alone one with compelling charm. As *Pastel*'s heroine says of her sister, people 'forget all about me when they meet her'. Frances is a new style of Heyer heroine. She is unlike any who have featured before, different from pretty, plucky Diana Beauleigh, successful writer Helen Marchant, or brave adventurer Prudence Tremaine. After *Pastel* came several quiet, self-effacing heroines who became favourites for many readers. One appeared only three years later, when Mary Challoner emerged from the shadow of her spoilt sister, Sophia (*Devil's Cub*). As in *Pastel*, a younger sister attracts the limelight. But while Mary tackles problems head on, Frances remains 'a shadow' of her sister.

Thankfully, she develops within her own story. To begin with, she doesn't know what she wants. She meets the man of her dreams, but he falls for her younger sister. Frances settles for a safe and familiar partner, but discovers that marriage requires effort. After a period of adjustment, she learns to appreciate what she has, and by becoming a mother, achieves fulfilment. But it is Georgette Heyer who is drawing this picture of domesticity, so *Pastel*'s plot may play safe, but its characters have three dimensions, she includes a scene-stealing Sealyham puppy (a breed much loved by the author), and her heroine lives in South Kensington after her marriage.

When Frances first sees athletic, charming and witty Oliver Fayre, he appears 'like a hero in fiction'. Inevitably, sparkling Evelyn enchants him, so Frances is 'sore and unhappy' about their courtship, convinced her 'one chance has slipped her by'. Patient Norman Acre remains in the wings. Although Frances thinks him 'dull', she believes 'if you don't marry you don't have a life at all,' so she marries him. Her parents regard Norman as an appropriate match for her, having viewed Evelyn and Oliver's marriage as 'ideal'. After Evelyn's grand wedding, she lives in a fashionable home with her handsome spouse. Frances believes they have it all. After she and Norman marry, they have to adapt to each other. Naturally frustrations occur. As individuals they have different personal habits, routines and tastes. He owns 'innumerable detective stories' and 'the works of Sir Walter Scott', whereas she has occasion to praise Jane Austen, one of Heyer's favourite writers.[1] A series of marital trials and tribulations – many amusing and all sharply observed – arise from their differences. Heyer shows how they negotiate everyday arrangements, covering everything from what each prefers for breakfast through to problems with household 'help'.

Frances is no feminist. She accepts the traditional role of suburban wife and mother. She flouts no conventions, although conservative values were challenged in contemporary society. Characters discuss old and new ideas about gender roles and equality at length, but none of the novel's major players approves of 'New Thought'. Heyer's affinity with traditional social structures translates seamlessly into her Georgian and Regency novels, but dates her in a twentieth century context. For all

---

[1] The influence of Austen on *Pastel* is unmistakable. Not only is Austen named, but turns of phrase (involving Lady Twyford as quoted later in this essay) also owe much to *Pride and Prejudice*. Frances even shares her first name and some of her problems with Fanny (properly Frances) Price, the quiet heroine of Austen's *Mansfield Park* (1814).

that, her creative experiment with Frances Stornaway paved the way not only for Mary Challoner's success as a reluctant heroine, but also for shy Hester Theale in *Sprig Muslin*, prosaic Drusilla Morville in *The Quiet Gentleman* and other leading ladies. They rise above a lack of classic personal beauty to win through with pragmatic good sense.

Heyer explores several male personalities in *Pastel* in fresh ways too. While Oliver has a matinee idol's good looks, he is not an ideal husband, despite what Frances thinks. After she sees his shortcomings at first hand, she accepts he is not perfect. She has already married Norman, whose appearance and abilities resemble those of Heyer's husband Ronald Rougier, as her brother Frank noted. Both Norman and Ronald enjoyed sport, and were tall, dependable, level-headed men aiming for successful careers. Fathers also appear in this novel, speak rarely, but are men of sense. Their down to earth reasoning supplies some light relief after intense exchanges, such as Frances has with her mother, and godmother, Lady Twyford.

Margaret Stornaway is an involved parent. She cares about both her daughters while not always sharing their opinions. Her maternal approach is conventional; she is unimpressed by 'new' attitudes that omit good manners and traditional roles. Heyer tells readers that Margaret believes ordinary 'nice' people bring 'a placidity to life that shade[s] off sharp edges, and neutralize[s] outstanding colours.' She dismisses as a passing 'girl's passion' Frances's heartache over Oliver.

Later, Margaret admits she doesn't 'really understand' Frances. Crossed wires probably featured in the relationship of Georgette and her mother. *Pastel* is dedicated to Sylvia Heyer, in hope that she would approve of at least some of it. Although Georgette had worshipped her father, and widowed Sylvia relied upon her daughter's financial support earned from novel-writing, she disliked that career choice. They had limited tastes in common. In *Pastel*, Margaret is aghast when Frances wants a low-key wedding 'in the city'; disconnected opinions occurred within the Heyer family too.

Lady Twyford (Aunt Mary) is her goddaughter's confidante. Heyer applies Austenian terms to her, so that [Mary] 'knew that a young man with money was nearly always more attractive than a young man without it'. After listening to Frances assess Norman's character prosaically, Lady T goes 'down to dinner in a depressed mood, and revoke[s] twice at Bridge afterwards.' Her warm heart would fit into any Heyer novel. Her early hopes for Frances and Oliver go awry; she understands exactly why Frances feels eclipsed by Evelyn. Mary is perceptive and witty, equally at home discussing wedding presents (a rose bowl for Evelyn, a Sheraton writing table for Frances), career women, spinsters and the generation gap. She is an early example of Heyer's mature, clear sighted, intelligent women, such as Mrs Tallant in *Arabella*, Lady Luttrell in *The Corinthian* and later, Cordelia (Consett) Morville in *The Quiet Gentleman*.

The Stornaway family has two daughters, whereas Heyer had two brothers. Happily, her good friends Joanna Cannan and Carola Oman (fellow writers) did have sisters. Georgette had already consulted Joanna extensively when writing *Instead of the Thorn*. *Pastel* highlights sisterly contrasts, but Frances and Evelyn have a family bond, seen clearly when Oliver treats his wife badly and Frances defends her sister.

Heyer's experiment with contrasting sisters in *Pastel* reaped rewards later. Many subsequent novels explore nuanced family dynamics. While the Merriville sisters are dissimilar in looks and actions, they have a caring mutual attachment in *Frederica* (1956). Selina and Abby Wendover (*Black Sheep,* 1965) have very little in common beyond shared family feeling, but stick together against the odds. Having written about the Stornaways in *Pastel*, Heyer devised complex sisterly relationships in her accomplished and celebrated Regency novels.

– *Ruth Williamson*

~ | ~

NONPAREIL

International Heyer Society Circular #10, April 2021

FROM THE PATRONESSES

Welcome once again to the monthly circular of the International Heyer Society!

Here we go in-depth into *Beauvallet*, Heyer's only novel set in the time of Elizabeth I, one of her few sequels, and the only one of her books featuring a pirate as its hero. Don't miss our Susannah Fullerton's rumination on its hits and misses, or the comprehensive listing of the notables referenced throughout. And, as always, there are reviews, locations, character bios and more.

> "Is he as mad as they say? They tell us, who have had dealings with him, that he is a man with black hair who laughs."
> White teeth gleamed for a moment. "Yes, he laughs, senor," said Sir Nicholas. A chuckle came, they little knew how audacious. "I dare swear if he stood in this room surrounded by his enemies at this moment, he would still laugh. It is a habit with him."
> — *Beauvallet*, Chapter IX

BEAUVALLET

MOST teenage readers of *Beauvallet* (which many of us were) probably missed the religious significance that underpins the plot. Other Heyer novels mention, to some extent, the cultural differences between Catholics and Protestants, not to mention the seeming impossibility of interfaith marriages, e.g. *The Talisman Ring* and *The Spanish Bride,* but only *The Great Roxhythe* deals with the very real, centuries-long (still ongoing) conflict between the two faiths as thoroughly. A later reading of *Beauvallet* shows that the topic is not even discussed in a terribly subtle way, but, in the book's opening chapters, the pre-story conversion of Spanish aristocrat Doña Dominica y Rada de Sylva from one religion to the other would very likely have gone over the head of anyone who didn't know what the word "Popish" meant.

And it is perhaps only when Sir Nicholas Beauvallet, having fallen for her and decided to undertake a foolhardy mission into the domain of his enemies to "make an Englishwoman" of her, tells his brother that she is "no Papist but a dear heretic," that the layperson will understand the significance of the book she'd hidden in her cabin, which she'd probably acquired from the Lutherans she was known to have consorted with, and that would have proven troublesome for her with the Spanish Inquisition (which, we are reliably informed, nobody ever expects).

One has to wonder: would the daring Sir Nick have so determinedly, dangerously pursued Dominica had she remained Catholic? Did the fact of her conversion make her more appealing to him, or would he still have chased after her, and merely considered it even more of a challenge? Either way, *Beauvallet* is a very eye-opening window into a topic that many readers may never have considered too deeply otherwise, and it is very much to Georgette Heyer's credit that in a swashbuckling romance of high adventure that would not have been out of place on the silver screen, with Nick played by Errol Flynn (if only!), she so easily slipped in yet more Learning! for us to take away from it.

— Clara Shipman

THE CHARACTERS

SIR NICHOLAS BEAUVALLET, AKA MAD NICK; EL BEAUVALLET; CHEVALIER DE GUISE
Daring, dashing and devilishly attractive, he is an enthusiastic corsair sailing the Spanish Main as captain of the Venture. Believed to be in league with Satan, he conquers all before him, even the heart of a Spanish aristocrat who should hate him.

GERARD, 7TH BARON BEAUVALLET
His far more staid older brother.

KATE, LADY BEAUVALLET
His good wife, a determined invalid and maker of potions. A romantic.

ADELA, LADY STANBURY
Their sister, mother to many girls and one boy.

EUSTACHE DE BEAUVALLET, MARQUIS DE BELRÉMY
A good friend of Nick's from their youth, he heads the French branch of the family.

SIMON, 1ST BARON BEAUVALLET
Their ancestor, a powerful noble soldier who brought a Frenchwoman home as his bride.

MARGARET, LADY BEAUVALLET, NÉE BELRÉMY
Said bride.

GEOFFREY, 2ND BARON BEAUVALLET
Their eldest son, always at loggerheads with his father.

HENRY, 3RD BARON BEAUVALLET
Geoffrey's eldest son.

MARGARET, LADY BEAUVALLET, NÉE MALVALLET
United the two houses with her marriage to her not-so-distant cousin, the third baron.

JOSHUA DIMMOCK
Nick's very proud personal servant, very thin with an extravagant moustache. Superstitious, loquacious, and endlessly loyal to his master.

CHEVALIER DE GUISE
A French noble on a secret mission to Philip of Spain. Attempted to steal Nick's horse and died for his trouble. (Might be real.)

HENRI DE LAUVINIÈRE
French Ambassador to the court of Philip II, very suspicious of Nick's disguise as one of the, er, de Guises.

DOÑA DOMINICA DE RADA Y SYLVA
Beautiful, proud and not averse to emotional manipulation, she is captured by Nick on the high seas, along with her ailing father. While she and Nick quickly fall in love, she cannot believe his promise to come into Spain to win her. She is wrong to doubt him.

DON MANUEL DE RADA Y SYLVA
Her honourable and loving father, who cannot help but respect Nick.

DOÑA BEATRICE DE CARVALHO
Dominica's jaded, intelligent, casually cruel aunt who is determined to marry Dominica (and her enormous fortune) to her son. She's very funny, though.

DON RODRIGUEZ DE CARVALHO
Her timid, rather ineffectual husband.

DON DIEGO DE CARVALHO
Their son, whom his mother clearly despises. A very exquisite caballero. Except for his penchant for abduction, of course.

DON MIGUEL DE TOBAR
Dominica's maternal uncle, whom she plans to ask for help against her aunt.

DON JUAN DE NARVAEZ
Captain of the Santa Maria, on which Dona Dominica sailed with her father.

LIEUTENANT CRUZADA
His subordinate.

MIGUEL DE VASSO
A crewman on the Santa Maria; locked Maria in her cabin.

DON MAXIA DE PERINAT
A Spanish captain defeated by Beauvallet who identifies him in Madrid and is considered mad, but he is absolutely right.

DON DIAZ DE LOSA
A gentleman of Madrid into whose care Nick, as the Chevalier de Guise, is placed.

DON JUAN DE ARANDA
A friendly gentleman from Adalusia who takes a liking to Nick in Madrid. The feeling is mutual.

DON LUIS DE NOVELI
Holds the party at which Nick is recognized by Perat and captured, much to his host's horror.

MARIA
Dominica's plump maid, wholly devoted.

MATTEO DE VAZQUEZ
Secretary to King Philip of Spain.

FATHER ALLEN
An English Jesuit priest, close to Philip of Spain.

FREY LUIS
A Spanish priest of the Dominican order, close to Philip of Spain. A true zealot.

DON CRISTOBEL DE PORRES
Commander of the Guards of Castile, and Nick's (temporary) jailer.

CRUZA
His lieutenant, very angry over Nick's escape.

LIEUTENANT RICHARD "DICCON" DANGERFIELD
Nick's lieutenant aboard the Venture, very susceptible to a pretty girl.

PATRICK HOWE
Master of the Venture.

CULPEPPER
An officer of the Venture.

WILLIAM HICK
A crewman on the Venture; attempts to force Dominica to kiss him.

JOHN DAW
A crewman on the Venture, forces a kiss on Dominica and apparently gets away with it.

RUSSET
Another crewman.

CURLEW
Ditto.

MASTER CAPPER
Parson on the Venture.

DAME MARGERY
Nick and Gerard's old nurse, still in residence at the Beauvallet estate in Hampshire.

MASTER DAWSON
Steward of the Beauvallet estate in Hampshire.

SAMSON
Gate-keeper at the Beauvallet estate in Hampshire.

CARMELITA
Another maid of Dominica's, old and wizened.

BARTOLOMEO
Don Manuel's man.

LUIS
Don Diego's valet.

~ | ~

CELEBRITY SIGHTINGS

CARRANZA, JERÓNIMO SÁNCHEZ DE
1539? - 1600?. A Sevillian nobleman who created the Spanish school of fencing known as Destreza, and author of the definitive text on the subject, *The Philosophy of Arms*.

SIR WILLIAM CAVENDISH
1505 - 1557. A courtier and accountant who helped in Henry VIII's dissolution of the monasteries and was accused of corruption, thereafter sent to Ireland. He had 16 children with his three wives, nine of whom survived infancy. Relative of the Dukes of Devonshire.

CROFT, SIR JAMES
1518 - 1590. An English politician known for his charm and double-dealing, he was a supporter of Lady Jane Grey and frequently switched sides in succession wars. He was eventually imprisoned in the Tower for his pains.

JOHN DAVIS
1550 - 1605. English sailor, Navy captain and explorer who was one of Elizabeth I's chief navigators. Sought the Northwest Passage to China on multiple Arctic voyages and discovered the

Falkland Islands. A childhood neighbour of Walter Raleigh. Also spelt "Davys"

SIR FRANCIS DRAKE
1894 - 1963. Captain of the Golden Hind, a famed explorer and sea captain (and, sadly, a slave trader), Drake was a favourite of Elizabeth I and was vice admiral of the English fleet in its victory over the Spanish Armada. Not all of his campaigns were as successful, however, and he died of dysentery following his failed attempt to take Panama and buried at sea in a lead-lined coffin. His body has never been recovered.

ELIZABETH I OF ENGLAND
1533 - 1603. Daughter of Henry VIII and Anne Boleyn, she was declared illegitimate when her parents' marriage was annulled following Anne's beheading, when Elizabeth was just two years old. She nevertheless succeeded to the throne in 1558, ruling with quiet good sense (aside from a few notable lapses in judgement, especially in regard to Mary, Queen of Scots) for 44 years and bringing some stability to a country plagued by infighting and religious schism. Known for or vanity, and as

the Virgin Queen, she never married or produced and heir, but she did expand England's influence greatly at home and abroad, and the Elizabethan era is remembered as a time of exploration, innovation and creativity.

FERRARA, ANDREA
?. A somewhat mysterious 16th-c swordsmith of probably Spanish origin who is believed to have killed his apprentice when he caught him spying on secret techniques. He then joined the court of James V in Scotland and taught the locals how to make high quality blades. Also known as Andrew.

FROBISHER, SIR MARTIN
1535 - 1594. Ship captain, privateer and explorer, he attempted to discover the Northwest Passage several times, and helped repel the Spanish Armada. Twice brought home tonnes of what he thought was gold from Canada, only to discover that it was worthless.

GILBERT, SIR HUMPHREY
1539 - 1583. Soldier, sailor and seaman, he stole lands in both the US and Ireland at the behest of Elizabeth I, and wrote a book in which he claimed

to receive visions from Biblical personages. Half-brother of Walter Raleigh.

HATTON, SIR CHRISTOPHER
1540 - 1591. One-time Lord Chancellor of England and favourite of Elizabeth I, despite being known to be a Roman Catholic in all but name. Never married, and remained loyal to his queen throughout his life. He was one of the judges who found Mary, Queen of Scots guilty of treason, which led to her execution.

HAWKINS, ADMIRAL SIR JOHN
1532 - 1595. Naval commander, privateer and early slave trader. Chief architect of the Elizabethan Navy, and directly responsible for the nation's superiority at sea for centuries.

HAWKINS, ADMIRAL SIR RICHARD
1562 - 1622. Son of Sir John, he too carved out a career on the seas, and wrote of the benefit of citrus fruits to treat scurvy a century before it was officially "discovered."

HAWKINS, WILLIAM
1519 - ?. Elder brother and business partner of John Hawkins. Family name also "Hawkyns."

HENRI I, DUC DE GUISE
1550 - 1588. Head of the Catholic League, which sought to keep a Protestant from inheriting the French throne, he was assassinated by bodyguards employed by Catherine de Medici, mother of Henri III of France.

HENRI III OF FRANCE
1551 - 1589. Fourth son of Henri II, he was not expected to inherit the French throne, and so accepted the throne of Poland, only to be recalled to France following a lot of fraternal death. Preaching religious tolerance, he was assassinated by a fanatical Catholic and succeeded by his cousin, who

converted to that religion and founded the Bourbon dynasty.

HENRY V OF ENGLAND
1386 - 1422. A famed soldier while still a teen, he continued to spend much of his life at war, either against rebellions at home or in the quest for the French throne. After five years of famously brilliant campaigning, Charles VI of France agreed to a truce in 1420, ending the Hundred Years' War. Two years later, Henry died suddenly and mysteriously, just two months before Charles VI.

HOWARD, CHARLES, 1ST EARL OF NOTTINGHAM, 2ND BARON HOWARD OF EFFINGHAM
1536 - 1624. Statesman and Lord High Admiral under Elizabeth I and James I. Led the fleet against the Spanish Armada in 1588.

MAROZZO, ACHILLE
1484 - 1553. Italian fencing master and author of The New Text on the Art of Arms.

MARY, QUEEN OF SCOTS
1542 - 1587. Daughter of James V of Scotland, she succeeded to the throne when just five days old. Married three times, dethroned twice, and imprisoned by her cousin Elizabeth I for 18 years before being executed. Held by many to be the rightful queen of England.

PARACELSUS
1493 - 1591. Philippus Aureolus Theophrastus Bombastus von Hohenheim was a Swiss physician, alchemist and theologian who is considered the "father of toxicology."

PHILIP II OF SPAIN
1527 - 1598. Son of Holy Roman Emperor Charles V, he was given Spain and Portugal to rule, and saw in the Spanish Golden Age. A devout Catholic, he

was a big fan of the Holy Inquisition. The Philippines were named after him. Sent the Spanish Armada to England.

RALEIGH, SIR WALTER
1552 - 1616. Best remembered for laying his cloak across a puddle for Elizabeth I (probably not true), he was a courtier, politician and sailor who popularized tobacco smoking in England. He was also an historian and poet who, some have claimed, may have had a hand in the writing of Shakespeare's plays.

VÁSQUEZ DE LECA, DON MATTEO
1542 - 1591. Rose from obscurity to become personal secretary to Philip II of Spain.

WADLOE
? A Simon Wadloe was known to keep as tavern called The Devil and Saint Dunstan, situated at 2 Fleet Street, London during the latter half of poet and playwright Ben Jonson's life, when he established the Apollo Club there (members included Shakespeare and Jonathan Swift). As Jonson was born in 1576 and our tale takes place in 1583, we have to assume that the Wadloe mentioned here is Simon's father, or even grandfather. The tavern was demolished in 1787 and Child's Bank now occupies the site.

WALSINGHAM, SIR FRANCIS
1532 - 1590. Remembered chiefly for his cunning (and his role in the execution of Mary, Queen of Scots), he was England's first "spymaster.". Well educated but from relatively humble origins, he quickly rose to being one of Elizabeth I's main advisors, and essentially ran all foreign policy for many decades.

~ | ~

My Lady Disdain! Give you a thousand good-morrows!
— *Beauvallet*, Chapter III

"Resolutions are made to be broken only."
— *Beauvallet*, Chapter XI

~ | ~

THE LOCATIONS

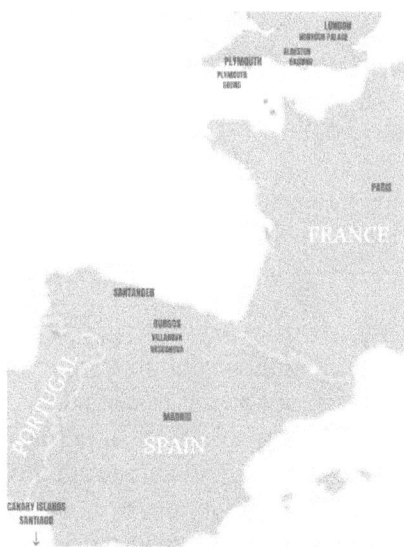

SANTIAGO
CANARY ISLANDS
SANTANDER
BURGOS
VILLANOVA
VASCONOVA
MADRID
- Inn of the Rising Sun, off the Puerta del Sol
- The Alcazar, Court of the Spanish King
- The Mentidero, at the entrance of the Calle Mayor

PARIS
LONDON
- The Tabard (outside London's walls)
- The Devil Tavern, East Chepe
- Paul's Walk (the central nave of Old St Paul's Cathedral)
- Westminster Palace

PLYMOUTH
- Plymouth Sound, off the coast of Plymouth
ALRESTON
In Hampshire, preferred country home of the current Lady Beauvallet
BASING
In Hampshire, site of Sir Nicholas Beauvallet's estate

WHAT THEY SAID

Contemporary Reviews of *Beauvallet*

The Times Literary Supplement, October 10, 1929

The hero of any story of English piracy (for such it really was, no matter how Protestant and patriotic it might be in the eyes of contemporary England) on the Spanish Main in the spacious days of Good Queen Bes, can hardly fail to run the risk of comparison with Amyas Leigh. Miss Heyer is to be congratulated on having produced in Beauvallet one whom the great exemplar would not have disdained. Indeed, he seems to have been a shipmate of Amyas Leigh's in the *Pelican*, and only Miss Heyer's silence on this important detail prevents the reader from comparing the worth of the silver ship in which Amyas Leigh and Salvation Yeo sailed into Bideford with that of the treasure brought by Beauvallet and his Joshua Dimmock into Plymouth after the sprightly knight had, in conformity with his promise, landed his future bride by night in Spain. Having done so, he naturally had to go back to Spain to find her, and Miss Heyer turns him into a gentleman of France, an identity thrust upon him complete with confidential dispatches by a fortunate by sanguinary hazard. In this guise Beauvallet is graciously received in audience by the gloomy King, whose beard he had been so busily engaged in singeing in propria persona at Vigo and in the Spanish Indies, and is able to set on foot his plans for an elopement. All goes well until Beauvallet is recognized by an astonished Don who finds masquerading as a French envoy from the Duke of Guise the man who was known all over the Spanish Main as a devil-inspired English pirate protected from all good Catholics by enchantment. Thereafter the story becomes cinematographic with escapes, kidnapping, galloping, sword play and a breathless elopement. Miss Heyer has produced quite a pleasing story of great days.

~ | ~

The Observer, October 13, 1929

This is gallantly So-hoish all through. From the imaginary family tree on the fly-leaf to the last marvellous triumph of Beauvallet it swaggers romantically. Beauvallet is a Dell hero in an Elizabethan ruff, and his Spanish lady is like the heroine of most "period" novels—proud and harsh at first, devout afterwards. Miss Heyer is a good storyteller, and some of her lesser characters—Philip of Spain, for one—are well suggested. But it is an odd thing that writers about the past think it was perpetually boisterous in act and emotion; as if nobody three hundred years ago, or even one hundred and fifty years ago, went to bed on a day of plain hard work without a cut-throat encounter in it.

~ | ~

Boston Evening Transcript, April 18, 1930

For several years Georgette Heyer has been proving herself a master of romantic fancy-dress fiction. What she does is always right, always highly flavoured of her period, so that in some odd fashion the whole era is actually alive before you, and that with few descriptions. It is so easy that you are assured of long study in preparation, while there is no faintest trace of effort. In her last book, *The Masqueraders*, the very essence of eighteenth century dandyism walked abroad; in this we have swashbuckling days on the Spanish Main, and the merry England of Good Queen Bess. The style itself changes to fit the mood, though never for a moment does she lose the sense of thrill. One cannot set down a book of hers if one loves the bright panache of days gone by, partly because the story is always too exciting to stop, and even more that the folk of the tale are too delightful to be lost sight of for a moment. Possibly—yes, of a certainty—it is that the spirit of one's own youthful dreams is here alive again, and one may dwell, for some three hundred and fifty large and well-written pages in one's own castles in Spain.

In the present story we are hurled at the beginning into a bloody, ravaging tornado of a sea fight, in which a mighty galleon is badly beaten by a small English vessel, which she unwisely attacks. The little Venture is the personal craft of that terror of the seas, Beauvallet, who had been pirate and privateer with Drake, and now runs the waters of the world for himself, preying upon the navies of Spain. His servant, Joshua, who followed him in all his adventures, lacked a family crest, but he had been told he should die in his bed, so he only worried about his master. Not that his faith in Beauvallet was dimmed, even by that frightful expedition into the heart of Spain, the jaws of the Inquisition, to steal a Spanish lady.

The lady, the lovely Dominica, was aboard the plundered Spanish vessel, with her father, an old Spanish governor of the West Indies, returning home very ill. Beauvallet, though five and thirty or more, had never before fallen to the wiles of a woman, but within twenty-four hours he announced his intention to make an Englishwoman of the lovely *signora* [sic]. If he came to Spain to seek her, he demanded, would she come away with him? And Dona Dominica, bowing proud head, promised to follow him across the northern waters.

Of Beauvallet's doings at home, in that pleasant English countryside where his brother was a lord, of his visit to court to see the queen, and of his subsequent merry but grim masquerade as an envoy from the House of Guise to the King of Spain, we may read with bated breath. And it is good to know, once more, that knights are brave and ladies beautiful.

~ | ~

WHAT A QUIZ!

Think you know your Heyer? These questions will test your knowledge...

1. In which year was *Beauvallet* first published?
2. To which novel does it stand sequel?
3. What relationship does Sir Nicholas have to the current baron of Beauvallet?
4. Name Nick's ship.
5. Name his faithful servant.
6. Name one of his nicknames.
7. Of what island was Dominica's father Governor?
8. With what does Dominica threaten to kill Nick?
9. How does Nick enter Spain?
10. Who does Doña Beatrice despise most, her husband or son?

ANSWERS: 1. 1929; 2. *Simon the Coldheart* 3. His younger brother; 4. The Venture; 5. Joshua Dimmock; 6. "Mad Nick," "El Beauvallet"; 7. Santiago; 8. His dagger; 9. With the papers of the Chevalier de Guise, on a secret mission; 10. Trick question: she pretty much despises everyone. (Except maybe Nick.)

~ | ~

"What I swear I will do that I shall certainly do, though the sun die and the moon fall and the earth be wholly overset!"
— *Beauvallet*, Chapter IV

~ | ~

SELECTED COVER GALLERY

Heinemann, UK
(1929)

Longmans, US
(1930)

Heinemann, UK
(1952)

Pan, UK
(1963)

Bantam, US
(1969)

Pan, UK
(1969)

Ulverscroft, US
(1969)

Pan, UK
(1976)

Bantam, US
(1983)

Mandarin, US
(1995)

Arrow, UK
(2000)

Harlequin, Canada
(2004)

Arrow, UK
(2006)

Thorndike, UK
(2007)

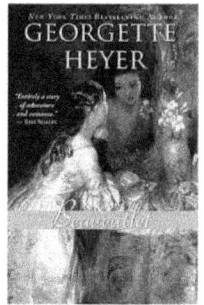

Sourcebooks, US
(2010)

SELECTED TRANSLATED EDITIONS

DUTCH: ZwarteBeertjes
(1978)*

GERMAN: Roman
(1980)

GERMAN: Roman
(1983)

GERMAN: Rowohlt
(1984)

ITALIAN: Mondadori
(2005)

* Much as this title appears like it should be *The Spanish Bride* (which is the direct translation), it is indeed *Beauvallet*.

BEAUVALLET: AN APPRENTICE NOVEL BY SUSANNAH FULLERTON

1929 WAS a busy year for Georgette Heyer. She published her contemporary novel *Pastel* and she also brought out *Beauvallet*. It was written in Macedonia, where she was adjusting to a new lifestyle.

Beauvallet is set in the days of Good Queen Bess and concerns the swashbuckling adventures of Sir Nicholas Beauvallet, friend of Drake and terror of the seas in his ship *Venture*. His character was modelled on that of Sir Walter Raleigh (though unlike Raleigh, Beauvallet does not write beautiful poetry). The story starts with a bang: "The deck was a shambles. Men lay dead and dying; there was split woodwork, a welter of broken mizzen and sagging sail, dust and grime, and the reek of powder." The reader is plunged into a dangerous sea battle in which Beauvallet and the crew of the *Venture* capture a large Spanish galleon and take prisoner all those still alive within her. His prisoners include the beautiful and spirited Doña Dominica de Rada y Sylva, who rages and spits against her captor, but inevitably falls in love with him.

Sir Nicholas might have reached the advanced age of five-and-thirty, but he has never been in love before. He is bluntly honest about his feelings and rapidly announces his intentions of making an English wife of her. But she is returning home with her gravely ill father, so Sir Nicholas nobly conveys her to her homeland, vowing that he will seek her out in impregnable Spain and take her back to England. After some scenes in England, Sir Nicholas then makes his way to Spain, into the very jaws of the Inquisition, facing duels, prisons, guards and many other dangers in order to win Doña Dominica. Of course, he does so successfully and together they return to England at the end of the novel.

The book sold 86,000 copies upon release and, as Jane Aiken Hodge states, "helped to consolidate (Georgette Heyer's) position as an author whose historical novels would sell themselves". Clearly it was popular with 1920s readers. However, I must admit, it has never been a huge favourite of mine – it's not one of the novels I visit regularly for a blissful reread. I find it a patchy book – good in parts, like the curate's egg.

I adore Georgette Heyer's use of Regency slang – for me it brings that era alive, adds a delightful quirkiness to her Regency novels, and it so colourful and vivid that I long for opportunities to use it in my own everyday speech. However, she is less successful with her Elizabethan language. 'Mad Nick' 'zounds', 'perchances', 'prithees' and 'forsooths' with the best of them, but the Elizabethan language appears slightly stilted and far less natural than the slang of the Regency novels. Here he is talking to his servant: "And stitch me these safe in a length of silk… What, do you tremble still. Cross yourself and say Jesu! It's in the part." We get some rather odd phrasing – "Marry, so would I know, Joshua", "Stay you in the lee of that hedge", 'Curb that prattling cheat of yours", "Fiend seize the princox" and "Beware your bed, dizzard, and get you hence." There are times when it simply feels like bad English. Reading it always gives me the sense that I am watching an Errol Flynn movie, with the sword fights and everyone just a little bit over-dressed and 'over-Elizabethan' in their language.

The plot is predictable – one knows that Nick will get his girl in the end – but then so it is in most of Heyer's fiction. It's the way she brings it all about which is what enchants, not any use of suspense. There's a nice link to one of her earlier novels – Beauvallet is a descendent of Simon the Coldheart. He is bursting with energy and vitality, and goes directly for what he wants – for him, 'failure is not an option". Dominica matches him in witty dialogue, holds her own with spirit, and then succumbs to his charm with a deep passion of her own, but I feel she fails to really come alive as a character. I miss the development of a romantic relationship, the sexy and moving growth of feeling one finds in beloved Heyers such as *Sylvester*, *Frederica* or *Arabella*. The sexual chemistry of Nicholas and Dominica lacks the wonderful subtlety of the developing relationships in *Venetia* or *Black Sheep*.

So those are my negatives. Yet there is Heyer magic in this novel too, even if it is fails to match her best. The story grabs you from the opening and continues at a cracking pace, sweeping the reader along. Heyer's always excellent use of historical detail makes you feel you are there on the decks, slippery with blood, of an Elizabethan privateer. She shows a good knowledge of the intricacies and intrigues of the Spanish court, gives us nice little cameo appearances of Philip of Spain and Queen Elizabeth I. Beauvallet meets Sir Francis Drake in Paul's Walk in London and the famous explorer and privateer is gorgeously described as "a bluff, square-set man, with a fierce golden beard, and long grey eyes set slightly slanting in a broad face. This man stood with feet planted wide, and arms akimbo … He wore a peascod doublet, hugely bombasted, and a jewel in one ear." As always, Heyer makes us see the man so clearly in just a few lines.

She provides wonderful domestic details - Sir Nick swings a pomander as he talks, rooms are furnished with chests and rich curtains, and the fabulously decorative Elizabethan clothing is described in all its richness. Heyer has an innate instinct about just the right amount of detail – she never overburdens her readers with pages of description (as Sir Walter Scott tended to do), but she gives enough to provide convincing background and local colour.

There are some vivid characters – I enjoy the servant Joshua Dimmick, who has been told by a fortune-teller that he will die in bed, so feels he can cope with anything when he is at sea or in the heart of Spain. He talks to himself in long monologues which are great fun, and he's a practical and down-to-earth contrast to Mad Nick's derring-do. There's also Dominica's cattish would-be mother-in-law in Spain, with all her machinations and sinister schemes. Dame Margery was once Nick's nurse and there's a nice scene where she pretends to scold him, while clearly delighted to see him back, and Nick's sister-in-law Lady Beauvallet is one of Heyer's fabulous hypochondriacs: "Not a second ague, I assure you, but more like the seventh, for, indeed, no sooner am I raised from one than another strikes me down."

Beauvallet is a rollicking romp, and there is much in it to admire. However, I can't help but see it as an 'apprentice novel' for Heyer – she was still finding, as an author, what historical era suited her best. Once she did, there was no stopping her. I enjoy *Beauvallet* but I infinitely prefer her Regency drawing rooms to the decks of a ship, the Spanish court, or an Elizabethan estate.

– Susannah Fullerton

~ | ~

"There is an old chronicle writ by one Alan, afterwards Earl of Montlice, wherein we learn that Simon, the first Baron of Beauvallet, took as his motto these words: 'I have not but still I hold.'" His voice rang out, and died again.

"Well, señor?" faltered Dominica.

"I have you not yet, but be sure I hold you."

— *Beauvallet*, Chapter IV

"Senor, Don Diego is somewhere at hand. Pray send for him."

"I have already had that pleasure, madame. I met your son upon the Mentidero yesterday."

"Ah, then you will not want to see him again."

— *Beauvallet*, Chapter X

~ | ~

NONPAREIL

International Heyer Society Circular #11, May 2021

FROM THE PATRONESSES

Welcome once again to the monthly circular of the International Heyer Society!

Here we go in-depth into Here we go in-depth into *Barren Corn*, Heyer's fourth and final contemporary novel. **PLEASE BEWARE OF MAJOR SPOILERS!** But don't miss scholar Maura Tan's appreciation of the story's underlying themes, and of the delicate character sketching and use of irony that she believes makes the book a forgotten classic. And, as always, there are references, reviews, locations, bios and more.

~ | ~

BARREN CORN

GEORGETTE was living in Macedonia through 1929 and perhaps it was the distance between her home there and her old life in England that set her thinking about class and the social hierarchy in which she had been raised. The novel she wrote in Macedonia set a new tone for a Heyer story and there is an element of deep honesty in *Barren Corn* that sets the book apart. This is Georgette's most ambitious and compelling contemporary story and the only one of her novels to deal so directly with the issue of class in English society.

The story is at first glance a simple tale of lower middle-class girl meets upper middle-class boy while holidaying on the French Riviera. Hugh and Laura fall for each other and, against her better judgement (because of the perceived class difference), she agrees to marry him. All goes well for as long as they are away from England and separated from his "people", but things begin to fall apart once he is reunited with his own "set". *Barren Corn* is a surprisingly empathetic novel and, whether she meant to or not, in telling Laura's story Heyer demonstrated a deep understanding of aspects of the human psyche and the kinds of mental traps into which individuals can fall when driven by love or sexual desire to act against their better judgement. She sees clearly the great class divide so prevalent in 1920s Britain. Among other things, *Barren Corn* explores the bitter consequences for Laura when she attempts to bridge the chasm of cultural and social difference that comes to lie between her and her selfish and insensitive husband. By the end of the novel, Laura is trapped in a kind of mental and emotional limbo – a personal hell from which there is no escape if she is to spare her own family pain and abide by the code of conduct laid down by her husband and his class.

Barren Corn is as much about snobbery as it is about the worth of the individual. Though often decried by Heyer lovers who prefer her lighter, wittier comedies of manners, *Barren Corn* is a remarkable book that shows the depth of Heyer's perception and her understanding of human nature. It was to be her final contemporary novel, however, and she never wrote in quite this way again.

— Jennifer Kloester

THE CHARACTERS

LAURA BURTON
30, beautiful and innocent, Laura gives up her happy life of work and family by her marriage to a dilettante of the moneyed classes.
MR BURTON
Laura's hard-working father. kindly and perceptive.
MRS BURTON
Laura's affectionate, understanding mother, awed by her daughter's new position in life.
GEORGE BURTON
Laura's stolid brother who fancies himself a wit.
MAY BURTON
Laura's younger sister, catty and jealous.
GLADYS JENKINS, NEE BURTON
Laura's other sister, to whom she is very close.
HENRY JENKINS
Her husband.
HARRY JENKINS
Their eldest son, doted on by the whole family. Fond of elephant rides.
"BABY" JENKINS
Adorable, apparently.
MADAME DUHAMEL
Proprietress of the hat shop in Nice in which Laura worked, solicitous of her best worker's health and even sends her to the seaside to recover from influenza.
GENEVIEVE
Works at the hat shop with Laura.
SOLANGE
Another hat shop worker.
FLORRIE HOPE
Another hat shop worker.
YVONNE
Would have lost her job, but Laura resigned.
MISS JACKSON
Runs Laura's boarding house in Nice, suspicious of her relationship with Hugh.
MRS. MILLER
Another resident, reader of *Who's Who*.
MISS DUTTON
Believes no good can come of Laura and Hugh's relationship. In fairness, she's right.
MRS. CROSBY
Very impressed with hunting as a hobby.

HUGH SALINGER
The spoiled nephew of a baron who fancies himself a painter. Unqualified snob.
EMMELINE SALINGER
His mother, a very pretty woman always in debt and dependent on her uncle. Unqualified snob.
JOYCE SALINGER
His younger sister, a "Modern", mean-spirited and surly. . Unqualified snob.
CHARLES HUMPHREY FORDYCE, LORD SALINGER
Hugh's uncle, a wealthy baron, clever and sardonic. Certainly a snob, but kind enough to hide it, which is almost worse.
HON. ROLAND GEOFFREY CHARLES FORDYCE SALINGER
Lord Salinger's son and heir, reportedly a very good sort of man, tragically killed in a riding accident.
LILIAN, LADY POWIS
Lord Salinger's forthright sister, mannish and managing, in charge of his household.
SIR JOHN POWIS
Her improvident husband, deceased.
JAMES "JIM" POWIS
Their unremarkable son.
HYLDA POWIS
Their daughter, an avowed and strident Communist who is a snob at heart.
PENNY
The butler at Alleyne, Lord Salinger's house.
STELLA HEPPLEWHITE
A neighbour at Alleyne and childhood friend of Hugh's with a secret love for him. A very decent human being, kind to Laura from the first, as much as her cool manner will allow.
MRS. HEPPLEWHITE
Her mother, a very soothing presence.
COLONEL HEPPLEWHITE
Her father, bluff and good-natured.
GEORGE HOPE
Avid hunter, has a house in Leicestershire where Hugh and Laura spend Christmas.
MRS. HOPE
His wife, a charming hostess.
MAURICE QUILLINAN

A good friend of Hugh's from the War, older than him, a distinguished writer. Doubtful about his marriage but hopes it will be good for him. One of only two truly decent people in Hugh's immediate circle.
GABRIELLE CRAWLEY
An acquaintance of Hugh's, chance met in Siena, who is introduced to Laura and finds her wanting. Inveterate name dropper.
JACK CRAWLEY
Her husband.
GEORGE CARRUTHERS
An acquaintance, now in a relationship with an actress, who is considered an object of pity.
MAISIE TRENT
The actress.
HILLIARD
A playwright, perhaps less clever.
LORNA PRAYLE
Actress in Hilliard's latest play.
WILLIAM WHITEMAN
Actor in Hilliard's latest play; mediocre.
LADY BARBARA "BABS" HANNERSLEY
A "modern" London acquaintance of Hugh's.
ADAM
Another London acquaintance, Laura's finds his "sexless"-ness confusing and challenging.
MEG
Another London acquaintance, always seems shocked when she runs into her husband.
DINGO
Her husband.
MAJOR LAWRENCE
A friend of the Hopes.
EMILIA
Caretaker of the house in Siena at which Hugh and Laura spend much of their honeymoon.
BIANCA
Her daughter.
BOWER
Butler forced upon Laura by Lady Powis.
MRS. BOWER
His wife, a cook, who dares cheek Laura about not being a 'lady" when caught stealing.

CELEBRITY SIGHTINGS

BAEDEKER, KARL LUDWIG JOHANNES
1801 - 1859. Descended from a long line of publishers and booksellers, his painstakingly produced travel guides set the standard for more than a century, and his name even became synonymous with the genre well after his death.
BOCCACCIO, GIOVANNI
1313 - 1375. Italian writer and poet renowned for the short stories comprised in *The Decameron*, as well as his book *On Famous Women*, detailing the lives of 106 famous women of myth and history, the first of its kind. Along with Dante and Petrarca, he is considered one of the "Three Crowns" of Italian literature.
CARUSO, ENRICO
1873 - 1921. An Italian tenor, he became internationally popular due to his 247 recordings, made between 1902 and 1920. He died after a bout of ill-health that was possibly caused by undiagnosed internal injuries following a stage accident.
CHAPLIN, SIR CHARLES SPENCER
1889 - 1977. English actor, filmmaker and composer who is an icon of cinema. His comedies are considered classics, both of the silent and "talkies" era. He co-founded United Artists, and

retained a remarkable control over his work. Controversy dogged him throughout his career, due to suspected Communist leanings and his marriage to an 18-year-old when he was 54. The couple had eight children, the last born when Chaplin was 73. Chaplin had been married three times previously, and had three other children.
KIPLING, RUDYARD
1865 - 1936. Indian-born English writer known for his works set in Colonial-era India. He won the 1907 Nobel Prize for Literature, the first English-language and still youngest to do so. Notable works include *Kim, Gunga Din* and *Mandalay*, but he is perhaps best remembered as the author of *The Jungle Book*, on which the Disney animated film is based.
LUINI, BERNARDINO
1480/82 - 1532. An Italian painter and student of Leonardo de Vinci, he is known for his graceful female figures. His son Aurelio was also a painter and draughtsman of some renown.
QUILLER-COUCH, SIR ARTHUR THOMAS
1863 - 1944. Known by his pseudonym "Q", he was a prolific poet and novelist as well as a professor of English Literature at Cambridge University. While his novels have fallen from common notice, his epic

work *The Oxford Book of English Verse 1250 - 1900* has endured, and is frequently updated. It is from one of his lectures at Cambridge that we have the famed writer's advice "murder your darlings."
THACKERAY, WILLIAM MAKEPEACE
1811 - 1863. Indian-born English author and illustrator best remembered for *Vanity Fair* and *The History of Henry Esmond*, in which he attempted to write in a 17th-century style.
VALENTINO, RUDOLPH
1895 - 1926. Born Rodolfo Alfonso Raffaello Pierre Filiberto Guglielmi di Valentina d'Antonguella in southern Italy, he emigrated to the US at 18 and found fame on the silver screen in silent films like *The Sheik* and *The Eagle*. Known for his dark good looks and potent sex appeal, he was labelled the "Latin Lover" and his early death due reportedly caused mass hysteria. 100 000 people lined the streets of Manhattan to witness his funeral cortege.
VILLANI, GIOVANNI
c. 1276 - 1348. A Florentine banker, official and diplomat who chronicled his city's history in the *Nuova Cronica* (*New Chronicles*), with a heavy emphasis on the role of God in the works of man. He died after contracting the Bubonic Plague while writing of the then-pandemic's disastrous effects.

THE LOCATIONS

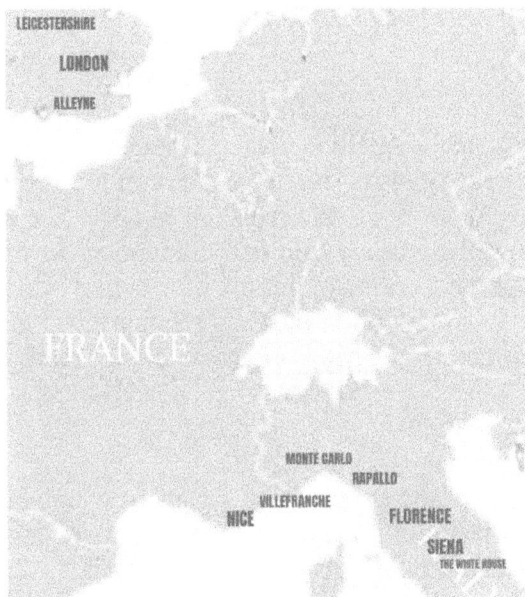

NICE
- Avenue de le Gare
- British Consulate
- Suzanne's Millinery
- Miss Jackson's Boarding House

VILLEFRANCHE
- Hotel de l'Univers

MONTE CARLO, MONACO

RAPALLO
FLORENCE
SIENA
- The White House, just outside Siena

LONDON
- Laburnum Avenue, Brixton, home of the Burtons
- Hans Place, home of Mrs. Salinger
- South Audley Street, home of Hugh and Laura Salinger

ALLEYNE
- In Sussex, between Arundel and Chichester

LEICESTERSHIRE
- Home of the Hopes, good for hunting

~ | ~

"That hidebound attitude infuriates me! Because Laura can't show a line of ancestors all more or less disreputable she is not to be thought a fit bride for me. Good God! does the accident of her birth make her nature less sweet?"

— *Barren Corn*, Chapter IV

"She began to think that perhaps from the very first she had cheated herself. He had never loved her as she understood love. Surely, surely, real love endured, and was not hurt by difficulties."

— *Barren Corn*, Chapter XXVIII

~ | ~

SELECTED COVER GALLERY

Longmans, UK
(1929)

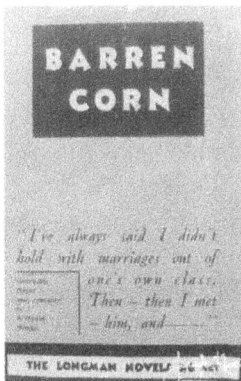

Longmans, UK
(1931)

Longmans, UK
(1934)

NO KNOWN TRANSLATED EDITIONS EXIST

WHAT THEY SAID

Contemporary Reviews of *Barren Corn*

Sydney Morning Herald, May 30, 1930

Georgette Heyer, with *Barren Corn*, has struck out on a story containing a theme that has come to be known lately as class consciousness. She makes a tragedy of it. The idle nephew of a baronet marries in a dash of emotionalism, a fine, handsome girl, working in a hat shop In Nice. She is afraid of the consequences of the Ill-assorted union, but is rushed into it by the ardent lover. Happiness unalloyed follows while they wander about the Continent, but the time comes when the enchantment passes, the music must be faced-the meeting with friends and relations, and the stern fact that a social law has been broken. The aristocrats and the bourgeoise do not readily mingle. In this story it is unusually difficult.

"She is a respectable young woman," says his baronet uncle.

"It sounds terrible," moans his mother.

There is some humour run into this tale. In the family of the husband is a socialistic daughter, who complicates matters with her arguments, but only tangles up the situation a little more, and shocks the English middle class sentiments, the carefully taught gentility, of the young wife, whose views about the definite place of a lord, and all that belong to him under the British Constitution, are badly shaken by this advanced enthusiast. The husband meets the problem no better than the wife. In fact he is made out to be rather a snob, and it is to be hoped the author is not claiming a true picture of English aristocracy.

The end is weak. The girl throws up her hand and puts an end to her troubles with a motor car, whereupon one's sympathies fade away suddenly. She might fairly have been expected to find a better solution. The author has widely diverged from her last book, *Beauvallet*. In this one, which is of a kind that will probably prove popular reading for her own sex.

~ | ~

The Scotsman, June 5, 1930

Hugh Salinger, trifling with art on the Riviera, encounters Laura Burton, a young woman assistant in a Nice hat shop. He is attracted by her, paints her portrait, thinks he is in love with her, but sees a wide gulf between their social standards. Laura is " genteel" in the true Victorian sense, but, though she turns down Hugh at first, their meeting after a separation convinces her that she is in love with him. Maurice Quillinan, a friend of Hugh's, has some plain truths to tell him—"She won't understand one tenth of the things that make up your world. Her education is naturally poor. How will you converse together when your love has grown more temperate? There is her outlook. I know her type... The niceties of social conduct as she understands them will constantly set your teeth on edge." "She will be shocked by the casual manner of our class; she has been taught gentility; to shake that off must go terribly against the grain." Yet Maurice advises Laura to marry Hugh. Almost from the beginning of their married life there are jars. Table manners, party episodes, Hugh's relatives worry Laura; her gentility that was her pride is only a vexation. Disillusion follows, and then an unexpected—in some ways an uncalled for—denouement. A story to read, and to talk about.

~ | ~

A FORGOTTEN WORK OF TRUE GENIUS BY MAURA TAN

THERE are some books you read again and again because they are enjoyable and engaging and, perhaps most importantly, comforting to revisit when you need something you know you love. Then there are the books you read again and again because of the depth of subtlety embedded in their pages, the nuance about time and place and the force of unspoken yet thoroughly understood ideas prevalent in any given society.

For me, Georgette Heyer's *Barren Corn* is one of the latter.

Upon first reading it I had not yet experienced the historical romances for which she is now so justly famous (see: *Heyer for Beginners*, by yours truly). I had, however, read her three other, earlier, contemporary efforts, *Instead of the Thorn* (1923), *Helen* (1928) and *Pastel* (1929), and so I thought I knew what I was getting myself into when I dove into this one.

I could not have been more wrong.

It is true that there are elements of the earlier works present here. The unequal marriage might not be quite so unequal, but it certainly exists in *Instead of the Thorn*, as does the childhood playmate who the family clearly believes should have been the bride. *Helen* gives us the leisured "Smart Set" in all its self-involved pomposity, and the rapture of a love that overcomes all common sense is a big theme in *Pastel*. (As, indeed, is that self-same "Smart Set.") But where *Barren Corn* differs so utterly from those previous works, not to mention from all of Heyer's other works, is that it is very, very serious in tone. Almost to the point of melancholy. Her deft characterization is all there on the page as vibrant as ever, but there is barely a clever bon mot or even a comical aside to raise a smile in the reader. A good percentage of the people we encounter in the novel are awful, but instead of redeeming them with clever wit (like, for example, with the Duke of Andover in *The Black Moth*) or making them adorable (like, for example, with Fanny Marling in *These Old Shades*), or even showing us their deep and abiding humanity (like, for example, with Jonathan Chawleigh in *A Civil Contract*), Heyer does not go out of her way to make anyone in the novel sympathetic in our eyes. She gives them to us whole, naked and unfiltered, almost without mercy, and we are left shaken and puzzled and conflicted by the experience.

Her heroine, in the 30-year-old millinery clerk Laura Burton, could easily have excited our unalloyed sympathy, what with her treatment at the hands of quite the most villainous "hero" to ever flow from Heyer's pen, Hugh Salinger. (And in this I am including William the Conqueror, who was, historically, an actual villain.) But Laura, too, is a problematic creature, and creation, and every time were are wholly on her side Heyer deftly pulls the rug out from under us by having her avow herself better than a barmaid, or look askance at actresses and independent women, or throw off her family because her unreasonable husband demands it of her.

It is almost unfathomable to the modern reader the idea that Hugh – not to mention his mother, and the rest of their family – holds, that, having married Hugh, a man born, if not of the nobility then of the gentility, she should no longer acknowledge her "lower-class" family, or have them as part of her life. When the couple pay a visit to his in-laws upon their return from their whirlwind courtship, nuptials and honeymoon in Europe, Hugh is somehow astonished that Laura should be happy to see her parents, siblings and their children, or to have missed them so terribly. "Did she then care so much?" he muses, as though it was an oddity that anyone might still retain an affection for their own relatives after having married into the lofty Salinger clan.

In one of the more galling scenes in the story, Hugh is scandalized when his mother happens to drop in at their apartment, unannounced, while he is away, and Laura has dared to invite her sister and nephew to tea in her own home. His mother complains how "impossible" Laura's sister is, and regards with horror the idea that someone else might have dropped in, and whatever would they think! This, coupled with the uninvited advent of the arch, unlikeable May Burton, Laura's other sister, into a cocktail party hosted by the Salingers, makes Hugh furious and he – who has been wanting to do it since the outset – forbids her relatives from coming to their flat. So, just in case someone should happen to be there and might judge him harshly for the Burtons' "commonness," Laura is never to have her family come to visit her in, again, her own home.

Infuriating, isn't it? And just one example of what makes *Barren Corn* such a truly excellent book.

Perhaps Heyer's best.

I know that is a bold and even controversial statement to make, as it is far from her most popular. But popular and best are very different things (see: enjoyable vs. admirable), and there is that in this exploration of class, self-confidence, control and mental illness that truly smacks of genius. She does not, as I have noted, rest on her singular skill with sprightly dialogue to make the story sing. Instead, she uses every word uttered like a scalpel, or perhaps a hammer, ruthlessly, remorselessly building up our sense of impending dread until the ending, suddenly seeming so inevitable no matter how much we wished it otherwise, breaks us, and our hearts.

That ending, for some, might seem a cop out, or even a judgement on those who might seek to marry, or live, "above their station." There is much in the book that can be taken in that light, and, indeed, has been. But the more I read it, the more I think that *Barren Corn* is not about class difference, but about how everyone is fundamentally the same. Everyone is a product of their upbringing. Everyone has their own social mores and strictures that don't always make sense to outsiders. Everyone believes themselves to be, in some way, more correct than others, whether it be in taste or education or religious belief or by some other arbitrary measure. We see Hugh and his family, and so-called friends, looking down on Laura due to her manner of speech and lack of clever repartee, but she, likewise, looks down on them for their casual manners and their taste in entertainments. Hugh's mother thinks she is so far above Laura's mother that she never even makes an attempt to meet her, but Mrs. Burton has taught her daughter to be loving, thoughtful and economical, which is more than the vain, selfish, spendthrift Mrs. Salinger has ever done for Hugh.

All of this duality of narrative is perhaps best expressed in Hugh's cousin Hylda, who claims to be a Socialist and a Feminist (Hugh's hatred of the latter is only matched by Laura's, another way in which Heyer deliberately makes her heroine not entirely sympathetic to us), but in her bones she believes she is being noble by claiming to consider those "lesser" than her as equals, and so is far from understanding the basic concept of equality. Hylda is, bar none, the most ironic, and quite viciously-drawn, character in the book. But it is Hugh, and his snobbery, not to mention superficiality, who is Heyer's most potent, and praiseworthy, creation in *Barren Corn*. From the first, we can't like him; he may be outwardly charming, but we are given entrée into his thoughts, and they are never a pleasant place to be. Even on his honeymoon he says to himself, quite candidly, that he will surely lose his love of Laura once her beauty is gone, and her "queenly" lines are turned to "coarse fat." He is Henry Higgins if Henry Higgins were even more of an elitist prig. He thinks that Cinema is "Bad Art" and doesn't even attempt to enter into Laura's interest in it, expecting her to confine her interests to his. (And then inwardly complaining that she has none, when it is he who has taken them all away.) He tells Laura she should be natural when in company, because when she is stilted she loses her charm, yet he is constantly correcting her, in either word or just with pained looks, making her even more self-conscious every time. Instead of trying to conform himself to any of her standards, he spends his time sure that his way is so much better than hers' that she must change, never he.

So when Laura calmly, methodically, decides to make the ultimate sacrifice on Hugh's behalf, so that he might be happy without her (since he has told her than a divorce is out of the question), you can understand how she got there. Removed from her family, under the thumb of a controlling despot who gives and then withholds affection depending on how well she has "pleased" him, knowing that the gentle Stella Hepplewhite is waiting in the wings (Stella, one of only two truly good people of Hugh's "sort" that we meet and who is, like Laura, far, far too good for him), and obviously suffering from depression, she both gains and loses our sympathy even as Heyer excites our unqualified admiration with her daring denouement. In all, *Barren Corn* is a truly magnificent accomplishment, and should be experienced at least once.

– Maura Tan

~ | ~

WHAT A QUIZ

Think you know your Heyer? These questions will test your knowledge...

1. In which year was *Barren Corn* first published?
2. In which town do Hugh Salinger and Laura Burton meet?
3. What is Laura's occupation?
4. What is Hugh's occupation?
5. Of what rank is Hugh's rich uncle?
6. What is the name of the "house of dreams" in which Hugh and Laura spend most of their honeymoon?
7. Name Laura's sisters?
8. Where does Laura's family live?
9. Who is Lady Powis?
10. What is the name of the country estate to which Hugh becomes heir?

ANSWERS: 1. 1930; 2. Villefranche, on the French Riviera; 3 assistant in a hat shop; 4 he doesn't have one, but fancies himself a painter; 5. Baron; 6. The White House; 7. Gladys and May; 8. Brixton; 9. Hugh's aunt, who runs his uncle's home; 10. Alleyne.

~ | ~

"If I had known there was you in the world, waiting for me, I – I would have waited, too."
— *Barren Corn*, Chapter VII

"This was the Might Have Been; in the contemplation of it bitterness grew up, insidious and deadly."
— *Barren Corn*, Chapter XI

~ | ~

"I find that sisters are worse than no good."
— *Barren Corn*, Chapter I

The taught lesson was useless.
— *Barren Corn*, Chapter VIII

~ | ~

"I may be wrong; I don't pretend to be infallible. But it seems to me that never were two people so badly matched. There's an immense gulf between you."

— *Barren Corn*, Chapter V

~ | ~

NONPAREIL

International Heyer Society Circular #12, June 2021

FROM THE PATRONESSES

Welcome once again to the monthly circular of the International Heyer Society!

Here we go in-depth into Heyer's most ambitious novel yet, *The Conqueror*, detailing William of Normandy's rise to power in the 11th Century. The research that went into this opus is extraordinary, and so too is our Celebrity Sightings section! Meanwhile, Rachel Hyland's essay wonders at the book's scope, and as always, there are references, reviews, (so many!) locations, and more.

~ | ~

THE CONQUEROR

GEORGETTE and Ronald returned from Macedonia early in 1930, after eighteen months away. Georgette had written two novels while overseas: the swashbuckling *Beauvallet* and the contemporary tragedy about class, *Barren Corn*, but although both books had done well, they were not where Georgette's literary heart lay. The previous year, her best friend Carola Oman had published a serious historical novel called *Crouchback* about Richard III and it was this that prompted Georgette to begin her own novel about an important historical figure. She chose William the Conqueror and immediately began researching his life and times. She had always been fascinated by the medieval era and her 1925 novel, *Simon the Coldheart*, had shown her that she was more than capable of bringing the period to life. Of course, *The Conqueror* was to be a very different undertaking, for Georgette wanted to tell the story of William from his birth in France in 1027 until his coronation at Westminster Abbey in 1066. It was immensely ambitious but she set about it with her usual thoroughness and determination. She and Ronald travelled to Normandy in order to see the places where William had lived and fought and ruled and she read every available text about his life and exploits. Ronald was a huge help and she would later write in his first-edition copy: 'Here is THE CONQUEROR for Ronald, with acknowledgements for his watchfulness & care in all such matters as Bear-fights, Cavalry-charges, Distances, & Male-Etiquette and with love from George.'

Though she had some momentary doubts about the book, she was encouraged by her friends Carola and Joanna [Cannan, also an author] to finish it, which she did late in 1930, and the dedication tells us a little of her feelings about the book: *To Carola Lenanton, In friendship and appreciation of her own incomparable work done in the historic manner dear to us both.* Years later, Georgette would remember writing *The Conqueror* and acknowledge:

> What a lot of work I put into it! And how difficult it was to correlate the various contemporary (and largely inaccurate) accounts of William's Life and Times – a task not made easier by the fact that, at that date, hardly anyone had a surname, and that the Chroniclers bestowed Christian names in a somewhat haphazard way, Ralph de Toeni, for instance, appearing, indifferently, as Ralph, Raoul, Reynaud, and Richard! And, even worse, that awful Fitz, meaning "the son of." All very well if the character was historically important, or if his father had an unusual name, such as Osbern; but although the student of the period knows All About William Fitzosbern, few could be expected to recognize William Fitzwilliam as his son. Well, not at a glance, anyway!

Today, *The Conqueror* remains an eminently readable account of William the Conqueror and reflects Heyer's remarkable ability to integrate history into fiction.

— *Jennifer Kloester*

THE CHARACTERS

RAOUL DE HARCOURT
A man of strong principle and fervent loyalty, he wants only peace and justice in a land and time that does not seem liked to give him either. Won over by one glimpse of William, the young Duke of Normandy, he enters his service and soon becomes indispensable, if not always approving, loving no one so much as his master until he meets his Saxon friend's sister, the lovely Elfrida. Nicknamed Watcher.

HUBERT DE HARCOURT
Raoul's father, a lord who owes fealty to Roger de Beaumont. Confused by his youngest son's sensitive nature, he is made proud by Raoul's standing in the Duke's circle.

GILBERT DE HARCOURT
Elder half-brother to Raoul, at first strongly opposes Duke William and even rebels against him before finally fighting at his brother's side. Attempts to abduct and rape a young woman from a neighbouring farm, but is stopped by an irate Raoul.

GISELA DE HARCOURT
Wife of Gilbert, who holds a rather inappropriate attraction towards Raoul.

EUDES DE HARCOURT
Raoul's other half-brother, not terribly clever but brave in battle.

GEOFFREY DE BRIOSNE
Neighbour of the de Harcourts, with whom he and his soldiers are in a perpetual feud.

GALET
The jester, or fool, in William's court; pretends to be half-witted, but is in face very perceptive and witty. Speaks truth to power with impunity.

WILLIAM D'ALBINI
Cupbearer to Duke William. Possibly a real person – records from a century after Hastings report a butler of that name in William's train, and a D'Albini (d'Aubigni) family rose to prominence in the time of King Stephen.

IVES
Page to Duke William, prone to seasickness.

EMMA
The midwife who delivers baby William.

EDGAR, THANE OF MARWELL
Given to Duke William as a hostage, he is a proud Saxon and strong believed in Harold Godwinsson who spends over a decade in Norman hands and forms strong friendships with among his captors, especially with Raoul de Harcourt, whom he considers a brother. He is overjoyed when Raoul wants to marry his sister Elfrida, despite the potential difficulties posed by the looming conflict between their two masters. He fights on Harold's side at Hastings and is killed, but not before he has a chance to say farewell to Raoul, and to save his life one last time.

ELFRIDA OF MARWELL
A sprightly Saxon beauty, sweet-faced and kind, sister to Edgar and beloved of Raoul de Harcourt. Gives into his pressure to marry him even though she literally just buried her father and brother, and it was his fellow Normans who killed them. She clearly really loves him.

DAME GYTHA
Aunt to Edgar and Elfrida of Marwell, hates Normans a lot.

EADWULF, THANE OF MARWELL
Father to Edgar and Elfrida, killed at the Battle of Hastings.

ALFRIC EDRICSSON
Saxon captured with Harold, a very good friend of Edgar's who finds him much changed by his years in the Norman court. Which, obviously.

OSWINE
Former betrothed of Elfrida, died of a wasting disease before she was old enough to marry.

HUNDBERT THE STRONG
Father to Oswine.

ERIC JARLSSEN
A Dane who was believed to have killed Oswine with witchcraft, and was stoned.

SIGWULF
A Saxon shipwrecked with Earl Harold, and a friend of Alfric.

EARNULPH
Another Saxon shipwrecked with Harold.

EDMUND
Yet another Saxon shipwrecked with Harold.

DROGO DE SAINT-MEURE
Called "Honest," he is among the drugged soldiers during Guy of Burgundy's unsuccessful assassination attempt on Duke William.

GODFREY OF BAYEUX
A soldier most likely involved in Guy of Burgundy's plot to murder William. Plays chess.

HERLUIN OF BONDEVILLE
The leader of three hundred knights who stave off the rebellion of William of Arques, giving Duke William time to arrive on the scene. (Possibly a real person.)

ROBERT
A Norman living in England who delivered news of Harold's movements to the invading Norman force, acting as a very effective spy.

PAPIA
Concubine to Archbishop Mauger who had earlier refused the advances of Duke William's cruel cousin.

GEOFFREY DE BERNAY
Nobleman unsure of William's military strategies. (Most likely fictional.)

BALDWIN DE COURCELLS
Another who does not like William's battle plans. (Also probably fictional.)

HUGH MAIGROT
A monk who acts as William's messenger to Harold before Hastings. Fluent in Saxon.

WILLIAM DE VIEUXPONT
Served under William at Hastings and was killed. Possibly based on a real person.

IVES DE BELLOMONT
Soldier beheaded in the Battle of Hastings, later discovered by Raoul.

ANGLESINE
A Saxon abbot who bravely demands religious rights from William following the Conquest.

ALRIC THE SCHOOLMASTER
Accompanies Edith Swan-neck to Hastings.

OSEGOOD CNOPPE
A monk, also accompanies Edith Swan-neck.

ETHELWULF
A Saxon, lives near Pevensey.

THE LOCATIONS

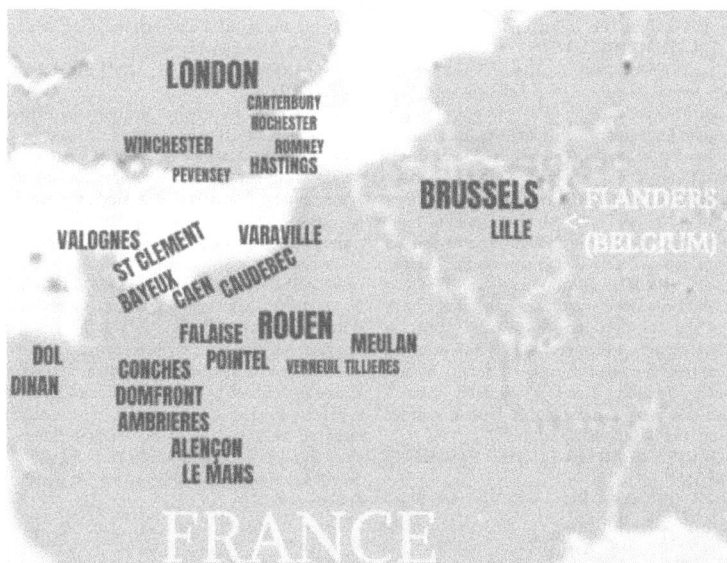

NORMANDY:

FALAISE
ROUEN
BAYEUX
VALOGNES
ST CLEMENT
CAEN
CAUDEBEC
POINTEL
CONCHES
DOMFRONT
AMBRIERES
ALENCON
MEULAN
VERNEUIL
VARAVILLE

BRITTANY:

DOL
DINAN

MAINE:

LE MANS
TILLIERS

FLANDERS:

BRUSSELS
LILLE

ENGLAND:

LONDON
HASTINGS
ROMNEY
ROCHESTER
WINCHESTER
PEVENSEY

CELEBRITY SIGHTINGS

ALFRED AETHLING (THE NOBLE)
c. 1005 – 1036. Son of Ethelred the Unready and his second wife Emma of Normandy, younger brother to Edward the Confessor, eventual king of England. Betrayed by Godwin, Earl of Wessex, after suggesting that they might retake the throne from the Danish King Canute. Alfred was blinded, tortured, and then died of his wounds. Edward never forgot, nor forgave.

ALFWIG
d. 1066. Abbot of New Minster and uncle of Harold Godwinson. Died at the Battle of Hastings.

ANJOU, FULK IV, COUNT OF
1043 – 1109. Called Foulques le Réchin, Fulk the Surly. Rebelled against his brother, Geoffrey III, defeated him soundly and cast him into prison. Cuckolded when his wife, Bertrade, "wed" Philip I of France, he nevertheless fought on the French side, and was a lifelong adversary of Duke William. Succeeded by his son, Fulk V.

ANJOU, GEOFFREY II, COUNT OF
d. 1060. Called Martel, or the Hammer, he was a warlike prince who joined with Henry of France to attack Normandy. He married four times, divorcing thrice, but died childless.

ANJOU, GEOFFREY III, COUNT OF
c. 1040 – 1096. Nephew of Geoffrey II, he was known as le Barbu (the Bearded). In 1067 he went to war with his younger brother Fulk, lost, and was imprisoned for 28 years.

AP LLEWELYN, GRYFFYD, KING OF WALES
c. 1010 – 1063. A renowned warrior, he fought many battles for land and titles throughout Wales, and allied himself with the Earl of Mercia, taking Edith (Ealdgyth) of Mercia as his bride. His expansionist policy was eventually ended by Harold Godwinsson, but not until Gryffyd had joined with Harold's brother Swegn in a rebellion against Edward the Confessor. In hiding, Gryffyd was killed and beheaded, presumably by his own men, and his head was presented to Harold as an act of good faith. Harold triumphantly displayed the head; he then married Edith of Mercia himself.

AQUITAINE, WILLIAM VII, DUKE OF
1023 – 1058. Born Peter and called the Eagle and the Bold, he was brother-in-law to the Holy Roman Emperor Henry III and stepson of Geoffrey Martel, Count of Anjou, whom he fought for his own territory. Joined with Henry of France against Normandy. He was married to one Erminsinde, and they are believed to have had at least two daughters.

BAYEAUX, ODO OF, EARL OF KENT AND BISHOP OF BAYEAUX
d. 1097. Younger half-brother to William, he was made Bishop of Bayeux in 1049 when still a teenager. A soldier and statesman, he is shown to be encouraging the troops at Hastings in the Bayeux Tapestry. Made Earl of Kent after the conquest, he was one of William's most trusted advisors and sometime regent whenever William was absent, but his greed and ambition soon overcame him. He was tried for embezzlement and later imprisoned after an ill-fated attempt to invade Italy, with the believed aim to become Pope. He sided with his nephew Robert in the tussle over the English throne, and was exiled to Normandy following William II's victory. He died on the First Crusade.

BEAUMONT, ROBERT DE, 1ST EARL OF LEICESTER, COUNT OF MEULAN
c. 1040 – 1118. One of only 15 proven companions of William at the Battle of Hastings, he commanded 1000 soldiers in his first campaign and emerged with a tremendous reputation for martial prowess. Becoming a trusted advisor to three English kings, he was renowned for his eloquence and wisdom. He and his wife Elizabeth had nine children, three of whom became different earls and one of whom was mistress to Henry I.

BEAUMONT, ROGER DE, LORD OF BEAUMONT
c. 1015 – 1094. Nicknamed La Barbe (the Bearded). Wealthy, influential and loyal, he was a great Norman lord and supporter of William. (Heyer also gives him Hubert de Harcourt, Raoul's father, as his vassal.) He was not at Hastings but underwrote the expenses, and contributed 60 ships to the endeavour. Two of his sons were later given English earldoms.

BELÉME (BELESME), WILLIAM, LORD OF
c. 1995 – c. 1060. Nicknamed Talvas, "Shield." Heyer tells us he swore allegiance to the infant William, but history suggests he cursed the child, instead. A powerful but unpleasant man, he is believed to have strangled his first wife on her way to church, and imprisoned and tortured a guest at his second wedding, among much other wickedness throughout his life. Father to the equally cruel Mabille (Mabel), wife of Roger de Montgomeri.

BIENEFAITE, RICHARD DE, LORD OF CLARE
c. 1035 – c. 1090. AKA Richard FitzGilbert, Richard d'Orbec, Richard de Clare, Richard de Tonbridge. Norman lord and son of Gilbert of Brionne, who was William's first guardian, he received much in the way of English honours from his distant cousin, the new King. By 1074 he was one of the Chief Justiciars of England. He and his wife Rohesia had at least 10 children.

BIGOD, ROGER DE
d. 1107. A Norman knight from an obscure family who rose to great prominence in England following the Conquest. Heyer gives us his name as the one who warned William of the plot by his cousin William Werlenc to overthrow him, but historical sources suggest this was actually a relation of his (perhaps his father) named Robert. Nevertheless, Roger was rewarded along with Robert with improved status in Normandy, and he would go on to act as Sheriff of Norfolk and Suffolk. He rebelled against William II in favour of Duke Robert of Normandy, and lost his considerable lands in consequence, but got them back after declaring fealty. His son was later created Earl of Norfolk.

BOHUN, HUMPHREY DE
d. c. 1113. Called "with the Beard," as Normans usually went beardless. An adherent of Duke William, he is the ancestor of the prominent Bohun family in England, which held the Earldom of Hereford for centuries. One of his descendants married Henry V.

BOULOGNE, EUSTACE II, COUNT OF
c. 1015 – c. 1087. Called aux Gernons (with Moustaches), he variously fought against and for William, most notably taking part on the Norman side in the Battle of Hastings, for which he was generously rewarded with lands and titles. (He is one of the few noblemen specifically named in historical records.) All of these he lost following yet another rebellion against William, though he was eventually forgiven. His first wife was sister to Edward the Confessor, and his brother married William's half-sister Adelaide.

BRIQUESSART, RANULF DE, VISCOUNT OF BESSIN
1050 - c. 1089. AKA Ranulf the Viscount. Stood with Guy of Burgundy against William but was eventually brought around to the Duke's side. He stayed in Normandy, where was an important statesman, landholder and jurist.

BRITTANY, ALAIN (ALAN) III, DUKE OF
c. 997 – 1040. Also Count of Rennes. Nephew to Richard II of Normandy, he rebelled against Norman rule following the succession of Robert I, but later pledged fealty. He was appointed guardian to the young Duke William following Robert's death, and died of suspected poisoning by those opposed to William just three years later.

BURGUNDY, GUY OF
1025 – 1069. AKA Gui of Brionne. Grandson of Richard II of Normandy, he plotted to oust William from his ducal seat under the grounds of his illegitimacy, but his attempts failed. Defeated by a joint army of Normans and French in 1047, he retreated to his castle at Brionne where he held out for three years, but was eventually starved out. He spent the remainder of his days under house arrest.

CNUT THE GREAT
d. 1035. AKA Canute. Son of Sweyn Forkbeard, he fought and/or inherited his way to becoming, in his own words, "King of all England and Denmark and the Norwegians and of some of the Swedes," all by the age of forty. Remembered as an effective ruler and a pious man, he was also a ruthless warrior given to torture and summary execution. He had two sons by his first wife, Aelfgifu, and a son and daughter by his second wife, Emma of Normandy, and was father to three kings. (He was married to both women at the same time.)

CONTEVILLE, HERLUIN OF
1001 – 1066. Stepfather to William, he was a minor nobleman in Robert of Normandy's court and married his lord's mistress Herleva in 1031. The couple had two sons and two daughters, all of whom rose to some prominence; Herluin had a further two sons with his second wife, whose fates are less well-known. Died in 1066, but unknown whether this was at Hastings; Herluin would have been at least 65 at the time.

D'AUFFAY, GILBERT, LORD OF SAINT-VALÉRY (ST. VALERI)
d. 1087. AKA Goubert D'Aufay. A Norman nobleman who fought with William at Hastings, but preferred to return to Normandy rather than attain lands and titles in England. Heyer gave him a friendship with her characters Raoul and Edgar; she also gave him six daughters and the hope for a son, but history differs on this point.

D'AVRANCHES, HUGH, 2ND EARL OF CHESTER
c. 1047 – 1101. Nicknamed le Gros (the Fat) and Lupus (the Wolf). He was possibly at Hastings, and was gifted the earldom of Chester in 1071. He fought many battles over land and dominance in Wales, and became a trusted councillor of Henry I. He was known for his large appetites. His son wed a granddaughter of William I, who may have been his cousin.

D'AVRANCHES, RICHARD, VISCOUNT OF
d. c. 1082. Norman nobleman, supporter of William. He sent 60 ships to aid the attack on England, but may not have been present in person. He is believed to have married William's half-sister Emma, with whom he had at least five children; this belief is somewhat disputed by his grandson's marriage to one of William's granddaughters, a close familial relationship anathema to the church at the time, but which could be overcome by special dispensation.

DE GACÉ, RAOUL, GOVERNOR OF NORMANDY

d. 1051. AKA Ralph de Gasie. Of the royal house of Normandy. Caused the assassination of Gilbert of Brionne, the young Duke William's first guardian, along with Thorkill, his tutor. Was persuaded to join William in battling against Henry of France, was victorious on the field, and came to form part of the Duke's inner circle.

DE MEULLES, BALDWIN

d. c. 1091. AKA Baldwin FitzGilbert, Baldwin the Sheriff, Baldwin the Exeter, Baldwin du Sap. Younger son of Gilbert of Brionne, Duke William's assassinated guardian. Formed part of the Norman host at Hastings. Awarded a castle in Exeter and made hereditary Sheriff of Devon.

DU PLESSIS, GRIMBAULT

d. 1047. AKA Grimault, Grimoald. Worked with Guy of Burgundy to assassinate the young Duke William, then only 19. After the rebellion's defeat at the hands of a united Normandy and France, he was taken captive, stripped of his lands, and was found dead in his prison cell on the day that he was to appear in a trial by combat.

EALDGYTH, QUEEN OF ENGLAND

c. 1042–?. AKA Aldgyth, Edith (and Aldgytha by Heyer), she was daughter to Alfgar, Earl of Mercia, and married to Welsh ruler Gruffudd ap Llywelyn at fifteen. Widowed, she was taken as wife and queen consort by Harold, king of England in 1066; after the Conquest, she disappears from history.

EDGAR II, AKA EDGAR ATHELING (HEIR)

c. 1052 – c. 1125. Raised in Hungary due to his father's exile by King Canute, this son of the royal house was held by many to be the true heir of Edward the Confessor's throne. A teenager at the time of Hastings, he was elected as king by the Saxon lords following Harold's defeat, but did not rule. He continued to attempt to wrest the crown from William, but was unsuccessful. His sister Margaret became a saint.

EDITH OF WESSEX, QUEEN OF ENGLAND

c. 1025 – 1075. AKA Gytha, Ealdgytha. Daughter of Earl Godwin, she married Edward the Confessor. Well-educated, she spoke several languages and, despite her husband's antipathy towards her powerful family, eventually became one of his trusted councillors. The couple remained childless, and after Edward's death and William's conquest she was allowed to live out her days in comfort. It has been suggested that she might be the author of the Bayeux Tapestry.

EDITH THE FAIR

c. 1025 – c. 1066. AKA Edith Swan-neck, Edith Swanneshals, Svanneshals; "Gentle Swan." Handfasted first wife – in the eyes of the Church, mistress – of Harold Godwinsson. Very beautiful, the two had at least six children, and legend has it that it was she who identified Harold's mutilated body after Hastings.

EDMUND II OF ENGLAND

c. 990 – 1016. AKA Edmund Ironside. Son of Ethelred the Unready, he earned his nickname for his courage in repelling the initial invasion of Cnut of Denmark. With Ethelred returned to the throne, Edmund revolted against him, and married without permission the widow of an accused traitor, who had been imprisoned in a monastery. Crowned king after his father's death, Edmund then fought a number of pitched battles against Cnut, eventually being defeated and agreeing to divide the country; he and his heirs would take Wessex, and Cnut could have the rest. But when Edmund died suddenly just two years later, Cnut declared himself king of all England and exiled Edmund's children, one of whom came to be known as Edward the Exile, while his grandson Edgar the Atheling (heir) was briefly proclaimed king in 1066, before conceding to William the Conqueror.

EDWARD THE CONFESSOR, KING OF ENGLAND

c. 1003 – 1066. Seventh son of King Ethelred the Unready, but the first with his wife Emma of Normandy, Edward was forced into exile after the English throne was taken by Sweyn Forkbeard, also King of Denmark, in 1013. Ethelred returned to the throne after Sweyn's death in 1014, but when he too died, just two years later, Sweyn's son Cnut took the throne after the death of Edmund Ironsides only months later. Cnut married Emma of Normandy, killing Ethelred's remaining adult son Eadwig and sending Edward and his brother Alfred into exile. Upon Cnut's death, his and Emma's son Harthacnut took the throne of Denmark while England was held by his half-brother, Harold Harefoot. Harold's popularity alarmed Emma, who recalled Edward and Alfred; Alfred was tortured and blinded at Harold's order, and died of his injuries. Upon Harold's death in 1040, Harthacnut took the throne of England, which he bequeathed to Edward when he died in 1042. History remembers Edward as a weak king, but a pious one; he reigned for 24 years of relative peace, but as beset by much infighting and religious turmoil. He was married to Edith (Eadgytha), daughter of Earl Godwin, but the pair had no children. He was made a saint in 1161.

EDWARD THE EXILE, AKA EDWARD ATHELING (HEIR)

1016 – 1057. Son of King Edmund Ironside, he was sent into exile by King Canute when just a baby, and was raised in Hungary. He was made heir to the English throne by Edward the Confessor, but died mysteriously only days after reaching London. It is rumoured that Harold Godwinson, wanting the throne for himself, may have had something to do with his death.

ETHELRED, KING OF ENGLAND

c. 966 – 1016. Known as the Unready (which derives from "poorly advised" rather than from "ill-prepared"), he came to the throne at 12, after the assassination of his elder brother King Edward the Martyr. Not long after, raids from Danish ships began to ravage his coasts, and after decades of conflict, Sweyn Forkbeard at last conquered England, leading to Ethelred's exile in Normandy. He returned to the throne two years later when Sweyn died, then soon died himself. He reigned for 27 years, longer than any other Anglo-Saxon king, and was succeeded by his son Edmund Ironside, who was soon also succeeded by Sweyn's son, Cnut. Ethelred has been credited with formalizing the concept of the 12-person jury, which may or may not have been of his own creation.

EU, ROBERT, COUNT OF, LORD OF HASTINGS

d. c. 1093. A supporter of Duke William, Robert of Eu commanded 60 ships in the Norman conquest and was given the newly-build Hastings Castle as a reward for his services in 1068. He initially supported Duke Robert's claim to the English throne, but was driven to William II's side by Robert's debauchery, and even backed the latter's invasion into Normandy. Accounted a devout man, he and his wife Beatrix had six children.

FLANDERS, JUDITH OF

c. 1030 – 1095. Heyer claims that she is the daughter of Baldwin V, and thus sister to Matilda, but it is believed that she was actually his half-sister, only child of their father Baldwin IV and his second wife, Eleanor of Brittany, and cousin the Duke William of Normandy. She first married Earl Godwin's son Tostig, who was later created Earl of Northumbria, and was widowed when Tostig attempted to take the English crown from his brother Harold in 1066; some years later she married Welf I, Duke of Bavaria. She possessed a large collection of books, rare for the times, which she bequeathed to the church upon her death. Two

known volumes still exist, held at the Morgan Library and Museum in New York City.

FLANDERS, MATILDA OF, DUCHESS OF NORMANDY AND QUEEN OF ENGLAND

c. 1031 – 1083. AKA Mathilde, Machteld, Mald, Maud. Daughter of Baldwin, Count of Flanders and granddaughter of Robert II of France, and a descendent of Charlemagne, the story goes that she at first refused the suit of William of Normandy on the grounds of his inferior birth. To this William reportedly took exception and rode into her father's keep to either beat her or threw her to the ground by her braids, after which she decided to marry him after all. She bore William at least nine children, two of whom became kings and one the mother of a king; she spent most of her later years in Normandy, where she acted as regent while William spent most of his time in England.

FLANDERS, ROBERT I, COUNT OF

c. 1035 – 1093. Called Robert the Frisian, he was the younger son of Count Baldwin V and wrested control from his teenage nephew Arnulf III, breaking his oath to protect him in a battle that saw him at odds with the Kings of France and England. With Arnulf killed in battle (probably due to friendly fire), he became Robert I, Count of Flanders. He allowed Flanders to become a haven for William's enemies, and allied himself with the Canute IV in a planned invasion of England in 1085, ultimately defeated by the assassination of Canute by, it is assumed, William's agents. He was succeeded by his son with Gertrude of Saxony (mother of Dirk V of Holland), Robert II.

GHERBOD THE FLEMING

Claimed by Heyer to be the first husband of Matilda of Flanders, though the existence of a previous husband is widely disputed by historians. There was a Gherbod the Fleming at Hastings with William, and who was later made Earl of Chester, but it seems doubtful that it is the same one.

GIFFARD, WALTER, LORD OF LONGUEVILLE

c. 1010 - 1084. A Norman baron and supporter of Duke William, he fought at Hastings and was gifted with lands and wealth in the new nation. His son was made Earl of Buckingham by William II.

GODWIN, EARL OF WESSEX

d. 1053. AKA Godwine. Rising to power under the Danish King Cnut, Godwin became the most powerful lord in England, and married his daughter Edith to Edward the Confessor. Edward blamed the Earl for the maiming and death of his brother Alfred, and there is some evidence to suggest that he was justified. Godwin had 11 children, five of whom held multiple earldoms and one of whom was, briefly, king of England.

GODWINSSON, GYRTH, EARL OF EAST ANGLIA

c. 1032 – 1066. Fourth son of Earl Godwin and his Danish wife, Gytha Thorkelsdóttir, a fierce warrior loyal to his brother Harold. He died at the Battle of Hastings, after reportedly urging Harold not to risk his life in the endeavour, too. Harold did not listen.

GODWINSSON, LEOFWINE, EARL OF KENT

c. 1035 – 1066. Fifth son of Earl Godwin, loyal to Harold, died at the Battle of Hastings. At one point he was Earl of Kent, Essex, Middlesex, Hertford, Surrey, and probably also Buckinghamshire.

GODWINSSON, SWEGN, EARL OF HEREFORDSHIRE

c. 1020 – 1052. AKA Swein. Eldest son of Earl Godwin and Gytha, after returning from battle in Wales he infamously abducted Eadgifu, Abbess of Leominster, in an attempt to force her into marriage and obtain her rich lands. Edward the Confessor refused to sanction the marriage, however, and Swegn was forced into exile, his lands divided between his brother Harold and cousin Beorn.

Forgiven by the king, he demanded his lands back and murdered his cousin Beorn when he was refused. Declared niðing, a man of no honour, he was again exiled, then exiled a third time, along with the whole Godwin family, just one year later. Claiming remorse, he undertook a barefoot pilgrimage to Jerusalem from Flanders (a return journey of over 8 000 kms), and was mysteriously killed upon his return. Swegn's son, Hakon, was a hostage in Normandy for many years, until brought back by Harold Godwinson after his own time imprisoned there; what happened to him after that is a mystery, though he may have perished at Hastings, along with his uncles.

GODWINSSON, TOSTIG, EARL OF NORTHUMBRIA

c. 1023 – 1066. Third son of Earl Godwin and Gytha, he was as ambitious as he was a reckless and unsuccessful military commander who frequently got into unnecessary fights he couldn't win. He wed Judith, half-sister (it is believed) of Baldwin V of Flanders, and when he was exiled, largely due to poor estate management and the levying of ruinous taxes on his people, he took refuge with his brother-in-law, then took an invasion force into England to demand the return of his lands. He was unsuccessful. After his brother Harold was crowned king in England, Tostig greatly weakened his army by attacking him, alongside the Norwegian King Harald Hardrada, which no doubt contributed to Harold's loss at the Battle of Hastings. But Tostig would not live to see his brother's defeat, having been killed nineteen days earlier, during his own (failed) invasion.

GODWINSSON, WLNOTH

1040 – 1094. AKA Wulfnoth. A hostage from the age of 11, to first Edward the Confessor and then William of Normandy, Wlnoth was never released from his constant captivity, right up until the time of his death. Heyer tells us that he was richly robed and well treated, and it is to be hoped that, at the very least, he liked the food.

GRANTMESNIL, HUGH DE, LORD OF

1032 - 1098. From a family famous for warhorses and a supporter of William, but was still exiled for 5 years. Reconciled, he went on to fight at Hastings, where he was injured when his horse (apocryphally) ran away with him. He took the city of Leicester and was installed as governor. He later returned to Normandy, often forced to defend his lands. He died in England, leaving his family and descendants to be continually betrayed by successive Kings of England and Dukes of Normandy.

HAROLD I OF ENGLAND

d. 1040. Called "Harefoot," probably meaning he ran fast, he was a son of Cnut the Great and was elected regent after his father's death in 1035, nominally holding the throne for his brother Harthacnut, busy in Denmark. In 1037 he had himself crowned king, then died mysteriously only three years later, just as his brother was preparing an invasion force to take back his throne.

HAROLD II OF ENGLAND

c. 1022 – 1066. Second son of Earl Godwin and Gytha, he is accounted to have been a leader of men and beloved figure throughout England, known for his strength, courage and personal charm. In 1064, Harold's ship foundered the coast of Ponthieu (he may have been attempting to free his brother and nephew from Norman captivity), and he was taken prisoner by Count Guy I. Duke William ransomed him and took him as a hostage, even knighting him and sending him into battle, but effectively keeping him prisoner until, the story goes, he at last swore upon holy relics to relinquish all claim to the throne of England. (This might be Norman propaganda.) Returning to England, Harold was crowned king after the death of Edward the Confessor, but was forced to defend his throne twice in a month, once

against his brother Tostig and Harald of Haradra of Norway, and then again against Duke William. He famously died in the Battle of Hastings, the Bayeux Tapestry claiming that he was shot in the eye by an arrow, though this has now been disputed. Harold had two wives, one, Edith (Swan-neck) considered his mistress as they were handfasted in "the Danish manner"; the other, Ealdgyth (Edith) of Mercia. He had at least 5 sons with Edith I, and one with Edith II, but despite their best efforts to retake England, none managed to inherit his throne.

HENRY I OF FRANCE

1008 – 1060. King of the Franks from 1031 until his death, he was the son of King Robert II. Seen as a weak king, he saw his domain shrink throughout his lifetime, and his unsuccessful attempts to oust Duke William from Normandy further eroded his prestige. He was succeeded by his son with Anne of Kiev, Philip I.

L'AIGLE, ENGENUFE DE

c. 1010 - 1066. AKA Engenulphe, Engenulf, Euguenulf, and Enguerrand. Died at the Battle of Hastings, leaving behind his wife Richeveride (what a name!) and three sons.

LACY, WALTER DE

d. 1085. While he may not have been William's strongest supporter in Normandy, he was rewarded with rich lands and titles in England following the Conquest, when he continued to battle against domestic incursions. He died when he fell from a ladder while inspecting a priory he had endowed.

LANFRANC

c. 1005 – 1089. An Italian jurist who became a monk and opened a school at Bec in Normandy, eventually becoming a trusted advisor to William despite his initial opposition to the Duke's marriage to Matilda of Flanders, based on kinship closeness. It was he who gained Papal dispensation for the marriage, and through his offices that William was given the support of the Church to take the throne of England. After the conquest he was made Archbishop of Canterbury.

MAINE, HERBERT II, COUNT OF

d. 1062. Called Heribert (by Heyer). Heir to Maine, he was ousted by Geoffrey Martel, Count of Anjou, and asked aid of Duke William. He was betrothed to William's daughter Adeliza, but died before she came of marriageable age.

MALET, WILLIAM, LORD OF GRENVILLE

d. 1071. Reportedly of mixed Saxon and Norman blood, he was an adherent and favourite of Duke William, and fought at the Battle of Hastings. He was gifted with many lands and was appointed High Sheriff of Yorkshire, intended to save defend York from Danish raids. At this he was unsuccessful, but he went on to be High Sheriff of Norfolk and Suffolk instead. He was reportedly entrusted with King Harold's remains by William himself.

MAYENNE, GEOFFREY II, COUNT OF

1030 – 1098. Joined with Geoffrey of Anjou in invading Normandy, which angered Duke William. Taken prisoner, he was not released until he at last paid homage to the Duke. He broke his word when he rallied the barons after the death of the Count of Maine; William's counter-attack drove him back to his castle in Mayenne, where he was eventually starved into submission.

MONTBRAY, GEOFFREY DE, BISHOP OF COUTANCES

d. 1093. Norman nobleman, warrior, jurist and advisor to William of Normandy. Respected more for his martial than ecclesiastical abilities, his career as a bishop has often been called into question by history. After William's death he rose against William II in favour of Robert, Duke of Normandy, though he surrendered within a year, after doing much damage to Somerset and surrounds, including burning the city of Bath (!).

MONTDIDIER, RAOUL IV, COMTE DE

VALOIS

c. 1025 - 1074. AKA Ralph the Great. Staunch French royalist, fought at the side of Henry I against Duke William. Upon Henry's death he married his widow, Queen Anne of Kiev and became advisor to the young King Philip I. Holder of a multiplicity of titles and lands.

MONTFORT, HUGH DE

d. c. 1088. An early supporter of Duke William, he fought beside him against Henry I of France and provided 50 ships and 60 knights to help invade England. He was rewarded with lands and titles.

MONTGOMERI, MABILLE DE

c. 1030 – 1079. AKA Mabel. Heiress of Bellême, she married Roger de Montgomeri and over time showed herself a poisonous troublemaker and a deadly opponent of any who would stand in her way. She is reported to have caused much suffering to many nobles in Normandy, and was eventually decapitated in her own castle by Hugh Bunel, whom she had deliberately bankrupted. He is believed to have escaped justice.

MONTGOMERI, ROGER DE

d. 1094. AKA Roger de Montgomery, Roger the Great. A principal councillor to Duke William, it is not certain whether he was at Hastings, but instead may have remained in Normandy as co-regent with Duchess Matilda. His worth to William was so great, however, that he was awarded lands and titles to amounted to 3% of the new nation's wealth. He and Mabille had at least six children; he remarried after her murder, and had at least one more with his new wife, Adelaide, whose character has gone unrecorded to history.

MORTAIN, WILLIAM, COUNT OF

c. 1020 – c. 1068. Called the Warling. Son of Archbishop Malger, he was grandson to Richard I of Normandy and rebelled against his cousin William's rule, believing himself a legitimate heir. His rebellion was quickly ended, and his lands and titles were given to Duke William's half-brother, Robert.

MORTAIN, ROBERT, COUNT OF

c. 1031 – c. 1095. Half-brother to Duke William, son of Herleva and Herluin de Conteville, he was granted lands and titles in both Normandy and England in return for his lifelong loyalty, though he later rebelled against William II in favour of his elder nephew, Robert. Described by his chaplain as dull and stupid, and given to domestic violence.

MORTEMER, ROGER DE

990 – 1074. A Norman lord who espoused Duke William's cause, but who also aided some of his enemies to escape following a defeat in battle, for which he was exiled for a time, and his lands held forfeit. He and the Duke eventually reconciled, and after the Conquest he was awarded considerable lands and titles in England. The Mortemer family eventually took the title Earl of March, which culminated in the taking of the throne, with the crowning of Edward IV.

MOULINES-LA-MARCHE, WILLIAM OF

? Called William Sanglier, for bringing down Harold's royal standard at Hastings. Maternal cousin of Duke William, angry and cruel. Became a large landholder in England after the Conquest.

NORMANDY, MAUGER OF

c. 1019 – 1055. AKA Malger. Younger son of Duke Richard II of Normandy and his wife Papia, he was uncle to the young Duke William, but was never one of his supporters. After a rebellion instigated by Mauger's brother William of Talou was defeated, Mauger was stripped of his bishopric and exiled to the Isle of Guernsey, where he reportedly took a wife with whom he had many children, and begun studying the occult, before apparently going mad and drowning.

NORMANDY, ROBERT I, DUKE OF

1000 – 1035. Called Robert the Magnificent and

Robert the Devil. He was the younger son of Richard II of Normandy and brother to Richard III, against whom he rebelled, but was defeated. Less than a year later, Richard III died – somewhat suspiciously – and Robert I took the reins, in 1027. He quickly became very involved in local politics, giving aid and shelter to Flanders and France, as well as the exiled sons of King Ethelred of England. He plotted an invasion to restore their thrones, but first he wanted to undertake a pilgrimage to Jerusalem—upon which he died, leaving behind his infant, illegitimate eight-year-old son, William, as his sole direct heir.

NORMANDY, ROBERT II, DUKE OF

1051 – 1134. Called Robert Curthose, a nickname apparently bestowed by his father. Eldest son of Duke William and Matilda of Flanders, he was quarrelsome and entitled. Angered by his father's failure to punish his brothers for a prank he raised a rebellion against him in 1077, but was defeated and fled Normandy. Father and son were at war for over a decade, until reconciled by Queen Matilda, but William still split his domains between his sons Robert and William Rufus. Many of England's barons attempted to put Robert on the throne, but were unsuccessful. Meanwhile, Robert mortgaged his duchy to his brother in order to finance the First Crusade. As he was returning, William Rufus died suddenly, and their younger brother, Henry I, took the throne. Robert invaded but was defeated due to his own poor strategy, and eventually Henry took Normandy, and imprisoned Robert, who died a quarter century later, well into his 80s.

OSBERN, SON OF HERFAST, SENESCHAL OF NORMANDY

d. c. 1040. Steward of Normandy under Robert the Magnificent, he was made a protector of the young Duke William and was murdered by one William de Montgomeri in the child's very bedroom. His son, William FitzOsbern, went on to likewise hold a very privileged position in the Duke's household.

PHILIP I OF FRANCE

1052 – 1108. Called the Amorous. Ascending to the throne at only the age of 7, his mother acted as his regent (the first French queen to do so), along with Baldwin V of Flanders, until he turned 14. He married Bertha of Holland in 1972, but after their son was born he repudiated her (claiming she was "too fat") in favour of Bertrade of Montfort, who was married to Fulk, Count of Anjou. Their bigamous marriage caused Philip to be excommunicated by the Pope several times, but he refused to give her up. It was under Philip's rule that the First Crusade was launched.

PONTHIEU, GUY, COUNT OF

c. 1025 – 1100. Captured by Duke William after his participation in the French attack on Normandy in 1054, Guy of Ponthieu was held prisoner for two years before he finally agreed to pay homage to William in exchange for his freedom. In 1064, Harold Godwinsson's ship washed up on the shores of Ponthieu, and Guy took him hostage, but released him into William's care upon request. This tableau is in the Bayeux Tapestry, in which Guy is called Wido.

RIE, HUBERT, SIEUR OF

c. 1008 – 1086. Reportedly gave aid to the fleeing Duke William after Guy of Burgundy's failed assassination attempt, and misdirected the pursuers to give him more time to escape. He had four sons - - Ralph, Hubert, Adam, and Eudo – about whom not much is known, except that the latter seems to have founded the church of St. Peter in Colchester, and that they might all have been present at Hastings.

RENNES, CONAN II OF, DUKE OF BRITTANY AND COUNT OF RENNES

c. 1033 – 1066. Inheriting the duchy as a minor, his uncle Odo was made regent but then refused to give up power when Conan reached his majority. Conan eventually defeated his uncle, whom he had chained and imprisoned. In 1064, Brittany went to war with Normandy after William supported an insurrection within the region (Duke William famously invited Harold Godwinson, his prisoner at the time, to join the battle) and Conan later refused to join the Norman conquest of England, due to the suspected poisoning of his father at Norman hands a quarter-century earlier. Conan soon died of suspected poisoning himself, possibly from laced riding gloves, possibly at William's order.

RENNES, ODO (EUDON) OF, COUNT OF PENTHIEVRE

c. 999 – 1079. Son, brother and uncle to Dukes of Brittany, he acted as regent to his nephew Conan II but wanted to keep control for himself. Eventually defeated, after he was released from imprisonment he pledged support of William's conquest of England, for which he provided some 5 000 trained soldiers. He had at least fourteen children, and is the 28th great-grandfather of supermodel Cindy Crawford.

SAINT-SAUVEUR, NEEL (II) DE, VISCOUNT OF COTENTIN

d. c. 1094. AKA Chef de Faucon. While originally opposed to the young Duke William, and even an active campaigner in the rebellion against him in 1047, this Norman lord was recalled from exile in 1054 and invited to join William's army. He went on to distinguish himself as a battlefield commander under William, was richly rewarded for his service, and is alleged to have died in the same unknown Welsh battle that it is claimed also took the life of Hugh de Gournay, along with Roger de Montgomeri.

STIGAND

d. 1072. A churchman who, by 1020, was a trusted councillor to the kings of England. Raised to the Archbishopric of Canterbury, he retained his Bishopric of Winchester, and was thus excommunicated by five successive Popes. He is believed to have embezzled huge sums, and at one time held the third richest property in England. Following the Conquest he was quick to submit to William, but in 1070 was deposed by Papal legates, his lands and wealth confiscated. He died in prison at Winchester, penniless.

TAILLEFER, FULK, COUNT OF ANGOULEME

c. 1015 – c. 1087. Allied with Henry I of France against Normandy. Succeeded by his son William.

TALOU, WILLIAM OF, COUNT OF TALOU, AKA ARQUES

Before 1035 – 1086. A son of Richard II of Normandy, he was uncle to William of Normandy and declared his right to rule following his brother's death, but was unsuccessful in his challenge. He eventually betrayed and then rebelled against William on multiple occasions until at last being exiled.

TEONI, RAOUL DE, SEIGNEUR DE CONCHES-EN-OUCHE

1027 – 1102. An adherent of Duke William whom we know definitely fought at his side at Normandy and was richly rewarded in the aftermath. He got into a war in Normandy with his neighbour the Count of Évreaux because an undisclosed rift between his wife Isabel and the count's wife Helvise. The matter was eventually settled, after a deal of bloodshed.

TOENI, ROGER DE

d. c. 1040. AKA Roger of Tosny, Roger of Hispania. Father of Raoul de Teoni, he did not support the young Duke William, due to his irregular birth, and led an early unsuccessful rebellion against him. He was and was constantly invading his neighbours' lands, and was slain in battle by one of the aggrieved parties.

MAINE, HERBERT II, COUNT OF

d. 1062. Called Heribert (by Heyer). Heir to Maine, he was ousted by Geoffrey Martel, Count of Anjou, and asked aid of Duke William. He was betrothed to William's daughter Adeliza, but died before she came of marriageable age.

TESSON, RAOUL I DE, LORD OF TURIE-EN-CINGUELIZ

c. 1000 – 1066. AKA de Taisson, de Roche-Tesson. Initially opposed to Duke William, he switched sides during the Battle of Val-ès-dunes, helping to defeat that rebellion. He became one of William's trusted advisors and generals; he is thought to have died at Hastings, but that may have been his son, Raoul II. Or perhaps they both died there, history is unclear.

THORIGNY, HAMON-AUX-DENTS, LORD OF

d. 1047. A Norman baron who fought and died rebelling against Duke William. Believed to be known as "aux Dents" because he was born with a full set of teeth.

THOUARS, AIMERY, VISCOUNT OF

c. 1024 – 1094. AKA Haimes, Aumari, Aimeri, Haimon, Amaury. Allied with Geoffrey Martel against Duke William, but was won to the Norman cause and is one of the few definitively known to be present at the Battle of Hastings. Assassinated by his own knights.

WARENNE, WILLIAM DE, 1ST EARL OF SURREY

d. 1088. A staunch supporter of Duke William, he is known to have been at the Battle of Hastings, after which he was granted extensive lands and titles, though he was created Earl of Surrey through his loyalty to William II during the rebellion in 1088. He was killed in battle only a few months later, at the First Siege of Pevensey Castle.

WILLIAM I, KING OF ENGLAND

c. 1028 – 1087. Son of Robert the Magnificent and his mistress Herleva, he was left as the sole heir to the duchy after his father's early death. Young and dismissed for his illegitimacy, he proved himself to be a brilliant military strategist and commander, and foiled multiple insurrections and assassination attempts before even reaching adulthood. Innovative and ruthless at war, William's military victories were legion, and he became determined to inherit the crown of England from his cousin Edward the Confessor, who was childless. Exacting a promise from the popular Saxon Harold Godwinsson that he would not contest William's right to the throne, he used the breaking of this so-called oath as an excuse to conquer England, which he famously did at the Battle of Hastings in 1066. He quickly took control of his new domain, gifting huge parcels of land to his favourites and supporters, and introducing new ideas to the government of nations. His later years were troubled by his fractious son Robert, the continuing threat of Danish invasion and assorted rebellions. He died on campaign in France, leaving Normandy to Robert and England to another son, William Rufus, who was succeeded by his brother Henry. He and his wife Matilda of Flanders had at least 8 children.

* See "ALSO MENTIONED…"

SELECTED COVER GALLERY

Heinemann, UK
(1931)

Heinemann, UK
(1933)

Heinemann, UK
(1952)

Pan, UK
(1962)

Pan, UK
(1965)

Dutton, US
(1966)

Bantam, US
(1968)

Bantam, US
(1972)

Pan, UK
(1972)

Bantam, US
(1974)

Bantam, US
(1985)

Arrow, UK
(1997)

Mandarin, US
(2001)

Arrow, UK
(2005)

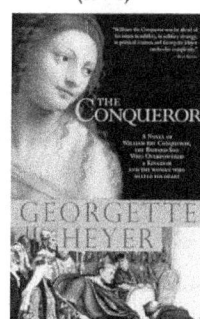

Sourcebooks, US
(2008)

SELECTED TRANSLATED EDITIONS

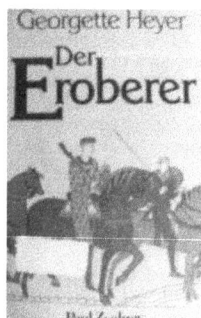

GERMAN: Paul Zsolnay
(1982)

GERMAN: Rowohlt
(1984)

German: Rowohlt
(1984)

GERMAN: dtv
(2002)

RUSSIAN: Великие
властители в
романах (2002)

WHAT THEY SAID

Contemporary Reviews of *The Conqueror*

Sydney Morning Herald **(Australia), May 15, 1931**

DUKE WILLIAM OF NORMANDY

In many school histories, William the Conqueror is exclusively associated with the dramatic events of 1066 A.D. and the beginnings of a system of national reorganisation in England. It is not always made clear that William had already completed several important conquests before he crossed the Channel, or that the Norman Conquest of England began long before Norman archers shot their arrows high into the air at Hastings. These points are carefully emphasised in Miss Georgette Heyer's historical romance, *The Conqueror*, in which the earlier career of William is narrated with especial thoroughness, together with the events which inevitably led up to the invasion of England. Like other stories by Miss Heyer, this book is full of hard galloping, brilliant pageantry, midnight escapes, sword-play, and romantic wooings. But the author has done full justice to the historical aspects of the plot, and gives a convincing study of William of Normandy from his illegitimate birth to the coronation at Westminster.

The outstanding incidents in *The Conqueror* are the plottings against young William when he first assumed his ducal power, his clashes with the King of France, the stormy wooing of the Lady Matilda, the visit to Edward the Confessor, Harold's forced oath to forego his claim to the English crown, the landing at Pevensey, and the English defeat by a narrow margin at Hastings. Miss Heyer takes pains to demonstrate how, when William made his landing in 1066, "he set foot on an island where, for a quarter of a century there had been a Norman party in politics, and where Norman methods and customs were known, feared, and admired." She skilfully relates this argument to the ineffectiveness of the overrated Edward, and the practical difficulties of Harold. It is, perhaps, regrettable that Harold is depicted as a lady-killer, but otherwise he suffers only in comparison with his all-conquering enemy from across the Channel. Running through the whole book is the story of William's trusted knight, Raoul de Harcourt, and his final conquest in true romantic style of the fair Elfrida.

~ | ~

The Sphere **(London, UK), March 13, 1931**

A full-dress historical novel of William the Conqueror from birth to education. It is excellent narrative, and Miss Heyer is a pioneer in a period strangely neglected and richly rewarding her graphic pen.

~ | ~

The Australasian, **May 30, 1931**

The task of the serious historical novelist is today much more exacting than it was when history and fable were in closer alliance. Not even the transcendent skill of Scott would raise his Norman barons and Saxon thanes much beyond the level of carefully costumed characters in a brilliant masquerade. But in Scott's time the fabulous element in historical romance still dominated, and the present age is one of cool skepticism and naturalistic criticism. In *The Conqueror*, Miss Georgette Heyer, while keeping this in mind, has over-reached herself a little. Carefully avoiding the stilted jargon of the 18th century romances, she attempts to give her story the flavour of the age by the lavish use of archaic terms. It is an ineffectual pretentiousness which translates pennon as "gonfanon," wolfhounds as "alaunt," warhorse as "destrier," hawk as "haggard," retainers as "raeinies," unlicensed castles as "adulterine fortalices," and so on. Furthermore, according to the evidence of the Bayeux Tapestry--that invaluable historical document in which the minutest differences between Norman and Saxon are noted, even to the way they cut their hair--the military equipment of these peoples was almost identical. Miss Heyer's Normans pit their lances and swords against the Saxon battle axes and javelins, and her careful emphasis on these points invites criticism. The story itself, however, concerned with the life of William I, from early manhood in Normandy to the conquest, is a fine piece of work. It is overweighted and overlong, but in spite of these handicaps it pulses with life and action. There is no better example of this sense of actuality than the description of the Battle of Hastings. The thread of the story is interwoven upon a tapestry that exhibits wars, plots, tortuous politics, courts, portraits of kings, nobles, priests, soldiers, and serfs, in order to bring out in relief the strong character of a man who drove to his goal through all this tumult, steadfast, calculating, unmoved by love or hate or fear of death, or by any discernible human weakness other than savage resentment of any mention of his humble origin.

~ | ~

Nottingham Journal (UK), April 17, 1931

Throws a good deal of light on the period of William the Conqueror. Shows the glory of a high-souled woman in her pure ancestry, and the determination of William to break it down. Miss Heyer is the author of *Beauvallet* which attracted wide attention.

~ | ~

WHAT A QUIZ

Think you know your Heyer? These questions will test your knowledge...

1. In which year was *The Conqueror* first published?
2. In which village was William of Normandy born?
3. Who was his mother?
4. How many brothers does he have?
5. To which king does he owe fealty?
6. With whom does he fall (quite literally) violently in love?
7. Who, according to the novel, saves him from an early assassination attempt at the hands of his cousin, Guy?
8. Which Saxon earl is shipwrecked and becomes William's prisoner?
9. How many men called Roger are in *The Conqueror*?
10. In what year did the Battle of Hastings take place?

ANSWERS: ANSWERS: 1. 1931; 2. Falaise; 3. Herleva, mistress of Duke Robert of Normandy; 4. Two half-brothers, Robert and Odo; 5. Henry I of France; 6. Matilda of Flanders; 7. Raoul de Harcourt and Galet, the fool; 8. Harold Godwinsson; 9. seven; 10. 1066.

~ | ~

UNMATCHED ATTENTION TO DETAIL BY RACHEL HYLAND

SAY what you will about *The Conqueror* (and I have much to say, I assure you), no one can deny the god tier scholarship on display throughout its considerable length. In the prologue alone there are dozens of words no longer in common use – chaffering, furmage, chanson, patins, to name but a few – and while their general meanings can mostly be garnered from context – chattering, a foodstuff, songs, plates – it is telling that Georgette Heyer makes use of archaic terms at every available opportunity, and even makes those opportunities for herself when she feels the need to throw in more local colour.

If anything defines Georgette Heyer's historical fiction above anything else, it is a hatred of anachronism. She would not use the word "horse" where "destrier" was more appropriate any more than she would say "market stall" when "sheld" was correct for the time and place.

The fact that said place is the ancient Duchy of Normandy in what is now Northern France and not her more usual English setting also affects the prose, and there are times when she has so clearly inhabited both the region and the era that you can feel the hubbub of the townsfolk, the stateliness of the court and the chaos of the battlefield, even though it all occurs in a time and place so alien from our own. (Not to mention in an alien language, which we must always bear in mind: Norman – or Norman French, as it is sometimes known – still exists in various subdialects and is spoken by about a hundred thousand people, but at the time of William the Conqueror it was, of course, the dominant language of the area.)

Heyer herself acknowledged the difficulty inherent in her task when she wrote, in later years, of how much "work" she put into this book, and how frustrating she found the nomenclature of Medieval people, with surnames - if, indeed, anyone had a surname - shifting with each generation, and the spelling of even first names so changeable across sources and centuries. I would add to this difficulty the multiple titles and nicknames by which people were known, in various languages, and how sometimes those nicknames would go on to effectively become that person's surname, but it would not pass down to their children (except, of course, that sometimes it did). In this, it is a little like reading a Russian classic, your head hurting until you gradually figure out that Alexei, Aloysha, Alyoshka, Alyoshenka, Alyoshechka, Alxeichick, Lyosha and Lyoshenka are all the same person. (To take a particularly irksome example from my own recent reading.)

What is quite remarkable about this, in regards to *The Conqueror*, is that Georgette Heyer somehow managed not only to keep all of these many identities of each of her characters – real people or not, in her hands they come alive as true characters – straight as she was writing the novel, and that without the aid of Ctrl+F, she even manages to mitigate against some of the inevitable confusion that arises in the reader, making it clear always who is whom even when their names, allegiances and titles always seem to be in a constant state of flux.

Of course, the sheer volume of real people namechecked in this book is almost overwhelming (see the FOUR PAGES of Celebrity Sightings as evidence of this), and likewise entirely remarkable. That she threaded in so many nobles, churchmen and warriors of the time is almost beyond belief, especially given that she was working with only pen and paper. Of course, other writers throughout literary history have pulled off similar feats, but I would argue that *The Conqueror* is at least as impressive, and potentially much more so, than even the most impeccably researched historical novel produced before it. And few, in my experience, are as impeccably researched as this one.

The problem with that, of course, lies in the fact that history is kind of dark and depressing, in a lot of ways, and the might-makes-right brutality of this era in Europe, in addition to the inhuman treatment of women, children, prisoners and the "lower" orders that was the norm, is often very hard to read about. And William himself, even before he got to conquering, is very much a product of his age, and so it can be difficult for the modern reader to entirely warm to him as a person.

Indeed, much of the book is rather excruciating to read due to William's fiery temper, as in fits of rage he orders appendages lopped off, kicks his disabled jester and heinously whips the woman he professes to "love" – but whom he really just desires, and wishes to possess – among much else. Indeed, Heyer's depiction of his savage, possessive pursuit of Matilda of Flanders is frankly abhorrent, and made all the more so by Heyer's attempt to justify the whipping – an historical fact, or as near to it as we have from the 11th Century – by suggesting that she was basically asking for it, that she wanted to provoke him:

> Such talk made Matilda lick her lips. To unleash the devil in a man was an ambition very likely to appeal to her. Had he a devil? Eh, what woman could resist the temptation to see for herself?

So, to wend this known fact into her narrative and yet create a picture of a successful marriage (which history, in fairness, reported to be the case – but which history, let us remember, was penned by men; we will never know the tears Matilda shed, nor the further suffering she was forced to endure), Heyer paints a picture of Matilda as a woman deliberately playing with fire, a woman who sought to be mastered and was even happy when she was, making of her an early exponent of Fifty Shades of Grey rather than a survivor of sexual harassment and violence. That might have been a more comfortable idea for Heyer, this suggestion that, in getting so viciously beaten in her own home Matilda got not only what she wanted but what she deserved – it is not for me, nor is it to most of us, I think.

Indeed, it is hard not to hate the book at times for its attitudes to women, which are dire and dismissive in the extreme. Even Raoul de Harcourt, Heyer's invention and a good and decent man whom we definitely like for most of the duration, says condescendingly "… for my part I judge it best to forget what women say," and calls a woman a "slut" because she has been forcibly taken as a mistress; while the Conqueror himself has a bunch of horrendous sayings – and doings – that just make you want to stab him with his own sword. When giving romantic advice to Raoul, he comes out with this offensiveness:

> "… women are not as men, and do not hate their conquerors. Tenderness is not so much their need as strength. You may use them ruthlessly, in such a way as must provoke in any man a bitter hatred and a desire for vengeance, and they will think no worse of you. Never waste gentleness to capture a woman's heart: she will deem you a weakling, and be done with you."

Okay, if you say so, William. That certainly does seem to be the case with Elfrida, the lovely Saxon maid with whom Raoul is in love, since he goes to her after the Conquest, when she is mourning the loss of her brother and father at Norman hands – not necessarily his hands, but they could just as easily have been – and demands she agree to marry him in quite the most insensitive way possible, which suddenly makes you hate Raoul, whom we had loved so well right up until his true colours are thus revealed.

Infuriating it may be to read, but as an example of the contemporary disregard for the feelings and personal liberty of women, it is spot on. And that is a big part of what makes this book so utterly brilliant, but also not very enjoyable. It is one of those books you cannot help but admire – the overriding reaction anyone must surely have to reading it is awe – but I don't think I could ever come to love it, nor could many of us.

And, perhaps not coincidentally, that seems to have also been true of William the Conqueror (AKA William the Bastard, Bastard of Normandy, the Fighting Duke, the Tanner of Falaise, Duke

William, William of Normandy – again, so many names, but at least with him, you immediately know who they're talking about). He was a man much respected for his cunning, his brilliant battlefield tactics, his courage and his fighting skill. But he was not beloved – except maybe by the fictional Raoul, and even then, not always – and despite Heyer's best efforts to, in some manner, redeem his reputation (along with that of Harold, his greatest rival; history believes them both to have been involved in more than one advantageous assassination, but she thinks them far too honourable to have done such a thing), it is just not possible to love the man, or his story.

But it is impossible not to respect both.

– Rachel Hyland

~ | ~

"You don't understand. Perhaps you have not seen him. He has that look in his face which draws me. A man might put his whole trust in him and not fear to be betrayed."
— *The Conqueror*, Part I, Chapter I
"I do not know if I love her. I only know that she is mine.

Mine, by the Rood, to hold in my arms if I will, locking my mouth to hers, or to break – yea, to hurt, to crush if that should be my will."
— *The Conqueror*, Part II, Chapter I

~ | ~

"Prowess in arms was the surest road to a Norman heart, and feats beyond their imaginings William showed them."
— *The Conqueror*, Part I, Chapter V

"I must die, but I will leave behind me a name that will endure, and a people made safe through mine endeavour."
— *The Conqueror*, Part IV, Chapter III

~ | ~

"If only I could be as they are, seeing one end alone worth striving for, not torturing my soul with thinking of what might have been, nor finding that my happiness tastes bitter on my lips after all because the price I had to pay for it was too heavy, and tore my heart in twain!"
— *The Conqueror*, Part V, Chapter I

~ | ~

* ALSO MENTIONED...

COUNTS OF: Asnieres, Avranchin, Cahagnes, Champagne, Chartres, Crevecoeur, Gascony, Guienne, Nevers, Poitou, Roumar, Saint-Pol, Soissons, Tournieres and Vermandois.

BISHOPS OF: Coutances, Lisieux (actually an Archdeacon), London, Worcester and York.

NONPAREIL

International Heyer Society Circular #13, July 2021

FROM THE PATRONESSES

Welcome once again to the monthly circular of the International Heyer Society!

Here we go in-depth into Heyer's first mystery novel, *Footsteps in the Dark*. In this month's essay, Clara Shipman gushes over the wry Charles Malcolm, whom she declares to be the true hero of the piece, and as always we have a breakdown of the characters, (few) references, locations and more.

~ | ~

"A very quaint old house. I was talking to Mrs. Bowers and she said you could lose yourself in the cellars."

"That's nothing," said Charles, getting up. "I lost myself getting from our room to my dressing-room. Of course it would simplify matters if we locked a few of the empty rooms, but I agree it would take away from the sporting element." — *Footsteps in the Dark*, Chapter 1

~ | ~

FOOTSTEPS IN THE DARK

BY the 1930s, the murder mystery had become a staple of best-seller lists on both sides of the Atlantic. The genre, which arguably began with Edgar Allen Poe's 1841 effort *The Murders in the Rue Morgue*, had been taken to new heights by Sir Arthur Conan Doyle and his Sherlock Holmes stories throughout the late Victorian era, and was even more greatly popularized by Doyle, Edgar Wallace, G. K. Chesterton and others in the early 1900s. By the time Agatha Christie published her first detective novel in 1921 – *The Mysterious Affair at Styles*, starring the flamboyant Belgian Hercule Poirot – female authors as acclaimed as Elizabeth Gaskell, Baroness Orczy and Mary Elizabeth Braddon had also all dabbled in the field.

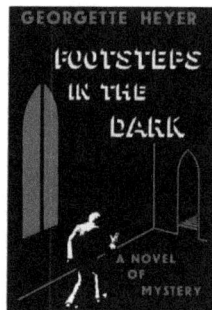

It only made sense, then, for Georgette Heyer to enter the lists as well, right slap bang in the middle of the Golden Age of Detective Fiction, especially as she (as she wrote in a 1931 letter to her agent, L. P. Moore) was then in need of funds:

> We are expecting an addition to the family in February – to my almost insane rapture…This, you see, accounts for my frenzied energy in writing this blasted thriller. I MUST HAVE MONEY. Like that. All in capitals. I pray to god to soften the hearts of an editor unbusinesslike enough to pay me an extortionate sum for the privilege of producing the thriller. [Ref: jenniferkloester.com]

But while it may have been a cash-grab that led Heyer to experiment with the genre, she proved to be quite adept at it. Despite becoming an exponent of the cozy murder mystery while its hard-boiled, stripped-down American offshoot was gaining traction, she rapidly carved out a reputation for herself as a mystery writer of unusual quality, and with a gift for humour and characterization second to none. Eventually given the moniker "Queen of Crime" (which, too, was Christie, among others), it all began with *Footsteps in the Dark*.

— *Maura Tan*

THE CHARACTERS

MARGARET FORTESCUE
Single, attractive and courageous, Margaret inherited the Priory, along with her siblings. Finds herself strangely drawn to the aptly-named Michael Strange, despite his evident shadiness...

PETER FORTESCUE
Brother to Margaret, with whom he lives in London, and Celia, he is a gallant and well-disposed young man, as yet unattached.

CELIA MALCOLM
Peter and Margaret's sister, a gentle but easily-frightened soul.

CHARLES "CHAS." MALCOLM
Celia's dashing, witty and intelligent husband, very tolerant of her whims. Known to be a rather brilliant solicitor.

LILIAN BOSANQUET
Margaret, Peter and Celia's aunt, a rather pompous and eminently practical woman who is nevertheless convinced of the supernatural when she believes she sees it.

BOWERS
Butler at the Priory, and butler to the Malcolms. Tends to believe in the presence of the ghost known as the Monk.

EMMA BOWERS
Housekeeper of the Priory, usually working in the Malcolms' London home. Formerly acted at nurse to the Fortescue children.

COGGIN
Works at the Priory.

JANE
Housemaid at the Priory, prone to hysterics.

FLORA HENDERSON
Deceased, former owner of the Priory.

COLONEL ACKERLEY
A retired soldier who settled in the vicinity of the Priory five years before the Fortescues arrived. Well-mannered, good company and very good at tennis, he quickly becomes a favourite guest of the town's newest residents.

LOUIS DUVAL
A French modernist painter of middle years who professes to believe in his own genius, but is actually quite insecure. Considered rather mad, he is humoured by the local townsfolk. An alcoholic and addict.

ERNEST TITMARSH
A rather scatty avid amateur entomologist always in search of rare moth specimens, he is often to be found on other peoples' property.

PENNYTHORNE
The vicar of Framley, a man of strong opinions.

MRS. PENNYTHORNE
His wife, an inveterate busybody who rarely has a good word to say about anyone. She is not popular in the town.

DR. ROOTE
Local physician in Framley, believed to be an alcoholic, rarely available for emergencies after hours, as he is probably drunk by then.

MRS. ROOTE
His wife, rather harsh-voiced and easily embarrassed by his behaviour.

WILKES
The genial publican of the Bell Inn in Framley, he professes to be certain of the ghost's existence.

SPINDLE
Barman at the Bell, an oddly anxious fellow.

MICHAEL STRANGE
A guest at the Bell Inn, he claims to be on a short holiday, but keeps turning up in the most unlikely places. Charles Malcolm finds him highly suspicious, but his sister-in-law Margaret does not agree, despite the evidence.

JAMES FRIPP
Travelling salesman staying at the Bell with a colourful lexicon; knows Michael Strange.

CONSTABLE HENRY FLINDERS
The local policeman of Framley, he is an earnest yet simple fellow very much afraid of the ghost allegedly haunting the Priory.

DISTRICT INSPECTOR TOMLINSON
Based in nearby Manfield, he listens to Charles and Peter's concerns about the doings at the Priory -- and about Michael Strange. But does he know more than he is saying?

SERGEANT MATTHEWS
Works with District Inspector Tomlinson.

DR. PUTTOCK
Based in Manfield, in charge of police autopsies.

BROWN
Private detective that Charles Malcolm asked to investigate James Fripp, salesman.

PEGGY MASON
A good friend of Margaret Fortescue.

BILL MASON
Her husband, once a suitor of Margaret's.

MILBANK
Kindly solicitor to the Fortescues, very active in their service.

MRS. MILBANK
His wife, with a great fondness for Margaret.

~ | ~

CELEBRITY SIGHTINGS

CROMWELL, OLIVER
1599 - 1658. General, statesman, and chief architect of the brief republican period in English history, after he deposed Charles I and was declared Lord Protector. A strict Puritan, laws under Cromwell were oppressive, and repressive, and genocidal towards Catholics. He died of malaria and was buried in great state, but after the restoration of the monarchy under Charles II he was exhumed and posthumously executed, hung as a traitor.

DICKENS, CHARLES JOHN HUFFAM
1812 - 1870. English writer, publisher, editor and social critic. Despite his lack of formal education, Dickens is one of the most famous and revered of all English-language novelists. His fifteen novels include some of the most beloved in all literature, including *Oliver Twist, David Copperfield, Great Expectations, The Pickwick Papers* and perennial holiday favourite, *A Christmas Carol*, .one of the most adapted books of all time.

WILLIAM I, KING OF ENGLAND, 7TH DUKE OF NORMANDY
c. 1028 – 1087. Coming to this dukedom very young and dismissed for his illegitimacy, proved himself to be a brilliant military strategist and commander. Innovative and ruthless at war, his military victories were legion, and he famously conquered England at the Battle of Hastings in 1066. He was succeeded as King by three of his sons, none of whom could claim his genius.

~ | ~

People in love became sloppy, she thought, and they were a nuisance to all their friends, which was a pity.
— *Footsteps in the Dark*, Chapter 9

"I see there has been fresh trouble in China. I feel one has so much to be thankful for in not being Chinese."
— *Footsteps in the Dark*, Chapter 6

~ | ~

THE LOCATIONS

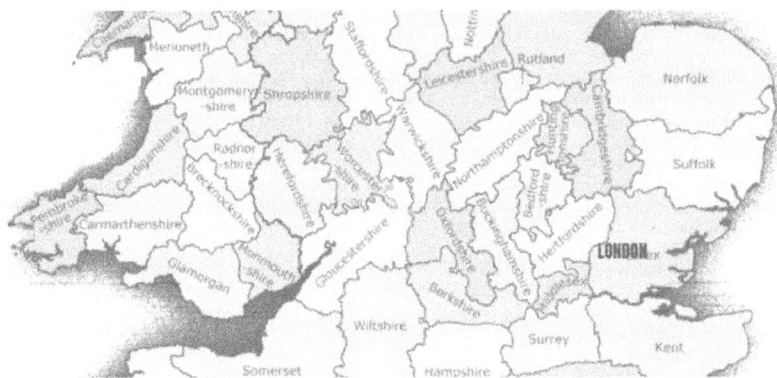

Unfortunately, we really have no idea where Framley is. We are given some clues: it's a little over an hour's drive from London, the distance varying greatly depending on what kind of car Margaret drives (which we don't know). We know it is picturesque enough to attract artists, but so are many places. We also know that the Manfield mentioned cannot possibly be the one in North Yorkshire, and that there is no such place as Tillingford Junction, which is the only other named nearby landmark. All we really know is that it's not on the coast, except... it might be. So just imagine Framley wherever you want it to be.

FRAMLEY
located a little over an hour from London, at 1930s driving speeds.

- The Priory
- Bell Inn
- The White House
Home of Colonel Ackerley

MANFIELD
Six miles east of Framley

- Police Station

LONDON
- Kensington
Home of Celia and Charles
- Knightsbridge
Home of Peter and Margaret
- Chelsea Embankment
Home of the Milbanks

WHAT THEY SAID

Contemporary Reviews of *Footsteps in the Dark*

Birmingham Daily Gazette (UK), February II, 1931

Haunted houses as a cover for crime are a familiar theme, but Miss Georgette Heyer gives to it several new twists in her *Footsteps in the Dark*. The author's skill in technique and in character-drawing is established by several non-sensational novels. They are not lost on this thriller, however--and one wishes these qualities were less rare in thrillers!

~ | ~

The Sphere (London, UK), February 13, 1932

Miss Georgette Heyer's *Footsteps in the Dark* is a conventional crime mystery story with a shameless use of the old constituents--a ghost, an old house, secret cupboards, a gang of counterfeiters operating, a lovely heroine. The secret is well preserved to the end, but the end seems hardly worth all the effort involved. If reading is for the sake of wasting time Miss Heyer's story fills its mission. There is some good writing thrown away.

~ | ~

Australian Woman's Mirror, April 5, 1932

Georgette Heyer has proved that she can write more than charming historical romances. Footsteps in the Dark is an exciting mystery revolving round an old stone mansion, the Priory, built in the early days when priests needed secret passages and sliding panels. Charles Malcolm and his wife Celia, her sister, Margaret Fortescue, her brother Peter, young people with a strong sense of humour, have thrilling adventures endeavouring to lay the Priory "ghost," a black-cowled figure of a monk who appears at the most unlikely moments. Stealthy footsteps, weird noises and sudden disappearances add to the eeriness of the book, and blend with the romance, mistaken identities, and surprises in plenty at the end. Other novelist may have used somewhat similar plots, but they could not have improved the telling.

~ | ~

The West Australian, (Perth, Australia), April 2, 1932

For the nonce Miss Georgette Heyer has forsaken the romantic period of *Powder and Patch* in favour of a modern mystery story. The result is an ingeniously constructed narrative written with a lightness of touch and a humour that distinguishes it above the usual efforts in this particular branch of contemporary fiction. For some considerable time 'The Priory,' an old country house where the scenes of the story are laid, has remained untenanted, until eventually it comes into the possession of Celia Malcolm and her brother and sister, Peter and Margaret Fortescue, through the testamentary dispositions of an uncle, recently deceased. From the very first, the new occupants of 'The Priory' are disturbed by mysterious nocturnal noises, which the rustic inhabitants of the neighbourhood attribute to the nightly perambulations of a phantom always alluded to by them as 'the Monk.' And as the ancient house is replete with priest-holes, vast underground cellars, sliding panels, and dark cavities, the inhabitants of this reputedly haunted house begin to think that there must' be something in these rumours of a restless apparition. Matters come to a climax with the kidnapping of Margaret and Peter while they are exploring a secret passage; and their rescue from a distinctly unpleasant predicament by Inspector Draycott, of Scotland Yard, who has been making investigations under an assumed name, leads up to the solving of a mystery which includes a plant for the printing of bogus bank notes and the identity of 'the Monk,' who turns out to be about the last person the reader would have suspected as the villain of the piece.

~ | ~

WHAT A QUIZ!

Think you know your Heyer? These questions will test your knowledge...

1. In which year was *Footsteps in the Dark* first published?
2. Around which village is the story set?
3. Who willed the Priory to Margaret, Peter and Celia?
4. Who is their local policeman?
5. What does James Fripp claim to be selling door-to-door?
6. Who is the owner of the Bell Inn?
7. What insects are the particular passion of Ernest Titmarsh?
8. What distinctive eyewear is worn by the vicar's wife, Mrs. Pennythorn?
9. What is the suspicious Michael Strange's real name and identity?
10. What simple mistake did Margaret and Peter make that allowed the Monk to guess they had escaped captivity, only to return?

ANSWERS: 1. 1932; 2. Framley; 3. Their aunt; 4. Constable Henry Flinders; 5. vacuum cleaners; 6. Wilkes; 7. moths; 8. pince-nez; 9. Inspector Michael Draycott; 10. They didn't drink any water.

~ | ~

SELECTED COVER GALLERY

Longmans, UK
(1932)

Longmans, UK
(1934)

Longmans, UK
(1943)

Amereon, US
(1976)

HarperCollins, US
(1985)

Berkeley, US
(1986)

Grafton, US
(1987)

Macmillan, UK
(1987)

Chivers Audio, UK
(1990)

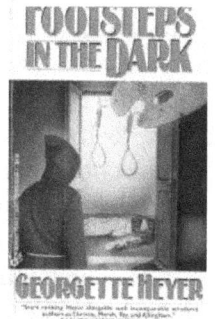

Berkeley, US
(1994)

Redwood, AUS
(2003)

BBC Audio, US
(2008)

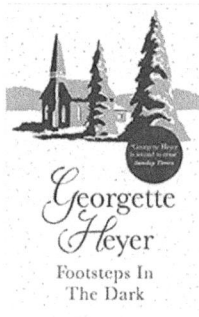

Arrow, AUS
(2018)

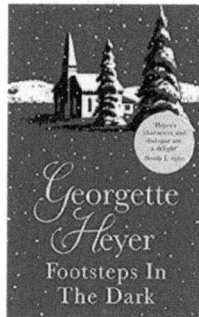

Cornerstone, UK
(2018)

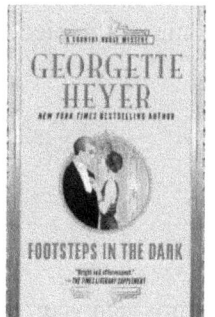

Poisoned Pen, US
(2019)

SELECTED TRANSLATED EDITIONS

GERMAN: Paul Zsolnay
(1986)

GERMAN: Rowohlt
(1988)

GERMAN: BEThrilled
(2017)

ITALIAN: Mondadori
(1994)

RUSSIAN: AST
(2017)

A LOVE LETTER TO CHARLES MALCOLM BY CLARA SHIPMAN

IT'S kind of a *Scooby-Doo* story, *Footsteps in the Dark*, isn't it? Of course, it predates Fred, Velma and the rest of the Mystery Machine gang by many decades, but when you read a book like this as a teenager, and you haven't then read the work of any other "country house" mystery writers before (or, frankly, since; I never could get into country house mysteries, aside from Heyer's), the thing that immediately comes to mind when you reach the inevitable unmasking is a *Scooby-Doo* villain being caught out under his unconvincing costume. Honestly, I half expected the culprit at the end of the tale to mutter about how he would have gotten away with it all if it weren't for those meddling Fortescues...

A bit about the book, to kick things off. Siblings Margaret and Peter Fortescue, along with their married sister Celia Malcolm (lucky, lucky Celia Malcolm; more on this in a bit), have recently inherited an old priory (cleverly named the Priory) from their deceased aunt. Though lacking modern conveniences – the place doesn't even have electricity – the trio nevertheless decide to spend the summer at their new country home, along with Celia's husband Charles (!!!) and their somewhat deaf but rather dear Aunt Lilian.

As newcomers to the village of Framley, on the outskirts of which the Priory lies, the party were unaware of the lore surrounding the house, but it turns out there is a famous ghost known to haunt the place, and multiple witnesses claim to have seen him in person. The ghost is known simply as the Monk, which makes sense when a) you discover his outfit is a robe and b) you learn what a Priory is. (Remember: I first read this as a teenager. And yes, Lord Damerel of *Venetia* also lived in a Priory, but I didn't know what one was when I read that book, either.) Soon, strange noises and eerie sightings and suspicious skeletons are everywhere, and it all seems a bit unlikely to be caused by a ghost, especially to the sensible and intrepid Charles Malcolm. (!!!)

But, wait. Let's first talk about that suspicious skeleton, because I have some thoughts. Upon my recent reread of *Footsteps* it really struck me as bizarre that, upon discovering human remains in a hidden room in their house (a priest's hole; also helpful to know what one of those is, when reading this book) that the decision was made to just... bury them. Just... find a human skeleton, and not inform the police and suddenly find your house under siege by CSI teams as they dust for prints and bring in sniffer dogs in case this is a serial killer case, or even alert the local historical society in case this supposedly centuries-old skeleton is of cultural significance, at all, but instead just bury it, like you would if it was the skeleton of, say, a dog. Was this really the cavalier attitude to human life that was prevalent in the time, or was this an error on Heyer's part, and in fact anyone happening upon ACTUAL HUMAN REMAINS even in the early 1930s would have felt naturally compelled to alert the proper authorities? Or have we, as a society, just gotten way more curious and/or precious about how and/or when dead and/or skeletal bodies have happened to turn up in our houses?

At least, when Charles (!!!) and Peter discover a second deceased person in the story – this one, a highly disreputable character who appears to have committed suicide – their first thought is to call the police and not just bury poor deluded M. Duval out of hand. That would really have been pushing things.

So, more than halfway into the story, we at last have a death, which is absolutely the opposite of how things work on *Law and Order* (and unless you count that skeleton, whose cause of death will forever remain unsolved), but is pretty common in Heyer's version of a murder mystery—though I don't think she ever again waits quite so long to deliver up the grisly discovery. And that is probably because Who Killed M. Duval? is not really the over-riding puzzle to be solved in *Footsteps*, but it is instead those very same footsteps... in the dark... and squeaking sounds... in the dark... and sightings of a monk-outfitted presence... in the dark... too.

I have to say, the actual causes of those footsteps, squeaks and spectres barely interested me, as the book went on. Not on my earliest reading, not in the ones since, and definitely not in my latest revisit. Who was the culprit and what (aside from murder) was the crime, I found mildly interesting, and the central couple of the story – Margaret Fortescue and her unreasoning but absolutely correct faith in the dubious Michael Strange, who of course turns out to be a renowned Scotland Yard detective – were cute and all, but they really didn't keep me too engaged with the story, either. Comic relief Aunt Lilian had her moments, as did the comically bumbling local constable, but really there is only one reason that *Footsteps in the Dark* is my favorite of all of Heyer's mystery novels, and one of my favorite Heyers in general: Charles. Malcolm.

Charles is one of those dapper, witty and sardonic gentlemen that Heyer excels at, and while he is pushed to the side lines for much of the book (and certainly in its concluding act), he absolutely steals every scene he is in. Like *The Black Moth*'s Duke of Andover before him and *Cotillion*'s Lord Legerwood after, Charles – Chas. to his friends; okay, I guess – hardly ever opens his mouth without a quip falling from it, and that is, of course, a huge part of his appeal.

But what he also has going for him is his wife, Celia. They are polar opposites in so many ways, she a fraidy cat more than half-convinced that the Monk is real, while he never doubts for a moment that human evil and not supernatural is at work; she not exactly an intellectual giant while he is a reputable barrister whose way with words suggests a towering intelligence.

The fact that Charles is so understanding of Celia, and does not pull a Mr. Bennet on her (their dynamic is not dissimilar), should not be to his credit, but for some reason, especially given the age in which this book was written, it feels especially noble of him. So, not only is he clever, funny and charming, he is also a good and loving husband – basically, the perfect man. And, to me, one of Heyer's very best husbands, actually.

Here are just a few of the moments that made me fall ever more in love with him...

This, when Margaret defends Michael Strange:

> "You both suspect Mr. Strange. Well, I'm sure you're wrong. Let the police take over before you both make fools of yourselves." She added apologetically: "I don't mean to be rude about it, but..."
> "I'm glad to know that," said Charles. "I mean, we might easily have misunderstood you. But what a field of conjecture this opens up! I shall always wonder what you'd have said if you had meant to be rude."
> – Chapter 4

And this, when Aunt Lilian proposes a séance:

> "Provided I am supplied with a comfortable chair I don't mind lending what I feel sure will be powerful assistance."
> Celia looked at him suspiciously. "If that means that you're going to fool about..."
> "Hush!" said her husband reprovingly. "For all you know I may be a strong medium. In fact I shouldn't be surprised if I went into a trance. Time will be as nothing to me. All the secrets of the future will be revealed to me." – Chapter 11

And this, when Strange's identity has at last been revealed:

> "A remark more calculated to provoke a peaceful man to homicide I've never yet heard."
> "Sorry," Michael grinned. "But it's important. Did either you or your sister, Fortescue, get any idea of the Monk's identity?"
> "What, don't you know who he is?" Charles demanded.
> "Not yet."
> Charles looked round at the others. "I don't believe he's a detective at all. Anyone got any wolfbane, or is that only good against vampires?" – Chapter 18

There is much, much more than this, of course, but these are the moments that have long stood out in my memory, even after the other events of the book in which they appear have faded. And the events of *Footsteps* do often fade, I find; every time I reread it, it's like reading it again for the first time... except for Charles, of course.

This is not to suggest that *Footsteps in the Dark* is a bad book, necessarily, although it is far from being among Heyer's best, even when it comes to the mysteries. (For me, that is *Envious Casca*, but your mileage may vary, as people used to say.) In fact, I would argue that having one stand-out character that can make me return again and again to a book I don't particularly care for, and otherwise find quite forgettable, makes *Footsteps in the Dark* kind of amazing. Because: Charles. Malcolm. (!!!) Right?

– Clara Shipman

NONPAREIL

International Heyer Society Circular #14, August 2021

FROM THE PATRONESSES

Welcome once again to the monthly circular of the International Heyer Society!

Here we go in-depth into Georgette Heyer's second sequel novel, *Devil's Cub*, which brings us the tale of the wicked Dominic Alastair, Marquis of Vidal, who is the son of some old and very dear friends. Check out Susannah Fullerton's deep appreciation of the novel, and, as always, there are character notes, historical references, reviews, locations and more.

DEVIL'S CUB

DEVIL'S CUB is often cited as a favourite by many a Heyer reader, but I have to say that it has never been one of mine. True, seeing Avon and Léonie and the gang from *These Old Shades* again was – and remains – a delight, and the developing relationship between the unruly Dominic Alastair, Marquis of Vidal and the seemingly-unequal (but more than equal to the task) Mary Challoner is perfectly played out. But what has always disturbed me about the novel, even leaving aside Dominic's deliberate seduction of teenage virgins and quite vicious abduction of Mary, is the way the book suggests that in running off with Mary, Dominic was in the wrong, because of her inherent quality, but had he successfully taken her younger sister Sophia away with him to France, as was his intention (and thence soon have abandoned her to a life of sex work, when he inevitably tired of her), it was no more than she deserved.

Look at the two girls. Sure, Sophia is an obvious beauty while Mary's attractiveness is much more subtle, and their manners are different, especially in their interactions with Vidal. But Sophia's only crime here seems to be that she never got the advantages of an elite private education in ladylike behaviour which was granted to Mary as the eldest, and funded by the girls' grandfather. Instead she has been left to her mother's devices, and the former Miss Simpkins has made of her youngest daughter a Lydia, while her time spent in the company of gentleman's daughters throughout her formative years has made of Mary an Elizabeth. Belatedly realizing that Mary's deportment and intelligence mark her as a gentlewoman, Vidal is ashamed of ruining her and insists she marry him, to save her reputation. But he would hardly have given the same consideration to Sophia, would he? Indeed, he deliberately plotted that young girl's ruination, and cared not a jot about what would become of her afterwards. No, he never promised her marriage, but arranging an elopement with her implied such, which makes this no better than Mr. Wickham's duplicitous treatment of the Bennets' youngest (again, teenage) daughter, after which they remained unmarried, and would have continued so, until Wickham was literally paid to wed her. And would Avon's old friend Sir Giles have gotten involved on behalf of his younger granddaughter, should she have been taken instead? We are given to believe... no, probably not.

The reformation of the rake is a popular trope in romantic fiction, and there are undoubtedly those who favour the Mr. Wickham archetype. But personally, despite my enjoyment of the journey through France, the comedic scenes (especially Lord Rupert and his wine), and my admiration of the redoubtable Mary, I find I just can't forgive this book for its victim-blaming of poor deluded Sophia Challoner. She's a foolish brat, yes, but she deserved better.

– Rachel Hyland

63

THE CHARACTERS

DOMINIC ALASTAIR, MARQUIS OF VIDAL
Headstrong, mercurial and ruthless, the young heir to the Avon dukedom is a gamester, rake, wastrel and a famous shot. Bur his life of wildness is forever changed when he abducts the practical Mary Challoner...

JUSTIN ALASTAIR, DUKE OF AVON
Dominic's now-aged parent, still as suave and omniscient as ever.

LÉONIE ALASTAIR, DUCHESS OF AVON
Dominic's French mother, still a great beauty and still as impulsive and bloodthirsty as ever.

LORD RUPERT ALASTAIR
Dominic's bachelor uncle, still always in debt and as under Léonie's thumb as ever.

LADY FANNY MARLING
Dominic's aunt, still as vain and ambitious as ever, very focussed on her daughter's future.

JULIANA MARLING
Fanny's daughter, a great beauty like her mother, and just as determined to marry the stolid man she loves rather than the brilliant match her mother envisages.

JOHN MARLING
Sensible and diligent but also judgemental and dull, Fanny finds her son a disappointment, despite the fact that he is very like his father and the love of her life, the departed Edward.

ELISABETH DE CHARBONNE
Dominic's generous and kindly but rather silly aunt on his French grandmother's side.

BERTRAND SAINT-VIRE, VICOMTE DE VALME
Ostentatiously charming son of Léonie's uncle, the Comte de Saint-Vire.

ARMAND DE SAINT-VIRE, COMTE DE SAINT-VIRE
His father, now tremendously large but still as gossipy as ever, we are told.

HORACE TIMMS
Vidal's valet.

RICHARDS
Vidal's groom.

FLETCHER
Vidal's London butler, much beset by Lord Rupert and the Duchess of Avon.

GASTON
Avon's corpulent valet.

MARY CHALLONER
Eldest daughter of a country gentleman and his merchant-class wife, Mary was educated to be a lady and doesn't fit in with her family. Determined, intelligent, practical and protective, she is also somewhat reckless, which leads to near-disaster...

SOPHIA CHALLONER
A great and spoiled beauty with little thought to her actions, her head is turned by the attentions of the Marquis of Vidal, which leads to her to make some very questionable decisions.

CLARA CHALLONER, NEE SIMPKINS
Mary and Sophia's mother, disapproved of by her husband's genteel family. She is determined to see her daughters wed to advantage, no matter by what means.

CHARLES CHALLONER
Her deceased husband, reckless and extravagant, a scapegrace son of the gentry.

GENERAL SIR GILES CHALLONER
Stern and straight-laced, he disapproved of his son's marriage to the ineligible Clara Simpkins, and cut off all financial support. He did, however, agree to pay for the elite education of his eldest granddaughter, Mary.

HENRY SIMPKINS
Clara's brother, a merchant.

BELLA SIMPKINS
His wife, fascinated with the doings of the nobility.

HENRY SIMPKINS
Their son, who has the good taste to prefer Mary to Sophia. Humourless and Puritanical, Mrs. Challoner thinks he is the best husband that her elder daughter will be able to find and is furious that Mary will not wed him.

ELIZA MATCHAM
Sophia's friend, always ready to help her sneak away to meet Vidal without her mother's knowledge, while also being very jealous of Vidal's interest in Sophia.

JAMES MATCHAM
Her brother, an unpleasant fellow.

PEGGY DELAINE
Their cousin.

BETTY
The Challoners' abigail, an untidy girl.

FREDERICK COMYN
The scion of an old though undistinguished family and an ambitious young man of a very serious turn of mind, he has won the affections of the beautiful and spoiled Juliana Marling, much to her mother's displeasure.

SIR MALCOLM COMYN
His eminently respectable father.

HUGH DAVENANT
The Duke of Avon's closest friend, somewhat disapproving of Vidal's behaviour. (As he had been of Avon's.)

MONTAGUE QUARLES
A hot-headed London gentleman at odds with Vidal. Red-faced and argumentative, he forces a duel onto Vidal and is shot accordingly.

JACK BOWLING
Attended Timothy's on the night of Vidal's duel with Quarles.

LADY MONTACUTE
Gave the drum to which Vidal was travelling when he shot the highwayman on Hounslow Heath.

CROSSLY
He and Vidal competed in a curricle race from London to Newmarket the day after Vidal's impromptu duel.

LEONARD HAMMOND
A Protestant cleric leading a young nobleman through his Grand Tour. Encountered at Dijon, he is outraged when asked to wed Frederick Comyn and Mary Challoner with so little ceremony.

LORD EDWARD CREWE
His charge, son of Lord Manton, a friend of Lord Rupert's.

M. PLANÇON
Landlord of the inn at Dieppe.

BOISSON
Landlord of the Rayon d'Or at Pont-de-Moine

CELESTINE BOISSON
His wife, outraged by females travelling alone.

JOHN
A lackey at Hôtel Avon in Paris.

MITCHELL
Another lackey at Hôtel Avon in Paris.

ROBERT
Another lackey at Hôtel Avon in Paris.

~ | ~

CELEBRITY SIGHTINGS

CHOLMONDELEY, GEORGE JAMES, 1ST MARQUESS OF CHOLMONDELEY
1749 – 1827. Succeeded his grandfather as fourth Earl of Cholmondeley in 1770, and was admitted to the Privy Council in 1783, though he left his post that same year and did not hold government office again until almost 30 years later. Notorious for his affair with married beauty Grace Dalrymple Eliot, which led to a scandalous divorce. Created marquess in 1815, he was a great-nephew of Horace Walpole.

COCCHI, ANTONIO
1695 – 1758. Italian physician and author of the influential text *Du regime de vivre Pythagoricien à l'usage de la médecine* (*The Pythagorean Diet, or Vegetables only conductive to the Preservation of Health and the Cure of Diseases*), among other books on then-modern health advice. A vegetarian, he was the first to suggest that scurvy might occur due to a lack of vegetables in the diet.

COKE, LADY MARY
1721 - 1811. Youngest daughter of the Duke of Argyll, she was pushed into marriage with the problematic Viscount Coke, who virtually imprisoned her at his estate for three years. Her family interceded, and eventually she was permitted to live with her mother until Coke's death, which came three years later. Independently wealthy, Lady Mary set out on a life of international travel and social success that was often marred by her self-importance and fantastic claims of victimhood, especially her suggestion that she had been secretly married to the Duke of York, and in her lifelong paranoid belief that her former friend, Empress Maria Theresa, was constantly plotting against her. Horace Walpole's The Castle of Otranto is dedicated to her, which he knew would gratify her need for attention. She is best remembered now for the decades of journals she left behind.

COVENTRY, MARIA, COUNTESS OF COVENTRY (née GUNNING)
1732 - 1760. Sister to Elizabeth, the beautiful Maria wed the Earl of Coventry in 1752. It was not a happy marriage, with the Earl taking up a mistress in the form of courtesan Kitty Fisher, much to Maria's distress. Maria, then already mother of three, died of lead poisoning (caused by makeup) at the age of 27. She was known as a "victim of cosmetics."

FOX, THE HON. CHARLES JAMES
1749 – 1806. Known for his wit, cleverness and compelling oratory, he was first admitted to parliament at 19, sponsored by his father, a prominent Whig politician. He spent most of his 38-year career in opposition and was the chief rival of Tory leader Pitt the Younger. Fox's personal life was plagued by gaming debt and scandal, yet he was well-liked in Society, where he had been a leader of the "Macaroni" fashion scene in his youth. A frequent victim of cartoonist Gilray, he was personally hated by George III and the monarchist Tory party.

HAMILTON, ELIZABETH CAMPBELL, DUCHESS OF ARGYLL AND 1ST

BARONESS HAMILTON OF HAMELDON (NÉE GUNNING)

1733 - 1790. An Irish beauty of no fortune, she and her sister Maria took London by storm in 1750. She wed the Duke of Hamilton on Valentine's Day, 1752, in a secret wedding only the month after they first met. The couple had three children. Upon widowhood she wed the Marquis of Lorne (later Duke of Argyll), with whom she had a further five children. Created a Baroness in her own right in 1776

DOUGLAS, WILLIAM, 4TH DUKE OF QUEENSBURY, AKA LORD MARCH

1724 - 1810. Cousin to the 3rd Duke, he had previously inherited the Earldoms of March and Ruglen from his parents. March, later fondly known as "Old Q", was famous for his love of gaming and was a great favourite of the Prince of Wales (George IV). He never married but had a daughter, Maria, who wed the Marquess of Hertford in 1798. and was the Duke's principal heir.

HOWARD, FREDERICK, 5TH EARL OF CARLISLE

1748 - 1825. Statesman involved in failed peace talks with the US which led to the American Revolution and with rule of Ireland during a particularly turbulent period. At one time was Lord Byron's guardian, and was much disliked by the young poet as a result.

MORE, HANNAH

1745 – 1833. Moralist, playwright, philanthropist and author, she actively campaigned against slavery and championed education for the underprivileged. Nevertheless, she was opposed to women's suffrage and even turned down membership in the Royal Society of Literature because she believed women were unqualified to join. Author of The Inflexible Captive, a book so worthy that it was approved of by John Marling.

PONSONBY, JOHN, 1ST VISCOUNT PONSONBY

1770 – 1855. Politician and diplomat of strong principles and address, Ponsonby is mostly remembered for having been extraordinarily handsome. There is a tale that he was saved from execution as an aristocrat during the French Revolution because the women in the mob objected to killing someone "so pretty."

RABELAIS, FRANÇOIS

c. 1483 - 1553. French scholar, writer and physician, he is known for his satirical works commenting on social depravity and excess. He was also a monk, and his professed faith and piety at times seems at odds with his often bawdy humour. The word "Rabelaisian," coined after him, is defined by Merriam-Webster as ""marked by gross robust humor, extravagance of caricature, or bold naturalism."

DE RUMIGNAY, LEGROS

1710 – 1770. Official hairdresser to the French court and author of *L'Art de la coiffure des dames françaises* (*The art of coiffure for French ladies*).

Popularly known as M. Le Gros.

WALPOLE, HORACE

1717 - 1797. Noted wit, gamester, epistolarian and author of *The Castle of Otranto*, generally regarded as the first Gothic novel.

WRAXALL, SIR NATHANIEL WILLIAM*

1751 – 1831. Son of a Bristol merchant, he entered the East India Company at the age of eighteen and quickly rose to the rank of judge-advocate and paymaster. Leaving the company when just 21, he set out on a tour through Europe, even being presented at the Portuguese court. Through keeping a thorough account of his travels he published several well-received books of memoirs, and garnered many wealthy and noble patrons throughout Britain and Europe. In 1777 Wraxall was given a lieutenancy in the British Army by George III, despite never undertaking any military service. He later entered parliament, spending fourteen years as a Tory representative. But it is his first-hand accounts of life in the Georgian era, most especially his works Historical Memoirs and Posthumous Memoirs, that proved to be his greatest contributions to posterity.

NOTE: The "Captain Wraxall" mentioned in the book may be fictional and not this gentleman at all, but he is quite remarkable, and his works were surely a reference source for Heyer.

~ | ~

The landlord was trying to explain that there were a great many English people in his house, all fighting duels or having hysterics.
— *Devil's Cub*, Chapter XVI

"I comfort myself with the reflection that your wife will possibly be able to curb your desire—I admit, a natural one for the most part—to exterminate your fellows."
— *Devil's Cub*, Chapter XIX

~ | ~

THE LOCATIONS

LONDON:

- Bloomsbury
Home to the Challoners
- Curzon Street
Home to the Duke and Duchess of Avon
- Half Moon Street
Home to Lord Rupert Alastair

NEWHAVEN

DIEPPE
ROUEN
PARIS
- *Hôtel Avon*
DIJON
PONT-DE-MOINE
Some 25 miles from Dijon
- Rayon d'Or

~ | ~

WHAT THEY SAID

Contemporary Reviews of *Devil's Cub*

The Bulletin (Australia), March 8, 1933

We first encounter the 24-year-old Marquis of Vidal in his coach on Hounslow Heath. Highwaymen! A shot from the coach. The Marquis draws his right hand from his pocket.

There was an elegant silver-mounted pistol in it, still smoking. The gentleman threw it on the seat beside him, and crushed the charred and smouldering portion of his greatcoat between very long white fingers.

Anticipating the methods of Chicago's quick-gunning gangsters, he has given the eighteenth-century racketeer the works from his pocket. A servant asks what he will do with the corpse. An expression of boredom flits across the dark and extremely handsome face of the Marquis. "My good fellow, are you suggesting I should carry a footpad's corpse to my Lady Montacute's drum?" He goes on like this all through the book – splendidly fearless, incredibly efficient, ineffably bored with his hectic life – and then comes lovely Miss Challoner, and Love. No such people ever lived, of course, but the world would certainly have been more picturesque if they had.

~ | ~

The Scotsman, December 12, 1932

Characters from the sphere of romance and from gilded scenes of English and French fashion of the pre-Revolution age blend in harmonious grouping and in dramatic action in Miss Heyer's novel, some of the figures in which are old acquaintances brought over from previous pictures of eighteenth century society from the same brilliant hand. The "Devil's Cub," the Marquis Vidal, comes upon the stage with an appropriate gesture and in well-fitting surroundings. He shoots a highwayman dead on Hounslow Heath, and he does not take the trouble of pausing to see what happens to the body. His time and his thoughts are wholly bent on the pursuits and pleasures of a high-born "Rake" of the period: on gaming and drinking with Charles James Fox, dancing and duelling with persons of ton, and scheming to kidnap women whose social rank falls short of his own. In all this he is a faithful follower—except when their wishes happen to clash—of his father who, however, as Duke of Avon, has "ranged himself" in a manner more beseeming one who has had the undeserved good fortune to love and marry a woman with a surpassing charm and spirit of the Duchess Leonie.

The victim whom Vidal has specially marked down for himself is a wealthy "Cit's" daughter, young and lovely but frivolous and designing. But Sophie's elder sister—an altogether different proposition in womankind—flings herself in his path, and is carried off to France instead. Thereupon ensues a conflict of will and wits, with imperious whim encountering real passion in which one cannot fail to find both entertainment and an interest which deepens, if it is made more complicated when the scene moves to Paris and to Dijon, and the Duke and the Duchess and the aunts, uncles, cousins, and other relations of the pair, arrive to play their parts. The Devil's Cub, as soon appears, has some redeeming graces apart from his quenchless courage and élan, while Mary Challoner is a woman among a million, in the high spirit, coolness, and resource she summons to meet dangerous situations, and in her power of seeing the humorous side of human frailty, while sternly holding the line of rectitude.

~ | ~

In reading one of Miss Heyer's novels one does not look for, nor expect to find, anything in the nature of subtlety of characterisation, or psychological insight into human conduct and motives. But what one does anticipate — and never yet has Miss Heyer failed her readers in this respect — is a thoroughly well-constructed story, with bright and sparkling dialogue, and characters who are not automata, but living flesh and blood creatures of like passions unto ourselves. Especially may this be said or her 'Powder and Patch' romances, of which *Devil's Cub* is perhaps the best of the several examples she' has given us of her work in this 'genre.' The young and headstrong Marquis of Vidal is indeed a personality of a marked distinction; and even when he 'pinks' or 'wings' his man on this or that trifling occasion, he may still be certain of holding the suffrages of all readers of the gentler sex, who are notoriously the most bloodthirsty of the novelist's patrons. And when the 'Devil's Cub' abducts the shrewd and sensible and not unattractive Miss Mary Challoner in mistake for that young woman's dollishly pretty and perfectly brainless sister, and takes her with him into France, the astute (and fair) reader will perceive, at the very beginning of the terrible coil this impetuous action on the part of the young Marquis brings about, that a happy 'denouement' is likely to develop as the upshot of this—at first sight— unpromising association. Among other interesting and, in some instances, charming personages introduced by the author into her spirited tale are Vidal's parents, the Duke and Duchess of Avon, his uncle, Lord Rupert Alastair, the sententious Mr. Comyn, and Leonie [sic] Marling and her mother, Lady Fanny Marling.

~ | ~

WHAT A QUIZ!

Think you know your Heyer? These questions will test your knowledge...

1. In which year was *Devil's Cub* first published?
2. How many sequels had Georgette Heyer published previously?
3. How many characters from *These Old Shades* appear?
4. At which gentleman's club does Vidal fight his impromptu duel?
5. In which vehicle does he undertake a race the next day?
6. Where do the Challoners live?
7. From which English port city does Vidal's ship depart?
8. What is Mr. Comyn's first name?
9. Why was Lord Rupert so happy to have gone to Dijon?
10. Why did Vidal think his mother would especially like Mary?

ANSWERS: 1. 1932; 2. 0; 3. 6: Duke and Duchess of Avon, Lady Fanny Marling, Lord Rupert Alastair, Hugh Davenant, Gaston; 4. Timothy's; 5. curricle; 6. Bloomsbury; 7. Newhaven; 8. Frederick; 9. He found good wine there; 10. Because Mary shot him.

~ | ~

"God knew she would ask nothing better than to be his wife, but she had sense enough to know that nothing but unhappiness could result from it. If he had loved her, if she had been of his world, approved by his family – but it was useless to speculate on the impossible."

— *Devil's Cub*, Chapter XIII

SELECTED COVER GALLERY

Heinemann, UK
(1932)

Heinemann, UK
(1951)

Penguin, UK
(1953)

Peacock, UK
(1963)

Bantam, US
(1967)

Pan, UK
(1969)

Pan, UK
(1983)

Arrow, UK
(1991)

Signet, US
(1992)

Arrow, UK
(2005)

Arrow, UK
(2004)

HQN, Canada
(2008)

Sourcebooks, US
(2009)

Windsor, US
(2012)

Sourcebooks, US
(2019)

SELECTED TRANSLATED EDITIONS

FINNISH: Uusi
kirjakerho (1982)

DUTCH: DeKern
(1983)

JAPANESE:
ハーレクイン (2011)

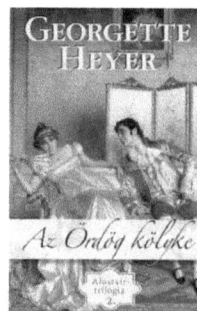

HUNGARIAN:
GABO (2012)

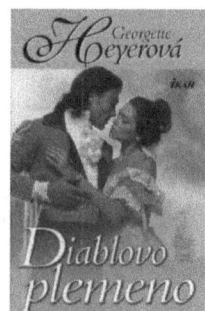

SLOVAK:
Ikar (2012)

DEVIL'S CUB: AN INSTANT SUCCESS BY SUSANNAH FULLERTON

PUBLISHED in 1932, Georgette Heyer's *Devil's Cub* has never been out of print. It was a sequel to her wildly popular 1926 novel, *These Old Shades* (set in 1755), and is set in the 1780s, so is a Georgian novel, not a Regency one. It was followed up by *An Infamous Army*, published in 1937, and set in 1815 at the time of the Battle of Waterloo.

Being a person who loves lists, I frequently make lists of my 'Top Ten' Heyer novels. These lists change often, usually depending on which Heyer I happen to be reading at the time, but one novel that never moves from the 'Top Five' is *Devil's Cub*. At the risk of upsetting those who are in love with the Duke of Avon and Léonie, I actually prefer it to *These Old Shades*.

So why do I love this novel so much? Well, the plot of the novel is started by a duel. Dominic Alastair, Marquis of Vidal (how can you not love a hero with such a fabulous name, I ask?) is involved in a duel after a game of cards and too much drink. The duel means he must flee from England. I adored writing about duels in my book *Jane Austen and Crime*, where I examined the place duels held in Georgian England, and the consequences of fighting one. Georgette Heyer, as always, has her facts right and is very aware of Dominic's position after he has shot at Mr Quarles in a "discreet-looking establishment" just off St James. Mr Quarles has not died, but is in great danger of doing so. The book actually begins with highwaymen (another chapter in my book was devoted to these gentlemen of the road), and gambling, abduction and attempts at murder, which all feature in *Devil's Cub*, are also discussed in my analysis of crime in the Georgian period. I like to think that Heyer would have found my book a useful reference guide while she was writing *Devil's Cub*.

Vidal has been indulging in flirtation with the lovely, but mercenary, Sophia Challoner. When forced to leave England, he decides that he might as well take this beautiful girl along with him for some light amusement. Sophia is from the bourgeoisie, and it never occurs to him that he might offer her marriage. But Sophia's strait-laced and intelligent sister Mary intercepts his note, and (heavily masked) sets off on the elopement instead of her sister, intending to thwart Vidal's dastardly plan. But Mary does not yet understand the Marquis's temper – in a fury at being hoodwinked, he drags her on to the boat for France, and she finds herself in an unexpectedly difficult situation.

It is at this point that we get what is possibly my favourite scene in all of Heyer. Poor Mary has been suffering from seasickness (her furious abductor has been forced to hand her a bowl into which she can be sick), but is yet determined to cling to her virtue:

> He was advancing towards her. She brought her right hand from behind her, and levelled the pistol. 'Stand where you are!', she said. 'If you come one step nearer, I shall shoot you down.'
>
> He stopped short. 'Where did you get that thing?', he demanded.
>
> 'Out of your coach', she answered.
>
> 'Is it loaded?'
>
> 'I don't know', said Miss Challoner, incurably truthful.
>
> He began to laugh again, and walked forward. 'Shoot then', he invited, 'and we shall know. For I'm coming several steps nearer, my lady.'
>
> Miss Challoner saw that he meant it, shut her eyes and resolutely pulled the trigger. There was a deafening report and the Marquis went staggering back. He recovered in a moment. 'It was loaded', he said coolly.

Mary has wounded Vidal and he grows weak and ill as a result – she has to nurse him. Forced to submit to her care, the Marquis learns many lessons, about himself and others, and he comes to appreciate her intelligence and her sense of humour. Trapped together due to circumstance, they both change and adapt. Vidal, so arrogant and sure of everything when we first meet him, comes to feel that Mary is "infinitely above" him, and is reduced to begging her to accept his hand. I love the transformation of his character throughout the novel. Mary, with her cool grey eyes and practical intelligence, has all the qualities of a true Heyer heroine – independence of spirit, a sense of fun, and loyalty. Heyer has named her so aptly – flightier characters in the novel can be called Juliana or Sophia, but the plain and respectable 'Mary' is exactly right for this heroine.

Devil's Cub offers such a fabulous supporting cast. The Duke of Avon and his Léonie are there to delight us once again, there's Lord Rupert Alastair popping in and out of the story, and there's Vidal's temperamental cousin Juliana and the man she loves, Frederick Comyn, who reveals unexpected depths. In contrast to the aristocratic characters, we have the cits – "stout and affluent" Joshua Simpkins, unbecomingly clad in puce, grasping and mercenary Mrs Challoner (who bears a striking resemblance to Jane Austen's Mrs Bennet), and selfish Sophia with her "limpid blue eyes", her calculations, and her lack of morals. There's a hilarious scene between Mrs Challoner and Lady Fanny Marling, fraught with misunderstandings (Lady Fanny thinks Mrs Challoner is talking about the Duke's bastard child), in Heyer's best comic style. There are the usual excellently drawn servants, including Vidal's Fletcher, who comes to view Miss Challoner "with dawning respect".

This novel also takes us travelling. Mary is taken from Bloomsbury to Newhaven on the coast, and thence in the Marquis' private yacht, the Albatross, to Dieppe. From there, they travel to Paris "by easy stages", stopping in Rouen. In that city, Mary slips away to admire the cathedral, which results in a "furious tirade" from Vidal because she could easily have been spotted by English tourists. In Paris they go to the Hôtel Avon. Mary flees from Vidal with Mr Comyn and the final scenes of the book take place in Dijon, the name of which place provokes bewilderment and even mirth in some of the characters. At the Dijon hostelry we have another duel, and this time it is Mary who is wounded, though it is only a scratch. The inn's landlord is at a loss, "trying to explain that there were a great many English people in his house, all fighting duels or having hysterics". The Duke of Avon and Duchess Léonie arrive on the scene (and we are treated to a marvellous dialogue between Mary and her future father-in-law), more misunderstandings ensue but are finally resolved, Rupert finds a superb wine to enjoy, and Vidal promises to take his Mary into Italy for a wedding tour.

Devil's Cub was an instant success, demanding a reprint in the same year. It has remained a top favourite for many of us. It is a novel that displays so much of Heyer's brilliance – deftly drawn characters whom we would recognise by their speech, even without any 'he said' or 'she said', a grand denouement with all the characters gathered together in mutual misunderstanding (such as we also find in *The Grand Sophy*), a sound knowledge of historical era and of location which is in evidence on every page, but most of all, it gives us a memorable and vivid hero and heroine, whose sparky encounters, learning-curves, and growing awareness of passion never fail to delight.

– Susannah Fullerton

~ | ~

"This is my cousin, by the way. I dare say you know of him. He is very wicked and kills people in duels."
— *Devil's Cub*, Chapter I

"I am not in a heat at all," Léonie said with great precision. "I am of a coolness quite remarkable, and I would like to kill that woman." — *Devil's Cub*, Chapter XI

NONPAREIL

International Heyer Society Circular #15, September 2021

FROM THE PATRONESSES

Welcome once again to the monthly circular of the International Heyer Society!

Here we go in-depth into Georgette Heyer's second crime novel, *Why Shoot a Butler?*, in which she really began to hit her stride in the genre. Check out Rachel Hyland's analysis of detective fiction's predilection for looking down on local law enforcement (as exemplified by the novel's hero), and as always, there are character notes, references, reviews, locations and more.

WHY SHOOT A BUTLER?

GEORGETTE HEYER'S second mystery novel does what many second attempts fail to do – it improves dramatically on her first. So often, all the good ideas seem to be used up by an author's debut, which has doubtless been puzzled over and plotted out painstakingly over what is probably years, while follow-ups tend to be produced far more quickly, and often suffer by comparison. "Second album syndrome" is how it is known in musical circles; elsewhere it might be called a "sophomore slump". Neither term was in ready use in Heyer's era, and nor, in her case, was it needed. Her second Georgian romance was the novel now best known as *Powder and Patch*, which most of us would consider at least equal to, if not better than, *The Black Moth*. Her second try at historical fiction resulted in the weighty, incurably faithful *The Conqueror*, assuredly more, well, assured than *The Great Roxhythe*. And her second mystery is leaps and bounds ahead of *Footsteps in the Dark*, which was a pleasant enough diversion, but was also far more enjoyable due to its snappy dialog and the undoubted superiority of side character Charles Malcolm (see: *Nonpareil* #13 for evidence of this) than the actual crime element—which might possibly be considered a flaw in what is allegedly a crime novel. But in reading *Why Shoot a Butler?* (while, yes, there is also snappy dialog and an adorable side character there, too; Tony Corkran, I love you!), there can be no doubt that Heyer was able to write Crime extraordinarily well, especially in its back third, which is all thrilling housebreakings and abductions, chases and deductions, leaving even the most inveterate of the genre's readers with no clue as to who actually dunnit and exactly why until the very last minute (which was certainly not the case in *Footsteps*.) An exhilarating and unusual country house murder mystery, *Why Shoot a Butler?* proves that Georgette Heyer was someone who, with practice, always just got better and better.

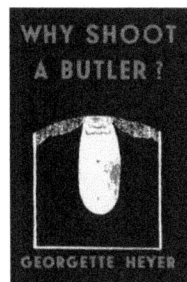

– Clara Shipman

~ | ~

"All the same," said Felicity irrepressibly, "we've never had so much excitement here before. It'll be frightfully dull when it's all over. I mean, just think of the past fortnight! We've had three deaths and two burglaries. I call that pretty good for a place like this."

— *Why Shoot a Butler?*, Chapter 15

THE CHARACTERS

FRANK AMBERLEY
An accomplished barrister whose powers of deduction are well-regarded, even as his habitual rudeness of manner is considered infuriating by pretty much everyone he has ever worked alongside. He is drawn into a web of mystery when he stumbles upon a dead body when on his way to visit his aunt, and along with the body finds a lovely young woman in possession of a gun...

MARION, LADY MATTHEWS
His aunt, kindly and seeming vague, but with a keen perception that even Amberley admires.

SIR HUMPHREY MATTHEWS
Her somewhat prosy and easily irritated husband, a Justice of the Peace and bibliophile who is also very interested in game and land management at his estate, Greythorne.

FELICITY MATTHEWS
Their sprightly daughter, great friends with her cousin Frank.

JENKINS
Butler at Greythorne.

LUDLOW
Chauffeur at Greythorne.

MOLLY
Housemaid at Greythorne.

BASIL FOUNTAIN
A bluff and aggressively sociable man who inherited Norton Manor from his uncle, and has apparently not been very happy about life ever since.

JOAN FOUNTAIN
His stepsister. They are not close. Good friends with Felicity Matthews.

ANTHONY "TONY" CORKRAN
Her fiancé, a charming, considerate and amusing gentleman who has no great liking for his prospective brother-in-law. Was at school with Frank Amberley.

DAWSON
The newly-deceased butler of Norton Manor.

ALBERT COLLINS
Basil Fountain's sinister valet, inherited from his uncle along with the estate.

ALICE
A housemaid at Norton Manor.

BAKER
The new butler at Norton Manor, who seems more than a bit suspicious...

COLONEL WATSON
Chief Constable of the area, officious and somewhat bumbling, ill-equipped to deal with multiple murders in his jurisdiction. Requests help from Amberley.

SHIRLEY BROWN
A lovely and mysterious young woman who claims to be visiting the country, and yet who happened to be found with a dead body on a lonely road one night. Clearly distressed but refuses to explain herself.

MARK BROWN
Her brother, an alcoholic.

MRS JONES
Helps with the cleaning at the cottage they have taken for a month.

INSPECTOR FRASER
Accepts Amberley's help with the murder case, but resents his attitude.

SERGEANT GUBBINS
Develops a comradely, if often contentious, relationship with Amberley as they work on the case together.

CONSTABLE TUCKER
Tasked with keeping an eye on the Browns; fails spectacularly in both cases.

CONSTABLES:
HARPER, HENSON, PARKINS, PHILPOTTS, WALKER, WESTRUPP and **WILKINS**, all of Upper Nettlefold, working under Gubbins.

PEABODY
Sailor employed by Amberley at Littlehaven.

~ | ~

CELEBRITY SIGHTINGS

ANANIAS OF DAMASCAS
? According to the Bible, a disciple of Jesus Christ who is depicted restoring the sight of Saul of Tarsus in the Book of Acts.

AUSTEN, JANE
1775 - 1817. Daughter of a clergyman, her first novel, the witty and often caustic yet very romantic Sense and Sensibility was printed anonymously in 1811. Five more novels followed, all of them now considered classics.

BURTON, ROBERT
1577- 1640. An English writer and Oxford scholar, he is best remembered for his 500,000-word epic The Anatomy of Melancholy, which is essentially a treatise on depression and its treatment, inspired by Burton's own struggles.

D'ISRAELI, ISAAC
1766 - 1848. English writer, scholar and noted bibliophile who is perhaps best remembered as the father of British Prime Minister Benjamin Disraeli. His miscellany masterwork Curiosities of Literature, featuring anecdotes, reviews and observations on rare books, among much else, is his most enduring literary legacy.

FAUST, JOHANN GEORGZ
c. 1480 – c. 1541. A German alchemist, astrologer and magician, he is the basis for the folkloric character who makes an unfortunate deal with the Devil and sells his soul in such works as Christopher Marlowe's play The Tragical History of the Life and Death of Doctor Faustus (1604) and Johann Wolfgang von Goethe's drama Faust (1808).

POISSON, JEANNE-ANTOINETTE, 1ST MARQUISE DE POMPADOUR
1721-1764. Mistress of King Louis XV of France she was among his most trusted advisors right up until her death.

MARY, QUEEN OF SCOTS
1542 - 1587. Daughter of James V of Scotland, she became queen when just 5 days old. Married three times, dethroned twice, and imprisoned by Elizabeth I for 18 years.

WOLSEY, CARDINAL THOMAS
1473 - 1530. Catholic Archbishop of York influential in the court of Henry VIII. Unable to obtain an annulment of Henry's marriage to Catherine of Aragon, he was exiled from court and later accused of treason, but died before he could defend himself against this charge.

~ | ~

Wolf was Felicity's Alsatian. When fetched from the stables he evinced his satisfaction by bounding around his mistress and barking madly for the first hundred yards of their walk. Exercising him was not, as Frank knew from experience, all joy, as he was not in the least amenable to discipline, had to be caught and held at the approach of any motor vehicle, and had a habit of plunging unadvisedly into quarrels with others of the canine race.

— *Why Shoot a Butler*, Chapter 2

"Bill was sniffing suspiciously at Tucker's ankles. Tucker made propitiating noises and wondered why the young lady couldn't have had a nice little Pekingese. He advanced a nervous hand towards Bill, assuring him that he was a good dog. Bill was more interested in trying to assert whether he was a good man. He came to the conclusion that no steps need at the moment be taken to evict the constable and went off again to continue operations in the back garden.

— *Why Shoot a Butler?*, Chapter 16

~ | ~

THE LOCATIONS

UPPER NETTLEFOLD
In Sussex
- Greythorne
Home to the Matthews
- Norton Manor
Home to the Fountains
- Ivy Cottage
Rented by the Browns
- Pittingly Road
Site of Dawson's murder
- The Boar's Head

LONDON
- The Temple
Home to Frank Amberley

LITTLEHAVEN

WHAT THEY SAID

Contemporary Reviews of *Why Shoot a Butler?*

The Times Literary Supplement (London, UK), May 4, 1933

There were plenty of reasons for shooting this one, though it would be unfair to disclose them. Other people in the book also deserve shooting and receive their just desserts. There are a new and ingenious amateur detective, a suspected heroine, more foolish than most heroines and more attractive than the heroines of most detective stories, a motor race on land and sea, and a motive which, granted the obtuseness of most of the characters, becomes almost plausible. The story is readable and, in parts, amusing.

~ | ~

Kingston Gleaner (Jamaica), April 22, 1933

Despite the title, *Why Shoot a Butler?*, Georgette Heyer's latest book is quite a worthy successor to her long list of crime novels successes, and on the whole is one of the few 'thrillers' that stand out so far in this year's publications so far. Her story is ingenious and well-told, and the moment interest is likely to flag over the original murder she conveniently introduces another and yet a third in happy and obliging sequence. It is not so involved as to make reading an effort and one can follow the story with interest and pleasurable anticipation from beginning to end. Neither is it one of those stories in which the perpetrator of the murder is made obvious in the second chapter. It is not until one is well over half way through the book that one can even hazard a guess, and then it is probably wrong. The authoress, like the great majority of crime writers, appears to have scanty respect for the capabilities of the police, and leaves the ultimate solution of her intricate mystery to a young barrister who, quite in the accepted style, rescues the girl in the case from certain death and, it is to be presumed, marries her. *Why Shoot a Butler?* is well-written and the interest never flags, and I can confidently recommend it to all who enjoy a good mystery story.

Brisbane Telegraph (Queensland, Australia), May 13, 1933

TANGLED SKEIN

When a novelist of the capacity of Georgette Heyer sets her hand to the writing of a mystery novel it may be taken for granted that the job will be accomplished with restraint and literary skill. These are definitely qualities of this admirably constructed book in which all the materials of sensationalism are utilised with an avoidance of melodrama which is remarkable in its completeness. The reason for the murder of a butler, with which the crime story opens, and the why and the wherefore of the presence near the dead man of a nice girl who chooses to be mysterious about her movements is very skillfully kept from the reader until a whole succession of exciting chapters have been digested and all sorts of theories formed and dismissed. The motive for the original crime and for some subsequent killings proves more substantial than is sometimes the case in mystery thrillers, and one comes to admire wholeheartedly the resource and penetration of Mr. Amberley, a criminal barrister who investigates the affair at the instigation of the police. The books is one of the most absorbing stories of its kind for a long time.

~ | ~

Daily Mirror (London, UK), February 20, 1933

The butler was "bumped off" because he knew too much. But two other victims follow him in due course. Why were they dispatched? And why is the heroine abducted and towed out to sea in a tug? These and other mysteries make good reading in one of the best thrillers that have come our way in a long time.

~ | ~

WHAT A QUIZ!

Think you know your Heyer? These questions will test your knowledge...

1. In which year was *Why Shoot a Butler?* first published?
2. Name the butler who was shot?
3. What is the profession of Frank Amberley, who steps in to solve the crime?
4. How does Amberley know Tony Corkran?
5. Why is Tony staying in the neighbourhood?
6. Where do the Fountain siblings live?
7. Who is the police sergeant Amberley tasks to help him with his inquiries?
8. Who's presence at the scene of the crime does Amberley conceal?
9. Why does he do it?
10. How many deaths occur in the book?

ANSWERS: 1. 1933; 2. Dawson; 3. 6: He is a barrister; 4. They went to school together; 5. He is engaged to Joan Fountain; 6. Norton Manor; 7. Sergeant Gubbins; 8. Shirley Brown's; 9. He fell in love with her at first sight; 10. Four - three murders and a suicide, plus the attempted murder of Shirley Brown several times, as well.

~ | ~

SELECTED COVER GALLERY

Longmans, UK
(1933)

Longmans, UK
(1937)

Penguin, UK
(1945)

Panther, UK
(1963)

Heinemann, UK
(1966)

Panther, UK
(1969)

Dutton, US
(1973)

Bantam, US
(1977)

Amereon, US
(1979)

Grafton, US
(1987)

Arlington, UK
(1990)

Berkley, US
(1994)

Arrow, UK
(2006)

Sourcebooks, US
(2009)

Sourcebooks, US
(2018)

SELECTED TRANSLATED EDITIONS

SPANISH: Ediciones
Agora (1945)

FRENCH: Editions
du Masque (1994)

ITALIAN: Mondadori
(2005)

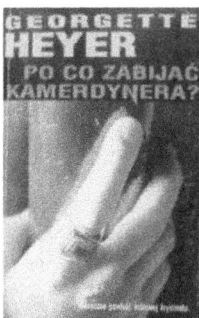

POLISH:
Mitel (1992)

RUSSIAN:
(1995)

DRAT THE POLICE BY RACHEL HYLAND

IT is a truth universally acknowledged that a crime committed in a small English village will not be solved by the local police. Universally acknowledged by crime writers, that is, who so often fashion for themselves an eccentric or irreverent or brilliant (or all three) amateur detective who comes upon the scene – quite often by chance – and gets to the bottom of things with intuitive acts of deduction that mere trained and experienced professionals in the field apparently cannot hope to emulate. Beginning with 1868's *The Moonstone* by Wilkie Collins, generally considered to be the first detective novel, in which a country house robbery is made harder to solve by some bumbling locals, it is a storytelling tradition that is so deeply rooted in the popular consciousness that the idea of any countryside crime actually being solved without the intervention of some insightful big-city sophisticate imported to the area seems almost outlandish. Through the great Sherlock Holmes making fools out of lesser minds everywhere in Arthur Conan Doyle's landmark stories; through Agatha Christie's Miss Marple rendering redundant the neighbourhood constabulary in her quaint village of St Mary Mead; through the aristocratic Lord Peter Wimsey heading out of his habitual London milieu to also prove rural authorities wrong in the works of Dorothy L. Sayers; the inherent uselessness of country police officers when pursuing a murder suspect had already become a rather established concept even in the heady Golden Age of Mystery days when Georgette Heyer first tried her hand at the form.

What is interesting is that British detective fiction, in many ways, owes its existence to the police themselves. In "The creation of the police and the rise of detective fiction" (2014), Judith Flanders argues that Charles Dickens's fascination with the 1829 establishment of London's new enforcement body led to his inclusion of Mr. Bucket in *Bleak House* (1852), whom she claims as the first fictional detective. (Though the first work of detective fiction is actually credited to Edgar Allan Poe and his short story "The Murders in the Rue Morgue", which appeared in 1841 and features the exploits of Parisian amateur sleuth Le Chevalier C. Auguste Dupin.) Like Sergeant Cuff in *The Moonstone*, Mr. Bucket was apparently inspired by a real Scotland Yard detective, Inspector Jonathan Whicher. Dickens and Collins were friends – *The Moonstone* even first appeared in serialized form in Dickens's magazine *All the Year Round* – and so it can certainly be argued that the genre, in Britain at least, was born out of their mutual interest in, and, let us presume, respect for, this one particular representative of the Law. But that respect would not go on to be extended to others who pursued the same vocation. Especially if they had the misfortune to live and work outside of the metropolis.

A lot of this can be attributed to classism, of course. By the time of the 1920s and 1930s, most detectives created by English crime authors were refined and educated scions of well-heeled and/or well-bred families (Poirot being a notable exception) so naturally they were to be considered superior in all ways to the countrified locals who perhaps had never been further afield than the nearest market town, and who were likely descended from peasant stock. Even in Georgette Heyer's first attempt at detective fiction, the short story "Linckes' Great Case" (published in *Detective Magazine* in 1923), our untried police detective hero is almost immediately established as worthy when it transpires that his father was at college with the government minister he is tasked to assist, the fabled old boy network very much in evidence. Her second attempt, the 1932 novel *Footsteps in the Dark*, gave us an attractive and well-spoken London detective in disguise whose efforts to uncover a sinister plot are constantly undermined by the officious Constable Flinders, the earnest but simple provincial who just wants to do his "dooty", the poor dear, but who mostly just ends up irritating everyone.

Then we come to her second mystery novel, *Why Shoot a Butler?*, in which Georgette Heyer takes this prevailing scornful attitude towards country police to a whole new – and in this case, almost wholly unjustified – level.

Here we have as our somewhat reluctant hero and lead investigator Frank Amberley, a barrister from London who happens upon a murder most foul in the most accidental of plot device-y ways. Confused over the shortcut he has been told to take to get to his aunt's country house, he takes a wrong turning and discovers a parked car replete with a dead body, and a beautiful girl replete with a gun. We soon learn that Amberley, in addition to his thriving law practice, is something of an amateur gumshoe and has even had occasion to assist (read: shame) police in the district with their inquiries before. Perhaps the kindest thing one could say of Frank Amberley's manner is that he is lacking in tact; it would be rather more accurate to say that he is a rude and arrogant jerk who shows a complete disregard for both the feelings and capabilities of others. (So far, so Sherlock.) So when he decides to withhold crucial evidence from those nominally investigating the murder and then, in a rather drawn-out and insufferable denouement, goes on to show off to the much put-upon Sergeant Gubbins about how he solved not only the titular butler shooting but also some previous and subsequent crimes, he displays a stunning lack of remorse over his role in the events that have rocked the formerly sedate community of Upper Nettlefold.

Take, for example, the death of Mark Brown. For all that Mark's sister Shirley (whom Amberley later claims to love) seems largely unaffected by this, it is still very possible that, without Amberley's ill-thought out intervention, she would not have had to suffer such a loss. If he had told the police all of his observations and suspicions, they might have taken better care of Mark; they would at the very least have investigated the Brown siblings, and perhaps have even come to the same realization that Amberley did as to their true identities. This revelation made earlier might even have prevented our ultimate villain from going full Dark Side, and leaving yet another sister brotherless (and also not too bothered about it) in this book. But Amberley is so convinced of his own moral rectitude and mental acuity, and so contemptuous of everyone else's, that he is reckless in the extreme, and in the end, gets more than one person killed, and the woman he loves abducted. If he had trusted to the local police more, had helped rather than hindered in their own investigations... but then, this would not be what it is, a crime story with a quirky amateur stepping in to show up the professionals, a trope very popular at the time. (And, indeed, now.)

Later, of course, Heyer would go on to feature intelligent police officers as the heroes of her crime novels once again, with Inspectors Hannasyde and Hemingway et al. of Scotland Yard called in to solve some of the knottier murders in assorted country houses throughout England. Indeed, *Why Shoot a Butler?* would go on to become her only crime novel starring an amateur detective. But that disdain of local law enforcement never goes away, and that just feels so unfair. Sergeant Gubbins and his ilk deserve better, don't you think?

– Rachel Hyland

~ | ~

"Among the most soughtafter guests for this season's house parties is Mr. Anthony Corkran, whose ready tact and savoir-faire make him so universally popular."
— *Why Shoot a Butler*, Chapter 6

"I can think of a lot of people who might get shot – gangsters and cabinet ministers, and all that push – but not butlers. After all, why shoot a butler? Where's the point?"
— *Why Shoot a Butler*, Chapter 2

NONPAREIL

International Heyer Society Circular #16, October 2021

FROM THE PATRONESSES

Welcome once again to the monthly circular of the International Heyer Society!

Here we take a look at *The Convenient Marriage*. Check out Maura Tan's conflicted feelings about it, and, as always, there are character notes, references, reviews, locations and more.

THE CONVENIENT MARRIAGE

IT has always seemed remarkable to me that Georgette Heyer wrote *The Convenient Marriage* while living in a simple country inn. To have written such a sparkling historical novel without the benefit of her library, her reference books or anything other than her remarkable memory and her knowledge of the whims, fashion and society of eighteenth-century England, seems extraordinary. She was a true artist, however, and already mistress of her craft and over the years she would prove herself adept at writing wherever she was. In 1933, she and her husband, Ronald, with baby Richard, had left Southover, the home they had rented for a year in the nearby hamlet of Colgate, and moved into the Sussex Oak Inn at Warnham while they looked about for a new house to rent. They lived at the inn for several weeks and Georgette put the time to good use writing her sixth Georgian novel. A radiant comedy with a young and rather surprising heroine in the stammering Horry Winwood and an omniscient but charming hero in the memorable Earl of Rule, *The Convenient Marriage* seems to have been one of those books that slipped easily from Georgette's pen onto the page. She clearly enjoyed writing the novel and wrote enthusiastically about it to her agent, L.P. Moore. As always when she wrote, her characters lived for Georgette. She was enthusiastic about the book and took the time to copy out several excerpts for her agent's amusement, commenting along the way about the Earl of Rule's mistress, the beautiful but scheming, Lady Caroline Massey. Georgette had the habit of writing as she spoke and would often pen her letters in an amusing, stream-of-consciousness way as though the person she was writing to were actually present and in conversation with her. Georgette writes to Moore about Lady Massey as if she were a real person:

> 'Yes, isn't it sad about Caroline Massey? Not a Nice Woman at all, & do you know I'm afraid she's going to have a liaison with Lord Lethbridge as well as with Rule? I do hate promiscuity, don't you? Her husband was in Trade, you know, & of course that was a Grave Drawback, & she never got herself received in the very best circles, but she had a lot of money, & gave lavish parties, & people who liked deep basset used to go to her house a lot. She had a good cellar, too, which attracted people like Lethbridge.'

Georgette wrote her new novel with pen and ink, for her typewriter days still lay several years ahead. For the modern reader it may be hard to imagine writing by hand, but Georgette not only wrote *The Convenient Marriage* quickly and while suffering all the inconveniences of living in a country inn with a small child, she also wrote it with such confident ease that her first drafts were often her final drafts. It seems incredible, but those hand-written excerpts that she copied out for her agent's entertainment are word for word what appears in the final published book.

– Jennifer Kloester

THE CHARACTERS

HORATIA "HORRY" DRELINCOURT, COUNTESS OF RULE, NÉE WINWOOD
Just turned seventeen, Horatia - Horry, to her friends and family - volunteers to marry the wealthy Earl of Rule in place of her beautiful eldest sister. Short of stature, with a stammer and determinedly straight black eyebrows, her attraction lies in her fearlessness, artlessness and incurable honesty.

ELIZABETH WINWOOD
Her eldest sister, the beauty of the family, who is in love with a much less eligible suitor than the Earl of Rule.

CHARLOTTE WINWOOD
The middle Winwood sister, who speaks in Capital Letters and has decided to Devote her Life to her Sainted Mama.

LADY WINWOOD
Their Sainted Mama, very prone to bouts of nerves, who has endured much privation due to the gaming addiction first of her deceased husband, and now of her reckless son.

PELHAM "PEL" WINWOOD, VISCOUNT WINWOOD
Her reckless son, an avid gamester with little regard for the practicalities of feeding, clothing and housing his female dependents, but who is so charming, kind and endearing that no one can find it in them to condemn him for it.

SIR ROLAND "POM" POMMEROY
His best friend, and best of good fellows, always ready to help Pel and Horry.

EDWARD HERON
Sharing a long-standing affection with Elizabeth Winwood, he is a younger son and a lieutenant in the Army.

MARCUS DRELINCOURT, EARL OF RULE
Elegant, intelligent and supercilious, but with a certain appreciation for the ridiculous, he has decided the time has come to settle down to a life of indifferent matrimony. Little does he expect to fall in love with his new wife...

LADY LOUISA QUAIN
His sister, happily married and determined to see Rule be the same. Carries a secret scandal in her past.

SIR HUMPHREY QUAIN
Her husband.

ARNOLD GISBORNE
A serious young man from a good but straightened family who acts as Rule's secretary, and has political ambitions.

CROSBY DRELINCOURT
Cousin to Rule, a spendthrift known for his acid tongue and his extravagant taste in fashion. Heir-presumptive to Rule's title and assets, he is furious when his status is threatened by Rule's marriage.

LADY CAROLINE MASSEY
A lovely widow, her merchant husband left her with the appearance of wealth, but she is not quite accepted in the first circles. Captivating and rapacious, she is Rule's mistress, but hoped to be made his wife.

MISS JANET
Her live-in companion, for propriety's sake.

ROBERT, BARON LETHBRIDGE
Dangerously attractive, but vicious to the bone, he pursues Horry's friendship in an attempt to gain revenge on Rule for a long-ago slight, and manipulates her into compromising herself. Truly loathsome.

THERESA MAULFREY
The Winwoods' cousin, rather pushing and judgmental. Not a favourite of anyone.

EDWARD HAWKINS
Highwayman and gun-for-hire, he is employed by Lord Lethbridge to hold up Horry's coach and is later employed by Pel to hold up Lethbridge's coach. Speaks in colourful cant at all times.

MISS LANE, "LANEY"
Former governess to the Winwood sisters, now retired to Kensington.

CAPTAIN FORDE
One of Crosby Drelincourt's seconds in his duel with Pel. Very enthusiastic about the fight.

FRANCIS PUCKLETON
Crosby's other second. Far less enthusiastic, as he fears the sight of blood.

LORD CHESTON
Pel's other second (next to Pom, of course).

BOULBY
Attempts to calm the situation when Pel is outraged by Crosby's insults towards Horry.

JEFFRIES
Groom to the Earl of Rule.

CORNEY
Pel's valet.

JACKSON
Pel's groom.

MOXTON
Lethbridge's butler.

CATTERMOLE
Publican of the Sun Inn at Maidenhead, very loyal to Rule.

COPPER
Landlord of the Crown Inn at Slough.

~|~

CELEBRITY SIGHTINGS

ALMACK, WILLIAM
1741 – 1781. Believed to be from Yorkshire – though some accounts call him Scottish – he was once valet to the 5th Duke of Hamilton before he bought a tavern and then opened a very successful gaming house, Almack's Club, in 1763. In 1765 he opened his purpose-built Almack's Assembly Rooms in King Street, to great success, although he did not live to see the height of their popularity in the Regency, under the iron rule of the lady patronesses. Almack's remained a stalwart of the London social scene until 1840 – the site is now an office building named Almack House.

ANGELO, DOMENICO
1717 – 1802. Also known as Angelo Domenico Malevolti Tremamondo, he was an Italian swordsman and fencing master who taught the London aristocracy and is the author of the 1763 illustrated instruction manual *L'École des armes*.

DOUGLAS, WILLIAM, 4TH DUKE OF QUEENSBURY, AKA LORD MARCH
1724 - 1810. Cousin to the 3rd Duke, he had previously inherited the Earldoms of March and Ruglen from his parents. March, later fondly known as "Old Q", was famous for his love of gaming and was a great favourite of the Prince of Wales (George IV). He never married but had a daughter, Maria, who wed the Marquess of Hertford in 1798. and was the Duke's principal heir.

FOX, THE HON. CHARLES JAMES
1749 – 1806. Known for his wit, cleverness and compelling oratory, he was first admitted to parliament at 19, sponsored by his father, a prominent Whig politician. He spent most of his 38-year career in opposition and was the chief rival of Tory leader Pitt the Younger. Fox's personal life was plagued by gaming debt and scandal, yet he was well-liked in Society, where he had been a leader of the "Macaroni" fashion scene in his youth. A frequent victim of cartoonist Gilray, he was personally hated by George III and the monarchist Tory party.

GLUCK, CHRISTOPH WILLIBALD RITTER VON
1714 - 1787. Born in what is now Germany and raised in what is now Poland, he was a composer of Italian and French opera who first came to fame in Austria, but was soon renowned throughout Europe. He was something of an opera revolutionary, shortening the typical length of his pieces as well as producing musical dramas and ballet pantomimes, among other radical works. He instructed the young Marie Antoinette in the harp, harpsichord and flute. A fire in 1809 destroyed half of his work; still, 35 full operas and about a dozen other works remain.

GRAHAM, DANIEL
c. 1695 – 1788. Apothecary to George III, son of Thomas Graham, apothecary to George I and II. Achieved long-lasting fame through his children, who were captured in portrait by William Hogarth; The Graham Children is considered to be one of the artist's best works.

HANDEL, GEORGE FRIDERIC
1685 – 1759. Born Georg Friederich Händel in what is now Germany, he began to receive music lessons after he was heard playing a church organ at the age of 9 by a local nobleman. He moved to England after George I took the throne, starting the Royal Academy of Music and becoming the nation's leading composer. His is perhaps best remembered for his Messiah, but he made many other lasting contributions to ecclesiastical music, including the perennial favourite Christmas carol "Joy to the World." He also wrote Water Music, and the UEFA Champions League anthem was based on his work Zadok the Priest. His body is interred at Westminster Abbey, his state funeral attended by three thousand mourners.

HAWKINS, SIR CAESAR
1711 - 1786. Fashionable London surgeon attached to St. George's Hospital and personal physician (Serjeant-Surgeon) to both George II and George III. Created a baronet in 1778. His grandson, also called Caesar Hawkins, went on to become Serjeant-Surgeon to Queen Victoria.

HOWARD, FREDERICK, 5TH EARL OF CARLISLE
1748 – 1825. Statesman involved in failed peace talks with the US which led to the American Revolution and with rule of Ireland during a particularly turbulent period. At one time was Lord Byron's guardian, and was much disliked by the young poet as a result.

JAMES, ROBERT
1703 – 1776. English physician best known as the author of the three-volume Medical Dictionary – with the help of childhood friend Samuel Johnson – and inventor of a popular fever powder that is believed to have contributed to the death of writer Oliver Goldsmith.

RUSSELL, GERTRUDE, DUCHESS OF BEDFORD
1715 - 1794. Second wife of John Russell, 4th Duke of Bedford. Called "stingy" and "avaricious" by Horace Walpole, she was nevertheless an accomplished hostess and diplomat.

SELWYN, GEORGE AUGUSTUS
1719 - 1791. Wit, politician, and great friend of Horace Walpole, with whom he shared a frequent correspondence. Despite his reputed intellect, he spent 44 years in the House of Commons without making a speech. An avid member of the Hellfire Club, he had a keen interest in the macabre and loved executions.

WALPOLE, HORACE
1717 - 1797. Noted wit, gamester, epistolarian and author of The Castle of Otranto, generally regarded as the first Gothic novel. Youngest son of the first British Prime Minister, the 1st Earl, he succeeded to the title in 1791, upon the death of his nephew. His house at Twickenham, Strawberry Hill House, was an early example of Gothic revival architecture and kickstarted a trend that lasted over a century But it is his Letters – he wrote thousands, many of which have been preserved – that remain his lasting legacy, as they form the basis of much of the sociological history that now exists of the time.

~ | ~

THE LOCATIONS

LONDON
- South Street
- Grosvenor Square
- Half Moon Street
- Jermyn Street
- Curzon Street
- Astley's Amphitheatre
- Almack's
- White's
- Ranelagh Gardens
- Vauxhall Gardens
- Drury Lane
- Richmond House
- Hounslow Heath
- Hercules Pillars Inn, Hyde Park

SLOUGH
- The Crown Inn

MAIDENHEAD
- The Sun Inn

MEERING
Near Twyford, in Berkshire
Country seat of the Earl of Rule

WHAT A QUIZ!

Think you know your Heyer? These questions will test your knowledge...

1. In which year was *The Convenient Marriage* first published?

2. Name Horatia Winwood's two sisters?

3. In what period is the novel set?

4. What is the Earl of Rule's first name?

5. Name Rule's sister.

6. Why does Lord Lethbridge want revenge on Rule?

7. Which three gentlemen dress as highwaymen to retrieve Horry's lost brooch?

8. Which famous wit is Horry's godfather?

9. To whom does Horry lose a lock of her hair at play?

10. Who is the Earl of Rule's heir-presumptive?

ANSWERS: 1. 1934; 2. Elizabeth and Charlotte; 3. 6: Georgian; 4. Marcus (his surname is Drelincourt); 5. Lady Louisa; 6. Rule prevented him from marrying Lady Louisa; 7. Pelham, Viscount Winwood, Sir Roland Pommeroy and Edward Heron; 8. Horace Walpole; 9. Her husband; 10. His cousin, Crosby Drelincourt.

WHAT THEY SAID

Contemporary Reviews of *The Convenient Marriage*

The Sydney Morning Herald (New South Wales, Australia), March 30, 1934

The fact that Georgette Heyer's plot in *The Convenient Marriage* has seen service on innumerable occasions should on no account deter those who enjoy a fast-moving, eventful romance. Stage and screen comedies and countless novels have described how, after a marriage of convenience, husband and wife discover themselves to be desperately in love with one another, yet pride will suffer neither to admit the fact—not, that is, until five acts or several hundred feet of film or 300 pages of fiction have narrated the mistakes, manoeuvres, and intrigues essential as a prelude to the grand declaration at the end. So it is with the wealthy Earl of Rule and the portionless younger sister of Viscount Winwood. His lordship desired to marry one of the Winwood sisters, being sublimely Indifferent as to which of the three should accompany him to the altar, and Horatia elected to sacrifice herself in the cause of the family mortgages. No sooner had the match been made, and the marriage settlements drawn up to the profound satisfaction of the Winwoods, than the familiar comedy begins, the earl busying himself with the wooing of his own wife, who, for her part, finds surprising difficulty in maintaining her predetermined aloofness.

Miss Heyer very properly gives her romance an eighteenth century setting, the social amenities of that period being better suited than a later date to the pretty complications invariable in such a romance. And, although this is no "historical" novel, the background has been sketched in both light and convincingly. We have the England of Horace Walpole and Fox, burly bucks and simpering macaronis, cardsharpers, duellers, and highwaymen. Ladies are kidnapped, gilded gentlemen draw their swords upon the slightest provocation, stage coaches are held up on Hounslow Heath, and queer things happen during mask and domino balls at Ranelagh. Everybody knows the glamour which this romantic apparatus lends to such a story. Just as everyone will be thoroughly familiar with the theme of post-marital wooing. Yet somehow the whole business seems quite fresh and acceptable as Miss Heyer presents it, probably because she knows her period so well and can make her characters vigorously alive.

Horatia is a charmingly spirited young heroine, all the more attractive by reason of her stammer. But her noble husband Is her intellectual superior, and can always outdo her in the verbal duels that frequently ensue and others as well. For instance, the villainous Lord Lethbridge, a social outcast, desires to make Horatia's acquaintance. He therefore hires three footpads to hold up the lady's coach, and himself stages a "rescue" single-handed. But Rule sees through the ruse, and seeks out Lethbridge.

> "I am quite lost in admiration," said Rule to Lethbridge "To tackle three—It was three, was it not? Ah, yes!—to tackle three desperate villains single-handed argues an intrepidity—or should I say a daring?—you were always daring, were you not, my dear Lethbridge?—a daring, then, that positively takes one's breath away."
>
> "To have succeeded," said Lethbridge, still smiling, "in depriving your lordship of breath is a triumph in itself."
>
> "Ah!" sighed the earl. "But you will make me emulative, my dear Lethbridge. "More of these deeds of daring and I shall really have to see if I cannot—er— deprive you of breath."

Politely insulting speeches like this, and others salted with eighteenth century wit, come easily from Miss Heyer's pen. She thus keeps her entertainment going merrily, between encounters of the more violent sort, and the result is an exceptionally diverting tale.

***The Scotsman*, February 15, 1934**

Lovers of romances with a strong eighteenth century flavour, complete with duels, highwaymen, abductions, and expensive young ladies addicted to the gambling table and fine feathers, will be rewarded by dipping into Miss Georgette Heyer's new novel. Having dipped, moreover, they will read to the end of the story, for although Lord Rule is just the sort of strong man with a dash of nonchalance about him that one would expect to find in such a novel, his young wife, Horatia, has more character and spirit than is usually allotted to the heroine. Her persistent habit of stammering proves tiresome, and might well have been left to the imagination, but the tale goes with a good swing and is shot through with refreshing shafts of humour. That it is highly improbable troubles no one, least of all the reader.

~ | ~

Western Mail **(Wales), July 30, 1934**

Miss Heyer is an old hand at historical romance. and experience enables her to fix her story into its background so that the two are indissolubly one. The eighteenth century is the only time and place for *The Convenient Marriage*. The artifice of marriage de convenance is really only at home in an age when dress, speech, manners, and morals were also so many artifices to decorate that vulgar business—life. Here, these artifices are delineated with accuracy and wit. The least real person in the book is the hero, Lord Rule, who marries his wife for her blue blood and is rather a water-colour portrait of the Scarlet Pimpernel. The heroine, Horatia, is a delightful person. Her behaviour in Chapter 11. is ravishing. In fact, Chapter 11. is high-water mark: so good, that it prepares us for really perilous seas which, disappointingly, die down into mere stormy millponds, or more aptly, artificial waters. However, this is a very readable story and a faithfully amusing account of eighteenth century modes and manners.

~ | ~

Daily News **(London, UK), February 26, 1934**

I liked Georgette Heyer's book, *The Convenient Marriage*. It is not a very important contribution to literature, but it is a gay, pleasant story of Georgian days.

Both the hero and the heroine are charming: if he is a little too reminiscent of Sir Percy Blakeney, she, with her slight provocative stammer, is sufficiently original. The dialogue is delightfully crisp and to the point, the story often exciting and often amusing.

If this is what one likes, and I do like it, it is very well done.

THEODORA BENSON

~ | ~

SELECTED COVER GALLERY

Heinemann, UK
(1934)

Pan, UK
(1964)

Bantam, US
(1967)

Bantam, UK
(1982)

Mandarin, US
(1993)

Harlequin, Canada
(2000)

Arrow, UK
(2001)

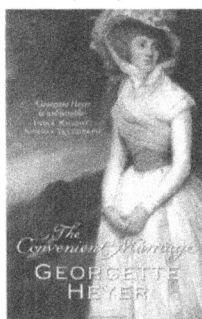

Arrow, UK
(2005)

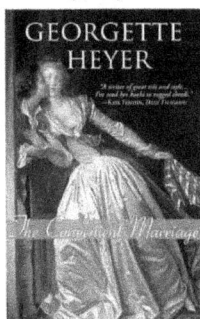

Sourcebooks, US
(2009)

Arrow, UK
(2013)

Thorndike, US
(2016)

Arrow, US
(2018)

Chivers Audio, UK
(2010)

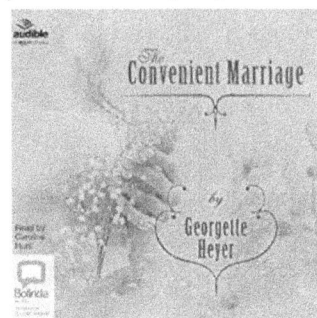

Bolinda Audio, Australia
(2018)

SELECTED TRANSLATED EDITIONS

GERMAN:
Bertelsmann (1960)

ITALIAN:
Mondadori (1977)

PORTUGUESE: Circulo
de Leitores (1978)

RUSSIAN:
(1996)

BAHASA: Nourabooks
(2016)

PEL AND POM: A TRIBUTE BY MAURA TAN

I HAVE written before, and at length, about the disturbing age difference between our main couple in *The Convenient Marriage*. When, in the book's second chapter, the Earl of Rule tells Miss Horatia Winwood, the young girl who has just – rather scandalously – come to his house to propose to him, that "... thirty-five makes a poor husband for seventeen," it is hard to disagree with him. The fact that this is a reality that plagued women throughout history and remains true in the present day; the fact that girls even younger than Horry were, and are, all-but sold into marriage with older men to secure their families wealth, prestige or even just one less daughter to feed; makes *The Convenient Marriage* even harder to take, because it is such an unpleasant reminder of this harsh truth. At least here, Horry has made the decision for herself, as ill-informed and dubious a decision as it might have been. It all turned out happily for her fictional self, but just two years before this book is set, the real-life Lady Georgiana Spencer married the 25-year-old Duke of Devonshire on her seventeenth birthday, and that marriage was far from a happy one. History is littered with more Georgianas than Horrys, sadly, and that is something that often sets sensitive teeth on edge about this tale. Enough that one might think anyone who feels this strongly about it would never want to read it again.

But in thinking that, one would be reckoning without Pel and Pom.

Pel and Pom! Otherwise known as Pelham, Viscount Winwood and Sir Roland Pommeroy. These two best friends, drinking buddies and (sad to say) gambling addicts are such a bright spot in this otherwise generally upsetting narrative – there is not only the age gap, but also the vile and villainous Lord Lethbridge's abduction and planned rape of Horry to contend with – and it is for them that I have gone back to this book more than once, and probably will again. And again.

Yes, I do realize that it is largely due to Pel that Horry (or, at least, one of his sisters; it isn't to be supposed he cares too much which) must marry Rule, or some other rich man who can pay up handsomely for the privilege, and so bring his family out of their current embarrassments. Embarrassments caused at least in part by Pel's extravagant spending habits and total disinterest in trying to reform his ways. He, like the entire Belmanoir family before him and his spiritual heir Viscount Dysart after (not to mention real people like Charles Fox – who appears in this book – and Beau Brummell, who appears in many more), seems to believe that, since a passion for gambling is "in the blood," there is no need for him to attempt to curb his enormous appetite for it. As the aforementioned real people illustrate, this is absolutely true to life, and it is not like there were yet any 12-step programs or counselling hotlines back then; nor are those things always successful, even now. But, for all that Horry seems to believe that genetic excuse with her whole heart, it should be difficult to not only like but love a character who cheerfully sacrifices his sister on the (literal) altar of his own selfishness and seems to bear little guilt about the stressful financial straits to which he has reduced his mother.

Yet, I do love Pel. And I love his friend Pom just as much – actually, maybe more, since as far as we know, he is not heedlessly leading his dependents into the poorhouse, all for his own pleasure. I love how Pel is always trying to help Horry (except for helping her to stay single until she is out of her teens, that is), and I love how Pom is immediately ready to help her, too. I love how Pel leaps to Horry's defence at all times, even if that defence isn't especially wise. And I especially love how Pel and Pom drunkenly descend upon a very weary and defeated Lord Lethbridge and somehow become convinced that he is giving a party of some sort, to which they have been invited, even though he isn't and they have not.

"If a man gives a party, he ought to know what kind of party it is," argued the Viscount. "If you don't know, how are we to know? It might be a damned soirée, in which case we wouldn't have come."

That whole scene is a delight, and never fails to make me laugh out loud. From Pom's theory of how Horry, who has just escaped Lethbridge's clutches, might have killed him ("She walked home. Passed Lethbridge's house. Went in. Hit him on the head with the poker. Came out...") to their disappointment that Lethbridge is still alive, it has made of *The Convenient Marriage* a comfort read for me, because I will happily slog my way past the age factor, the Massey, Charlotte's dreariness (why is she Like That? And wouldn't she and Rule's excellent secretary Arnold make a satisfying pair?), and Rule not telling Horry important things because I love to come upon that scene (all Pel/Pom scenes, really) organically, and be won over by them anew.

And Heyer does this kind of thing *a lot*.

In her essay on *Footsteps in the Dark*, Clara Shipman wrote that she rereads it solely for the character of Charles Malcolm, but finds the rest of the book "forgettable." I often find myself rereading this book that I cordially dislike because I love Pel and Pom. What a rare, and special, gift Georgette Heyer had. And what gifts she gave to us.

– Maura Tan

~ | ~

"God love yer, do ye take me for a mill ken?" demanded the visitor, affronted. "Lordy, them as is on the rattling lay don't take to slumming kens!" With which lofty but somewhat obscure remark he took himself down the steps...   — *The Convenient Marriage*, Chapter VII

Glamour might still have clung to a rakehell who abducted noble damsels, but no glamour remained about a man who had been pushed into a pond in full ball-dress.   — *The Convenient Marriage*, Chapter XIV

~ | ~

"The Viscount stepped into the room. "Came to see if you was dead," he said. "Laid Pom odds you weren't."

Lethbridge passed his hand across his eyes. "I'm not," he replied in a faint voice.

"No. I'm sorry," said the Viscount simply. He wandered over to the table and sat down. "Horry said she killed you, Pom said So she might, I said No. Nonsense."

Lethbridge still holding a hand to his aching head tried to pull himself together. "Did you?" he said. His eyes ran over his self invited guest. "I see. Let me assure you once more that I am very much alive."

"Well I wish you'd put your wig on," complained the Viscount. "What I want to know is why did Horry hit you on the head with a poker?"

Lethbridge gingerly felt his bruised scalp. "With a poker was it? Pray ask her, though I doubt if she will tell you."

"You shouldn't keep the front door open," said the Viscount. "What's to stop people coming in and hitting you over the head? It's preposterous."

"I wish you'd go home," said Lethbridge wearily.

— *The Convenient Marriage*, Chapter XV

~ | ~

NONPAREIL

International Heyer Society Circular #17, November 2021

FROM THE PATRONESSES

Welcome once again to the monthly circular of the International Heyer Society!

Here we go in-depth into Georgette Heyer's third crime novel, *The Unfinished Clue*, which was once described by industry luminary Dorothy L. Sayers as "pure joy from start to finish." Check out Jennifer Kloester's look at Heyer's ever-developing flair for the genre, and, as always, you will find extensive character notes, references, reviews, locations and more.

THE UNFINISHED CLUE

I READ all of Heyer's mystery novels about twenty years ago and enjoyed but didn't love them. Since then, I've focussed on her historical fiction and had rather forgotten about the mysteries. However, a recent rereading of her 1934 novel *The Unfinished Clue* has left me wanting more of them, as I enjoyed it far more than expected. I couldn't remember who committed the crime, so there was some suspense, and I enjoyed the classic scenario of various ill-assorted characters trapped at a country house party where one character has been fatally stabbed while sitting at his desk in the study. Before him on the table is the start of a word he tried to write in his last moments - the 'unfinished clue' of the title. The novel has a satisfying love story, some humour, a varied cast of characters and a good resolution. I finished the book feeling astonished that Heyer could turn from sparkling historical fiction to well-plotted and convincing murder mysteries. What an amazing mind and skill she had!

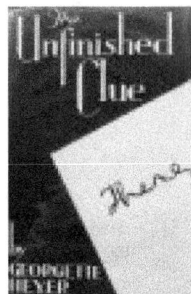

As always with Heyer, she makes us see her characters so clearly. This is one:

> "She was a thin woman of about fifty, with a weather-beaten complexion, and hair of that pepper-and-salt variety that might in her youth have been almost any colour. Kindly people said she must have been pretty once, but she had not worn well, and did nothing now to improve her appearance. She wore pince-nez, despised face powder and curling-tongs, and had a genius for acquiring frocks made according to the last fashion but one. Her weak-sighted eyes had a trick of peering, which gave her an inquisitive air, and she had a voice that had probably, in her girlhood, been a childish treble, and had become, in the process of time, merely sharp."

While telling us how this woman is dressed, Heyer also shows us her personality and the way others respond to her. The 'heroine' of the novel is Dinah Fawcett, who has an alibi and so can never be considered a suspect. Dinah has a sense of humour and, like many a Heyer heroine, often gurgles with barely repressed laughter. The hero is Inspector Harding, whose steady eyes and air of command tend to quell troublesome culprits and suspects. Put them in an empire gown and a pair of buckskin breeches, driving in a carriage instead of a car, and both would be completely at home in Heyer's Regency world.

I am now looking forward to further excursions into Heyer's world of mysteries, having so much enjoyed *The Unfinished Clue*.

– Susannah Fullerton

THE CHARACTERS

GENERAL SIR ARTHUR BILLINGTON-SMITH
An autocratic and mean-spirited retired Army officer prone to sudden rages. Very rich and can appear charming, but is an unmitigated bully.

GEOFFREY BILLINGTON-SMITH
His son, a hopeful writer, who's sensitive nature is a disappointment to the General.

CAPTAIN FRANCIS BILLINGTON-SMITH
The General's nephew, dependent on his uncle for financial support, which he has often received because he went into the Army.

STEPHEN GUEST
A distant connection of the General, he often visits the Grange due to his interest in the General's wife. Well-travelled, clever and kind, he is desperate to save her from her situation.

FAY, LADY BILLINGTON-SMITH
The General's much younger wife, very pretty and gentle, beaten down by his horrible treatment. Not-so-secretly in love with Stephen, but is scared to run away with him.

DINAH FAWCETT
Her sister, an intelligent and straightforward young woman who does not understand how her sister can put up with such treatment. Dislikes the General very cordially.

MRS. FAWCETT
Their incredibly selfish mother.

JULIA TWINING
A neighbour to the Billington-Smiths, but only recently moved into the area, she has known the General for years and is the only one for whom he seems to have any respect.

THE REVEREND HILARY CHUDLEIGH
The local vicar, very earnest and is especially set against divorce. A vegetarian.

EMILY CHUDLEIGH
His wife, a fussy busybody very full of her own importance, but genuinely devoted to her husband. And Geoffrey, for some reason...

CAMILLA HALLIDAY
A guest, she allows the General to flirt with her shamelessly.

BASIL HALLIDAY
Her husband, who is unhappy about this.

LOLA DE SILVA
A beautiful Mexican cabaret star, and Geoffrey Billington-Smith's magnificently selfish fiancée.

CONCETTA
Her voluble maid, necessary to her comfort.

SAMUEL "SAM" LEWIS
Lola de Silva's aggressively American agent.

DR. RAYMOND
Local doctor called to the General's murder.

HORACE TREMLOWE
The General's solicitor, called from London.

DETECTIVE-INSPECTOR JOHN HARDING
Brought in from Scotland Yard to investigate the murder, he is young, well-spoken and really seems to enjoy the company of Dinah Fawcett...

SUPERINTENDENT LUPTON
Of the Ralton Police, very hostile to Harding.

MAJOR GRIERSON
Helpful Chief Constable, knows Harding.

SERGEANT NETHERSOLE
Diligent, very honoured to work with Harding.

CONSTABLE FLETCHER
Of the Ralston Police. Lola does not care for him.

CONSTABLE HAMMOND
Of the Ralston Police, engaged to a Grange maid.

FINCH
Butler at the Grange.

MRS. MOXON
Housekeeper at the Grange.

LESTER
Head gardener at the Grange.

PEACOCK
Chauffeur at the Grange, can't wait to leave.

MISS PECKHAM
Head housemaid at the Grange.

JOAN DAWSON
Housemaid at the Grange.

CHARLES THOMPSON
Footman at the Grange.

~ | ~

CELEBRITY SIGHTINGS

DICKENS, CHARLES JOHN HUFFAM
1812 - 1870. English writer, publisher, editor and social critic. Despite his lack of formal education, Dickens is one of the most famous and revered of all English-language novelists. His fifteen novels include some of the most beloved in all literature, such as The Pickwick Papers, David Copperfield, Great Expectations, and the perennial holiday classic A Christmas Carol, which has been adapted for stage, film and television more than 250 times. A social critic and reformer, Dickens's progressivism has been outshone by his literary legacy, but he was also an avid philanthropist in his time.

VÉLEZ, MARIA GUADALPE VILLALOBOS
1908 – 1944. Known as Lupe Vélez, she was a Mexican actress and singer who made her way to Hollywood in 1927 after several years spent in vaudeville in her homeland. She there starred in many silent films, and then easily made the transition to "talkies," her popularity reaching its height in the 1940s in the six-movie Mexican Spitfire franchise. Romantically linked to Charlie Chaplin, Clark Gable and Gary Cooper, she later married Tarzan actor Johnny Weissmuller; when she petitioned for divorce after only ten months, she cited "cruelty." Tragically, she died of an overdose at just 36.

SCOTT, SIR WALTER
1771 - 1832. Famed Scottish historical novelist, playwright and historian best remembered for the sweeping epics Waverley, Rob Roy and Ivanhoe, in addition to his narrative poems Lady of the Lake and Marmion; his non-fiction histories were considered masterpieces. Often called the founder of historical fiction, he had a direct influence on writers as diverse as Balzac, Dostoevsky, Dumas and several Brontës, among many others. By profession a lawyer and judge, he was made baronet in 1820, in thanks for his aid in rediscovering the Crown Jewels, lost for over a century.

~ | ~

"When a woman powders her nose, Inspector, she loses count of time. My own estimate would be a moment or two; almost any man, I feel, would probably say, ages."
— *The Unfinished Clue*, Chapter 9

""Really, I don't know what the world is coming to if I am to be suspected of staring in at windows!"
— *The Unfinished Clue*, Chapter 13

~ | ~

"For me this is an affair extremely terrible. It is known that the General – whom, however, I forgive, for I am a very good Christian, I assure you – has been most cruel to me. Certainly the police must ask themselves if it is not I who have stabbed the General."

— *The Unfinished Clue*, Chapter 6

THE LOCATIONS

LYNDHURST
In Hampshire*
- The Grange
Home to the Billington-Smiths
- Blessington House
Home to Mrs. Twining, 3 miles from the Grange
- Lyndhurst Vicarage
Home to the Vicar and Mrs. Chudleigh

RALTON
- The Crown
- Ralton Police Station

LONDON
Home to Inspector Harding

* We actually can't be sure in which county the Lyndhurst described here can be found. There *is* a Lyndhurst in Hampshire, but there is no place called Ralton nearby, nor any towns called Bramhurst or Laxton. There *is* a Laxton in the UK, but it is in the north, heading towards Manchester, and that seems a less likely locale. So let us place our scene in Hampshire, because it might as well be there as anywhere else.

~ | ~

WHAT THEY SAID

Contemporary Reviews of *The Unfinished Clue*

US Syndicated Column, March 4, 1937

The Unfinished Clue by Georgette Heyer is another topnotch yarn by the author of those enthralling volumes, *Merely Murder, Behold, Here's Poison*, etc. No one surpasses Miss Heyer in sketching character through witty dialogue, and in bringing together between the covers of a book some of the most charmingly acidulous people in modern fiction. There never is a dull moment in this one. - E. M. T.

~ | ~

Hampshire Telegraph (UK), April 20, 1934

When an unpleasant person is stabbed to death his enemies may secretly rejoice, but the law has to get to work and find out which of them did the deed. In the case of the General in *The Unfinished Clue* the task was not easy, for 11 persons were more or less suspect. Georgette Heyer, who tells the story, manages it with a skilful hand and gives the reader a pleasantly puzzled time. This is the best of her detective stories so far, though the others are notably clever.

~ | ~

The Telegraph (Brisbane, Australia), May 5, 1934

Not for the first time Georgette Heyer has put her literary talents to use in the writing of a detective story. Since the public like murder mysteries and read them with avidity there is no reason why they should not be taken in hand by people of literary reputations. Indeed did not Sir Conan Doyle build his great reputation on the back of a singular amateur detective? And has not G. K. Chesterton amused himself with the "Father Brown" stories? Miss Heyer has preceded the murder and the mystery with a most amusing picture of a country house party which is made colourful by he irrepressible furies of the pompous General Billington-Smith and by the folly of his son

Geoffrey, bringing down for approval an entirely self-centred cabaret star far introduction to the family as his future wife. Before the week-end is over the general has behaved disgustingly to his beautiful young second wife, has got himself into the toils of a designing woman, has disinherited his son, has refused to pay any more bills for his scapegrace nephew, and has aroused the ire of a travelled young man who is silently and devouringly in love with Lady Billington-Smith. This picture of domestic infelicity, greatly enlivened by the fearless candour of Lady Smith's sister, is achieved with masterly strokes and the atmosphere is ideal for the plunging of the household into the consternation and suspicion caused by the discovery of the general stabbed to death in bis study. The subsequent unravelling of the mystery at this crime - a task ingeniously managed by Inspector Harding - occupies the larger half of the book and is sustained with sufficient dramatic tension to keep one on tenterhooks as to the identity of the murderer. The eventual solution is rather incredible, but more it would be unfair to say. The book will probably command a vogue.

~ | ~

Sunday Times (Perth, Australia), May 6, 1934

From the pen of Georgette Heyer comes *The Unfinished Clue*, an addition to the thrillers, *Footsteps in the Dark* and *Why Shoot a Butler?*. Miss Heyer has presented an Ingenious plot. When General Billington-Smith was stabbed in the neck with a dagger, no one wept salt tears. Eleven people were week-ending in his house at the time. Everyone hated him, and had just reason to do so. There was his wife, at whom he shouted In public; his son, whom he had disinherited in a violent scene; his son's fiancée, whom he disliked without concealment; his nephew, who was in financial straits; his sister-in-law, who—worst offence of all—was not in the least afraid of him. One of them stabbed him. Who?

~ | ~

WHAT A QUIZ!

Think you know your Heyer? These questions will test your knowledge...

1. In which year was *The Unfinished Clue* first published?
2. Who is the victim in this novel?
3. What is the name of the country house that is the scene of the crime?
4. How many of the guests are related to the victim?
5. Who discovers the body?
6. Name the Scotland Yard inspector who comes to investigate?
7. From which country does cabaret star Lola de Silva originate?
8. Who is the only guest at the house party who has a solid alibi?
9. Who falls in love with her?
10. How many other deaths occur in the book?

ANSWERS: 1. 1934; 2. General Billington-Smythe; 3. The Grange; 4. 3: his son, his nephew and a distant cousin; 5. Mrs. Twining, a neighbour and old acquaintance; 6. Inspector Harding; 7. Mexico; 8. Dinah Fawcett, the General's sister-in-law; 9. Inspector Harding; 10. Just one: a suicide.

~ | ~

SELECTED COVER GALLERY

Longmans, UK
(1934)

Doubleday, US
(1937)

Penguin, UK
(1945)

Grafton, UK
(1964)

Panther, UK
(1964)

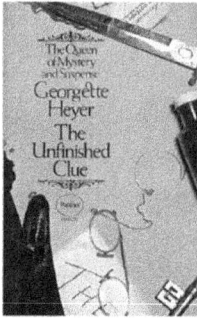

Harper Collins, UK
(1969)

Dutton, US
(1970)

Bantam, US
(1971)

Heinemann, UK
(1971)

Holt, US
(1985)

Audio Partners, US
(2001)

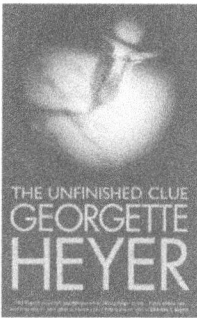

House of Stratus, UK
(2001)

Arrow, UK
(2007)

Sourcebooks, US
(2009)

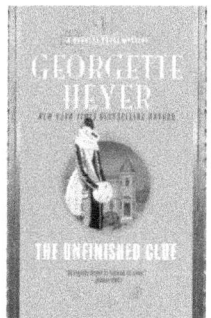

Sourcebooks, US
(2018)

SELECTED TRANSLATED EDITIONS

GERMAN: Rowohlt
(1976)

ITALIAN:
Mondadori (1983)

FRENCH: Fayard
(1991)

GERMAN:
Rowohlt (1995)

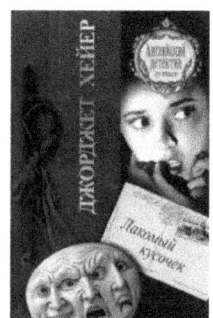

RUSSIAN: Astrel
(2012)

FINDING HER VOICE BY JENNIFER KLOESTER

BY the early 1930s Georgette Heyer was writing prolifically, with an average of two books a year between 1928 and 1933. She had moved from London to Sussex in 1931, given birth to a son in 1932, and scarcely missing a beat, published two novels that year, followed by a single book, *Why Shoot a Butler?* a year later. In 1933 the Rougiers moved house again and Georgette found in Blackthorns the perfect writing retreat. It was a pleasant, two-storey house, set in fifteen acres of woodland with a large garden and it perfectly fulfilled Georgette's need for privacy. With a nanny for Richard and a housekeeper and a maid to run the house she could concentrate on her writing. This was vital because the money coming in from Ronald's sports store was not enough to cover the family's outgoings and her writing royalties had become their main source of income.

Having written a good part of *The Convenient Marriage* while living at an inn, it must have been a relief to move into Blackthorns where she could write in much greater comfort. Her first novel in her new home was to be another detective story. Georgette had enjoyed good success with both *Footsteps in the Dark* (1932) and *Why Shoot a Butler?* (1933) and her publisher, Longmans, was eager for a third detective story. Initially she planned to call the new book Murder on Monday but eventually changed the title to the more apposite *The Unfinished Clue*. The novel would be something of a departure from her first two detective-thrillers, for she now focused less on the "thriller" angle and more on the murder mystery. Reading those early mysteries it is easy to see that Georgette had not fully developed her voice for the genre in her first two thrillers, but she did so in *The Unfinished Clue.*

Like so many of the novels of the Golden Age, *The Unfinished Clue* is a weekend country-house party murder mystery. Set at "the Grange", its owner is the loathsome General Sir Arthur Billington-Smith. A wealthy landowner and an ex-soldier, he bullies his fragile wife, Fay, despises his son, Geoffrey, and is impatient with anyone who does not conform to his rules. Being heartily disliked by almost everyone means that, when Sir Arthur is stabbed to death in his study, there are plenty of suspects. Fay's sister, Dinah, cool-headed, intelligent and possessing far more courage than her shy, shrinking sibling, is the story's heroine and she is instantly drawn to the novel's hero, Inspector Harding of Scotland Yard. Charming and perceptive, had Heyer chosen to use Harding again, he might have become another of the 1930's iconic detectives.

Despite its rather gruesome murder, *The Unfinished Clue* is a humorous novel with several excellent character studies – not least of which is Lola, the Mexican dancer. Heyer's first biographer, Jane Aiken Hodge, described *The Unfinished Clue* as 'a thoroughly good country house mystery with an intricate plot based on timing, a romantic interest for the gentleman detective, and what Georgette Heyer herself later described as "a superb lady called Lola".' Georgette was not the only one to think Lola a delightful comic creation. Dorothy L. Sayers, writing in *The Sunday Times*, observed frankly that:

> I said last week that good writing would often carry a poor plot, and here is a case in point. Reduced to its main outlines *The Unfinished Clue* has the stamp of stereotype all over it. Here is the same old week-end party: the disagreeable rich man, who is stabbed in the study, the down-trodden wife, the rebellious son with the undesirable fiancée, the hard-up nephew, the wife's lover, the husband's petting-partner and her husband – all the stock characters, including the mysterious widow out of the victim's past and the gentlemanly detective with the sugary love affair, together with a solution which had grown whiskers in the sixties [1860s!] and is as preposterous now as it was then. And yet, simply because it is written in a perfectly delightful light comedy vein, the book is pure joy from start to finish. Lola, the fiancée, by herself is worth the money, and, indeed, all the characters from the Chief Constable to the Head Parlourmaid, are people we know intimately and appreciatively, from the first words they utter. Miss Heyer has given us a sparkling conversation-piece, rich in chuckles, and all we ask of the plot is that it should keep us going until the comedy is played out.

In the years to come, Heyer would become known as the "wittiest of detective writers" and it would be her humour that would set her apart from her detective-writing peers. While she never attained the icon status of a Sayers or a Christie, she easily sat alongside along Ngaio Marsh and Margery Allingham and the quality of Georgette Heyer's detective fiction would ensure her place among the "Golden Age of Detective Fiction Writers".

– Jennifer Kloester

NONPAREIL

International Heyer Society Circular #18, December 2021

FROM THE PATRONESSES

Welcome once again to the monthly circular of the International Heyer Society!

Here we go in-depth into Georgette Heyer's fourth crime novel, *Death in the Stocks*. Check out Jennifer Kloester's fascinating recounting of the American attempt to bring the story to the stage, and, as always, you will find extensive character notes, references, reviews, locations and more.

DEATH IN THE STOCKS

ONE of the great joys of reading works set in the period in which they were written – what we experts like to refer to as "contemporary" novels; you may have heard the term – is how much they reveal about the lives lived at the time. For many years, really until my enforced discovery of Georgette Heyer (enforced by one of this Society's venerable Patronesses, who, I don't know how many of you know Rachel personally, but she is so persuasive that it almost amounts to sorcery), I held a contemporary scholar's disdain for works of historical fiction, believing them to be a mere shadow of their counterparts. How, I was heard – and read – to argue loudly and often, could one compare actually being there with the rose-coloured-glasses, 20/20-hindsight, Monday Expert version of events that was the product of authorial imagination rather than lived experience? I still feel that way, to a degree, but what is fascinating about Georgette Heyer is that the reader feels just as much there in her Regency drawing rooms and medieval royal halls as they do in the studio flat of the often repellent Vereker siblings, Kenneth and Antonia, in 1930s Chelsea. Some of the hallmarks of Heyer's social satire are certainly present, as is her way with a witty rejoinder, devoted retainer, and devil-may-care gent hard up for cash but still spending pretty liberally (because one just does, you know). But what is perhaps particularly notable is the romance between first cousins that is presented to us as completely natural and desirable, as is the case with much of the literature of the time. (First cousin marriage does still occur in much of the world, and though it is now often seen as a social taboo, it is legal in most countries, including the UK.) To the modern reader, Antonia's choice of beau is icky in the extreme, but to this lover of contemporary fiction, it is exactly as it should be.

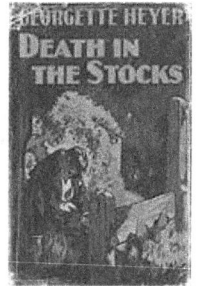

– Maura Tan

~ | ~

"Don't you talk like that, Master Kenneth! How would you like to have a knife stuck in you? Nasty, underhand way of killing anyone, that's what I call it."

"I don't see it at all," objected Kenneth. "It's no worse than shooting a person, and far more sensible. Shooting's noisy, for one thing, and, for another, you leave a bullet in your man, and it gets traced to you. Whereas a knife doesn't leave anything behind, and is easy to get rid of."

– Death in the Stocks, Chapter 4

THE CHARACTERS

ARNOLD VEREKER
An unlikeable and easily-angered businessman who, as the eldest son, inherited his father's mining company, which has since become enormously successful. Miserly with his siblings, he is hated by most people who have ever met him. Fond of pretty young women, whom he frequently takes to his vacation home for overnight stays.

ROGER VEREKER
His scapegrace younger brother, an alcoholic and a gambler, who disappeared for many years, and was long believed dead. Quite charming and shrewd, in his way.

KENNETH VEREKER
Their younger half-brother, an artist and connoisseur of beauty. He tends to affect an attitude of careless insouciance. In need of funds. Engaged to the beautiful Violet Williams.

ANTONIA VEREKER
Kenneth's very pretty and insouciant sister, who lives with him in a flat in Chelsea. She is furious when Arnold, her guardian, forbids her proposed marriage. Breeds bull-terriers.

GEOFFREY VEREKER
Their deceased father.

MAUD VEREKER
His first wife, mother to Arnold and Roger.

VIOLET WILLIAMS
Kenneth's beautiful fiancée, whom he appears to hold in equal affection and disdain. A very determined young woman whom most of Kenneth's acquaintance believe to be a gold-digger and their social inferior.

RUDOLPH MESURIER
An accountant at Arnold Vereker's mining company, he is engaged to Antonia Vereker, but his employer does not approve. Especially as there seems to be something wrong with the figures...

LESLIE RIVERS
A long-time friend of the younger Verekers, very obviously in love with Kenneth. Hates Violet Williams with a passion.

MURGATROYD
Former nurse and now housekeeper to Kenneth and Antonia Vereker. Fiercely loyal to both, and not especially fond of the police. Is certain neither of her charges could ever have committed any kind of crime.

MR. PETERS
Resident in Chelsea, owns the garage where the younger Verekers park their cars.

ROSE MILLER
Arnold Vereker's cold, composed and competent secretary.

HAROLD FAIRFAX
Deputy manager and long-time employee of the Shan Hills Mining Company, serving under Arnold Vereker.

MRS. BEATON
Charwoman for Arnold Vereker at Riverside Cottage. A disappointing witness.

BEATON
Her son, gardener at Riverside Cottage.

GILES CARRINGTON
A cousin to the younger Verekers, he is also their solicitor, as well as an executor of Arnold Vereker's estate. Called in following the murder, he turns his shrewd brain to the problem of proving that, if no one else, Antonia Vereker certainly did not do it. Becomes very friendly with Superintendent Hannasyde of Scotland Yard, and so is given access to much privileged information. Often acts as an interpreter and liaison between his cousins and the police.

CHARLES CARRINGTON
His father, a bluff and rather forgetful solicitor who is quite indulgent where his son is concerned, though he hides it under much bluster.

JANET CARRINGTON
His wife, sister to the young Verekers' mother.

JACKSON
Chauffeur to Arnold Vereker, recently fired and thus with a motive to kill him.

TAYLOR
Sour butler at Arnold Vereker's Eaton Place residence. Very put out by the presence of what he sees as presumptuous police officers.

MATTHEW
Footman at Arnold Vereker's Eaton Place residence.

GORDON TRUELOVE
The other executor of Arnold Vereker's will, alongside Giles Carrington.

FLOSSIE (OR FLORENCE)
A sex-worker allegedly employed by Roger Vereker.

HORACE DUKE
Lives near Ashleigh Green with his wife. Is disturbed by the police after the body is discovered.

PHILLIP COURTENAY
Former secretary to Arnold Vereker.

CEDRIC JOHNSON
Had an appointment with Arnold Vereker on the day before his death, questioned as to what he might have heard regarding a meeting between the deceased and Rudolph Mesurier.

SIR HENRY WATSON
Had an appointment with Arnold Vereker right before Rudolph Mesurier.

MISS SUMMERTOWN
A friend of Violet Williams who provides her with an alibi.

FRANK CREWE
A friend of Kenneth's.

THE DAWSONS
Mutual friends of Giles and Antonia.

THE HON. THOMAS DREW
Attended a Charity Ball with Kenneth and Leslie. (Lives at Albany, a favourite spot of Heyer's.)

GERALD HERSHAW
With his wife, also attended a Charity Ball with Kenneth and Leslie.

PAULA
Also attended a Charity Ball with Kenneth and Leslie.

MR. WESTLEY
He and his wife, too, attended the Charity Ball with Kenneth and Leslie.

SUPERINTENDENT HANNASYDE
A good humoured and deceptively mild Scotland Yard investigator with a keen insight into human nature and a gentle wit. Not afraid to ask for help when he needs it.

SERGEANT HEMINGWAY
Hannasyde's trusty sidekick, with his genial nature and everyman vocabulary, he works very hard in the background, tracking down alibis and clues.

INSPECTOR DAVIS
Of Scotland Yard.

DR. STONE
The London police surgeon who performs Arnold Vereker's autopsy.

CONSTABLE DICKENSON
Discovers Arnold Vereker's body on Ashleigh Green.

SERGEANT HOLLIS
Expert in fingerprint analysis for the Hanborough Police.

SERGEANT HAMLYN
Of Hanborough Police, takes the phone call reporting on the dead body in the stocks. Breeder of Airedales.

COLONEL AGNEW
Chief Constable at Hanborough.

INSPECTOR JERROLD
Of Hanborough Police. Very brusque.

HILL
His driver.

DR. HAWKE
Hanborough police surgeon who first examines the body.

JOHN FOTHERINGHAM
A former fiancé of Antonia's.

MAXTON
A tradesman to whom Kenneth owes money.

BILL
One of Antonia's three bull-terriers.

MR. JACKSON
Manager of the building where Roger Vereker lives.

MR. AND MRS. CHOLMONDELEY
Tenants in the same building

MRS. DELAFORD
Tenant in the same building.

MISS TURNER
Her maid.

ADMIRAL CRAVEN
Tenant in the same building

SIR GEORGE FAIRFAX
Tenant in the same building, along with his wife.

MR. MUSKETT
Tenant in the same building, along with his wife.

MR. TOMLINSON
Tenant in the same building, along with his wife.

MR. HUMPHRIES
Tenant in the same building.

MISS MATTHEWS
Tenant in the same building.

~ | ~

"I do want to know who did kill Arnold. I've often said I'd like to, but I never did, somehow."

— *Death in the Stocks*, Chapter 2

"I never in my life met a fellow with a worse heart, or a worse temper, or worse manners, or more obstinate, pig-headed—"

— *Death in the Stocks*, Chapter 7

CELEBRITY SIGHTINGS

CHEKHOV, ANTON PAVLOVICH
1860 - 1904. Russian playwright and short story writer. His most famous plays, *The Seagull, Uncle Vanya* and *The Cherry Orchard*, are still frequently performed, and are notable for their complexity and the rudeness of his characters. He is considered an early modernist of the theatre, and is ranked alongside Ibsen and Strindberg. Chekhov also wrote over 500 short stories, many of which are now considered among the best, not only in Russian but in all literature. He married his wife Olga in 1901; he died just three years later, of tuberculosis.

DOYLE, SIR ARTHUR IGNATIUS CONAN
1859 - 1930. British physician and famously the author of the Sherlock Holmes detective stories, as well as of many other works in many other genres, including novels of fantasy, romance and science fiction. Doyle was especially interested in spirituality, psychic powers and clairvoyance, and was even friends with escapologist Harry Houdini. He married Louisa in 1885, and together they had two children; after her death from tuberculosis, he married again, and had a further three children. All five of them survived to adulthood, but they all died childless. Doyle died of a heart attack at the age of 71. His last words are believed to have been "You are wonderful," directed to his wife.

MATHERS, EDWARD POWYS
1892 - 1939. Known as "Torquemada", he was a translator and poet best remembered for his work as a compiler of cryptic crosswords, his pseudonym implying that they were so difficult, they were like torture. It is under this name that he also reviewed detective fiction. John Steinbeck's novel Cannery Row quotes liberally from his translation of 11th-century Kashmiri poet Bilhana's work *Caurapâñcâśikâ*, which he entitled *Black Marigolds*.

MILTON, JOHN
1608 - 1674. English poet best remembered for his epic work *Paradise Lost*, a blank verse poem considered by many to be among the greatest works of English literature. At the age of 35, while a schoolmaster, he married the 16-year-old Mary, who left him to return to her parents after a month, only returning years later at the outset of the Civil War. (And turning him into a proponent of divorce.) Outside of the Arts, Milton was a prominent Puritan and civil servant who was a strong supporter of Oliver Cromwell, turning his creative talent towards writing pamphlets and treatises in praise of Puritan ideals. Widowed twice, he married his third wife at the age of 55, when she was just 24. Having lost his vision completely by 1652, his work was thereafter dictated to a series of secretaries. He was arrested after the Restoration in 1660, but was freed by one of his former secretaries, who was then an MP. He was trilingual - writing in English, Latin and Ancient Greek - and went on to be revered by famed English poets Dryden, Wordsworth and Blake. He continues to inspire poets to this day.

SHAKESPEARE, WILLIAM
1564 - 1616. Considered the greatest playwright in the English language, Shakespeare's origins were humble. Son of a glove-maker, he married at 18, but 10 years later he had left his wife at home to pursue an acting career in London. Over the decades he produced dozens of plays, from histories to comedies to tragedies, and was so prolific and brilliant that much debate still rages over the true authorship of his works. He also wrote poetry, and his Sonnets are considered some of the most romantic, and are certainly the most famous, in all literature.

WALLACE, RICHARD HORATIO EDGAR
1875 - 1932. Born illegitimate, he was adopted into a semi-literate family as an infant, leaving school at the age of 12 and working in a variety of menial occupations before joining the British Army - under this assumed surname - at the age of 21. He met Rudyard Kipling in South Africa, who inspired him to write; after leaving the army he stayed in Africa and became a correspondent during the Boer War. Returning to England, debt-ridden, he began writing thrillers to make money quickly; he eventually self-published his debut novel in 1905, which sold well but left him in more debt. After years of struggling, he signed with Hodder & Stoughton in 1921, and by 1928 it is estimated that one in four books read in Great Britain was his. He was enormously prolific, writing across multiple genres, and by the time of his death he had produced more than 170 novels, 18 stage plays, and 957 short stories. He also wrote the original draft of the film *King Kong*. He died of complications from diabetes at the age of 57.

~ | ~

"What's the use of Arnold's being murdered if we're saddled with Roger?"

— Death in the Stocks, Chapter 13

~ | ~

THE LOCATIONS

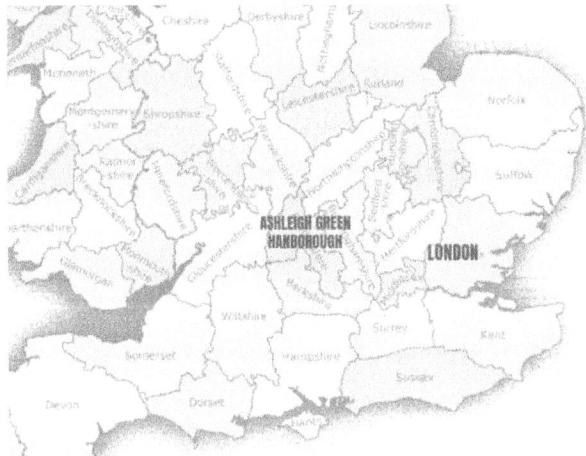

ASHLEIGH GREEN
Village close to Hanborough
- Riverside Cottage, holiday home of Arnold Vereker
- Pennyfarthing Row, home to his housekeeper

HANBOROUGH
There is a Long Hanborough, in the parish of Hanborough, in Oxfordshire. We're assuming this is it.
- The King's Head
- Hanborough Police Station
- Hanborough Court House

LONDON
- Eaton Place, home of Arnold Vereker
- Chelsea, home of Kenneth and Antonia Vereker
- Embankment, home of Violet Williams
- Adelphi Terrace, office of Giles Carrington
- Scotland Yard

~ | ~

WHAT THEY SAID

Contemporary Reviews of *Death in the Stocks*

Melbourne Herald (Victoria, Australia), July 4, 1935

In *Death in the Stocks*, Arnold Vereker is found dead in the early hours of the morning with his feet imprisoned in some old stocks. Three people immediately become suspects, all of whom have a strong motive and no alibi. Later their number is added to by a fourth man. Three of the four suspects take an impish delight in long and amusing discursions, in which they prove entirely to their own satisfaction, but hardly to that of the police, the guilt of the others. And no malice is borne on either side.

Kenneth Vereker and his sister, Antonia, are a very unusual and original young couple with a complete disregard for each other's feelings or anyone else's for that matter.

The police are completely at sea when coping with the Vereker family, for Kenneth and Antonia and later, Roger, make no attempt to conceal their hatred for their half-brother or their unbounded delight at his death. They refuse absolutely to behave with the conventional decorum of bereaved relatives or the gravity which is usually associated with those strongly suspected of murder.

This odd family and their little ways keep one chuckling all the time, while one is still keenly interested in trying to unravel the mystery of who really did kill Arnold Vereker.

~ | ~

Auckland Star (New Zealand), June 15, 1935

Death in the Stocks, by Georgette Heyer, is an entertaining, quite thrilling and exceptionally well-written detective story. The authoress has drawn the attention of a large number of readers by her historical romances, as well as her stories of modern crime. Where she scores is in her style. So many writers of so called "thrillers" rely only on the plot. Miss Heyer introduces humour, insight and shrewd character drawing. Her young, smart people are really quite bright in their repartee, and there is hardly a page in *Death in the Stocks* where you will not get a chuckle. As the title suggests, a body is found dead in the stocks. Everyone comes under suspicion; even the attractive Antonia, with the copper curls and the large and brilliant dark eyes. Death is accepted in detective story books, but why the stocks? That is what Georgette Heyer in her refreshing and very clever way explains.

~ | ~

Sunday Post (Lanarkshire, Scotland), April 28, 1935

Shows that a woman can write a thrilling detective story. Sparkling dialogue, good love story, startling surprise at the end.

~ | ~

Daily News (London, UK), April 10, 1935

A man found dead with his feet in the stocks, fantastic false trails — Miss Heyer's tale is original from the beginning, and exciting till the end.

~ | ~

New Zealand Herald, May 11, 1935

Among present-day novelists Miss Georgette Heyer must be ranked in the first flight for versatility at least. Her attractive and well-written historical romances are equal to the best fiction of their kind, while the author's stories of modern life are excellently done and extremely entertaining. Miss Heyer's latest publication, *Death in the Stocks*, is a mystery story that her many readers will welcome with enthusiasm. Naturally enough in the true Heyer style, it is something entirely new in murder mysteries. There is no straining for effect with gruesome detail or sensational incident. Certain matters of a morbid nature have to be discussed, of course; but here a commendable restraint is exercised. Actually the murder theme of the book is merely a background used by a clever writer to introduce the reader to a most interesting circle of people, and to meet them is so refreshing that it might be regarded in the light of privilege. Certainly the reader will be indebted to them for much amusement. The Verekers are a quaint family, frank and honest almost to the point of foolishness, with a high standard of decency and a sense of "playing the game" that is not at first apparent because they choose to pose as callous "moderns" with not a thought for anything but their own comfort in life. At the same time the mystery side of the story is expertly handled, and few will be able to "spot" the assailant before the author chooses to impart this particular knowledge. Apart from the fact that Superintendent Hannasyde of Scotland Yard suffers foolishness, if not fools, a trifle too gladly for an officer of his standing, the book is more or less a flawless piece of masterly story-telling, written with ease and skill that makes for bright entertainment. There are those who will say perhaps that Antonia Vereker could have been presented in a more pleasing light had Miss Heyer chosen to tone down some of the ultra-modern "slanguage " attributed to this charming girl.

~ | ~

WHAT A QUIZ!

Think you know your Heyer? These questions will test your knowledge...

1. In which year was *theb* first published?
2. Where are the stocks of the title?
3. Which siblings are the initial chief suspects of the crime?
4. Which family member is also later implicated?
5. How much does the victim's heir stand to inherit?
6. Which Scotland Yard officer makes his first of six appearances in this novel?
7. With the help from which fellow officer?
8. How many times is Antonia Vereker engaged in this novel?
9. Who actually solves the crime?
10. What is his profession?

ANSWERS: 1. 1935; 2. Ashleigh Green; 3. The victim's half-brother and -sister, Kenneth and Antonia Vereker; 4. The victim's brother, Roger Vereker; 5. £250,000, mostly in mining stocks; 6. Superintendent Hannasyde; 7. Sergeant Hemingway; 8. twice; 9. Giles Carrington, the Verekers' cousin; 10. He is a solicitor.

~ | ~

SELECTED COVER GALLERY

Longmans, UK
(1935)

Doubleday, US
(1935)

Sun Dial, US
(1935)

Penguin, UK
(1942)

Heinemann, UK
(1952)

Dutton, US
(1962)

Panther, UK
(1963)

Grafton, UK
(1963)

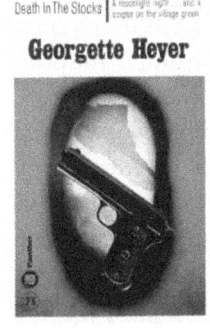

Panther, UK
(1966)

Harper Collins, UK
(1968)

Berkely, US
(1986)

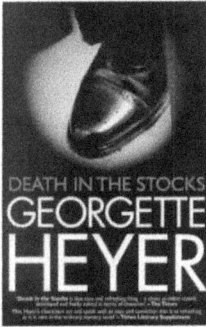

House of Stratus, UK
(2002)

Arrow, UK
(2006)

Sourcebooks, US
(2009)

Sourcebooks, US
(2018)

SELECTED TRANSLATED EDITIONS

GERMAN: Econ & List
(1976)

DUTCH:
Westfriesland (1990)

FRENCH: Poche
(2002)

SPANISH:
Salamandra (2008)

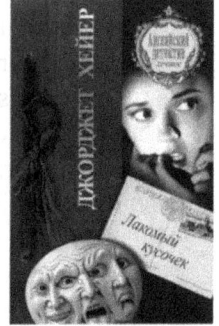

JAPANESE: 東京創元社
(2011)

DEATH IN THE STOCKS ON THE STAGE BY JENNIFER KLOESTER

DEATH IN THE STOCKS was written in 1934. It was Georgette Heyer's fourth detective novel and is regarded by many readers as her best. It was the last of her books to be published by Longmans & Co. and the only one of her detective stories written without her husband, Ronald Rougier's, assistance. He had "had a hand" in her first three mysteries and would again help with the "how dunnit" of seven of the remaining eight detective novels that Heyer would eventually write (*Penhallow* was different). *Death in the Stocks*, however, was hers alone. It would prove to be a very successful book and its publisher, Longmans, tried hard not to lose her. Her editor, Kenneth Potter, wrote Georgette enthusiastic letters assuring her that the firm would do their best for her new novel but her mind was made up: "You ought to see Potter's latest effusions! He 'feels sure he can sell *Death in the Stocks*'! Ha, Ha!" Two months before *Death in the Stocks* was published under the Longmans banner, she signed a contract with Hodder & Stoughton for "her next four new and original 'modern' novels"; they would publish her next five detective novels and lose her over *Penhallow*.

Georgette had enjoyed writing *Death in the Stocks* and it shows in the novel's dark comic vein wherein, despite a rather nasty murder, her prime suspects enjoy cracking jokes about the crime, pointing out to the police just how easy it would have been for any one of them to have "dunnit", and pointing the accusatory finger at whomever it suits them to do so. Published in Britain in April 1935, *Death in the Stocks* was the first of Georgette's detective novels to be published in America. In September 1935, Doubleday Doran brought out the book under the new title of *Merely Murder* with a quotation on the cover that read: "A rare and refreshing novel of mirth and murder among the mad young Verekers". The American edition enjoyed good sales and Doubleday would go on to publish eight more of her murder mysteries and six of her historical novels before she moved to Putnam in 1946.

Although Longmans UK had brought out five of her novels in the States, Georgette had not had an American publisher since 1926 when Small Maynard had published *These Old Shades*. Although she had no great expectations of her American publisher it was still a feather in Georgette's cap to be published there.

The following year she was equally pleased when *Merely Murder* caught the attention of the the successful playwright and screenwriter, A.E. Thomas (1872-1947). Thomas had recently adapted the play *No More Ladies* into a script for a film of the same name starring Joan Crawford and Robert Montgomery. Struck by the wit and vigour of Heyer's dialogue, he thought that *Death in the Stocks* would make a successful Broadway play. In 1936, the theatre and film director, writer and producer, Edward A. Blatt, came on board and it was he who would forward the script drafts to Georgette.

At first she held high hopes for the play version of her novel, but by November 1936, she was becoming increasingly disillusioned. As her own writing success proved, Heyer had a keen ear for dialogue as well as an acute sense of what worked in both plot and character. As she pointed out to her agent: "the original reason for dramatizing the book lay in the quality of the dialogue", as well as in the personalities of its main characters and the reader's uncertainty about Kenneth Vereker's guilt or innocence.

Unhappy with the first script, she was equally disappointed with the second:

> I send you back the second script herewith. If you can say to Mr Blatt without offence I should like him told that I do not care for this version. It differs only slightly from the first, & its differences, which are interpretations, do not seem to me felicitous. The introduction of a Butcher

& a Musical Stranger are, I believe, egregious mistakes. The Butcher's purpose is to show the audience that Kenneth is hard-up. This is bad psychology, & rather poor technique. To begin with, men of Kenneth's type are not disturbed very much by being in debt to tradesmen. To go on with, the paltry motive of a butcher's bill unpaid, even assuming that all the other tradesmen are also unpaid, is not sufficient to give a motive for murder. Had the sum in question to be gained by murder been a few hundred pounds the butcher might have been relevant. But no man needs a motive of that nature for murder with a large fortune at stake. Therefore I would say, Out with the butcher! He is unnecessary. If an additional reason for dispensing with him is needed, I would suggest that no trusted family retainer, or in fact any well-trained servant, would usher a dunning tradesman into her master's presence.

[Georgette Heyer to Norah Perriam, 8 November 1936]

One advantage to reading Heyer's criticisms of the new script is the insight it offers her readers into her own sense of language as well as her sense of her audience:

The more Mr Thomas touches Murgatroyd up the worse she becomes. There is no point in the scene where she becomes drunk, & I think it will be very distasteful to most people. It is not in the part, & serves no useful purpose. What I should like to do with the final script would be to rewrite all Murgatroyd's speeches. The polyglot language she now speaks is quite painful to anyone moderately familiar with the Cockney, Irish & Scotch tongues. It strikes me, with reference to the two additional characters, that Mr Thomas has perhaps got the thing a little out of focus. He very rightly took Kenneth for the main figure, but what he does not seem to me quite to grasp is that the public is going to be interested, not in red herrings, but in the main problem, which is: Did this young man do it or did he not? Readers of the book, I found, practically disregarded the other suspects, & I think audiences of the play would be inclined to do so too. If additional subjects are wanted there are enough already.

Sadly, she was not to be satisfied by any script produced by A. E. Thomas. She felt sure that she could amend it herself for a better result but, as she explained to Norah Perriam, that required a collaboration which in turn meant travelling to America:

I quite see that I ought to go to New York, but I can't possibly do it. This play is not going to be as good as I could make it. To correct by correspondence is very difficult, as I don't wish to hurt Mr Thomas's feelings. The ideal thing would have been for us to have worked together – he to plot the sequence me to write the necessary dialogue.

Reading this 2nd version has made more than ever determined to do Behold, Here's Poison myself. The more Mr Thomas deviates from my text the worse the play grows. It must, of course, be exceedingly hard to write convincing dialogue for another person's characters.

In the end, Georgette was proved correct. *Merely Murder* opened on Broadway at the Playhouse Theatre on 3 December 1937. Three performances later, it closed.

– Jennifer Kloester

~ | ~

THE WEEKLY POST, VOL II.

#1 – A PROPER HIGH BRED 'UN BY RACHEL GRANT

Friday, January 8, 2020

> 'Eh, lad, you've got a proper high-bred 'un here!'
> 'Do you like him?' Richmond asked eagerly. 'He's young – pretty green still, but a perfect mover! I broke him myself.'
>   - *The Unknown Ajax*

Around the turn of the 17th century, three Arab stallions were brought to England. They were Byerly Turk, Darnley Arabian and Godolphin Arabian (Barb). They were bred with strong, calm, "cold-blooded" English mares (actually of Irish Hobby and Connemara stock) and the result was the perfect sporting horse, the Thoroughbred. All thoroughbreds are descended from the three sires, and these magnificent horses appear with great regularity in the pages of Georgette Heyer's novels. Many of her heroes ride and drive high-couraged beautiful steppers. From Lord Worth's magnificent chestnuts to the Hon. Nicholas Carlyon on his stylish bay, and from Sir Nugent Fotherby on a showy chestnut to Lady Cardross behind her match greys, the characters are elucidated and given depth through descriptions of their horses.

So what makes a Thoroughbred so special? They are true athletes, loving to compete and to win, which makes them ideal as racehorses. They are versatile, energetic and high-spirited with great heart. Physically, the thoroughbred is large and powerful, yet elegant with long legs and a lean body. The head is refined and the eyes wide-spaced, with a long arched neck and well-defined high withers. (Withers are the ridge between the shoulder blades. It is the standard to measure a horse's height from the ground to the withers. Measurement itself is in 'hands' - originally the breadth of a human hand but now standardised to 4 inches. Most thoroughbreds are 15-17 hands). Thoroughbreds have deep sloping shoulders, a short and evenly curved back with a high croup and a broad chest. (The croup is the top line of the horse's hindquarters from the hip to the dock of the tail.)

> Miss Thane took no part in the recital, but derived considerable amusement from watching Shield's face while he tried to resolve two conversations into their component parts.
> '- like his knee action - came to murder Ludovic - had a thoroughbred hack like him once - he had a dagger - kept on throwing out a splint - tried to stun Sir Hugh - took his fences as well standing as flying - wore a mask - had a slight curve in his crest!' announced Eustacie and Thane in chorus.
>   – *The Talisman Ring*

Thoroughbreds come in a variety of colours but are predominantly Bay, Chestnut or Brown.

Bay: reddish-brown or brown body colour with black points (the mane, tail, ear edges and lower legs).
Chestnut: reddish to brown body colour with the mane and tail the same colour or lighter. No black hair.
Brown: similar to bay but with more black colouration. True black thoroughbreds are very rare.
NB. A Grey horse has white hair (actually depigmented) over black skin.

> "You are to drive away in a carriage, behind a pair of beautiful grey horses!"
> "I am driving my chestnuts today,' said Mr Beaumaris apologetically. 'I am so sorry, but I feel I should perhaps mention it!"
> "You did very right,' said Arabella approvingly. 'One should never tell untruths to children! Chestnuts, Jemmy, glossy brown horses!"
>   – *Arabella*

Georgette Heyer mentions many different breeds of horses from common hacks to Welsh ponies. Some of these animals, as Master Edmund Rayne disparagingly says, are "bone-setters". But for the heroes and heroines riding through the pages, only the best "out-and-outers" will do. A thoroughbred it has to be!

                                     – *Rachel Grant, Animal Correspondent*

#2 – MISS BROUGHTY'S WEDDING PRESENT BY SUSANNAH FULLERTON

Friday, January 15, 2021

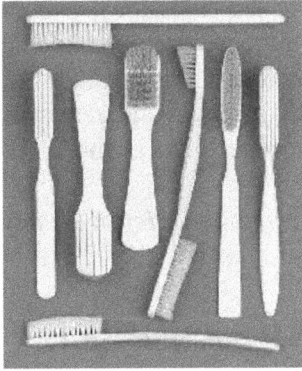

When Miss Olivia Broughty of *Cotillion* is setting off on her elopement with her beloved Camille, the ever-practical and totally gorgeous Freddy Standen reminds her that she has not packed a toothbrush. They stop off at Newton's Emporium in Leicester Square so that he can hurry in and buy this practical object for her. When she protests that she hasn't the money to pay for it, Freddy announces laconically that the toothbrush can be a wedding present. Surely the most unusual wedding gift in all of Georgette Heyer's fiction!

We tend to shudder when we think of the personal hygiene habits (or rather, the lack of them) of the Georgians, but oral hygiene was attended to by those of the ton, like Freddy, and the middle classes (to which Olivia Broughty belongs). To clean their teeth our ancestors used devices now known as chew sticks – a twig with a frayed end, with which teeth and gums were brushed. The earliest chew sticks found in ancient graves date from 3500 BC and came from Mesopotamia, but other similar devices were discovered in Egyptian tombs and are mentioned in Chinese records. The Romans and Greeks seem to have preferred toothpicks. The very first toothbrush with bristles (the hair came from hogs) are from China and date from around 700, with the bristles attached to a piece of bamboo or bone. Gradually European travellers, impressed by such a useful implement, carried it back to Europe. Throughout the 17th century, toothbrushes became common in shops, with bristles made of horsehair or boar's hair. The first recorded use of the word 'toothbrush' in Britain was in 1690, when a Mr Anthony Wood mentions buying one from J. Barret.

By the time of the Regency era those, like Freddy, wishing to purchase a toothbrush could buy a mass-produced one. These became available in England in 1780, produced by entrepreneur William Addis (1734 – 1808). His invention came about because he spent time in prison for being involved in a riot. Trying to clean hie teeth in his cell, using rag and soot, he grew convinced that there had to be a better way. He saved a bone from his prison dinner, and then tied into the tiny holes in the bone little tufts of bristles that his guard helpfully provided. Using some glue, he sealed all into position. Once released from prison, he set to work to manufacture his toothbrushes, growing rich as a result (the business he started remained in family ownership until 1996). Freddy had choices when he bought Olivia a toothbrush – a more costly one with badger hair for its bristles, or a cheaper one with pig bristles. But then we know Freddy always goes for quality! The handle could have been bone, wood, ivory or even silver. Today the Addis Collection at the Hertford Museum has about 5000 toothbrushes on display.

Freddy does not mention the purchase of tooth powder, but we can assume that was added to the neat parcel he hands to Miss Broughty. The Ancient Egyptians used a powder composed of an amazing range of abrasives – ashes, ground ox hoof, powdered eggshells, pumice and even myrrh. The Greeks used crushed bones and oyster shells. The Islamic world had available from the 9th century some form of toothpaste which was evidently 'pleasant to the taste', but its ingredients have not been recorded. In Britain tooth powders came into general use and were commercially available in the 19th century. Those living in the country would have made their own, using baking soda, chalk, salt and even pulverised bricks, but Londoners could buy various brands (though some of these might well have done more harm than good). With the increasing use of sugar in foods throughout the Georgian era, a good brush and some form of cleansing agent were badly needed. Manufacturers of tooth powder promised that their products would sweeten the breath, polish the teeth, and even help to fasten teeth that were coming loose! A widowed Mrs Trotter sold her tooth powder at 2s 9d a box in London, while one of her toothbrushes would have set Freddy back one shilling. Most apothecaries, and some doctors, would have sold tooth powder and each person who made the product jealously guarded their recipe.

Oliva Broughty sets off for France and we learn nothing more of how she cares for her teeth there. Freddy Standen, as Kitty notes, may not be a man who can slay dragons, but who needs a dragon-slayer when there are more practical problems to be solved? Georgette Heyer uses the purchase of a simple toothbrush to show her readers just what a thoughtful, practical and generous man Freddy Standen is. No wonder he was chosen as the No. 1 Favourite Hero at the 2019 Georgette Heyer conference in Sydney!

– *Susannah Fullerton, Patroness, International Heyer Society*

~ | ~

#3 – HEYER'S HOUSES #1: WIMBLEDON BY JENNIFER KLOESTER

Friday, January 22, 2021

67 Ridgway Place, Wimbledon Village, SW19. Charming double fronted Victorian terrace in Wimbledon Village. savills

It is always fascinating to visit a place where a beloved author once lived and worked. I have been lucky enough to visit nearly all of the houses and apartments in which Georgette Heyer wrote her novels and each one has given me a little more insight into the personality of this reclusive writer.

Growing up, Georgette lived at a number of different addresses. As a friend of her childhood explained, "They seemed to move about and travel a lot"; she also described Georgette's father as "A bit of a rolling stone". Most of the houses in which the Heyer family lived were in Wimbledon, just a few miles south-west of London.

It would have been at 11 Homefield Road in Wimbledon that Georgette wrote out the fair copy of her first novel, *The Black Moth*, before sending it to Constable, who published the book in September 1921. By then she was living at Melcombe House in Oatlands Avenue, Weybridge, another dozen miles further southwest. In 1923, the Heyer family moved to 5 Ridgway Place in central Wimbledon and it was there that Georgette completed her first contemporary novel, *Instead of the Thorn* and where she would also write her first medieval novel, *Simon the Coldheart*.

Number 5 Ridgway Place is now 67 Ridgway Place (the numbers were changed after the 1920s) and is an attractive, three-storey Victorian Terrace house which I was lucky enough to visit thanks to the kindness of its current owners. It was a strange experience to be in a house where Georgette Heyer had lived and walked, slept, laughed and conversed with her parents and two brothers and where she had put her powerful imagination to work and written two of her early novels.

5 Ridgway Place was also the site of Georgette's greatest tragedy for it was there that on 15 June 1925 her father so unexpectedly died. He died from a heart attack in front of his only daughter. There was nothing she could do to save him and the cataclysmic experience forever changed her.

– *Jennifer Kloester, Patroness, International Heyer Society*

~ | ~

#4 – HEYER'S HOUSES #2: AFRICA AND MACEDONIA BY JENNIFER KLOESTER

Friday, January 29, 2021

Although I have been lucky enough to visit a number of Georgette Heyer's homes, I have not (so far) made it to either of her overseas ones. Georgette wrote four of her novels while living abroad and, while some readers might have expected the exotic locations to have influenced her writing in some way, this does not seem to have been the case. Indeed, the novels written while she was in Africa and Macedonia are demonstrably English. Three of these books were contemporary novels with English protagonists having typical (of the time) middle and upper-middle class conversations.

In late 1926, Georgette travelled by boat to Kenya in East Africa, there to meet her husband Ronald Rougier in Mombasa. Their new home was in Kyerwa, a remote part of Tanganyika (modern-day Tanzania) and miles from the nearest town. Georgette's house was a grass hut built inside a compound surrounded by a tall fence made of elephant grass. It was in this very basic accommodation that Georgette wrote her most autobiographical and cathartic novel, *Helen*, and one of her most romantic novels, *The Masqueraders* – a joyous Georgian novel featuring a pair of cross-dressing siblings. *Helen* was Heyer's second contemporary novel and not only her tribute to her father but also a way of coming to terms with the shock of his sudden death.

After eighteen months in Tanganyika Georgette and Ronald decided that his quest for striking it rich via tin-mining had proved futile and in June 1928 they returned to England. A few months later, Ronald took a job working in the lead mines in Macedonia. Left alone in England while her husband found them somewhere to live, Georgette wrote her third contemporary novel, *Pastel*. Like *Helen,* the novel contained many autobiographical moments, including a portrait of a marriage, elements of which bore strong similarities to Georgette's own.

Late in 1928, she travelled out to Macedonia and settled into her new home in Kratovo a small village east of the city of Skopje. Here, Georgette wrote first *Beauvallet* and then her fourth and final contemporary novel, *Barren Corn*. *Beauvallet* was another of her fast-paced adventure stories but with a dashing sea captain for a hero and an Elizabethan setting which reflected nothing of Georgette's personal circumstances. It is only in *Barren Corn* that one may discern a possible effect of distance from home on Georgette. It is in this novel that she most forcefully questions the social hierarchy that was so powerful in contemporary England, but it was the last time she would attempt such a thing. Ultimately, neither the remoteness of her location nor the exotic nature of either setting seemed to affect Georgette's ability to write very English novels. Perhaps it was the very difference between her birthplace and the places in which she found herself that made her cleave to the world she knew best – England and the English.

– Jennifer Kloester, Patroness, International Heyer Society

~ | ~

#5 – HEYER'S HOUSES #3: KENSINGTON BY JENNIFER KLOESTER

Friday, February 5, 2021

By April 1930, the Rougiers were back in England and deciding what to do next. Georgette wished to start a family and was determined that this could only happen if they were settled in England.

They rented an apartment at 62 Stanhope Gardens in Kensington. The building is still there and the apartment would have been a pleasant one with high ceilings, a fireplace, and plenty of light. Interestingly, it is located around the corner from where Georgette's son, Sir Richard Rougier, would one day have a flat of his own.

Georgette and Ronald lived in London for a year while Ronald tried his hand at various jobs and she went on with her writing. It was at Stanhope Gardens that Georgette wrote *The Conqueror*, her remarkable medieval novel that retold the life-story of William of Normandy and his triumph over the British at the Battle of Hastings. She had rejoined the London Library on her return from Macedonia and could easily catch the tube from Gloucester Road to St James's Park from where it was just a short walk to that marvellous repository of books.

There is no doubt that Georgette used the London Library both when she was living overseas and also while in London and later in Sussex, but it is not clear whether she spent time poring over books there or whether she took her reader's allowance home with her. But whether she read her reference materials in situ or whether she took them home, there is no doubt that Georgette made good use of the library's resources.

That year, she and Ronald also travelled to France in order to visit the many sites relating to William the Conqueror's life and exploits. Work for a mining engineer was not easy to find within a reasonable distance of London and within a year of their return from Macedonia Ronald had taken a lease on a sports store in Horsham in Sussex. In April 1931, Georgette and Ronald left the metropolis and began the next phase of their lives together.

– Jennifer Kloester, Patroness, International Heyer Society

~ | ~

#6 – HEYER'S HOUSES #4: SWAN KEN, BROADBRIDGE HEATH BY JENNIFER KLOESTER

Friday, February 12, 2021

Having returned from Macedonia in 1930, Georgette and Ronald lived in London for over a year. She wrote *The Conqueror* in their flat in South Kensington but, after a year of city living, they decided to move to the country.

The move was not so very surprising. Georgette had grown up in Wimbledon at a time when it still retained its country charm with its fields of wildflowers, blossoming hedgerows and the great expanse of Wimbledon Common. Georgette's childhood homes nearly all had gardens, while visits to her favourite grandmother – Grannie Watkins – meant playing in the garden of her palatial house in Eltham, south of Greenwich. Georgette loved gardens and after her years living overseas in Africa and Macedonia likely found city living too far removed from the more tranquil and aesthetically-pleasing environments she had grown used to.

In early 1931, Ronald took a lease on a sports store in Horsham, Sussex and on the 30th of April he and Georgette left London. They found accommodation at Swan Ken, Broadbridge Heath, just a couple of miles from Horsham (currently a one-hour train journey from London), and here Georgette began writing a new book. It was to be her first detective novel and early in September she told her agent, Leonard Moore, that *Footsteps in the Dark* was 'developing into a remarkably fine effort'.

Despite moving house several times, Georgette Heyer would prove remarkably prolific in the 1930s. This last letter (extant) written from Swan Ken also delivered three important bits of news: she and Ronald had taken a furnished house for a year and would move in on 28 September; she had a new book in mind and triumphantly told Moore that, 'I've got something far more amazing up my sleeve. What price a sequel to *These Old Shades*?'

And, perhaps most importantly, she and Ronald were expecting their first child in February.

– Jennifer Kloester, Patroness, International Heyer Society

P.S. The exact location of Heyer's Swan Ken is currently a bit of a mystery, but we do have a working theory. The attached pictures are of a lovely period home called Swan Ken, on Broadbridge Heath Road in what is now Bailing Hill, in the parish of Warnham, an area commonly known as Broadbridge Heath in the 1930s. Conclusive evidence does not exist, but it is likely that this was the Rougier residence of the time, whether they settled in the main house (5 bedrooms, worth over £1 million in today's property market) or perhaps in a smaller building on the same property. *– Rachel Hyland*

~ | ~

#7 – HEYER'S HOUSES #5: SOUTHOVER, COLGATE BY JENNIFER KLOESTER

Friday, February 19, 2021

On the 28th of September, 1931 Georgette and Ronald moved into Southover, a large, two-storey brick house in Springfield Lane, Colgate, about five miles east of Horsham. Springfield Lane was very private, being a dead-end, and Colgate was a tiny hamlet with just one pub, The Dragon, on the corner of the lane. Georgette and Ronald enjoyed a drink and no doubt visited the Dragon on more than one occasion.

They had rented Southover, fully furnished, for a year and it was here that Georgette would write her promised sequel to her bestselling novel, *These Old Shades*. She was enthusiastic about the new novel, believing that it 'will be well subscribed, especially if Heinemann advertize it cleverly.' She had great fun telling her agent (with her tongue firmly in her cheek and using even more than her usual number of exclamation marks) just how her publisher might go about it:

> If Heinemann advertized after the manner of the talkies they could puff the tale I meditate after this manner:- "Read this dynamic story of love in the eighteenth century!! You'll laugh, you'll cry, you'll thrill!! Don't miss it!!!! It is a story of how a wicked young rake found love after hair-raising adventures & poignant heart-searchings!!!!! You will adore Dominic Alastair & his beautiful bride Helen!!!!!! A Romantic Yell! The finest thing published for years!! Laughs on every page!!! A Riot of Fun!!!! An all-talking, all-laughing, all-fighting Furore!!!!! The Book the World has been Waiting For!!!!!

Georgette eventually changed her heroine's name from Helen to Mary and, after humorously suggesting titles as varied as *Dominic, Son of Leonie*; *Wolf of Avon*; *These Old Shadows* (suggested by her brother, Boris); *The Son of the Duke*; *More Old Shades* and *The Son of Satanas*, she finally decided that 'it needs the sort of title that will tell the expectant world that here at last is more about Avon & Léonie'. In the end, she called her book, *Devil's Cub*.

It was also while living at Southover that on the 12th of February 1932, Georgette gave birth to her son, Richard, whom she later described as 'my most notable (indeed, peerless) work'. It was also on that day that her first detective-thriller, *Footsteps in the Dark* was published. Twenty years later Georgette noted that: 'This work, published simultaneously with my son on Feb. 12th 1932, was the first of my thrillers, and was perpetrated while I was, as any Regency character would have said, increasing. One husband and two ribald brothers all had fingers in it, and I do not claim it as a Major Work.'

The detective-thriller did well, however, and its success inspired Georgette to write a second novel in that genre. *Why Shoot a Butler?* was to be her third and final book written at Southover, because in the spring of 1933, the Rougiers would once again move house.

– Jennifer Kloester, Patroness, International Heyer Society

~ | ~

#8 – HEYER'S HOUSES #6: THE SUSSEX OAK INN, WARNHAM BY JENNIFER KLOESTER

Friday, February 26, 2021

In May 1933, Georgette and Ronald left Southover, their rented house in Springfield Lane, Colgate, and moved into rented rooms at the Sussex Oak Inn in Warnham, just a few miles away on the other side of Horsham. Ronald was still running the sports store and he and Georgette wished to remain in the area; living at the inn gave them time to look around and try to find a house in which to raise their son, Richard.

He was now fifteen months and, as his mother described him, 'lusty and belligerent'. It cannot have been easy living with a toddler in an inn, especially while trying to write a novel. However, it was in this two-storey, seventeenth-century inn with its Horsham slab roof and casement windows that Georgette began writing her sixth Georgian and tenth historical novel. She would call the book *The Convenient Marriage* and it is possible that her rustic surroundings helped to inspire this delightful tale of young Horatia (Horry) Winwood with her stammer and her eyebrows and her unlikely marriage to the Earl of Rule.

It is not known if Georgette wrote her novel in her bedroom upstairs at the Sussex Oak or in the public rooms downstairs. By 1934, she had become a very private person and she hated people knowing what she was doing or asking her questions about her novels either past or present. While she and Ronald very likely enjoyed a drink in the bar in the evening and probably took their meals in the inn's main room, it is hard to imagine Georgette writing there – though she may well have done so. As was her way in those years, she wrote by hand and quickly; finishing the first few chapters in a matter of days and including excerpts from them in her letters to her agent, Leonard Moore.

Writing her novel, house-hunting and caring for Richard when his nurse was not available – all while Ronald was away working in the sports store – must have been a challenge. Georgette's brother Boris was also employed in the shop but making a go of it was not easy and there was continual pressure on Georgette to keep producing the novels that increasingly were an important part of their income. She wrote every day and frequently stayed up all night.

Despite having lived at four different addresses between April 1931 and May 1934, Georgette managed to write five very different and very successful novels. The 1930s were to be her most prolific decade and in their next house, Georgette would write as never before.

– Jennifer Kloester, Patroness, International Heyer Society

~ | ~

#9 – THE DANCING BEAR BY RACHEL GRANT

Friday, March 5, 2021

Here we begin a break from Jennifer Kloester's fascinating series "Heyer's Houses" to bring you a dispatch from our Animal Correspondent…

> "You see, there was a performing bear"
> "Oh!" said Carlyon. "I see."
> Nicky grinned at him. "I knew you would!"

When the Hon. Nicholas Carlyon is rusticated from Oxford for "borrowing" a bear to frighten his professors, a chain of events is set in motion in *The Reluctant Widow*. Nicky's insouciant and light-hearted attitude to the incident of the performing bear hides the darker reality of life for these animals in Georgian times.

For centuries, dancing or performing bears were used as entertainment in the marketplaces and town squares of England, and indeed, the whole of Europe. Mostly Black or Brown bears were captured when young, or born and bred in captivity, and prepared for the dance. Their claws were cut back or removed and often teeth were removed too. A metal ring was placed through the nose and a rope or chain could be fed through it to control the bear. Training was carried out by the infliction of pain. The bear was taught to dance by standing it on a metal platform over a log fire. As the metal warmed up, the bear would rise up on its hindquarters and then hop from one paw to another, trying to escape the burning heat. Drum music was played during this procedure and eventually the bear learned by association to "dance" whenever it heard the drum.

Bears were also kept in public menageries such as the Tower or the Exeter 'Change. They were considered fierce and dangerous creatures. People would prod them with sticks through the cage bars, trying to provoke a reaction.

Bear-baiting, where the animal is tied to a stake and then attacked by a pack of aggressive dogs, was very popular and drew large cheering crowds. However, bears were more valuable alive than dead and this extremely cruel sport became less prevalent as time went on.

Commercial bear breeding also took place and bear fat was used for greasing wigs and moustaches. The famous bearskin headdress of the Grenadier Guards has its origins in the Battle of Waterloo and yes, the hats are still made of bearskin today, using culled Canadian Black bears.

Life was anything but a dance for the bears of Georgian England but attitudes to animal welfare were changing and in 1835 bear-baiting was made illegal by the British Parliament. It took until 1911 for bear "dancing" to also be outlawed. *– Rachel Grant, Animal Correspondent*

#10 – THE BLACK MOTH NEW COVER REVEAL!

Friday, March 12, 2021

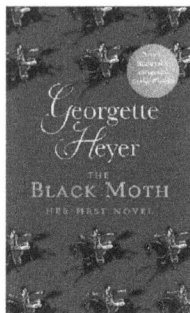

As Heyerites everywhere continue to celebrate a centenary of *The Black Moth*, we are so pleased to share with you a first look at the new edition cover, to be released in paperback by Georgette Heyer's official publishers on August 26, 2021. Aren't the colours gorgeous? And what do you think about Jack (all the Jacks!), pistol(s) drawn?

We also have some incredibly exciting news! Our very own Society Patroness Jennifer Kloester has been invited to pen the Afterword to this new edition. And given that she is second to none in her knowledge of all things Heyer, it will be a thrill to discover what further insights she has to share about this incredible debut novel.

In the meantime, let us take a look at some of the rather... less successful, not to mention far less sumptuous, covers that this classic novel has been subjected to over the past several years, in various unauthorized and/or public domain forms:

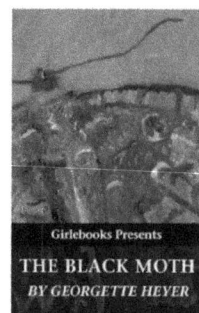

No, your eyes do not deceive you. These all literally have black moths on them! What's next? A *These Old Shades* cover featuring a pair of scratched-up sunglasses? The *April Lady* cover showing a calendar flipped to the fourth month next to the Disney dog? On *The Toll-Gate*, just an old photo of New York commuters paying to cross the George Washington Bridge? And as for these terrible moths... no! I very much prefer the multiple Jacks, and I hope you do, too. (The scratched-up sunglasses one would be pretty funny, though.)

– Rachel Hyland, Patroness, International Heyer Society

~ | ~

#11 – WHY I (SOMETIMES) STILL READ BARBARA CARTLAND BY RACHEL HYLAND

Friday, March 19, 2021

Whenever I think back to my earliest forays into historical romance, four authors immediately come to mind. Georgette Heyer, of course. She was my first, and shall be forever unsurpassed. Then came Clare Darcy, a kind of Heyer-lite, and thereafter Marion Chesney (aka M. C. Beaton), who scandalized me with her characters' brazenness and whom I have ever since disdained.

And then, my friends, came Barbara Cartland.

We all know the legend. We know that she is among the world's most prolific authors, having produced more than 700 books, almost all of them romances – along with some self-help titles, several biographies, four autobiographies… and even a few cookbooks, for some reason.

We also know that she still holds the world record for the most books produced in one year—a staggering 27, in 1982, thirteen of which included the word "love" in their title, and one of which is the enigmatic-sounding *Book of Celebrities*. There have long been rumours that she employed as many as six secretaries at any one time, all of them taking down her thoughts—either simultaneously or concurrently—as she worked on numerous manuscripts, all of them containing barely discernible differences. She was Princess Diana's step-grandmother, and was descended from the ducal house of Hamilton.

She liked pink.

Indeed, I defy any of her readers to think of her and not immediately recall the assorted bedazzled, Barbie-worthy ensembles in which she posed for the pictures that adorned the back of her paperbacks for the latter half of the 20th century, her face a waxwork nightmare of pancake powder, red lacquered lips and pencilled eyebrows—a bit rich coming from the author of *Look Lovely, Be Lovely* (1958), *Book of Beauty and Health* (1972), and *Getting Older, Growing Younger* (1984).

Nowadays, the name Barbara Cartland has become a byword for manufactured pulp—and moralistic, derivative pulp besides. She is decried for her elitist attitude and virginal heroines as much as for her flagrant plot recycling and stilted, nonsensical dialogue. Her language is dismissed as flowery yet dull, her incessant use of ellipses… is… a…perpetual… joke… and her later works (from the 1990s onward; Cartland died in 2000, leaving some 160 unpublished manuscripts behind, all since published posthumously) are justifiably accused of being nothing more than a series of seemingly unrelated sentences masquerading as paragraphs.

Heyer famously considered suing her for plagiarism – and she would surely have won.

But what we may little suspect – at least, those among us who haven't read three out of four of those autobiographies of hers… unlike, I'm afraid to say, me – is that the young Miss Cartland was something of a scandalous, even salacious, figure to 1920's London society. She spent a year as a gossip columnist; her first novel, *Jig-Saw*, has been described as "a risqué society thriller"; and among her non-fiction output are such titles as *Love, Life and Sex* (1957) and *Sex and the Teenager* (1964). Whether she's for it or against it I can't say, not having read the book in question, but my guess? She's for it, as long as they're first married to a viscount who is at least thirty and who until recently despised them.

Yes, let's talk her characters. The heroines small, big-eyed and helpless, owning to the most ridiculous of names almost always ending in an "a"—Richenda, Arilla, Zenobia, Loelia, Dorina, Rozella, Salrina, Elmina, Florencia, Illita, Aldora… I could go on forever—and the heroes domineering, sardonic and freakishly tall for their era. Everyone had high cheekbones, and at least one of the couple was in penury or in peril, which only True Love could make right in the most contrived and yet oddly captivating of ways.

Her plots cleaved almost exclusively to a few familiar patterns, and for the loyal Cartland reader it became almost a game, when picking up a new title, to guess what familiar form this latest adventure would take. Forced to Marry was a big favourite of hers (and, indeed, mine), with young innocents being sold into advantageous matches to pay gambling debts, forge dynastical alliances or similar, while younger, plainer sisters would beg to take the place of their elders, who were always in love with someone else (hello there, Horry!). Improvident fathers were a major theme, as were evil step-mothers, notorious fortune hunters and the inevitable elderly lechers who lusted after our ethereal innocents'…er…innocence. There was often a mystery—who killed the late earl? What are those mysterious lights out at sea? Who is the Rightful Heir?—and frequently a Lost Treasure. Highborn governesses abounded, as did virtuous young ladies of uncertain parentage who ended up being born of the nobility, and were therefore worthy of titled husbands.

At times we'd travel to the Exotic East, and be called upon to marvel at the wonderful strangeness of it all, even as we gloried in British Imperialism. Royalty from remote, largely fictional, nations was also popular: in danger and incognito, a princess would meet a Big, Strong Englishman who would undertake to get her to safety, and along the way lose his embittered, aristocratic heart; or a king would encounter a disguised scion of a rival house, and fall in love with the seeming peasant girl before discovering she was every bit as blue-blooded and inbred as he.

American railroad and/or mining heiresses were also a bit of a thing, and yet they were never as nice as their English counterparts. Who can say why?

And almost every Cartland courtship ended with the couple sharing a moment of post-coital (assuredly post-wedlock) exuberance, while birds sang, breezes wafted and stars twinkled in the Heavens. The manner of these passionate declarations was so similar in almost every instance that, to this day, my best-friend and I end our conversations like this:

> Me: Heart of my Heart.
> Her: Soul of my Soul.
> Me: Light of my Life.
> Her: Love of my Life.
> Me: My love!
> Her: My wife!

We read a lot of Barbara Cartland together throughout our school holidays. (For Christmas some years ago, this same friend gave me a CD I will always cherish, entitled *Barbara Cartland's Album of Love Songs*, on which Cartland herself atonally sings/recites/Def Poetry Jams over assorted standards, backed by the Royal Philharmonic Orchestra. Oh, yeah. We read her *a lot*.)

It was in our teens that we also discovered on VHS the TV movie version of that seminal Cartland masterwork, *A Hazard of Hearts* (1987), starring a young Helena Bonham Carter. Hugh Grant showed up in the not-quite-as-successful adaptation of *The Lady and the Highwayman* (1989), and three other Cartland movies yet exist: *The Flame is Love* (1978), *A Ghost in Monte Carlo* (1990) and *Duel of Hearts* (1991).

One has to wonder at the fact that there are *five* Barbara Cartland film adaptations, and yet the only Heyer we have on screen is 1950's unfortunate attempt, *The Reluctant Widow*.

One also has to wonder what made those five particular stories so attractive to producers (much like with *The Reluctant Widow*, actually), ahead of all the other hundreds upon hundreds of variations on their themes. Oh, I doubt I have read all of her output—although, looking over the book synopses, I feel as though I might as well have—but off the top of my head I can easily think of five other Cartland novels that would have made superior movies. I couldn't necessarily give you their titles (though odds are, alliteration, the word "love" and/or some variation of a nobleman's title appears in them prominently), but whether it had been *The Ruthless Rake* or *The Penniless Peer*; *The Odious Duke* or *The Wicked Marquis*; *The Mask of Love*, *The Tears of Love*, *The Wings of Love*, *The Wild Cry of Love* or even—and yes, this is real—*Love and the Loathsome Leopard*, I am all but certain that pretty much any Cartland novel would have done just as well as those chosen to be immortalized in film.

Why? Because, in so many ways, they really are all the same.

And that's okay. I always enjoyed my time spent leafing through the pages of those slim, similar volumes, and every now and then, when I delve into the recesses of my bookshelf and drag out some of my old favourites (*Enchanted, The Taming of Lady Lorinda, Love Climbs In, The Saint and the Sinner*, or even—and yes, this is real—*The Vibrations of Love*), I smile as I recall the many happy hours I spent as a youngster immersed in these cookie-cutter perfect tales of endangered virtue, missing jewellery, foreign travel and disillusioned dukes won over by sundry simpletons to whom they'd been reluctantly wed. Who cares if all the books blend amorphously into one another over time, that the women are all girls and the girls are all naive, that the men are mostly jerks, and that both sexes actually sit around shamelessly calling each other things like "Soul of my Soul"?

Because… fun! And so very funny.

And that is why I (sometimes) still read Barbara Cartland. It's the same reason I (sometimes) watch Z-Grade monster movies, and (often) listen to bubble gum pop music with lyrics that make no sense. There is no universe in which a Cartland novel stacks up to Heyer – not even the "good" ones of her youth, her contemporaries, come close to *Pastel* or *Helen* – but sometimes, a little nonsense is just what you need. Heyer is the Oscars, Cartland is the Razzies, and I've learned that there is room in my life, and heart, for both.

Sure, they're silly love stories. Very, *very* silly love stories. But what's wrong with that, I'd like to know?   – *Rachel Hyland, Patroness, International Heyer Society*

~ | ~

#12 – HEYER'S HOUSES #7: BLACKTHORNS BY JENNIFER KLOESTER

Friday, March 26, 2021

Georgette and Ronald moved into Blackthorns in 1933 after a sojourn at the Sussex Oak Inn where she had written most of *The Convenient Marriage*. Set on the outskirts of a tiny hamlet called Toat Hill (toat being the Saxon word for 'lookout') in the parish of Slinfold, Blackthorns was on the opposite side of Horsham from their previous house, Southover, and just four miles to the west of the market town. Like Southover, the new house was set well back from the road and was quite private with a long driveway and a great many mature trees along the road to shield it from public view. For Georgette, it was a convenient location far enough removed from Horsham and the local scene to ensure her privacy, but only thirty-three miles from London by road and forty-two miles by train. In the 1930s, Slinfold even had its own railway station on the Horsham and Guildford branch of the Southern railway, with a train service that would take Georgette to London in just over an hour.

In November 2009 I was lucky enough to visit Blackthorns. I had been to the house a few years earlier but, not knowing the owner, had ventured no further than the gate (which was locked). I did meet her son, however, and he suggested that I write to his mother and explain why I was so keen to visit the house. This I did and his mother, Jane, kindly replied and turned out to be the loveliest woman. She invited me and my friend jay Dixon (who generously drove me around West Sussex to many of the inns and houses with Heyer connections – such a wonderful day!) to lunch so that we might see the house where Georgette Heyer wrote thirteen books and several short stories.

The mature trees still lined the roadway, making it impossible to see the house until you were a little way up the curving driveway. When it came into view we could see the house set in a pretty garden and surrounded by fifteen acres of woodland. Blackthorns was still very much as it would have been when the Georgette and Ronald lived there. The house is red brick with two storeys and a lovely verdant outlook. We ate lunch in the elegant dining room and, with Jane, tried to work out exactly what alterations Georgette had made to the house in 1936. It had always seemed odd to me that she chose to spend a large sum of money on a rented house but it must have been important to her. She and Ronald spent over £800 on the builders, painters, plasterers and carpet-layers hired to renovate Blackthorns and Georgette even bought a Vi-Spring mattress – a luxury brand made in England since 1901 and used on the *Titanic* and the *Queen Mary*. Although she moved out for the worst part of the refurbishment, Georgette still managed to write a couple of short stories and make a start on *Behold, Here's Poison* during that time.

Georgette wrote most of her detective novels while living at Blackthorns and managed to produce two books a year there for five years. Of course, she had domestic help which made life easier. Until the War broke out in September 1939, she and Ronald had a cook, a nanny for Richard (he was three when they moved to Blackthorns), and at least one maid. As Georgette once explained, "I *loathe* domesticity!" but the reality was that cooking and cleaning interrupted her writing and they needed the income from her books. Between 1936 and 1939 Ronald was reading for the Bar and thus precluded from earning an income. This meant that in the years leading up to the War, Georgette was the sole family breadwinner. One can easily understand how the additional domestic duties caused by the loss of her cook and maid increased the stress in her life. By1940 and with no new cook on the horizon Georgette and Ronald decided to give up Blackthorns and move to a service flat in Brighton.

Their residence at Blackthorns was to be the last time that they would live in a house.

– Jennifer Kloester, Patroness, International Heyer Society

~ | ~

#13 – HEYER'S HOUSES #8: STEYNING MANSIONS, BRIGHTON BY JENNIFER KLOESTER

Friday, April 2, 2021

By the middle of 1939, Georgette and Ronald had been living at Blackthorns, their large rented house in Toat Hill near Horsham, for six years. They had enjoyed the peace and privacy afforded by the large garden and surrounding woodland and Georgette had produced almost a dozen novels. But War came in September and with it came new anxieties. Horsham was on the bombing run to London and their young son, Richard, nearly eight, was still living at home. The War also made it increasingly difficult to hire servants. Georgette had long had the benefit of a cook and at least one maid, but more and more women were leaving "service" and finding work in factories or on the land doing War work. By the time the War began in earnest in May 1940, Georgette was struggling to care for Richard, manage the house, cook, and write the books that were their main source of income. As the year progressed she began to think seriously about moving. In October, Georgette and Ronald sent Richard to boarding school in the Malvern Hills – well out of the way of German bombers. His departure meant one less responsibility and by October she had decided that a service flat in Brighton – just twenty miles away – would ease the rest and enable her to continue writing.

On 19 December 1940, the Rougiers moved into Apartment 2B, Steyning Mansions, King's Cliff, Brighton: telephone number 6461. Steyning Mansions is a grand building and it is likely that Georgette's second-floor apartment had a view over the sea. Not that she could visit the beach or the famous Brighton pier, however, for months earlier the War Office had issued strict instructions closing the pier for fear of a German invasion. Concerns that the pier might be used as a landing-stage had also seen a large section of it removed and orders given that it be guarded around the clock. On 2 July 1940, the War Office ordered the beach closed and laid with mines and barbed wire to prevent the enemy gaining access to the town should they successfully cross the Channel. Brighton had been bombed in September 1940, but Georgette appears to have been unfazed by the threat of further bombing raids. Settled into her new home with its private bathroom and all meals provided, she got on with her writing. By April 1941 she had finished *Envious Casca* and was thinking about a new novel. In July she began writing *Faro's Daughter* straight to the typewriter. By 10 August – less than four weeks later – she had written 88,000 words and finished her new novel! Only a month later, she moved again.

This 1948 advertisement for Steyning Mansions is probably similar to the one that caught Georgette's attention in 1940.

> **STEYNING Mansions Hotel, Brighton. Kings Cliff. Sea front near bathing pool. Unique comfort and excellent cuisine. Every room has own private bathroom "en suite," G.P.O., phone, wireless and elec. fire. Lift. Garage. Fully licensed. Brochure... Tel. 2589.**

– Jennifer Kloester, Patroness, International Heyer Society

~ | ~

#14 – HEYER'S HOUSES #9: ADELAIDE CRESCENT, HOVE BY JENNIFER KLOESTER

Friday, April 9, 2021

After nine months living at Steyning Mansions on Kings Cliff, Brighton, Georgette and Ronald decided to move again. The reasons for this are not clear but it may have had something to do with the War, although they did not go far to their new home. In September 1941, the Rougiers moved a couple of miles further west to the town of Hove. Georgette knew this part of England's south coast from her childhood for her paternal grandparents had lived at Worthing as had her Aunt Ilma, her father's sister. Georgette's brothers, Boris and Frank, had also attended Lancing College, which was only a short drive inland from Hove.

The Rougiers' new home was an apartment in Adelaide Crescent. Located immediately behind the Hove seafront, Adelaide Crescent is an impressive building of grand design. Built between 1831 and 1860 it consists of several elegant sections with a long curving arm of four floors looking out over the sea. They lived here for just over a year from September 1941 until November 1942. As in Brighton, their apartment was serviced, with their meals brought to them by their landlady, Mrs Isabella Banton. Five days a week Ronald commuted by train to his office in London, beguiling the tedium of the journey by playing bridge with three friends at their reserved table in the first-class carriage. Georgette continued writing. It was while living at Adelaide Crescent that she wrote *Penhallow*. Unique in the Heyer canon, the novel compelled and obsessed her. Years later, Isabella Banton vividly remembered Georgette sitting by the fire writing and "and living with real people" – the Penhallows.

Georgette and Ronald did not stay long on the seafront; they lived in Hove from September

1941 until November 1942, when they finally moved to London. These were not easy times for people in England. The War was a time of great hardship, anxiety and dreadful tragedy. Georgette was stoic but there is no doubt that she, like so many others, felt the strain. Their time at Hove was not easy. In the first few months of living there she was treated with arsenic for a skin complaint which (unsurprisingly) made her very ill, her blood pressure continued to be low and she contracted shingles. She was only just beginning to recover when Ronald's mother became very ill and needed a great deal of attention. Much of this responsibility fell to Georgette who found it very difficult watching her mother-in-law suffer and reported feeling "worn to shreds with anxiety".

When Jean Rougier died on 31 December 1941, Georgette told a friend that it "was a most merciful release and no occasion for mourning". Though she recovered from her own health issues and early in 1942 was writing again, Georgette never really took to living in either Brighton or Hove and before the year was over she and Ronald finally found their ideal home.

– Jennifer Kloester, Patroness, International Heyer Society

~ | ~

#15 – HEYER'S HOUSES #10: ALBANY PART 1 BY JENNIFER KLOESTER

Friday, April 16, 2021

By the middle of 1942, Georgette and Ronald had begun to seriously think about moving to London. The Blitz had ended and the danger of being bombed had lessened – at least for now. Ronald had passed his final examination for the Bar in 1939 and was working as a barrister in central London. His daily commute by train to his office in the Paper Buildings in the Inner Temple, though not difficult (he and three friends spent the hour-long journey playing bridge in the first-class carriage), had become tedious, while Georgette was missing her friends and the easy access to the London Library and her agent.

Her friend and publisher, A.S. Frere, and his wife, Patricia Wallace (the writer Edgar Wallace's daughter) lived in London in an apartment in Albany. This famous building was located on Piccadilly, just a few hundred yards west of Piccadilly Circus and across the road from the famous grocer, Fortnum and Mason. Originally built in 1771, Albany was designed as a grand house for Lord and Lady Melbourne. In 1791, however, they sold the property for £23,570 to the Duke of York and Albany and ten years later – beset by ever-increasing debt – he sold it to developer Alexander Copeland. In 1803, Copeland converted the mansion into thirteen apartments and built two more buildings at the rear of the original house. These two new parallel buildings faced each other across the "Rope Walk" and between them offered residents a choice of 54 new apartments. The Freres lived on the ground floor of one of these two buildings and in September 1942, they invited Georgette and Ronald to visit their "set" (as Albany apartments are called) known as "E.1.".

Georgette was entranced. She found the building enchanting and told her agent that: "I rather fell for it. If we could get a large set we might consider it, as it isn't expensive, & it's wonderfully cloistral. Frere has Macaulay's chambers - very nice, but not quite large enough for us." She was right in thinking it wasn't expensive. Incredibly, to rent a set in Albany in 1942 cost only £125 per year! [£6,000 in today's money.] And once she had seen this oasis in the heart of London, Georgette set her heart on it. After some negotiation and time spent seeing if they could have a new kitchen installed in one of the apartments, the Rougiers eventually settled on F.3. Albany.

This set was at the rear of the building on the west side of the Rope Walk with views over Vigo Street and the window where Georgette had her desk may be seen from this vantage point. F.3 was on the second floor up a double flight of narrow concrete steps – 70 in all – leading to an elegant front door with a brass knocker. During my many research trips to England I had several times walked along Piccadilly to the front entrance of Albany, crossed the large square cobbled courtyard and knocked on the door of the porters' lodge. The porters were always pleasant and polite, but without an invitation from a resident they were never going to let me past the entrance. I was allowed to peep inside the grand foyer and to catch a glimpse of the Rope Walk beyond, but not until I had corresponded with the Trustees and with the current occupant of F.3, did I have a hope of seeing the set where Georgette Heyer wrote twenty-two of her finest novels.

– Jennifer Kloester, Patroness, International Heyer Society

~ | ~

#16 – HEYER'S HOUSES #11: ALBANY PART 2 BY JENNIFER KLOESTER

Friday, April 23, 2021

In January 2008, I finally achieved my long-held ambition of seeing inside Georgette Heyer's beloved home at F.3 Albany. My letter to the current tenant had borne fruit and he had very kindly invited me to visit. What excitement I felt as once again I trod across the cobblestone courtyard to the porters' lodge. This time, I had an entrée and would not be turned away as I had been on my previous visits. Now the porter had my name and with a nod and a smile he directed me down the famous Rope Walk to the stairs that Georgette Heyer has so often used to climb to her set.

Delighted to follow in her footsteps, I walked slowly down the Rope Walk, drinking in the sights, sounds and smells of the scenery around me. I could see at once why Georgette had loved Albany so much. It was quiet and on either side of the long covered walk there was a well-kept garden broken every so often by right-angled paths which gave access to the staircases leading Albany's other apartments. Georgette's staircase was towards the rear of Albany and I remember being very surprised by it. Although in her Heyer biography Jane Aiken Hodge had accurately described it as "a gruelling flight of concrete steps", for some reason I had always imagined them as a set of wide, graceful stone steps leading easily upwards to an elegant front door. Jane was right, however. The steps were concrete and narrow and steep and there were seventy in all. No wonder that by 1966, at the age of 64 and with worsening health, Georgette decided she could no longer manage the steps at Albany! I *was* right about the elegant front door though and what a thrill it was to ply the polished brass knocker and have the door opened and to be graciously ushered inside.

F.3 Albany is not large by modern standards but it is elegantly appointed and it suited the Rougiers perfectly. The entrance hall runs the length of the apartment and at the end of it is the room which Georgette and Ronald used as their bedroom. A small room off to the left of the hall had been used as a bathroom in their day but under the new tenant this room had been converted into a modern kitchen. When Georgette lived in F.3. the kitchen was most inconveniently located up a set of curving narrow stairs and took up most of the small upper floor. Apart from its location, peaceful atmosphere and privacy, what must have drawn her to the apartment was the spacious and well-proportioned dining room and large adjoining sitting room. The latter has a large window overlooking Sackville and Vigo Streets. It was here that Georgette had her desk. Two large bookcases stood either side of the wide opening between the sitting and dining rooms and from 1959 Georgette's portrait hung above the mantelpiece in the dining room.

F.3. Albany was where Georgette Heyer lived the longest. For twenty-four years, between 1942 and 1966, she enjoyed the amenity of this quiet paradise in the heart of London writing twenty-two novels and hosting family and friends to dinner parties, cocktail parties and three wedding receptions.
– Jennifer Kloester, Patroness, International Heyer Society

~ | ~

#17 – TOP 10 FILMS FOR THE HEYERITE BY RACHEL HYLAND

Friday, April 30, 2021

It is a frequent cry among Heyer readers that *there should be films!* Or a television show, like Netflix's recent crossover hit *Bridgerton*… or a short web series… or it could even be an anime, we don't care, we just want to see our beloved stories brought properly to life, all the better to share our love of Heyer's magical worlds with the general populace. (Most of whom, sadly, still do not recognize either her name or genius.)

The rights to many of her novels have been acquired over the years, all to no avail – except, of course, for the ill-fated 1950 version of *The Reluctant Widow*, and the 1959 German adaptation of *Arabella* – but while we wait for that pleasant someday when things will be different, in the meantime we at least have other, vaguely Heyer-adjacent, films to watch and enjoy. My recommendations:

10. A HAZARD OF HEARTS (1987)
I have mentioned before my frankly unashamed infatuation with Barbara Cartland's particular brand of Regency-set wackiness, and even if you (rightly) disagree, it is hard not to enjoy the outlandish melodrama of this film adaptation of her first "costume book," as Lord Vulcan (Marcus Gilbert) saves the innocent Serena (Helena Bonham-Carter) from a shady gamester, while she saves him from his callous mother (a truly magnificent Diana Rigg). Pure, if very silly, fun.

9. THE DUCHESS (2008)
The dark side of a Brilliant Match is portrayed perfectly in this account of the life of Georgiana Cavendish, Duchess of Devonshire (Kiera Knightley), based on the biography by Amanda Foreman. The Georgian-era costumes are stunning, the performances heartbreaking, and the details are reproduced so lovingly that Georgette Heyer herself might have been in charge of set design. Definitely a must-see. But have tissues – or even some smelling salts – ready to hand.

8. THE MADNESS OF KING GEORGE (1994)
The steady decline of King George III's faculties is impeccably displayed in this bittersweet dramedy about family, duty and the pitfalls of primogeniture. Set amid the Regency Crisis of 1788-89 – in which interested parties in Parliament argued to set aside the King (Nigel Hawthorne) in favour of his son (Rupert Everett); an action that would, as we know, indeed take place some two decades later – the film shows us the Court in all its pomp and circumstance, and the ably illustrated backroom dealings among courtiers and councillors are all very Roxhythe-ian. Helen Mirren as Queen Charlotte is wondrous, as always.

7. AGAINST ALL FLAGS (1952)
This Errol Flynn nautical adventure also gives us the captivating Maureen O'Hara as Prudence "Spitfire" Stephens, a pirate queen second to none. The dashing Flynn is Brian Hawke, a British naval officer tasked with infiltrating a pirate hideout off the coast of Madagascar. There are

swordfights, and Mughal princesses, and forbidden love, and it's all very exciting—very much a tale for the *Beauvallet* fans out there.

6. THE KING (2019)

From the swashbuckling Sir Nick Beauvallet to his cold-hearted ancestor, this recent account of the ascent to the throne of Henry V (Timothée Chalamet) shows us the harsh realities of Simon's battlegrounds—if not too many historical realities, it must be said. The script was based more on Shakespeare's *Henry*s than the actual men, and a lot of detail has been added, shaded or eroded entirely. Nevertheless, it is an enjoyably cinematic vision of the titular hero's transformation from pleasure-loving prince to warrior king.

5. THE ABDUCTION CLUB (2002)

While it is difficult to think of abduction as anything other than anathema, in this romantic comedy adventure it is somehow delightful. In 1780s Ireland, pockets-to-let bachelors Garrett Byrne (Daniel Lapaine) and James Strang (Matthew Rhys) set their sights on the fortunes of wealthy sisters Catherine (Alice Evans) and Anne Kennedy (Sophia Myles), and so plan to marry them out of hand. But their cavalier abduction soon turns into a reluctant road trip as they are chased across the country by a furious suitor, and even framed for murder. *Way* more romantic than it has any right to be. Also – Ireland is so pretty!

4. BELLE (2013)

The true-ish story of Dido Elizabeth Belle (Gugu Mbatha-Raw), daughter of British naval officer Sir John Lindsay (Matthew Goode) and Maria Belle, an African slave in the West Indies. Brought to England by her father in 1765, while just a child, she was raised by his uncle and aunt, Lord and Lady Mansfield (Tom Wilkinson and Emily Watson), alongside her cousin, Lady Elizabeth (Sarah Gadon). A sumptuous production exploring race, nobility and family, the film also includes a truly lovely romance that is even grounded in reality. (As much as such things can be, of course.)

3. AMAZING GRACE (2006)

Another biopic, and another discussion of race in the Georgian period, this film follows the career of activist William Wilberforce (Ioan Gruffudd) as he seeks to abolish slavery in the British Empire. With much told in flashback, and with Wilberforce nearly abandoning all hope, his meeting with the beautiful Barbara Spooner (Ramola Garai) reignites his efforts, and watching his political manoeuvring among familiar political figures is much more thrilling than that sounds like it could be. An important film, and quite a remarkable one.

2. KITTY (1945)

Set in the 1780s, and based on the novel by Rosamund Marshall, this *My Fair Lady*-esque story gives us the beautiful but lowborn Kitty (Paulette Goddard) caught trying to pick the pocket of painter Thomas Gainsborough (Cecil Galloway) and then asked to pose for him, as penance. (Because of the beauty.) There, well-dressed and even more stunning, she excites much attention, particularly from the sardonic Sir Hugh Marcy (Ray Milland)—who employs her as a scullery maid. But when the success of her portrait offers him a chance to introduce her to a rich peer for his own profit, he teaches her to be a lady! Hard to find, but worth the effort.

1. BEAU BRUMMELL (1954)

Based on an 1890 play, this tale of the rise and fall of George Bryan "Beau" Brummell (Stewart Granger) is just as elegant, entertaining and ultimately cruel as the Arbiter himself. Much of it does not have basis in fact – the inclusion of one Lady Patricia Belham (Elizabeth Taylor) as his conflicted love interest, for one; the historically impossible reunion of Beau and Royal Patron, for another – but from the cut of his coats to the fall of his cravats to the delivery of his *bon mots*, the film is otherwise entirely good *ton*.   – *Rachel Hyland, Patroness, International Heyer Society*

* Most, if not all, of the many Jane Austen adaptations are also highly recommended, obviously, but they will have to wait for their own list. A "Top 10 TV Series for the Heyerite" is also forthcoming.

#18 – HEYER'S HOUSES #12: JERMYN STREET BY JENNIFER KLOESTER

Friday, May 7, 2021

By 1966, Georgette and Ronald had enjoyed almost twenty-four years of life in Albany. Their move there in 1942 had proven to be a great success and, as her friend and publisher A.S. Frere asserted, Georgette had found her "apogee" while living at Albany. She wrote twenty-two novels at her desk in the sitting-room of her apartment at F.3, among them some of her finest and funniest Regency novels. It was while living at Albany that she eventually devoted her writing time to her forte – the Regency novels for which she would become most famous. It must have been with mixed feelings that the Rougiers received the news that their lease on F.3 would not be renewed upon expiry in November 1966 as the owner, Lady Hooper, had decided to move in. After almost a quarter of a century it would be a wrench but it was also true that Georgette's uncertain health had made the daily climb up the seventy stone steps to her front door increasingly difficult. She still did her own shopping and found carrying the bags – even from Fortnum & Mason just across Piccadilly – a strain on her lungs. She had never given up her lifelong habit of smoking two packets of cigarettes a day and the demands of those seventy steps often left her breathless and uncomfortable. Her search for a new flat took some time but by August she was able to tell Max Reinhardt, her publisher at The Bodley Head (where she had moved in 1963),

> that we have practically taken a flat in Jermyn Street, & expect to get possession at the end of September…It has constant hot water, & central heating, & if I had Domestic Difficulty I could run it with one hand tied behind me.

Her new address at Flat 4, 60 Jermyn Street, was only a stone's throw from Albany. Jermyn Street is just one block south of Piccadilly and conveniently close to St James's Square and the London Library and so Georgette would happily remain in familiar environs. Having found a new home, Georgette decided they needed to renovate. She had agreed to pay for some of the fixtures already in the apartment, but wanted a number of additional "improvements". Accordingly, she called in the £3000 advance for *Black Sheep* to pay for the tradesmen, painters and removalists needed for the move to Jermyn Street. She aimed to have everything completed by December, but this proved a vain hope, as only a week before Christmas she told Reinhardt that she was "being driven mad by Decorators!" and "I feel that if I see one more Workman on the premises I shall drum with my heels." And it was not only the task of getting the new flat ready for the move, Georgette also had to face the daunting task of packing up F.3 Albany. This was not easy, and in late September she told Reinhardt that she was 'engaged on the ghastly job of Turning-Out. After 25 years, the accumulation of junk is appalling. I am becoming ruthless about it!' Only a few weeks later her resolve to be ruthless was tested when she found herself faced with the challenging task of dealing with the

> stacked piles, in every edition & every language of My Works!…What <u>am</u> I to do with them? I can send the foreign to a certain hospital, but what about the Duttons, Penguins, Pans, Aces, Bantams, Longmans, & God Knows how many Differently priced editions???

Georgette had long had the habit of keeping copies of her published works *behind* the books on her library shelves and had likely taken to storing her books in Richard's attic room after he married Susanna Flint in 1962. The move from Albany demanded most of Georgette's time and attention but the task was not without its lighter moments. In October, while she was 'in the midst of the toil, trouble, & general horror of the approaching move,' she was stunned to receive a phone call from Buckingham Palace. The caller was Sir Mark Milbank, the Master of the Household, and he was phoning to ask if Georgette would "lunch informally with the Queen & the Duke" on 3 November? Sir Mark also told her that, "We are all madly keen on your books here!" Thrown off her balance (as she said), Georgette meekly replied that she would "be honoured". Two weeks prior to this flattering event, Georgette and Ronald held a "house-cooling" party for seventy friends. It was an evening filled with wine, caviar, conversation and laughter; it must also have been an occasion tinged with sadness as Georgette bade farewell to her beloved home at F.3. Albany.   – *Jennifer Kloester, Patroness, International Heyer Society*

~ | ~

#19 – HEYER'S HOUSES #13: 28 PARKSIDE, KNIGHTSBRIDGE BY JENNIFER KLOESTER

Friday, May 14, 2021

Through the late 1960s, Georgette's health had become increasingly precarious. By 1970, she was struggling with cardiovascular issues and over the next four years she would suffer from various injuries and ailments, all of which increasingly affected her writing life. Georgette Heyer was by nature stoical, however, and if she could write, she would. She finished her penultimate novel, *Charity Girl*, in the first half of the year and her agent, Joyce Weiner, encouraged her to start thinking of a new novel for publication in 1971. After four years at 60 Jermyn Street, Georgette was finding the flat too noisy and by autumn she and Ronald had decided to move. They found a large, spacious, elegantly-appointed apartment in Knightsbridge and by November had once again packed up their paintings, books, bags, furniture and *objets d'art* and this time moved a few miles to the west. Once the disruption of the move was behind her, Georgette found the new apartment at 28 Knightsbridge "beautifully spacious and blessedly quiet". The building was a large one and, like Albany, had a staff of day and night porters to help with the residents' needs. Best of all it had lovely views of Hyde Park that could be seen from their sitting-room, their bedroom and also from Georgette's study.

The park was an oasis and an escape from the increasing noise and traffic that had become a part of life in London. Georgette loved Hyde Park and would often walk there, finding it "a blessed relief to be surrounded by grass, and trees, and flowers, instead of houses!" In those last few years of her life she was easily exhausted and more easily overwhelmed by modern life. She found that she could not cross the busy roads alone and was glad when Ronald finally gave up his legal practice and could walk with her in Green Park or to Harrods. In January 1972, a few months after moving into Knightsbridge, Georgette and Ronald gave a lavish cocktail party for sixty guests. It was a huge success but it was to be last time they would play host to such a gathering. In future they would only have friends and family to dinner, lunch, or occasional drinks. Georgette broke her leg that year and never really recovered. She was writing again and, despite her ill-health, was finding enjoyment in the process. She had always loved writing and making up stories but *Lady of Quality* was to be her last completed novel. It came out in October 1972 with huge sales and good reviews. With her book finished, Georgette did think of writing another, but her health would not allow it.

She and Ronald continued living at 28 Parkside, Knightsbridge, until May 1974 when, at last, her many bouts of ill-health finally overtook her and she was admitted to Guy's Hospital with severe pain in her back and legs. She died there with Ronald by her side on 4 July 1974; she was not quite 72. She left a rich and lasting literary legacy to the world of 55 novels, more than a dozen short stories, and a genre – the Regency – which over the years would produce many imitators though none to touch her for wit, humour, plot, character or that extraordinary sense of "being there". There will only ever be one Georgette Heyer.

– Jennifer Kloester, Patroness, International Heyer Society

~ | ~

#20 – THE WORKING DOGS OF HEYER'S REGENCY WORLD BY RACHEL GRANT

Friday, May 21, 2021

In Regency times, the idea of keeping a dog as a lap-dog or companion was well established. However, working dogs were more prevalent and of more importance. Let's put aside the collies, terriers and shepherd dogs belonging to the lower orders and take a look at the hounds and spaniels of the Georgian aristocracy.

FOXHOUNDS

The English Foxhound is a medium sized dog with a smooth glossy coat of black, tan and white. It's origins are in France and it is a mix of Bloodhound (for scent trailing) and Greyhound (for speed). The Foxhound has great stamina and is a tenacious and determined hunter. Packs of hounds could be followed by riders on horseback, and fox hunting became one of the most popular sports of the era. It was particularly enjoyed by the gentry and aristocracy, who had the means, money and land with which to indulge in this pastime. Aristocrats including the Dukes of Beaufort and Rutland established and scientifically bred foxhound packs, and pedigrees started being recorded from 1787.

Eye-watering sums were spent on the hounds. The Duke of Richmond paid £10,000 for the architect-designed kennels on his estate. The Duke of Bedford's hounds were kept in kennels at Woburn Abbey that had been designed with lighting, ventilation and temperature control in mind. There were drinking fountains, special lodging rooms for pregnant females and young dogs, feed rooms, hospital rooms and even apartments for two human "kennel keepers". The largest estate kennels could house 60-70 couples (2 matched hounds) and often 20-30 couples could be used at each hunt. The hunting season ran from late October through to March/April, and the diet of the dogs was carefully adjusted to keep them in prime condition for the long gruelling days following the fox. It is highly possible that these dogs lived in better conditions than many of the human tenants!

Today, some Foxhounds are still kept for hunting, but they are also kept as companion animals. They require a huge amount of exercise and they are a pack animal – they hate to be alone. Training can be challenging; once they are on the scent, they are almost impossible to recall!

SPANIELS

The Spaniel originated in Spain and is described in the Oxford English Dictionary as "a breed of dog with a long silky coat and drooping ears". Most of the modern spaniel breeds were developed in Britain, specifically to flush game out of hiding places and also to retrieve it after it was shot. Spaniels are adept at getting into, and through, thick foliage and brambles. They are much slower than Foxhounds and can be followed on foot by the hunter.

Originally, spaniels were divided by the game they flushed, not by the breed. Cockers for

Woodcock and Springers for partridge, pheasants and hares. They were also specialised into water and land breeds. The "toy" spaniels such as the Cavalier King Charles Spaniel were never hunters and were developed as companion dogs. Today, spaniels of all breeds are extremely popular as pets.

Spaniels are clever dogs – Sylvester's unnamed liver-and-white spaniel knows his wardrobe intimately and can recognise when he is not dressed for hunting "...and she knew well that pantaloons and Hessian boots meant that the most she could hope for was to be permitted to lie at his feet in the library" – but there are exceptions to every rule...

THE 'NOT WORKING SO WELL' DOGS

- **Flurry from _Venetia_:** an "amiable if vacuous spaniel... being of an excitable disposition (and) incurably gun-shy", Flurry, although "much addicted" to flushing out game, is useless as a hunting dog because he is afraid of the sound of a gun.
- **Bouncer from _The Reluctant Widow_:** the pride and joy of the Hon. Nicholas Carlyon, Bouncer is half Lurcher half Mastiff. Lurchers are clever and cunning sighthounds and are used for hunting (and poaching) rabbits, hares and game birds. Mastiffs have great strength and endurance and are used for hunting and for blood sports such as bear and bull baiting. They make excellent guard dogs too, as Bouncer over-enthusiastically demonstrates!
- **Poodle Byng's Poodle from _Arabella_:** Poodles originated in France and were developed to retrieve game birds from the water. Frederick Gerald Byng's poodle is an elegant carriage dog and was probably not used in a hunting capacity. NB. It is claimed that Poodle Byng was given his nickname by Beau Brummell!
- **Lufra from _Frederica_:** The famous Baluchistan Hound is definitely not a working dog. His attempt to herd cows in Green Park ends in disaster. Unfortunately this breed is an on-the-spot invention of the Marquis of Alverstoke, so Lufra's true origins must remain shrouded in mystery.

– Rachel Grant, Animal Correspondent

~ | ~

#21 – CHICKS IN PANTS – CROSS-DRESSING HEROINES IN HISTORICAL ROMANCE BY JANGA

Friday, May 28, 2021

Note: Romance novel enthusiast and critic Janga was a stalwart of Romancelandia for several decades. A contributor to Heyer Society – Essays on the Literary Genius of Georgette Heyer, _before her untimely demise she very kindly gave that collection's editor, Society Patroness Rachel Hyland, permission to reprint some of her lost pieces, as the occasion might arise. This is one of those pieces, and certainly one of those occasions, presented here with much fondness for this beloved kindred spirit._

Cross-dressing heroines, or "Chicks in Pants" books as they are popularly known, are among my favorite reads when they are done well. _Twelfth Night_ has long been my favorite Shakespearean comedy. One of my favorite 19th-century popular novels is _The Hidden Hand_ by Emma Dorothy Eliza Nevitte "E. D. E. N." Southworth (1819-1899), one of the most widely read and highest paid authors in America during her period.

The Hidden Hand (serialized 1859; published as novel in 1888) features a heroine whom readers first meet when she is masquerading as a boy in order to survive. When orphaned street waif Capitola Le Noir, also known as Cap Black, realizes that boys are earning money carrying parcels, blacking boots, and shoveling snow on the streets of New York, jobs denied her solely because of her gender, she disguises herself as a boy. She has no regrets: "The only thing that made me feel sorry was to see what a fool I had been, not to turn to a boy before." Even after she is rescued by a wealthy relative and restored to her female identity, she rejects conventional feminine behavior—confronting villains, fighting a duel, rescuing an imprisoned maiden, and expressing herself without reservation.

The romance novels of Georgette Heyer are far removed in time and place from Southworth's gothic tale, but Heyer too utilized cross-dressing heroines. In fact, she created three of them, all of which I have read and reread and reread... Léonie de Saint-Vire of *These Old Shades* (1926) is the flame-haired street urchin Léon when she meets the Duke of Avon and becomes his page. Two years later, in *The Masqueraders*, Heyer chose a pair of cross-dressers: Prudence Marriot is disguised as handsome Peter and her brother Robin, who "was made to be a breaker of hearts," assumes the identity of a fashionable, flirtatious beauty. And in *The Corinthian* (1940), Penelope Creed masquerades as a boy in order to escape a forced marriage.

In all three books, the heroine has a particular reason for assuming a male identity, she experiences a freedom in male attire that she could never know as a woman, and the hero sees through the disguise early in the story. For me, Heyer is the gold standard for all such novels, and these elements are essential to my appreciation of other books with heroines disguised as males.

Here are some favorites, which I highly recommend:

VALENTINE LANGLEY, FOOL'S MASQUERADE (1984), JOAN WOLF
Valentine runs away after her father is killed at the retreat to Corunna rather than be sent to her estranged grandparents. Since she has a gift for horses, she disguises herself as a boy and finds work as a groom on the Yorkshire estate of Richard Fitzallan "Diccon", Earl of Leyburn. Although Diccon discovers her gender easily, the two have time to know each other before Valentine's identity is revealed.

ELLEN GRIMSLEY, MISS GRIMSLEY'S OXFORD CAREER (1992), CARLA KELLY
Students at Miss Dignam's Select Female Academy in Oxford study French, watercolors, and embroidery, but Ellen Grimsley longs to study geography, geometry, and Shakespeare at Oxford University. Her brother, in his first year of study at Oxford, wants only to join a cavalry regiment. He persuades Ellen, who bears a marked resemblance to him, to dress in clothing and a scholar's robe borrowed from one of his shorter friends and to attend a tutorial in order to write his essay on A Midsummer Night's Dream. One essay turns into three before Ellen is discovered, forced to deny authorship of the essays, and banned from Oxford. But all is not lost. She has met her true love, a marquess and a Shakespearean scholar who realized she was female almost immediately and took her to a taproom anyway. Moreover, he promises after their marriage "to stand up every year in the House of Lords and rail on and on about the need for equal education for women."

CHASTITY WARE, MY LADY NOTORIOUS (1993), JO BEVERLEY
Chastity Ware, disgraced after she refuses to marry the man her father has chosen for her and desperate to help her sister and infant nephew escape the control of her brother-in-law, dresses as a highwayman and kidnaps a coach. Inside the coach is a bored Cyn Malloren who realizes that his kidnapper is a woman. For his own amusement, Cyn agrees to help the women but chooses not to reveal that he knows "Charles" is a woman in men's clothing. Despite the real villainy the heroine is battling, the novel edges into farce when Cyn dons women's clothing and Charles becomes his footman. Some of the most sensuous food scenes in romance fiction are a bonus as the two defeat their enemies and head toward their HEA.

ROSENCRANTZ, THE GREATEST LOVER IN ALL ENGLAND (1994), CHRISTINA DODD
An orphan brought up by actor Danny Plympton, Rosie masquerades as a boy playing women's roles in her foster father's acting company. When Danny's life is endangered by his knowledge of a plot against the queen, the company leaves London for the estate of Sir Anthony Rycliffe, the master of the Queen's Guard. Tony recognizes Rosie is a woman within minutes of meeting her. This one is unusual in its Tudor setting and in the fact that Rosie in disguise as a boy plays a male actor who plays women's roles, including Ophelia in Hamlet, written by her honorary "Uncle Will."

ANNE WILDER, ALL THROUGH THE NIGHT (1997), CONNIE BROCKWAY

There is nothing typical about this dark, intense romance. Anne Wilder is known to society as a gentle, wealthy widow who is chaperoning a debutante. No one knows she is Wrexall's Wraith, a cat burglar who dresses in black and moves unseen along London rooftops at night in order to steal from the wealthy for the charities they ignore and to experience the sense of truly being alive only when she risks losing her life. When she is caught in an act of theft by Colonel Jack Seward, Whitehall's Hound and England's greatest spy, she uses her body to distract him and escape. He is shocked to learn that the Wraith is a woman, one who has humiliated him and one he cannot forget. Thus, obsession begins.

ALYS WESTON, THE RAKE (1998), MARY JO PUTNEY

Strickland, the estate that Reginald Davenport has just been given, is a model of agricultural production and contented tenants, thanks to the practices instituted by the steward, A. E. Weston, who is thought to be a man. Alys is an unusual cross-dressing heroine in that although she wears men's clothing on the job, she makes no attempt to disguise herself as man. The tenants address her as "Lady Alys" and Reggie's first view of her brings an immediate appreciation of her long legs and the fit of her shirt. He promises to "treat her like a man," but it soon becomes clear he is unable to keep that promise.

SYLVIE GEORGIANA, THE WICKED LOVER (2004), JULIA ROSS

Robert Dovenby returns home to find his mistress burning his clothes and a young man tied to his bed. The young man claims to be George White who has stolen into Dove's home to steal a cravat on a wager. Dove realizes "at second glance" that George White is a woman, but he forces George to become his secretary. In that guise, she accompanies him to masquerades and coffee houses. George is actually a spy working for a man bent on destroying Dove. The story is a perfect set up for trust issues to war with the wild attraction that exists between the two.

HARRIET, DUCHESS OF BERROW, DUCHESS BY NIGHT (2008), ELOISA JAMES

Tired of her uneventful life, Harriet accompanies her friend Isidore, Duchess of Conway, to the home of the scandalous Lord Strange whose ongoing house party includes guests from powerful politicians to actresses. Isidore is courting scandal for her own purposes, but Harriet, to protect her reputation, is disguised as Harry Cope, a young relative of the Duke of Villiers, whose invitation gives this odd trio entrance to the party. Villiers is still recovering from a serious illness and turns Harry over to Jem, Lord Strange for instruction in manly pursuits. It takes Jem a while to realize that Harry is Harriet, and the interval before recognition is played for laughs with Harriet enjoying the freedom of a young man and dealing with an actress interested in more than flirtation and Jem disturbed by his attraction to this feminine young man. Harry's response to riding astride for the first time is a particularly funny scene.

AYISHA, TO CATCH A BRIDE (2009), ANNE GRACIE

For six years, since her father's death, Ayisha has disguised herself in male clothing to evade the men to whom a young virgin is a valuable commodity to be sold to whoever will pay the highest price. With the help of a big-hearted, childless widow, she survives, just another street urchin in Cairo. Rafe Ramsey, younger son of the late Earl of Axebridge, arrives in Egypt to search for the missing granddaughter of Lady Cleeve, a friend of his grandmother's. When Ayisha steals into the house where Rafe is staying to rescue a friend, Rafe catches her. She fights so ferociously that Rafe is forced to punch her, a blow that knocks her cold. Looking at her unconscious face, he is struck by the delicacy of her features and he wonders. A flat chest fails to answer his question, but a more intimate examination proves the urchin is definitely not male. A closer look at her face persuades him that she is the girl he has come to rescue, and another battle begins.

ELIZABETH SMITH, THE EDUCATION OF BET (2010), LAUREN BARATZ-LOGSTED

The illegitimate, orphaned daughter of a maid, Bet is brought up by Paul Gardner, who rescues her when he comes to the aid of his grand-nephew, Will, whose parents perished in the same epidemic that killed Bet's mother. Will is a poor student who dreams of being a soldier. Bet, bright and ambitious, is relegated to learning needlepoint and other domestic skills. She comes up with a plan that will allow her and Will to achieve their goals. She will take Will's place at his boarding school, and he will be free to enjoy military life. But Bet is unprepared for the bullying and violence that are part of public school experience for boys in Victorian England, and she's unprepared for the feelings awakened by James, her good-looking roommate, who is just as unprepared to discover that his roommate who is surpassing him in academic standing is a girl.

If you love Léonie, and Prudence, and Pen, you will most likely love these Chicks in Pants as well.   *– Janga, Special Contributor, in memorium*

~ | ~

#22 – WHY SOME WRITERS LIVE ON BY JENNIFER KLOESTER

Friday, June 4, 2021

'Every now and then an artwork comes along that consoles you for a lifetime: heals heartbreak, banishes loneliness, and even enlightens the end-of-days gloom of a global pandemic.' So wrote Amanda Hooton in a recent newspaper article in Melbourne's *Age*. She was talking about Patrick O'Brian's Aubrey-Maturin series, but she could just as easily have been describing Georgette Heyer's historical novels.

I have long been fascinated by books and authors and in particular by the fact that in each generation of successful novelists, only a handful live on beyond their lifetime. Among my large collection of Georgette Heyer novels are many hardback editions, each with a distinctive dustjacket on the back of which there is sometimes printed a long list of books and their authors. Of these, I recognise a few names: W. Somerset Maugham, Thornton Wilder, Margaret Kennedy and J.B. Priestley, but most of those listed – though famous in their own time – are now long forgotten.

Georgette Heyer, however, is one of the chosen few of her literary generation whose books continue to be read long past her death in 1974. She once said 'most of my works would die with me, I fear' but time has proven her wrong. Today fifty-one of her fifty-six novels continue to sell and she would undoubtedly be delighted to know that her books are still read and loved decades after her passing. After all, isn't this why so many people write? That they may achieve a little bit of immortality; that when they are no more, some part of their mind and soul will remain. Heyer readers know why her novels endure: it is the luminous writing; the vivid recreation of past eras; the humour and the sparkling wit; the glorious language; the clever plots and the living, breathing characters who remain with you long after the last page is turned. Now, more than ever, in these days of Covid-19 and lockdowns and self-isolation and the sadness of losing loved ones, we need books to cheer and comfort us.

This is what Georgette Heyer's wonderful novels do. As Rachel Law, Lady Ellenborough, once said of her:

> Only one author has made me so oblivious of my surroundings as to laugh aloud shortly before the tumbrils arrive which carry hypodermics and which herald trolleys. That author is Georgette Heyer … Comic characters are more enduring and archetypal than tragic ones. Tears may fall from heaven but laughter is the earth's underground, inexhaustible spring… and always her pure, truly classic style of perfect, ironic prose. In technique she is the equal of any writer in the language.

May we all have a Heyer novel to retreat to when life becomes too serious, too grim or too overwhelming. She is there for us in the good times and the bad and, simply because her books bring comfort and light and laughter, I suspect she will continue to be that rare thing among authors – an enduring bestseller who lives on long beyond her life and century.

– Jennifer Kloester, Patroness, International Heyer Society

#23 – TOP 10 FRIENDSHIPS IN HEYER BY RACHEL HYLAND

Friday, June 11, 2021

In this era of social distancing, travel restrictions and often limited in-person contact with our loved ones, it is only natural that we begin to value our friendships more than ever. In many ways we are lucky, because despite the difficulties, at least we can stay in touch via assorted user-friendly mediums – social media, video calls, even the old-fashioned telephone. But there is nothing quite like *being there* to share the everyday trials and triumphs of those we care for, and whenever we can't (and, as I live in the oft-lockdowned Melbourne, *can't* feels like it has been more often than not, this past year or so) I have found myself taking great comfort in the rereading of Georgette Heyer, and, moreover, have found myself gravitating towards those of her novels that feature strong friendships.

Of course, many of Heyer's friendships lead to love, but that is the topic of another list – Top 10 Friends-to-Lovers in Heyer, perhaps – and will have to wait for another time. There are also many siblings who share great affinity throughout the novels, but that is another list, as well.

And so, with those caveats in place, here are my favourite (entirely platonic, non-related) friendships in Heyer…

10. CHARIS MERRIVILLE AND CHLOE DAUNTRY, *Frederica* (1965)
The great beauty of debutante Charis is, we are told, enough to make any competing woman hate her, but the gentle Chloe – newly out, and quite taking in her own right – is too sweet to have any such envious animosity occur to her; on the contrary, she admires Charis tremendously. Charis, meanwhile, though not a great thinker or conversationalist, is likewise very sweet-natured, and the two strike up a friendship on the periphery of the story that is quite lovely, if almost entirely incidental. And their bond serves as an important reminder that there is someone for everyone out there; that intellect and humour aren't everything. Sometimes two people connect with one another simply because they are both really very nice.

9. KITTY CHARING AND MARGARET "MEG", LADY BUCKHAVEN, *Cotillion* (1953)
The newlywed Meg, expecting her first child, has been left alone in London while her older husband sees to apparently urgent diplomatic duties. Fearful of being sent to the country, she is trying hard to hide her loneliness under a veneer of fashionable gaiety, but when her brother Freddy foists his "fiancée" into her care, Meg rediscovers joy: first, as a mentor to the country-raised Kitty, and then, as her true companion. Meanwhile, it is when Kitty comes to realize that her masquerade will end up hurting Meg, whom she has come to love so well, that she decides to end it, no matter what the consequences might be to her own happiness. True friendship, indeed.

8. PHILIP JETTAN AND COMTE LOUIS DE SAINT-DANTIN, *Powder and Patch* (1923)
After his arrival in Paris in search of a retaliatory full-body makeover, country bumpkin Philip Jettan proves to be a prodigy and soon finds a place in Parisian high society. Among his large acquaintance, Saint-Dantin stands out as a staunch ally and devoted friend, as well as one who will happily indulge his Philippe's every whim – except, perhaps, when it comes to poetry. Saint-Dantin also displays a very proper dislike of the despicable Henry Bancroft, so he is clearly a judge of character *par excellence*.

7. SARAH THANE AND EUSTACIE DE VAUBON, *The Talisman Ring* (1936)
When the excitable Eustacie de Vaubon finds her way to the inn at which the quick-thinking Sarah Thane is passing a rather dull time, little do either of them know that it is the beginning of what will quickly become a strong *amitié*. Sarah might be older and wiser, but she enters so thoroughly into Eustacie's schemes – and dreams – that the two are revealed to be kindred spirits; and while

there is often an element of amusement in Sarah's interactions with Eustacie, especially when it comes to her wilder ideas, there is also an enormous fondness that will clearly never fade.

6. JUSTIN ALASTAIR, DUKE OF AVON AND HUGH DAVENANT, *These Old Shades* (1926)

On the surface, these two practically define the concept of *opposites attract*, as surely none could seem more entirely incompatible than the cold, calculating, cynical duke and his kind-hearted sidekick. But is that really true? It is certain that Hugh knows Avon better than anyone, and has no compunction in taking him to task when he is being particularly heartless, though many quail before the cutting words and gaze of the so-called Satanas. It would be intriguing to read a prequel where we see just how these two vastly different people – split by age, personality and rank, among much else – somehow ended up so close. Fanfic writers, get to work!

(Special note should be given here to this friendships' progenitors, Tracy Belmanoir, Duke of Andover and his similarly opposite number, Frank Fortescue. But Justin and Hugh have the edge here, I think.)

5. AMANDA SUMMERCOURT AND HILDEBRAND ROSS, *Sprig Muslin* (1956)

Demanding and entitled, runaway schoolgirl Amanda can be difficult to endure, but the snarky, snappy relationship she quickly develops with chance-met traveller (and near age-mate) Hildebrand is nothing short of delightful. As the two bicker and argue their way past his initial infatuation and her outright lies, they develop an easy – if contentious – camaraderie that you can easily imagine lasting long after Amanda's marriage to her soldier, and eventual return from the Continent. If nothing else, she will always be very honest with him, and if that is not a sign of true friendship then I don't know what is.

4. SIMON OF BEAUVALLET AND ALAN OF MONTLICE, *Simon the Coldheart* (1925)

Meeting as adolescents, Alan, son of a great lord, and Simon, his new servant, develop a topsy-turvy but intense friendship based on Alan's worship of Simon's martial skill and cold demeanour, and Simon's tolerance of said worship. By the time the two become inseparable comrades-in-arms – Simon, the general, Alan, one of his most trusted lieutenants – they are as close as brothers, and it is his fear for Alan's safety that leads Simon into some rather muddy waters, honour-wise, as he confronts the woman who holds Alan captive. When it comes to Alan, at least, Simon's heart is not so cold, after all.

(Special note should be given to the pair's friendship with Sir Geoffrey of Malvallet, the third member of their triumvirate, but since he is Simon's half-brother, he is disqualified from this list.)

3. JOHN "JACK" CARSTARES, EARL OF WYNCHAM AND SIR MILES O'HARA, *The Black Moth* (1921)

These two haven't seen each other in several years – not since Jack fled from Polite Society, having nobly taken the blame for a cheating-at-cards incident – but that distance of time and apparent social standing has no impact on their patent feelings for one another when they do meet again. Miles, to whom the criminal Jack has been remanded to custody, shows no compunction in letting him off the hook due to their prior connection, and they immediately fall back into what is clearly a familiar pattern, sharing a sense of humour and bantering with one another almost ceaselessly. Miles's absolute faith that Jack could never have done the dastardly deed attributed to him is also very touching.

2. VISCOUNT "DY" DYSART AND CORNELIUS "CORNY" FANCOT, *April Lady* (1957)

This comedic duo carouse up a storm throughout London's bachelor hotspots, as well as getting into more than one scrape together while (foolishly) attempting to come to the aid of Dysart's sister, Lady Cardross. Their drunken exploits are particularly entertaining – especially when they are confused as to where they are, and foist themselves into more than one scene they shouldn't –

and the fact that they not only enter strongly into all of each others' interests but are also rarely seen without the other in company is true #friendshipgoals.

(Special note should be given here to this friendships' progenitors, Pelham "Pel", Viscount Winwood and Sir Roland "Pom" Pommeroy, of *The Convenient Marriage* fame. Also very adorable!)

1. PHOEBE MARLOW AND TOM ORDE, *Sylvester* **(1957)**

These childhood friends are so close that, although he does not in the least want to, Tom is even prepared to marry Phoebe to save her from an unpleasant betrothal, if he must. In the end, all he is really asked to do is help her to run away from the Duke of Salford's imminent advances, and while it turns out to have been entirely unnecessary, Tom was not to know that. He is the keeper of her secrets, the supporter of her choices and the shoulder on which she leans – he is also not afraid to tell her when he thinks she is being unreasonable and works very hard to make sure she gets her happy ending. In all, Tom Orde is the ultimate best friend, and Phoebe... well, she likes him a lot, too. Here's hoping everyone in the world has their own Tom Orde...

– Rachel Hyland, Patroness, International Heyer Society

~ | ~

#24 – JUSTICE FOR GIL BY CLARA SHIPMAN

Friday, June 18, 2021

Don't get me wrong, I really enjoyed reading Rachel's *Weekly Post* last week about friendships in Heyer, but I just could not believe it when I reached the ending, and that is why we are gathered here together today.

Even as the numbers counted down – 5. Amanda and Hildebrand, fine… 4. Simon and Alan, sure… 3. Jack and Miles, okay… 2. Dy and Corny, absolutely – I thought to myself, huh, it's weird not to have Phoebe and Tom Orde on the list, but I guess…

WHAT? Phoebe and Tom Orde are NUMBER 1?!?

I immediately scanned up, to make sure I hadn't missed something, but no, I had not. Rachel had given space to CHARIS MERRIVILLE on her list but not – *not* – the best friend *ever*, one Mr. Gilbert Ringwood, of *Friday's Child*? Was she kidding me right now?

I wrote to her:

> *Are you kidding me right now?*

She didn't even have to wait for my clarification:

> *"Gil? Heh, sorry. It's not that he's not great, it's just that I couldn't choose between the friendships in that book. And, honestly, I might have gone for Sherry and George over Gil and… well, everyone, anyway."*

I say again… WAIT, WHAT?

Sometimes, she makes me so mad…

Of course, I'm aware that it's more than a little bit ridiculous that I have gotten myself so worked up over this. These are fictional characters, and tastes are subjective, and sure, it's kind of cute the way Sherry and George begin the book as rivals in love but still hang out, and how George is always threatening to murder everyone, and he could totally do it, but no one pays any attention to his histrionics because he is, hands down, the biggest drama queen in Heyer.

But how can anyone not appreciate what a stand-up guy Gil Ringwood is?

And by far the best friendship in that book – for sure eclipsing every other (platonic, non-related, to quote Rachel) friendship in all of Heyer's books – is between Gil and Hero.

Let us first take a look at Gilbert Ringwood, Esq. Stylish, sensible, impeccably-mannered and kind, he is the heart of his friendship group, comprising the frenzied George, Lord Wrotham, the mercurial Anthony Verelst, Viscount "Sherry" Sheringham, and the somewhat simpleminded Honourable Ferdinand "Ferdy" Fakenham. Being able to navigate three such uneven and quite opposite temperaments is no mean feat, but add the fact that two of their number – and the most violently emotional two, at that – happen to be in love with the same woman can only make an already seemingly impossible balancing act that much harder.

Look at when we first meet Gil.

> "Gil, you're a knowing one: I want your help!"
> Mr. Ringwood was so much moved by this unexpected tribute that he blushed, and dropped the *Morning Chronicle*.
> "Anything in my power, Sherry! Know you've only to give it a name!" he said.

And that is how, in typically brilliant Heyer fashion, we get to learn exactly who Gil Ringwood is, and how thoroughly he is to be depended on. We also learn that he is not routinely given his due from his friends, particularly not from Sherry, who undoubtedly takes him, like he takes everything, for granted. And yet Gil's first thought is always how he can help, despite what appears to be habitual ingratitude on Sherry's part, and that is just so *lovely* of him.

Of course, the help asked of him is in the procurement of a Special License, that Sherry might wed his childhood friend and teen runaway Hero Wantage, and Gil is understandably taken aback. He expostulates, checks on Sherry's bride's pedigree, and though he does not, in fact, know where one finds a Special License, he is kind enough to consult his man, Chilham, on the matter.

> "Extraordinary fellow, Chilham! Knows everything!"

Gil says, readily ceding his place as the most "knowing one" of Sherry's acquaintance.

Into this scene walks George, furious in the knowledge that Sherry has recently proposed to the divine Isabella Milborne, the object of both their affections. George, always boiling for a fight, is not only told off in no uncertain terms by Gil:—

> "… sit down, George, for God's sake, and don't put yourself in a pucker over nothing! I never saw such a fellow!"

but is also given a lecture in how he is not the boss of Isabella:

> "Suppose she does mean to marry Severn? What of it? No harm in it, is there? Dare say she's taken a fancy to be a duchess. Anyone might!"

A perfectly reasonable response and one, moreover, that shows Gil has a greater understanding of Isabella's mind (at this point of the book, anyway) that this man who claims to love her so utterly.

As the story progresses, we get to see more of Gil's exceptional personality, and we fall in love with him again and again as he takes care of Hero in big ways and small, accompanying her to buy clothes – his excellent taste coming into play – and teaching her to drive – his nonpareil, FHC-worthy driving skills being put to use – and advocating for her to her oblivious husband.

> "Wouldn't say she wanted to go if you didn't, Sherry. Noticed it often. Always does what you wish. Mistake if you ask me." He recruited himself with another pull of his glass. "Selfish," he produced.
> "Who is?" demanded his lordship.
> "You are," said Mr. Ringwood simply.

He also becomes Hero's closest confidante, and is the person in whom she has the most faith, because when she feels forced to leave Sherry – he has told her that he made a mistake in marrying her, and she is sure he will never love her, and would be much better off without her – she goes straight to Gil, for his counsel. And it turns out that not only does Gil know exactly what to do for her, but also that he has been worrying about Hero and Sherry for a while, and wondering whether Sherry truly knew the depth of his own feelings for his wife.

His plan is a solid one – send Hero to his grandmother in Bath, where she can act as companion and be tutored in the ways of being a lady. Meanwhile, Sherry goes slowly mad with worry, realizes he does indeed love his wife, and is overcome with jealousy when he learns that she has captivated another man, who, unaware of her marital status and caught up in the romance of Hero's imaginings, carries her off to what he hopes will be a happy ever after.

The fact that Hero and Sherry find their happy ever after is almost entirely the result of the care and attention given to them both by Gilbert Ringwood, Esq. and it is for this reason that we love him, and that I declare him the very best friend in all of Heyer, with apologies to *Sylvester*'s Tom Orde, who is also a wonderful friend, as well.

Though would the two of them have been friends, had they met? Now that is a Heyer fanfic *I* want to read! — *Clara Shipman, Guest Contributor*

~ | ~

#25 – CLASS DIFFERENCES IN HISTORICAL ROMANCE BY JANGA

Friday, June 25, 2021

The theme of love powerful enough to overcome the boundaries of class is rooted deeply in the tradition of romance fiction. Whether one views the title character in Samuel Richardson's *Pamela, or Virtue Rewarded* (1740) as hypocritical schemer or moralistic prig, the virtuous maid "tames the rake" and marries the master, a decidedly upward move in the class hierarchy given Pamela's poverty and low social status and Mr. B.'s estates in Bedfordshire and Lincolnshire and his connection with the peerage.

The class distinction between Elizabeth Bennet and Fitzwilliam Darcy in Jane Austen's *Pride and Prejudice* (1813) is far more subtle than the gap between Mr. B. and Pamela. As Elizabeth says of Darcy to Lady Catherine de Bourgh, "He is a gentleman; I am a gentleman's daughter; so far we are equal." Although Darcy is wealthier, he and Mr. Bennet both belong to the landed gentry. However, more than a difference in income separates the two men. Mr. Bennet married the daughter of an attorney, a *mésalliance* that is compounded by their differences in temperament and intelligence. Darcy's father married the daughter of an earl. Charlotte Brontë held a poor opinion of Austen's novels, but she pairs her most famous heroine with a hero who is considered her social superior throughout most of the novel. By the time the heroine says "Reader, I married him" in the first sentence of the final chapter of Jane Eyre (1847), she has reversed the inequalities that marked her position for most of the novel, but by that time the impression of Jane as poor, plain, and powerless has been memorably established.

Feminist publisher Carmen Callil, finding the plots of Georgette Heyer's novels lacking, said "She just used *Jane Eyre* and jiggled it around 57 times." Although Heyer herself acknowledged that her Mark I heroes owed a debt to Charlotte Brontë's Rochester, Jane Austen's influence was at least as great, and hundreds of romance writers have read and emulated Heyer's "jiggling." Like Austen and Brontë, Heyer dealt with cross-class relationships, most notably in *Devil's Cub* (1932) and *A Civil Contract* (1961), a more thorough and complex treatment of a cross-class marriage. When Adam Deveril's father dies unexpectedly, Adam is forced to leave his regiment and return to Fontley Priory, the family estate, which is heavily mortgaged. He must marry a wealthy woman, even if it means forfeiting his dream of a life with the beautiful Julia Oversley, a childhood friend and near neighbor. He agrees to marry plump, plain Jenny Chawleigh, daughter of a wealthy merchant and to see that she is accepted into aristocratic circles. In exchange, Chawleigh settles the debts and mortgages that Adam has inherited. No makeover transforms Jenny into a beauty, and no epiphany reveals her to Adam as his True Love. Instead, the two become friends who understand one another, building a life of shared interests, gentle laughter, and quiet contentment. Some readers feel that Jenny is cheated out of a grand passion and insist this novel is no romance, but others declare this the best and most realistic of all of Heyer's romances.

Heyer established types and tropes that would become staples of romance fiction into the twenty-first century, and the cross-class romance was no exception, but perhaps no historical romance author has written more cross-class romances than has Mary Balogh, beginning with *A Chance Encounter* (1985). The basic premise of *A Christmas Promise* (1992) is similar to that of Heyer's *A Civil Contract*: Randolph, the Earl of Falloden, inherits a mountain of debt with his new title. Joseph Transome, a wealthy coal merchant, buys all Randolph's debts and offers to forgive them if Randolph marries Transome's daughter Eleanor. Similarities to Heyer end here, as misunderstandings and prejudices keep Randolph and Ellie from discovering any common ground. A Christmas house party that includes a group of Randolph's aristocratic friends and two dozen or so of Ellie's middle-class relatives proves surprisingly harmonious and provides a back drop for the marriage of convenience to become a love match.

A pair of books published the same year serve to show Balogh's range in using cross-class plots. *The Famous Heroine* (1996) pairs Cora Downes, the daughter of a wealthy Bristol merchant, with Lord Francis Kneller, a leader of fashion and connoisseur of beauty. Cora is constantly plunging into disasters from which Francis saves her even as she saves him from depression and ennui. They delight in one another's company, and the reader delights in this rare friends-to-lovers tale that recognizes the importance of shared laughter in developing intimacy. Sharing shelf space with *The Famous Heroine* in 1996 was *Truly*, a Welsh-set tale rich in the history of peasant rebellions known as the Rebecca Riots, that features Geraint Penderyn the new Earl of Wyvern, once an impoverished village schoolboy and his childhood friend, Marged Evans, who holds him responsible for her husband's death.

Balogh continued to make cross-class pairs her protagonists. In her popular Bedwyn series, three of the aristocratic Bedwyn brothers marry women of a lower class, and even Wulfric, the powerful head of the family, chooses a bride who is far from his equal in rank and influence. In *Slightly Married* (2003), Lord Aidan Bedwyn marries Eve Morris, a coal miner's daughter; in *Slightly Wicked* (2003), Rannulf marries Judith Law, a poor clergyman's daughter who has accepted a job as a lady's companion; and in *Slightly Sinful* (2004), Alleyne marries Rachel York, gently bred but formerly a lady's companion, who is living in the home of four prostitutes. In *Slightly Dangerous* (2004), Wulf, The Duke of Bewcastle, marries Christine Derrick, a village schoolteacher and widow of the brother of a viscount. Like Elizabeth Bennet, Christine is a gentleman's daughter but one nonetheless considered the social inferior of the hero.

Julie Anne Long is another author who has used the cross-class trope throughout her career. Her debut novel, *The Runaway Duke* (2004), could be described as a faux cross-class romance. When Roarke Connor Riordan Blackburn, heir to the Duke of Dunbrooke, is wounded in battle, he seizes a case of mistaken identity to escape a life he hates. Blackburn dies at Waterloo, and Connor Riordan survives to become a groom in the stables of Baron Henry Tremaine. After five years, Connor has risen to head groom, and he has become the friend and confidant of Tremaine's unconventional young daughter Rebecca. A misjudgement on Becca's part leaves her betrothed to a rake interested in her dowry and incapable of appreciating her intelligence and honesty, and Connor agrees to help her run away, planning to take her to his aunt and then leave for a new life in America. Of course, Connor ends up as a duke who wants Becca for his duchess, but for most of the novel he is a groom and she is a baron's daughter. There is nothing faux about the cross-class romance in *To Love a Thief* (2005), a *Pygmalion* tale that pairs Gideon Cole, a successful barrister and heir to a barony, with Lily Masters, a curate's granddaughter turned pickpocket to support her younger sister.

Stephen Sharot, who studied cross-class romances in movies released between 1915 and 1935 (*The Psychology of Love*, 2012), found that such romances typically feature a rich protagonist, generally male, paired with a poor protagonist, generally female. The heroine demonstrates what Sharot calls "disinterested love," that is, she subordinates considerations of class and status to the value and emotion of love, desiring the hero for what he is rather than for what he possesses. The wealthy hero proves that he is willing to forego the approval of his family—and even disinheritance—for love of the heroine, and the romance ends successfully with marriage or the promise of marriage. Although Sharot limited his study to films from two decades, which were contemporary stories, his conclusions apply as well to most historical romances published in the last quarter of the twentieth century and the first dozen years of the twenty-first century. This rubric can be identified in the novels by Mary Balogh and Julie Anne Long cited and to countless other cross-class romances. What distinguishes the mediocre from the excellent among these hundreds of books is the freshness the best authors add to the familiar pattern. In addition to the novels by Balogh and Long, I include the following baker's dozen of titles in the excellent, highly recommended category.

- *Reforming Lord Ragsdale* **(1995) by Carla Kelly:** John Staples, Marquess of Ragsdale and Emma Costello, an Irish indentured servant. Class and ethnicity separate Ragsdale and Emma, and the HEA between a lord and a servant seems impossible. But Kelly makes the happy ending believable and satisfying.
- *One Perfect Rose* **(1997) by Mary Jo Putney:** Stephen Kenyon, the Duke of Ashburton and Rosalind Jordan, an orphan adopted by the Fitzgeralds and reared as a member of their acting company. Stephen, whose life has been circumscribed by his position, interacts during what he thinks are the last months of his life with the vibrant Rosalind and her vital, funny family and falls deeply in love with Rosalind whom he insists on marrying. Only afterwards are her aristocratic ties revealed.
- *My Dearest Enemy* **(1998) by Connie Brockway:** Avery Thorne, a gentleman and an adventurer, and Lily Bede, a bastard and a suffragist. Some readers hate that Lily sold out her anti-marriage principles when she agreed to marry Avery, but I love this book with its epistolary element, the chemistry between Avery and Lily, and a couple of secondary characters about whom I still wonder.
- *Tallie's Knight* **(2001) by Anne Gracie:** Magnus, Earl of D'Avenville, handsome, titled, and wealthy and Thalia "Tallie" Robinson, poor relation and children's nurse. Cinderella tales abound in romance, but this is the only one I know where the prince's motive is a desire for a child—not an heir, but a child to love—and his proposal more arrogant that Darcy's, where Cinderella almost refuses, and where the couple takes a road trip to France and Italy.
- *The Rogue's Return* **(2006) by Jo Beverley:** Simon McBride, a McBride of Brideswell distantly related to nearly every and titled family in England and Jane Otterburn, orphaned daughter of a shopkeeper. Simon, who has spent five years in Canada, marries the niece of a dying friend in order to take care of her. He is concerned about how Jane will fit into his aristocratic circle when they return to England, and then he learns that his wife's lineage is even more humble than he supposed: she is not Jane Otterburn but her half-sister, product of their schoolmaster father's illicit union with the promiscuous Tillie Haskett, the best of a family of wastrels and vagabonds.
- *And Then He Kissed Her* **(2007) by Laura Lee Guhrke:** Harry, Viscount Marlowe, a peer denounced by the queen for his divorce and successful publisher of newspapers, magazine and

books, and Emmaline Dove, his super-efficient secretary who aspires to be an author of etiquette books. This Victorian take on the boss-secretary romance is the first and best of Guhrke's Girl Bachelor series.

- *Proof by Seduction* by **Courtney Milan (2010):** Gareth Carhart, Marquess of Blakely, a scientist who uses reason and logic to hold the world at arm's length, and Jenny Keeble, aka Madame Esmerelda, a young woman of uncertain parentage who earns her living as a fortune teller. Class is a topic Milan has explored in a number of her books, but this one stands out for me because Jenny's choice of a way to survive in a world that limited a woman's choices so strictly is so far removed from the usual choices of governess or courtesan.

- *Seduction in Silk* (2011) and *Scandal Wears Satin* (2012) by **Loretta Chase:** Gervaise Angier, the seventh Duke of Clevedon, and Marcelline Noirot, an ambitious dressmaker; Harry, the Earl of Longmore, best friend of the Duke of Clevedon, and Sophy Noirot, sister of Marcelline and partner in the dress shop, Maison Noirot. Not only is it unthinkable that a duke marry a dressmaker but Clevedon is also informally pledged to marry the sister of his best friend, a young woman whom he has loved most of his life. To complicate matters further, the patronage of his almost-betrothed is Marcelline's goal, a vital step in becoming the "greatest modiste in all the world." In the second book, Sophy, intelligent, competent, and something of a chameleon, and Harry, an easy-going guy a bit reminiscent of Heyer's Freddy Standen, work together to save Harry's sister Freddy from marriage to a loser who has compromised her and through Clara save Maison Noirot which is being avoided by the tonnish ladies shocked by Clevedon's marriage to a modiste. Both are wildly improbable tales but wholly delightful examples of Chase's wit and winning characters.

- *A Lady's Lesson in Scandal* (2011) by **Meredith Duran:** Simon St. Maur, the new Earl of Rushden in need of an heiress, and Nell Whitby, a factory girl from a London slum who believes she is the by-blow of the previous Earl of Rushden and who bears a marked resemblance to a missing heiress. What sounds like another trite tale becomes something extraordinary as Duran shows Nell's adjustment to her new life and the mix of emotions her new status evokes.

- *A Gentleman Undone* (2012) by **Cecilia Grant:** Will Blackshear, a younger son of an aristocratic family and a veteran of Waterloo trying to atone for an error in judgment, and Lydia Slaughter, a woman of gentle birth who becomes a prostitute. Grant has a gift for taking the conventions of romance and giving them a twist that produces something exciting and different. She does that in spades with this tale of hero who accepts estrangement from most of his family as the price of marrying the woman he loves, who not only is the mistress of another man when he falls in love with her but also actually enjoys sex with the other man (gasp!).

- *Ravishing the Heiress* (2012) by **Sherry Thomas:** George Edward Arthur Granville Fitzhugh, Earl Fitzhugh, a nineteen-year-old newly ascended to his title and in need of an heiress, and Millicent Graves, only daughter of a wealthy manufacturer of "tinned goods and other preserved edibles." This is one of my top twenty-five all-time romances, and one reason I love it is that it feels to me as if Thomas has rewritten Heyer's *A Civil Contract* and given the heroine the joyous HEA that Heyer denies her Jenny.

- *Any Duchess Will Do* (2013) by **Tessa Dare:** Griffin York, the Duke of Halford, who is kidnapped by his mother and taken to Spindle Cove, that haven of misfits and unattached maidens, to choose a duchess, and Pauline Sims, a barmaid who dreams of owning a bookshop. Not many authors could make me suspend disbelief and accept a duke paired with a barmaid. Tessa Dare does and makes me love it in this mix of humor and pathos.

And we must never forget Heyer's *A Civil Contract*, of course, without which it is very possible none of these books would exist.
                                                                    – *Janga, Guest Contributor*

#26 – BELINDA'S PURPLE GOWN BY SUSANNAH FULLERTON

Friday, July 2, 2021

One of the great delights of Georgette Heyer's 1948 novel *The Foundling* is the character of Belinda. Incredibly beautiful, pliable and brainless, Belinda's great goal in life is to own a purple silk gown. The first words she speaks within the novel concern this pressing desire: "He said I should have a purple silk dress when we was married", she tells the Duke. The purple dress is a constant refrain throughout the novel, wearying the poor Duke of Sale, who cannot understand Belinda's obsession, and causing all who talk with her to cut her off before the dress can again be mentioned. Invariably, the dress raises a smile in Heyer's readers - most of us love every single purple dress reference within the novel.

As Belinda grows more and more entrenched in the Duke's life, he begins to grow anxious:

> "What in heaven's name am I to do with you?", said the Duke, looking harassed.
> Belinda said hopefully: "You did say that you wished you might give me a purple silk dress," she suggested.
> He could not help laughing. "No, no, that is not what I meant."

He feels obliged to warn Belinda that she must not "go off with strange men just because they promise (her) silk dresses". When he passes her into the care of his betrothed, he warns Harriet about Belinda's shallowness:

> "Oh, the loveliest creature imaginable! he said gaily. "With not two thoughts in her head to rub together! No, I wrong her! There are just two thoughts! One is of golden rings, and the other of purple silk dresses."

Her obsession with the colour purple leads Belinda to ask the Duke if he "wears a coronet, and purple robe" – she is deeply disappointed to find his robe is a scarlet one! Once she is in Bath, Belinda goes shopping and espies her heart's desire in a Milsom Street establishment. Harriet, who accompanied her, describes it with horror: "It is of the brightest purple satin, with Spanish sleeves slashed with rows of gold beads, and a demi-train, and the bosom cut by far too low!" But Belinda is happy to run away with Lord Gaywood so long as he promises to purchase it for her, and she then has to be rescued from that entanglement. At the end of the story, dim-witted Belinda is married off to Mr Mudgley who, she acknowledges, she loves even more than purple gowns. On the last page, we learn that Belinda is to get her dress after all – Harriet plans to bestow it on her as a bride-gift. She knows the girl will look "quite shockingly" in it, but Jasper Mudgley loves her so much, he'll think her a vision of loveliness in any colour at all.

While the Duke, who is so rich he can buy anything he wants in whatever shade he chooses, cannot understand Belinda's fixation with purple, many people of the Regency era would have had no trouble sympathising with her desire to be so garbed. The colour purple was incredibly expensive to produce. It came from the glandular mucus of a sea snail called the murex and it took thousands of sea snails to extract enough of the pure dye to colour just one Roman toga. Extraction was labour-intensive, complicated, variable, and extremely costly. It often lacked stability and fastness (had Belinda washed her dress, it could well have faded into blotchy patches, or turned pale lilac – not what she wants at all!). The very earliest purple dyes date back to about 1900 BC.

Given how hard and expensive it was to create a small length of purple cloth, it's not surprising that purple was used for the clothing of emperors, magistrates and highly privileged individuals. For those in power in the Byzantine Empire and the Holy Roman Empire, for Roman Catholic Bishops, and in Imperial Japan, purple symbolised wealth and status. No country in the world has purple in its flag – this is because it was so costly, and also because of its exclusively royal associations. Through history, purple became a colour associated with rarity, mystery, royalty and money! Belinda's life might have mystery in it – she is a foundling and has no idea who her parents were – but she has no power, no money, no prestigious connections. Somehow, in her far from bright mind, she is aware of all she lacks and feels that wearing purple will provide what is missing in her life.

Belinda is very young in this Regency novel, and can expect (as Mrs Jasper Mudgley) to live well into the Victorian era. As an elderly lady, if she still hankers after purple, she could have her entire wardrobe filled with purple gowns at a very reasonable price. Interestingly, it was the colour purple that would bring about huge changes to fabric dyes and fashion, and it all came about as the result of an accident …

The discovery of a cheaper way of producing purple cloth took place in 1856. An 18-year-old student, William Perkin, was attempting to synthesise quinine for the treatment of malaria. His experiment (oxidizing aniline using potassium dichromate) did not achieve what he had hoped it would but, in cleaning out his flask at the end of the experiment, Perkin noticed traces of deep purple. He conducted further experiments and grew certain that aniline could be partly transformed into a crude mixture which, when extracted with alcohol, produced a liquid with an intense purple colour. This liquid proved to stain cloth indelibly, and it did not fade when exposed to sunlight or soap. Alert to the commercial possibilities of what he had discovered, he patented this dye as 'aniline purple' (later the name was changed to 'mauveine') and opened a dye works in Middlesex. He had to raise the money to produce the dye, work out how to manufacture it cheaply, adapt it to enable the dyeing of cotton, and create a public demand for the colour, but he managed all these tasks successfully. He built his factory, publicised his invention of the dye, and gave technical advice to the dyeing industry.

Both Queen Victoria and Empress Eugénie wore the new colour and it took off – Perkin grew rich on his accidental discovery. Suddenly purple, which had been prohibitively costly, was affordable, and women began to wear it on a regular basis. The streets of London must have been filled with 'purple Belindas'. *Punch* magazine even published articles poking fun at the great prevalence of the colour. By the 1870s synthetic dyes in other colours were being produced, but Perkin had laid the foundation for the synthetic organic chemicals industry and had helped to revolutionise fashion. He became Sir William Henry Perkin (1838 – 1907), was made a Fellow of the Royal Society, and today his Stepney home is marked with one of London's famous Blue Plaques.

I think Belinda would have approved!

– Susannah Fullerton, Patroness, International Heyer Society

~ | ~

#27 – TOP 10 TV SERIES FOR THE HEYERITE BY RACHEL HYLAND

Friday, July 9, 2021

As promised in the earlier list "Top 10 Films for the Heyerite", here you will find some recommendations for television series that somewhat evoke the same feel as the works of our beloved Georgette. Everyone's viewing preferences are different, of course, so I cannot guarantee that they will all make it onto your watch list, but I believe they are all worth a try for anyone who enjoys stepping into the past and experiencing the sights and sounds of times long gone.

Not all of these are available to stream, sadly, but all are to be found on DVD, should you still have one of those to play them on.

10. BRIDGERTON (2020 –)
Created by Chris Van Dusen; Based on the novels of Julia Quinn
Number of Episodes: 10 (in Season 1) | Netflix

It is much, *much* racier than Heyer's Regency, of course, and the devoted scholar of the period will note many an anachronism, both deliberate and incidental – are those young ladies actually not wearing court dresses at their presentation to the Queen? – but the show is nevertheless beautiful to look at, and the nearest thing we have yet seen to the exploits of Arabella, Kitty Charing and the Misses Merriville on screen. Worth a watch, even if the modern sensibilities the show (and, indeed, the books on which it is based) portray aren't quite to your taste.

9. CAMPION (1989 – 1990)
Created by John Hawkesworth | Based on the novels of Margery Allingham | 6 episodes | BBC
For fans of Heyer's mysteries this series adapting the Albert Campion series by contemporary Margery Allingham is sure to appeal. Just like *Footsteps in the Dark* and its compatriots, the show is very much a triumph of style over substance – tune in more for the stately surroundings, the vintage Lagondas and the elegant evening wear, just as one reads Heyer's mysteries for the characters and dialogue far more than the murder plots – but Peter Davison as our aristocratic, idiosyncratic gentleman detective hero is ever a delight.

8. GENTLEMAN JACK (2019 –)
Created by Sally Wainwright | Based on the diaries of Anne Lister | 8 episodes (Season 1) | BBC
No, this is not about the owner of a certain select boxing saloon in Regency London, but instead is the based-on-a-true-story dramatization of the life of one Anne Lister. A lesbian and sudden landowner after the death of her uncle, the worldly Anne heads to Yorkshire in 1832 to claim her inheritance and finds there not only enemies but a great love, in the person of neighbourhood heiress Ann Walker (Sophie Rundle). Suranne Jones is perfect as the charming, clever and determined Lister, and the show's exploration of gender politics and roles, both in history and in the present day, is very much on point.

7. BELGRAVIA (2020)
Created by Julian Fellowes | Based on the novel by Julian Fellowes | 6 episodes | ITV
Opening at the Duchess of Richmond's ball on the eve of the Battle of Waterloo (and it is stunning!), but soon jumping forward a quarter century, this story of a social climbing merchant, a lost heir, gambling debts and romance by the man best known for *Downton Abbey* is exactly as convoluted as you might expect, but with its pageantry, its lords and ladies all over the place and its simmering elitism, it is without a doubt a worthy watch for any Heyer fan. Indeed, it feels somewhat like a *roman à clef* one Phoebe Marlow might have written as a follow up to her debut bestseller. (We all think Phoebe continued writing after her marriage to Sylvester, right? I certainly hope so, at any rate.)

6. THE WHITE QUEEN
Based on the novels of Philippa Gregory | 10 episodes | BBC/Starz
Heyer never treated with the Wars of the Roses, but who knows if she might not have gotten to it if she'd had the chance to complete *My Lord John*, which deals with the ancestors of the House of Lancaster shown here. This series mostly deals with the House of York, however, as the young Edward IV (Max Irons) falls in love at first sight with unsuitable widow Elizabeth (Rebecca Ferguson) and marries her, thereby causing a series of quite calamitous events. Sensationalized and soap opera-ized in the same vein as *The Tudors* and *Reign*, et al, the show nevertheless grips with its political machinations and beautiful people, and Amanda Hale as the pious, ruthless Lady Margaret Beaufort both fascinates and infuriates in equal parts. An exhausting, exhilarating passage through history. Follow up series *The White Princess* and *The Spanish Princess* aren't necessary viewing, but aren't the worst way to spend a few idle hours either.

5. ARISTOCRATS (1999)

Created by Harriet O'Carroll | Based on the novel by Stella Tillyard | 6 episodes | BBC

Adapting the sweeping and compelling biography of the four surviving Lennox sisters, daughters of the 2nd Duke of Richmond, in 18th-century England, this Georgian series will gladden any Heyerite heart. Laden with historical references, sumptuous gowns, clever dialogue and the occasional scandal, the tale of these four very different women as they grow up, marry, triumph and suffer is truly like seeing history – and sociology – come alive. Among a very able cast it is worth noting that the previously mentioned Julian Fellowes (*Downton Abbey, Belgravia*) plays His Grace. Definitely worth tracking down!

4. ROOKIE HISTORIAN GOO HAE-RYUNG (2019)

Created by Sohn Hyung-suk | 20 episodes | Netflix

This historical drama from South Korea takes place in 1830 and gives us the spirited Goo Hae-rung (Shin Se-kyung) as one of four fictional female historians, recruited to help record the day-to-day doings of the royal court. Many lavish Korean productions are set in the Joseon period – which ran from 1392 - 1897, so there is a lot of scope there – but few also explore the taboos of outside cultures penetrating into the xenophobic nation, and the persecution of those who practiced Western religions. The costumes are beautiful as are the people (especially K-pop idol Cha Eun-woo, as a much-beset prince and secret romance writer), and the developing romance is very sweet. If you're new to Korean series, you might find some of the characters a bit shouty and the sound effects a bit disconcerting, but just know that their use in *Rookie Historian* is actually pretty moderate, comparatively. And I promise, you get used to it very quickly.

3. CRANFORD (2007)

Created by Sue Birtwistle and Susie Conklin | Based on Elizabeth Gaskell | 5 episodes | BBC

Melding together the characters and events of several Gaskell stories, this series gives us the carefully respectable village of Cranford, in 1840s Cheshire. Newly arrived in town is widowed Captain Brown (Jim Carter), and after a sudden tragedy he settles into town life with his daughter Jessie (Julia Sawalha – Lydia!) and is forced to navigate the levels of hierarchy, propriety and custom that rule over everyone. The cast is nothing short of spectacular – headed by Judi Dench – the costuming immaculate, the dialogue amusing and the social satire pointed, as one would expect from any series derived from a Gaskell work. A sequel series, *Return to Cranford*, doesn't quite match the original, but is still worth a look. (As, of course, is Gaskell's *North and South*, starring the compelling Richard Armitage, well known to Heyer readers as the wonderful audiobook narrator of some sadly abridged versions of her works.)

2. LARK RISE TO CANDLEFORD (2008 – 2011)

Created by Bill Gallagher | Based on the novels of Flora Thompson | 40 episodes | BBC

Set in the latter days of the Victorian era, a time of great upheaval and social change in England, we visit with the inhabitants of the rural hamlet of Lark Rise and neighbouring market town Candleford and see the world through the eyes of the innocent, helpful and adorable Laura Timmins (Olivia Hallinan) as she takes a job delivering letters under the aegis of her independent aunt, post mistress Dorcas Lane (Julia Sawalha again!). The trials and tribulations of the area's residents, across four seasons, always appeal, and the window into a lost world can only be appreciated by any reader especially enamoured of Heyer's country-set novels.

1. POLDARK

Created by Debbie Horsfield; Based on the novels of Winston Graham | 43 episodes | BBC

Army veteran Captain Ross Poldark (Aidan Turner) returns to his home in Cornwall in 1783, after the American War of Independence, and discovers his father dead and his inheritance in ruins. Determined to reinvigorate his family estate, he faces many obstacles presented by family, friends, business rivals and nosy neighbours, especially when he weds an ostensibly unsuitable woman.

Rarely spending any time in the more rarefied surrounds of Heyer's Georgian novels, the story nevertheless cannot help but capture the imagination of anyone with an interest in the period. The latter seasons also bring in the spectre of war with the French, giving them vague *The Spanish Bride* vibes that will greatly please any fans of that novel. And Aidan Turner is AMAZING.

– Rachel Hyland, Patroness, International Heyer Society

~ | ~

#28 – HEYER IN LOCKDOWN BY CLARA SHIPMAN

Friday, July 16, 2021

As much of the world continues to find itself in either permanent, intermittent or even voluntary lockdown due to the ongoing Covid-19 crisis, we must all seek comfort wherever we can find it to help us get through the days, weeks, months – and now it seems, years – of uncertainty brought about by this continuing threat, and by the long days stuck at home, often seemingly without end.

Like many of us, I have been turning to Georgette Heyer for my source of distraction and good cheer almost from the moment this all began at the start of 2020, but recently I have found that not all of her books make the best of pandemic reading. They did at first, with their lively humor and ability to take me out of reality, but as time goes on and a return to normality seems ever more distant, I have found that much of my reading matter has had to be carefully curated so that it does not cause me severe freedom envy.

And the works of Heyer are no exception.

To begin with, we can rule out all of her books that involve any kind of party, especially not successful ones like the grand balls given by the Marquis of Alverstoke in *Frederica* or Lady Bridlington in *Arabella*. Because anything that can be characterised as a "crush" or a "squeeze" is certainly not something we can even think about in this age of social distancing. Also out on that score: *The Grand Sophy*, *The Nonesuch* and *Cousin Kate*. (Oh no, however will I live without *Cousin Kate*?)

We can also bypass all of the books that involve international travel, since that is currently out of the question for most of us. So bye bye *Simon the Coldheart* and *Beauvallet*, and *These Old Shades* and *Devil's Cub*, and *An Infamous Army* and *The Spanish Bride*. Also necessarily eliminated are *The Great Roxhythe* and *The Conqueror*, but I find I'm okay with that. Ditto all of the contemporaries. (Scotland counts as international travel, right?)

Staying at hotels? Definitely triggering for me. So that leaves out *The Black Moth*, *Regency Buck*, *The Corinthian*, *Sprig Muslin*, *The Foundling*, *Charity Girl* and *The Talisman Ring*. (Though imagine how much fun it would be to quarantine with Sarah Thane!)

Indeed, we need to rule out all of the books that feature travelling any major distance from home, and also sight-seeing, since many tourist destinations remain resolutely closed throughout this time. So not today *The Toll-Gate*, *Cotillion*, *Friday's Child* and *Venetia*! (Also *Royal Escape*, but again, that's fine.)

Then there are the books that see people going to the theatre, the opera or any other form of public entertainment. So depressing that performances keep getting cancelled, isn't it? So that means we have to say goodbye to *A Convenient Marriage*, *Lady of Quality*, *Bath Tangle* and *Black Sheep*. (They always go to a lot of concerts when in Bath, don't they?)

A fan of game nights? Then you have to exclude *The Masqueraders*, *Powder and Patch* and, of course, *Faro's Daughter*, since so much of the action takes place at assorted gaming venues. (Of course, my preferred game nights feature more *Trivial Pursuit* and *Cataan,* and less hazard and piquet, but the principle is the same.)

Books with large house parties? No, they won't work either. And so we must bid farewell to *The Quiet Gentleman, A Civil Contract, The Reluctant Widow, False Colours, The Unknown Ajax* and pretty much all of the mysteries from the list.

What, then, are we left with?

None.

Not a single Heyer novel. Which shows you just how little the world has changed, since we all do the same things now that they did then – or, at least, we used to.

Forget it, then. I take it all back! Give me all the balls, soirees, theatre visits, extended stays at inns and house parties I can handle, and then some. And perhaps, if nothing else, all the very proper bowing and curtseying will break me of the habit I still have of reaching out to shake people's hands or go in for hugs, which is very much frowned upon in these troubled times.

The books that feature international travel are still off the list, however, since that is what I miss the most.

What are your most comforting Heyer reads? And do you have any you can't read right now, or is that just me?

– *Clara Shipman, Guest Contributor*

~ | ~

#29 – TOP 10 JANE AUSTEN ADAPTATIONS BY RACHEL HYLAND

Friday, July 23, 2021

As promised, and following on from the "Top 10 Films for the Heyerite" and "Top 10 TV Series for the Heyerite," here is a list of some truly remarkable adaptations of Jane Austen's timeless classics, found both on the page and on the screen. As we all know, Austen was among Georgette Heyer's very favourite authors, and was also – arguably – the biggest influence on her work, especially when it comes to her Regency romances. Of course, it would be hard to find the modern romance writer who was not also similarly influenced, wouldn't it?

I am aware that when it comes to Austen adaptations – of which there are many thousands, especially if one counts all of the *Pride and Prejudice* variations that exist – opinions are naturally bound to vary wildly. But here are mine:

10. PRIDE AND PREJUDICE – A COUNTING PRIMER (2011)
Adapted by: Jennifer Adams and Alison Oliver
From: *Pride and Prejudice* (1813)
Published by: BabyLit®

This adorable board book is the perfect gift for any Austen fan, whether they have young children or not. Sweetly illustrated and depicting one English village, two rich gentlemen and three country houses, all the way up to the humorous denouement at number 10 – can you guess what it is? – it is very clever, very cute, and the first outing in the very popular BabyLit® series, which also features *Sense and Sensibility – An Opposites Primer* and *Emma – An Emotions Primer*.

9. LOVE AND FRIENDSHIP (2016)
Adapted by: Whit Stillman
From: *Lady Susan* (1871)

As long as one can set aside the bizarreness of the title – why did they name this film after that unrelated piece of juvenilia *Love & Freindship* [sic]? *Why?* – one will surely enjoy this witty, elegant and stylish live action version of Austen's novella. Kate Beckinsale is perfectly cast as the widowed Lady Susan Vernon, who wants nothing more than to secure wealthy husbands for herself and her daughter by any means necessary. Charming, cunning and unspeakably beautiful, Lady Susan is as much of a textbook narcissist on screen as she is revealed to be through her letters in the original text—and the fact that the term was unknown in Austen's time makes the creation of his fascinating anti-heroine even more remarkable, especially since Austen most probably did so when still in her teens. (The novella is believed to have been written circa 1794, when Austen would not yet have been twenty years of age.)

8. ELIGIBLE (2016)

Adapted by: Curtis Sittenfeld
From: *Pride and Prejudice* (1813)
Published by Random House

The fourth of the anthologized *Jane Austen Project* titles (Joanna Trollope wrote the first) at last treats with *Pride and Prejudice*, bringing the author's satirical eye and sparkling wit to this updated tale of thirty-something journalist Elizabeth Bennet, who returns to her Cincinnati hometown due to her father's ill health and meets infuriating neurosurgeon Dr. Fitzwilliam Darcy. Much pride and prejudice thence ensue. (*Eligible*, by the way? The name of the dating reality game show on which Dr. Chip Bingley recently appeared. If that isn't enough to entice you into this *P&P* variation, then nothing will.)

7. SENSE AND SENSIBILITY: THE COMIC (2010)

Adapted by: Nancy Butler and Sonny Liew
From: *Sense and Sensibility* (1811)
Published by: Marvel Comics

A follow up to their 2009 release, *Pride and Prejudice: The Comic*, Marvel's second foray into Austen territory is a real winner; more than worthy of a place on this list. Writer Nancy Butler infuses Elinor and Marianne with proper Dashwoodiness and makes the devastatingly attractive Willoughby just as magnetically repellent as ever. (I think she did better with Lizzy and Mr. Darcy in the *P&P* comic – but then, *everyone* does better with Lizzy and Darcy, don't they?) But it is the cartoonishly agreeable art of Sonny Liew – who also did excellent work on the *P&P* covers – that makes this the superior effort: cleverly blending scenes from the book with iconic images from the assorted adaptations makes this illustrated adventure accessible to both the film-only and non-graphic novel fan, and a whole lot of fun for serious scholar and casual comic reader alike.

6. BRIDE AND PREJUDICE (2004)

Adapted by: Gurinder Chadha and Paul Mayeda Berges, directed by Gurinder Chadha
From: *Pride and Prejudice* (1813)

Bringing the story into the modern day (well, the modern day of 2004) and then setting it in India really makes sense when you think about it. When Mrs. Bennet becomes Mrs. Bakshi, the power she wields over her five daughters and her determination to see them all married well does not come off as anachronistic at all. The luminous Aishwarya Rai plays Lalita – whom, with apologies to this movie's version of Jane (Namrata Shirodkar as Jaya), surely no one could ever think was less beautiful than literally anyone – and when spoiled American hotel heir Will Darcy (Martin Henderson) arrives in her hometown of Amritsar to attend a friend's wedding, misunderstandings, both cultural and otherwise, conspire to keep them from ever seeing eye to eye. Especially with the arrival of the dashing Johnny Wickham… Enlivened by riotous colour, fantasy sequences, musical numbers and a good deal of preposterous impeccably-executed-though-apparently-spontaneous choreography, in true Bollywood fashion, the film captivates with its relentless energy and verve even as it retells a very familiar tale, making it all seem quite shiny and new again.

5. PRIDE AND PREJUDICE AND ZOMBIES (2009)

Adapted by: Seth Grahame-Smith
From: *Pride and Prejudice* (1813)

The instigator of the literary monster mashup craziness, *Pride and Prejudice and Zombies* was an instant classic, the kind of book that made you wonder why no one had ever thought of it before, and yet be astounded that anyone had thought of it at all. The perfect blend of outrageousness, parody, reverence, and homage, it quite rightly took the literary world by storm by not taking it— or itself—too seriously. Because it's *Pride and Prejudice*, and there are zombies in it! Simply, awe-inspiringly brilliant. For Mr. Darcy to meet Elizabeth for the first time and hold her to be tolerable enough but secretly admire her mad skill with a katana is both satisfying and surreal. Pliant Jane, flighty Lydia and Kitty, and even pious Mary wielding weapons of war with gay abandon is also a study in compelling contrast. The idea of such a measured and restricted society as that of genteel 19th century England being forced to deal with the unpleasantness of animated rotting corpses is just very, very amusing. And the pleasingly just punishment exacted upon the irksome Mr. Collins must surely gladden Austenite hearts the world over.*

* Excerpt taken from my book *Classics Gone Wild: Pride and Prejudice and Zombies and Beyond – A Guide to Literary Monster Mashups* (with Kate Nagy)

4. CLUELESS (1995)
Adapted by: Amy Heckerling
From: *Emma* (1815)

Take *Emma*, but make it Los Angeles in the 1990s, and in high school. That is the concept at the heart of *Clueless*, which sees the winsome Alicia Silverstone as teen Cher Horowitz, daughter of a Hollywood lawyer who never saw a thing she couldn't buy, or a person she couldn't charm. But her crusading one-time stepbrother Josh (Paul Rudd), newly in college and so certain of his own maturity, makes Cher begin to question her values, especially when Cher's makeover of transfer student Tai (Brittany Murphy) goes disastrously awry. Studded with quotable lines and beautiful people, *Clueless* is just a really good time, and holds up surprisingly well to this day. (Except maybe for the fashions. The fashions are a bit much.)

3. THE LIZZIE BENNET DIARIES (2012 - 2013)
Adapted by: Hank Green and Bernie Su
From: *Pride and Prejudice* (1813)

This webseries retells its source material through the vlog of graduate student Lizzie Bennet (Ashley Clements), with the help of her best friend Charlotte Lu (Julia Cho). Across one hundred short episodes, the whole story is told, often through re-enactments, though we do meet many of the people mentioned, notably Lizzie's gentle older sister Jane (Laura Spencer) and attention-seeking younger sister Lydia (Mary Kate Wiles), as well as Jane's new beau, medical student Bing Lee (Christopher Sean), and his friend, the heir to Pemberley Digital, William Darcy (Daniel Vincent Gordh). Lizzie, of course, hates Darcy almost immediately, but by the time he appears on screen it is clear that her opinion has started to change… An online phenomenon at its release, the series has accumulated hundreds of millions of views on YouTube and spawned several sequels and spinoffs, as well as a couple of novels, a line of merchandise, and even a DVD box set.

2. SENSE AND SENSIBILITY (1995)
Adapted by: Emma Thompson, directed by Ang Lee
From: *Sense and Sensibility* (1811)

Emma Thompson justly won an Academy Award for her sparkling screenplay of this masterpiece, in which she plays the sensible Elinor to Kate Winslet's sensibility-laden Marianne. Beautifully shot and masterfully rendered, the interplay between the sisters and especially between Elinor and

Edward Ferrars (played by a wonderfully restrained Hugh Grant) is so lovingly depicted that they come positively alive, and live long in your heart long after the film ends. Thompson's slight but significant changes and additions actually add depth and delight to the story, a far cry from some ill-fated attempts to do the same in other Austen adaptations I could mention (*cough*nosebleed*cough*), while her understanding of, and respect for, the source material can never be in doubt. Just magnificent.

1. PRIDE AND PREJUDICE (1992)

Adapted: by Andrew Davies, directed by Simon Langston
From: *Pride and Prejudice* (1813)

Is there a better go-to pick-me-up ever created than this acclaimed BBC mini-series of Jane Austen's most beloved work? From Colin Firth's dour but debonair Mr. Darcy to Jennifer Ehle's smart and sensual Elizabeth Bennet, and from David Bamber's creepy Mr. Collins to Julia Sawalha's outrageous Lydia, every role is perfectly cast; add to this the impeccable costuming, direction, scene selection and judicious screenwriting, and it is difficult to imagine a better, more satisfying adaptation of this – or, indeed, any other – novel. The five-hour running time means we don't miss much; we also get such vital additions to Austen's original narrative as the chaste marital kiss at the end and… well, a dripping wet Colin Firth doesn't hurt any, does it? All in all, this version of *Pride and Prejudice* trumps every other Austen adaptation in practically every way; almost thirty years on, and still nothing has even come close.

We can only wonder what Heyer would have thought of these adaptations, especially some of the more outlandish ones! *These Old Shades and Zombies*, anyone?

– Rachel Hyland, Patroness, International Heyer Society

~ | ~

#30 – TOP 10 BEST AND WORST JANE AUSTEN ADAPTATIONS BY SUSANNAH FULLERTON

Friday, July 30, 2021

Oh, where are the smelling salts? Someone please bring me a vinaigrette! I have just seen my esteemed fellow patroness Rachel Hyland's list of Top 10 Jane Austen Adaptations and feel palpitations, worse than any suffered by Mrs Bennet, coming on.

I've had to make a list, not only of my Top 10, but also of my Worst 10, in response:

TOP 10

10. MRS. GODDARD: MISTRESS OF A SCHOOL (1993)

Adapted by Joan Austen-Leigh, from Emma *(1815) | A Room of One's Own Press*
This is a clever re-telling of the plot of Jane Austen's *Emma* through the eyes of practical and sensible school mistress, Mrs Goddard. The author was a descendant of the Austen family, and she gets the style and tone just right.

9. PRIDE AND PREJUDICE – A COUNTING PRIMER (2011)

Adapted by Jennifer Adams and Alison Oliver, from Pride and Prejudice *(1813) | BabyLit®*
I agree with Rachel on this one – cleverly done and a delight for an Austen fan.

8. PRIDE, PREJUDICE AND JASMIN FIELD (2000)

Adapted by Melissa Nathan, from Pride and Prejudice *(1813) | William Morrow*
Actor Jasmin Field gets involved in a stage production of *Pride and Prejudice* and meets her match in the man playing Darcy. This is amongst the best modern adaptations of the novel.

7. LIZZY BENNET'S DIARY (2014)

Adapted by Marcia Williams, from Pride and Prejudice *(1813)* | *Candlewick*

Gorgeously produced with pull-out letters and other novelties, this is a charming re-telling of the plot of the novel as it may have appeared in Elizabeth's dairy. A lovely gift book for a younger reader.

6. CLUELESS (1995)

Adapted by Amy Heckerling, from Emma *(1815)*

Few film directors are able to catch the ironic voice of Jane Austen. This film, set in California, manages it and is an extremely witty and clever version of Austen's greatest novel.

5. MANSFIELD PARK (1983)

Adapted by Kenneth Taylor, directed by David Giles, from Mansfield Park *(1814)* | *BBC*

Incredibly faithful to the book, with an extremely strong cast, and lovely locations, this is a version I often return to.

4. BRIDE AND PREJUDICE (2004)

Adapted by Gurinder Chadha and Paul Mayeda Berges, from Pride and Prejudice *(1813)*

Like Rachel, I love this adaptation. Full of energy and colour, songs and even elephants, it's a romp, but also shows how well Jane Austen translates to modern India.

3. PRIDE AND PREJUDICE (1992)

Adapted by Andrew Davies, directed by Simon Langston, from Pride and Prejudice *(1813)*

A fabulous version, although for me Alison Steadman as Mrs Bennet ruined every scene she was in, and Jennifer Ehle is just not right for me as Elizabeth. Colin Firth is superb.

2. PRIDE AND PREJUDICE (1980)

Adapted by Fay Weldon, directed by Cyril Coke, from Pride and Prejudice *(1813)*

This is my favourite movie version of this novel. Elizabeth Garvie is the perfect Elizabeth Bennet and most of the characters are brilliantly cast.

1. SENSE AND SENSIBILITY (1995)

Adapted by: Emma Thompson, directed by Ang Lee, from Sense and Sensibility *(1811)*

In my view, the best movie adaptation of any Jane Austen novel.

WORST 10

10. PRIDE AND PREJUDICE AND KITTIES: A CAT LOVER'S ROMP THROUGH JANE AUSTEN'S CLASSIC (2015)

Adapted by Pamela Jane and Deborah Guyol, from Pride and Prejudice *(1813)* | *Skyhorse*

This is a mash-up of cats and Jane Austen, which achieves nothing, isn't even attractive to look at, and is simply an incredible waste of paper.

9. EMMA: A MODERN RETELLING (2015)

Adapted by Alexander McCall Smith, from Emma *(1815)* | *Pantheon*

Written in a few weeks (and doesn't it show), this book is wordy, dull and devoid of any real appreciation of the great novel, which is such a pity as McCall Smith can be an enjoyable writer and says he loves *Emma*.

8. JANE & D'ARCY (2017)

Adapted by Wal Walker

This piece of rubbish tries to argue, in two volumes no less, that Australian pioneer doctor D'Arcy Wentworth was the love of Jane Austen's life. Oh dear – smelling salts please!

7. ELIGIBLE (2016)

Adapted by: Curtis Sittenfeld from Pride and Prejudice *(1813)* | *Random House*

The Darcy and Elizabeth characters in this adaptation seem to delight in having 'hate sex'. They get all hot and sweaty together, while constantly insisting on how much they hate each other. Really??? Sorry, Rachel, but Georgette would surely turn in her grave over this book?

6. PRIDE AND PLATYPUS: MR DARCY'S DREADFUL SECRET (2012)

Adapted by Vera Nazarian, from Pride and Prejudice *(1813)*

Why on earth can't these authors just leave Jane Austen alone and write their own terrible books? Mr

Darcy is turned into a platypus whenever the moon is full. I wish the author would turn into some creature unable to hold a pen.

5. MANSFIELD PARK (2007)

Adapted by Maggie Wadey, directed by Iain B. MacDonald, from Mansfield Park *(1814) | ITV*

British movie with the unbelievably miscast Billie Piper as Fanny Price. She runs, romps, pouts and shows far too much bosom and anyone more unlike Fanny it would be impossible to find. I fancy the idea of pistols at dawn with the casting director!

4. PERSUASION (2007)

Adapted by Simon Burke, directed by Adrian Shergold, from Persuasion *(1817) | ITV*

How could they have done such a thing to such a gloriously beautiful novel?? Sally Hawkins never regains any bloom, goes through the entire film having bad hair days and looking grumpy, and then we see her in training for the Bath Marathon as she chases Captain Wentworth through Bath. Eeeeek!

3. SENSE AND SENSIBILITY AND SEA MONSTERS (2009)

Adapted by Ben H. Winters, from Sense and Sensibility (1811) | Quirk Books

May the creatures of the deep which Winters unleashes on the characters of Austen's rational, moving and glorious novel turn and finish him off for creating this abomination.

2. PRIDE AND PREJUDICE AND ZOMBIES (2016)

Adapted by Burr Steers, from Pride and Prejudice and Zombies *by Jane Austen and Seth Grahame-Smith*

The film made from the novel. Utter, utter trash and a waste of everybody's time and energy.

1. PRIDE AND PREJUDICE AND ZOMBIES (2009)

Adapted by Seth Grahame-Smith, from Pride and Prejudice *(1813) | Quirk Books*

Sorry, Rachel, but this is what really gave me palpitations. How could anyone who loves Jane Austen's characters and prose possibly like this truly ghastly piece of drivel? It has some good lines – all written by Jane Austen and just stolen by that appalling creature Seth Grahame-Smith. Pistols at dawn would be too good for him. I'd ask Vidal to simply run him through!

– Susannah Fullerton, Patroness, International Heyer Society

~ | ~

#31 –HEYER'S HOBBIES BY JENNIFER KLOESTER

Friday, August 6, 2021

A compulsive writer for most of her life, Georgette Heyer once said of herself: "I have no hobbies and play no ball-games". While the latter statement was certainly true for, despite growing up in Wimbledon, she did not play tennis, and although she sometimes walked the golf courses with Ronald and later Richard, she did not play golf. It was not true, however, that she had no hobbies. Of course, her statement was made in response to a request from one of her publishers for a biography – something Georgette loathed writing and only did so under duress! Where other authors wrote happily of their hobbies and how they loved fishing or sailing or hiking or stamp-collecting, Georgette found the sharing of such information distasteful. With the sole exception of fishing (which she had occasionally enjoyed), she did not participate in sport or see herself as someone who had "hobbies".

However, given that the dictionary defines a hobby as "an activity you do for pleasure when you are not working" then, despite her denial, Georgette Heyer actually had several different hobbies:

1. **Reading.** Georgette loved reading both fiction and non-fiction and she read widely and eclectically. Discounting the books she read in order to write her novels, she read not only the Classics including Austen, Dickens and Shakespeare, but also poetry and modern fiction, keeping up with the bestselling authors of the day such as Agatha

Christie, Somerset Maugham, Rebecca West, Margaret Kennedy, Stella Gibbons, Ivy Compton-Burnett, Alistair Maclean, E.M. Forster and Antoine Saint-Expéry, to name just a few.

2. **Letter-writing.** Despite an intense writing schedule, particularly in the first three decades of her writing life, Georgette regularly wrote letters. She cannot have ever thought of this activity as a hobby for she once told her agent that she thought her letters "peculiar" and even declared that "I write very few" – an astonishing statement given that there are over eight hundred letters extant and many of the letters she wrote are lost or destroyed. Georgette actually loved writing letters and frequently wrote as though she were speaking in a stream-of-consciousness style that is wonderfully revealing. Hobby or not it is definitely an activity for which those who love her books and want to know more about their author may be thankful!

3. **Bridge.** A popular card game and one which suited Georgette's ordered mind. She and her husband Ronald often played with friends and relatives. Although Georgette always said she only played "kitchen bridge", she loved the game and she and Ronald taught it to their son, Richard, when he was a boy. Richard went on to become a very fine competitive player and Ronald often played for stakes at his club. In the 1950s Georgette told a friend that she would "soon abandon bridge altogether, not being up to the standards now reigning in the home." She went on playing, of course, and also enjoyed games of piquet and cribbage – both of which often appear in her Regency novels.

4. **Patience (aka Solitaire).** Georgette's card game of choice when she was working out the plots of her novels. She would often sit on her Knowle sofa (upholstered in gold velvet in later years) and play complicated games of patience and think about her characters and the sorts of scenes into which she might plunge them. As she told her publisher in 1965: "I am playing a lot of patience" adding that this was a sure sign that she was "Revolving Plans for a Book!" Playing cards – as many a writer will tell you – seems to allow the mind to open to new ideas. Long before computer solitaire, Georgette Heyer was putting her pack of playing cards to good use and we have the cards to thank for many an imbroglio ending!

5. **Knitting.** It is not known exactly what Georgette Heyer knitted, only that she did so, especially when on holiday at Greywalls or when having "a quiet evening" at home alone. She knitted a good deal in 1966 after injuring her leg and finding herself spending a good deal of her time lying on the sofa. She found having to rest "a bore" but she did get "a lot of knitting done".

6. **Needlework.** This was an unexpected hobby which came about in 1955 while their chambers at Albany were being redecorated. As Georgette explained to her friends Frere and Miss Wallace:

> "I have been seized by unaccustomed energy. Did I tell you that I had re-covered an old screen? Well, I did – & it turned out to be Quite a job. But it is held to be very professional-looking, & it is certainly Rich & Magnificent. I'm recovering my chairs in beige damask [she means she's having them recovered, not that she's doing it herself!], & to add warmth & colour to the room conceived the happy notion of re-covering the screen in red & gold brocade & carrying this scheme out in new cushion-covers. So I then made covers, &, finding myself with lots of bits of silk on my hands, thought I'd use it up in a patchwork cushion. My first attempt at this work, which is fun. I've made a small cover in diamonds, & am so flushed with success that I'm doing another now in hexagons. I

really can't do much but sew with the place in this turmoil – & since I'm no needlewoman it affords me a lot of triumphant satisfaction."

The week before Christmas Georgette delivered one of the cushions to the Frere's at E.1. – their chambers at Albany – with a note: "This is a present for E.1 – so that Frere shall no longer be able to go about town telling people that the only thing Georgette Heyer can do is write frippery romances!"

7. **Jigsaws.** Georgette loved complicated jigsaws, and in 2007 I was given one of these. The story of that jigsaw complete with pictures of its progress as I put it together is the subject of next week's *Weekly Post*.

– Jennifer Kloester, Patroness, International Heyer Society

~ | ~

#32 – GEORGETTE HEYER'S JIGSAW BY JENNIFER KLOESTER

Friday, August 13, 2021

In January 2008, I travelled to England to attend Sir Richard Rougier's memorial service at the Temple Church. Richard was Georgette Heyer's only son and from our first meeting in April 2002 we had become good friends. He was always a great supporter of my research and writing endeavours: generously inviting me to stay at his home in Somerset and giving me – as he always said – *carte blanche* with his mother's notebooks, remaining manuscripts, the remnant of her library, her family photo albums and many other items of useful family ephemera such as the baby book her mother had kept for a few years after Georgette was born. Richard's memorial service was very moving and I felt privileged to be there. In the days following that final farewell to my dear friend I went down to Somerset to stay with his widow for a few days. While I was there she showed me Georgette's jigsaw puzzles in their much-loved boxes and asked me if I would like to have one.

Of course, I said yes.

I had often wondered about the jigsaws that Georgette had so much enjoyed. Richard had told me that his mother liked to puzzle them out while thinking up the plots for her books. Jigsaws and games of patience seemed to suit her remarkable brain! The author, A.S. Byatt, wrote of Georgette Heyer that, "In her private life, besides her work, she seems to have liked things that required skill, or style, or precision, from jigsaws, to cards, to complicated kitchen gadgets…" (A.S. Byatt, "The Ferocious Reticence of Georgette Heyer"). It was an astute observation, but until I actually owned and solved one, I never really understood the "jigsaw effect".

I carried that (slightly battered) gold cardboard box all the way back to Australia and spent several happy days putting it together. Last week, with only the faintest memory of the puzzle, I took out that jigsaw once again and began piecing it together for the second time. Owning and doing a jigsaw that Georgette Heyer herself had once owned and done is delightful. The jigsaw is one of the *Victory* "Gold Box" range and hard to date – though it was possibly bought in the 1950s. The box is a bit battered, but the puzzle is in excellent condition with all of its pieces and very little wear. It's plywood and very cleverly cut. It's also a genuine puzzle – as in it takes a lot of working out! Not only are there no "edge" pieces to get you started, there is also no picture on the box to guide you. The only clue is the name of the puzzle – in this case "CORNER SHOP RYE" which makes me wonder if Georgette had bought this particular puzzle during or after one of her visits to Rye in the 1950s. Or perhaps after writing *The Unknown Ajax*, which has several memorable scenes in that town.

Although it's only 500 pieces, the jigsaw is a challenging one and you have to credit the makers for their clever cunning in cutting it in such a way that many of the usual clues of colour and shape are difficult to discern. Some of the pieces are delightfully shaped into animals, birds, fish or people and it's great fun trying to figure out where these fit into the puzzle. After an hour of jigsaw puzzling (and slow progress) I returned to my desk to get on with writing my new novel. To my surprise, I found new insight into why Georgette Heyer did puzzles when working out the characters or plots for her novels.

I had always thought that she must have done this detailed working out while actually engrossed in the jigsaw. But when doing the jigsaw myself I found my brain engrossed by the pieces and the challenge of placing them – there was no room for thinking out the details of my novel. Of course, Georgette Heyer had a remarkable brain, so perhaps she was able to do what I could not. But then I made a discovery: I realised that the benefit (for me, at least) actually came *after* spending time on the puzzle. It was as if the challenge of working out the jigsaw acted like a springboard for the brain. On returning to my desk I suddenly found myself eager to write. The words came more easily, the plot evolved a little faster and the characters spoke with unusual fluency. Was this Georgette's experience, too? If it was then her love of jigsaws and patience became clear. We'll never know for sure, but I like to think that it was this mental shift between writing and puzzling that she found so beneficial. Either way, I loved doing her puzzle, knowing that her hands had also held the pieces. It wasn't easy, but it was great fun, and like Georgette Heyer, I eventually worked it out!

– Jennifer Kloester, Patroness, International Heyer Society

~ | ~

#33 –HEYER, TRANSLATED BY RACHEL HYLAND

Friday, August 20, 2021

It should surprise no one to learn that the works of Georgette Heyer have been translated into many, many other languages. There are the expected European languages, of course – Spanish, Italian, French, Dutch. She has long been especially popular in Germany. But there are also an abundance of Heyer novels that have been translated into Finnish and Swedish, Russian and Croatian, Czech and Slovak. Not to mention Japanese, which, actually, *is* quite surprising. And wholly delightful, as well.

One can only applaud the valiant translators who attempt to convey Heyer's very English world – and words – into other forms. How does one convey Regency cant in, for example, Japanese? Try putting the word "bosky" into Google Translate and you simply get ボスキー, or "*bosukī*", which, when translated back into English, gives us the rather nonsensical "boss key." Now, of course, a professional translator is unlikely to resort to such imprecise means as the ever-evolving hivemind that is the internet, but since so much of Heyer's dialogue is replete with phrases unfamiliar to most English-speakers, and that are probably entirely absent from any other lexicon, we can only assume that sometimes they have to look up the definitions before simply inventing the equivalent pretty much out of whole cloth. (For which phrase they might also have to do that.)

Or perhaps they don't try to do so at all. After all, it is most likely that "bosky" in Japanese would be given as nothing more complex than 酔っ払い ("*yopparai*"), which means "drunk." Which is entirely beside the point—but at the same time is also exactly the point.

Let us take for example this passage from Chapter 1 of *Arabella*:

> "Bertram, is it indeed true? Now, don't try to roast me – pray don't!"
> 　　"Lord, yes! But who told you?"
> 　　"Harry, of course," replied Sophia. "The children know everything in this house!"
> 　　Mr. Bertram Tallant nodded gloomily, and pulled up his sleeve a trifle. "You don't want him in here: shall I turn him out?" he enquired.
> 　　"Ho!" cried Harry, leaping to his feet, and squaring up to his senior in great good humour. "A mill!"

And now let's look at it in the 1950 Colleccion "La Nave" Spanish translation of *Arabella*, the earliest one we know about:

> —Bertram! ¿Es cierto, de veras? Oye, no te burles de mi…, te lo suplico.
> 　　—¡ Dios del Cielo, pues claro que es cierto! Pero ¿quién os lo ha dicho?"
> 　　—¿Quién quieres que fuse? Harry—contestó Sofia—. Lon niños son siempre los que se enteran primero de todo en esta casa.
> 　　Mr. Bertram Tallant asintío con un gesto sombrío de cabeza, molesto de que le hubiesen estropeado la noticia. Luego se estiró los puños levemente, y dijo:
> 　　—Esta estorbando aqui, ¿verdad? ¿Queréis que le eche?
> 　　—¡ Oh! —exclamó Harry, dando un brinco y haciendo una mueca de burla a su hermano— . ¡Ya serà menos!

The period terms we particularly want to look at there are "roast," "turn him out" and "mill." How has our intrepid translator dealt with those?

- "Now, don't try to roast me": *Oye, no te burles de mi* = "Hey, don't make fun of me."
- "Shall I turn him out?": *¿Queréis que le eche?* = "Do you want me to kick him out?"
- "A mill!": *¡Ya serà menos!* = (lit.) "It will be less!" (In context, more along the lines of: "I'd like to see you try!")

Of course, the flavours of any language cannot be understood by simple word-for-word comparison, but nevertheless this short passage is indicative of just how much of the nuance and yet precision of Heyer's period English – in particular – must necessarily go missing when the words and concepts are essentially untranslatable. The general vibe is there, but half of the appeal of Heyer is in her complete, almost unparalleled facility with the English language, so one can't help but feel that those who read her works in other forms are somehow being cheated out of experiencing their true splendour. The same can be said for any writer whose works are translated, of course, from Homer to Tolstoy to Laozi, but with Heyer the way she puts sentences together, and the particular era-appropriate synonyms and euphemisms she uses, just seem crucially important to the overall experience, don't they?

Meanwhile, along with these many translations often come the translated – and altered – titles, and that is where things can get very entertaining.

Frederica, for instance, is known variously as *Debutantes* (*Debiutantki*, Polish), *Marriage Mart* (*Heiratsmarkt*, German) and *Frederica's First Love* (Japanese).

Lady of Quality can also be found as *The Lady of My Heart* (*De liefde van een lady*, Dutch), *Chaperone* (*Przyzwoitka*, Polish), and *A Season in Bath* (*Una stagione a Bath*, Italian).

False Colours is *Swapped Twins* (Japanese), *Under False Flag* (*Under falsk flagg*, Swedish) and *For the Love of Cressy* (*Pour l'amour de Cressy*, French).

The Talisman Ring is *The Brazen Ingenue* (*L'ingénue effrontée*, French), *Happiness Ring* (*Onnensormus*, Finnish) and *Three Engagements* (*Verlobung zu dritt,* German).

Regency Buck is *Love and Defiance* (*Láska a vzdor*, Czech), *Unbearable Lord* (*Talumatu lord*, Estonian – truth!) and *Virgins' Trap* (*Die Jungfernfalle*, German). (!!!)

And *These Old Shades* is known as *This Wonderful Past* (*Ce merveilleux passé*, French), *The Pawn Exchanged* (*La pedina scambiata*, Italian), and *Duke's Protégé*, (*Hertigens skyddsling*, Swedish). Rumour has it that *These Old Shades* is also known as *The Decision Between Love and Revenge* in Mandarin – which is just excellent! – though a copy of this translation, apparently published in the 1980s, has so far proved impossible to find.

Cotillion, meanwhile, is known as *Lady's Choice* (*Damenwhal*, German), and there are two competing Russian versions, *The Marriage of Kitty* and *Innocent Deception*.

Indeed, there are some truly fascinating Russian titles for the novels, like *Love Test* for *Simon the Coldheart*; *Education of the Senses* for *Friday's Child*; *Confusion of Feelings* for *A Civil Contract;* and one version of *The Corinthian* is known in Russian, somewhat confusingly, as *Disastrous Passion*. Check out the cover for it! [Left.] Very misleading indeed.

Almost as misleading as the title *Insidious Seducer* for *Sylvester*. Say what you will about that man, but "seducer" seems uncalled for. "Insidious"… well, maybe. (That title would have worked fine for *Devil's Cub*, though.)

The mystery novels certainly have some unusual rebrandings, too, such as the Japanese version of *Death in the Stocks*, which, when translated literally into English, means *Gentleman and Moonlit Night Exposed Table*. (In Czech is it is known as the far more apt *Nobody Has an Alibi*). Also apt, not to mention perhaps overly literal, is the Polish version of *Envious Casca,* known as *A Crime on Christmas Eve*, and again Russian translators can only make us marvel at them, as that language's version of *Detection Unlimited* is given as *Who Got in the Way of Sampson Warrenby?,* and its version of *No Wind of Blame* is *It's Not Fair to Kill Like That!* (Which could be the title of any detective novel, really.)

Regardless of translation accuracy, title changes and dubious covers – oh, the covers! – however, we can only be grateful for the worldwide interest so roused by the enduring success of Georgette Heyer's novels across the last century that so many publishing houses across the globe have gone to the trouble to make them available to speakers of so many different languages. But have they gone far enough? How about Heyer in Korean, or Swahili, or Tamil? Heyer in Arabic, or Xhosa, or Bahasa? And more in Mandarin, of course, (assuming here that the aforementioned version of *These Old Shades* is not a mere urban legend). The more readers who can access the works of Georgette Heyer, the better.

Even if they are sometimes published with titles like *Forbidden Desires*. Take a guess which of Heyer's novels this Russian attempt applies to.

You are probably wrong.

– Rachel Hyland, Patroness, International Heyer Society

~ | ~

#34 – THE HISTORICAL NOVEL PRIZE IN MEMORY OF GEORGETTE HEYER BY SUSANNAH FULLERTON

Friday, August 27, 2021

From 1978 to 1989, The Bodley Head and Corgi Books sponsored a competition for an historical novel in memory of Georgette Heyer. What a lovely way of paying tribute to a wonderful writer, was my first thought about this competition, but I have now thought more deeply about the award and must admit to having some doubts.

The first winner of the prize in 1978 was the novel *Gallows Wedding* by Rhona Martin. It is described as "a dark novel of witchcraft and forbidden love set against the backdrop of religious upheaval in Henry VIII's times" – that description and the rather lurid cover seem to promise a novel more in the style of the Brontës than that of Heyer. However, I opened the book and began to read…

The very name of Georgette Heyer conjures up images of something light, bright and sparkling. Her name leads us to expect humour, witty dialogue and a cast of entertaining minor characters. You don't find any such things in *Gallows Wedding*. To be fair, the competition did not demand an imitation of Heyer's style in its rules. It was a contest for the publishers to discover new writing talent in the historical fiction genre. However, I felt something a little more cheerful could perhaps have been chosen as the inaugural winner. (**MAJOR SPOILERS FOR *GALLOWS WEDDING* FOLLOW**)

The heroine of this novel is called Hazel. Her father is killed, her mother (about to give birth to her thirteenth child) is accused of being a witch and, while struggling to give birth, is tortured and hanged. The baby drops from her body and is hurled into the fire that the villagers have lit. Hazel has to flee. She is then robbed, half-starved, raped and left pregnant. By chance she finds herself in a town where a hanging is about to take place. The outlaw Black John is the unfortunate gallows-victim. Hazel, however, decides to marry him (a gallows wedding saved the victim from his fate) and throws in her lot with John and his horse, Black Man. She gives birth to her son in a cave, and proceeds to fall in love with Black John. It turns out that he is actually a Cornish Lord, deprived of his rightful inheritance and determined to regain it. With Hazel's help, he secretly enters his ancestral home to get proof that he is the rightful heir. At last, I thought, poor Hazel will get a little bit of security and comfort and will find herself a Lady of the Manor. But … no such luck. I didn't think things could get much worse for this benighted heroine, but they do.

It turns out John is legally married, though his wife, thinking him dead, has wed the usurper. John's attempts to claim his inheritance fail disastrously and he is arrested. Hazel, like her mother, is branded a witch and is being tortured with hot metal rods. John is, once again, about to be hanged. Seeing Hazel and realising that he really does love her, he breaks free of his bonds, leaps from the tumbril and joins her. Gathering her into his arms and knowing escape is hopeless, he then snaps her neck to save her from the horrors of the burning. He himself then dies in agony and with "the stench of his own entrails". The stunned reader is left at the end of the book with every nice character dead (even the horse!) and only the loathsome characters still alive. This is NOT a book to be read during Covid. If you felt depressed at the beginning, you'll be in a truly dire state by the end. I'd always thought that Thomas Hardy's *Jude the Obscure* was the most depressing book in the English language, but *Gallows Wedding* can give it a good run for its money.

After reading the above, I'm sure you'll agree with me that anything less like the comforting, happy novels of Georgette Heyer it would be hard to imagine. It seems to me ironic that its cover should bear her name. There is good historical detail in the book and Rhona Martin's style is well-paced and convincing – I guess it was those things that won her the prize – but the plot was simply too dark, bleak, tragic and violent. As Black John is old enough to be Hazel's father, and she is about fourteen years old, the book also disturbed me with its (by today's standards) paedophilic romance. What Georgette would have made of this novel, I shudder to think.

After surviving my reading of *Gallows Wedding* (just!), I was not surprised to learn that almost none of the past winners of the Georgette Heyer Prize are still in print. Indeed, most seem to have virtually disappeared from sight, which makes one question the success of a project whose aim was to showcase new talent. All the books were debut novels. Perhaps it might have been safer and more worthwhile had the competition selected second or third books by writers who had already proven themselves able to attract readers? However, it should be noted that most of the authors did go on to write more fiction, and Norah Lofts and Susan Kay both became bestselling authors. The prize was being offered before social media could spread the word, yet seemed to attract a good number of entries. Perhaps today, with word being spread on-line, there could simply be too many entries for a group of judges to reasonably manage.

Here are the other books that won: *The Day of the Butterfly* by Norah Lofts (1979), *Children of Hachiman* by Lynn Guest (1980), *Zemindar* by Valerie Fitzgerald (1981), no award in 1982, *Queen of the Lightning* by Kathleen Herbert (1983), *The Terioki Crossing* (in the USA it was known as *The Three Passions of Countess Natalya*) by Alan Fisher (1984), *Legacy* by Susan Kay (1985), *The Cage* by Michael Weston (1986), *I am England* by Patricia Wright (1987), *Trust and Treason* by Margaret Birkhead (1988), and *A Fallen Land* by Janet Broomfield (1989). I have not read any of them, so do let me know if you are familiar with any? I think it is going to take me years to recover from *Gallows Wedding*, so I'm in no rush to make my way through the list.

The prize was discontinued after 1989. It seems that finding judges was a challenge, The Bodley Head was sold in the 1980s and no longer existed in the same form. There is still today a Sir Walter Scott Prize for Historical Fiction (a suitable choice, as it was Scott who made historical fiction both popular and respectable in Britain). But how much do literary prizes really count? A quick look at Booker winners from past decades reveals many novels I've never even heard of, let alone read. I don't tend to select a book to read because it has won the Sir Walter Scott Prize, or any other prize, for that matter. I have other criteria and prefer to do my own 'judging'.

– Susannah Fullerton, Patroness, International Heyer Society

~ | ~

#35 – THE ROMANCE OF RUDENESS BY RACHEL HYLAND

Friday, September 3, 2021

With the focus of this month's *Nonpareil* on *Why Shoot a Butler?*, naturally one's mind must turn to Georgette Heyer's tendency towards romanticizing rudeness. More than this, she somehow makes us love the rudest of gentlemen and want only happiness for them, despite the misery their sharp tongues so often inflict upon others.

In the case of *Why Shoot a Butler?*, of course, this rudeness is perpetrated by Frank – and rarely has a hero been so aptly named – Amberley, the brilliant barrister who happens upon a murder and ends up in love with its chief suspect. (Although only he knows she *is* the chief suspect.) Throughout the novel his rudeness is mentioned again and again, and we even see that he is little liked due to his magnificent disregard of the most basic of courtesies, but it doesn't seem to worry him any. In fact, he seems to take pride in his near-universal unpopularity. And when his contentious relationship with Shirley, the aforementioned suspect, at last leads to a declaration of love, he holds true to his nature and says it thus:

> "I don't like you at all. You're obstinate and self-willed and abominably secretive. Your manners are atrocious, and you're a damned little nuisance. And I rather think I worship you."

Sweet, right?

There can be no doubt that the Enemies to Lovers trope has long been enduringly popular in romantic fiction, with Jane Austen's *Pride and Prejudice* leading the vanguard into the genre as we know it today. Stories of snarkily bantering leads whose often instant attraction to one another is either heralded or disguised by their evident dislike populate the romance landscape, whether on page, stage or screen, and Georgette Heyer gives us several glittering examples of the form told remarkably well.

What Heyer does that so few authors manage to accomplish as effectively is to give us a completely satisfying redemption of our hero, whose often brusque manner is so frequently the reason for the enmity between the couple in the first place. The stern Charles Rivenhall's dictatorial attitude to his cousin Sophy kicks off their book-long feud; Max Ravenscar's outright insults ultimately lead to his own imprisonment by the slighted Deb Grantham; Lord Rotherham's thoughtless tirades make him seem an impossible match to, and for, Lady Serena Carlow; and Simon of Beauvallet holding a sword to her throat hardly endears him to the proud Lady Margaret Belrémy. But by the end of each of their narratives, we see that Charles and Sophy will be very content arguing their way through life together; that Max was smitten by Deb from the outset, and it was his disappointment in learning her identity that made him so cruel; that Rotherham is the only one who could ever be a match for Serena (and, frankly, that they deserve each other); and that Simon would rather die, or worse, bring trouble to his beloved king, than see even a single hair harmed on Lady Margaret's queenly head.

These four are among Heyer's less courtly heroes, but we nevertheless cheer for their happy endings. How much more, then, do we cheer for the successful courtships of their more debonair brethren, who are nevertheless just as facile with a cutting comment—perhaps, even more so?

Take Justin Alastair, Duke of Avon. One hesitates to call him rude, but at the same time, he is hardly nicely, or even kindly, spoken – he is no Freddy Standen, or Kit Fancot, or Gilly Ware. He wins us over with his ready wit, but so much of that wit is employed at the expense of others; just because he has an elegant suavity that is lacking in, say, Frank Amberley, and is entirely absent in his own son, the Marquis of Vidal (much as we may love Dominic, his brash outlandishness is a far different proposition from his smooth-tongued father), it does not mean that he, too, is not an example of Heyer's rudest of heroes. What may make him even worse is that his level of rudeness is mostly born out of a sense of superiority and a lifetime of entitled *ennui*, echoes of which can be found in the Marquis of Alverstoke and Lord Damerel, and certainly in Mr. Beaumaris, who even chooses to direct his hurtful remarks towards a rescued stray dog.

But if we are talking about Heyer's rudest romantic heroes, the Bath-visiting, spinster-wooing duo of Miles Calverleigh and Oliver Carleton must surely be at the top of anyone's list. These two take this "mark" of Heyer hero to its very extreme, as they both show no regard for convention, no compunction about their use of language, and no delicacy when it comes to conversational topics. They all-but attack with their words, and alternately send the independent ladies of means with whom they become enamoured – Abigail Wendover and Annis Wychwood, respectively – into paroxysms of outrage, confusion and amusement just by being so very different than anyone else either has ever encountered. This is not to suggest that Miles and Oliver are exactly the same character, though they are the closest kin of any of Heyer's leading men (just as *Black Sheep* and *Lady of Quality* bear the strongest resemblance to each other, as novels). But they do both start their books at odds with their ladies; both eventually win them over with their idiosyncratic views of the world; both declare themselves rather too bluntly, and perhaps prematurely; and both remain forthright almost to the point of open hostility all the way to the very end.

And yet we love them. Heyer makes us love them, in all of their flawed flawlessness—them, and her other comparatively rude heroes. We see our heroines match their wits against these powerful, razor-sharp minds, and often come out victorious; we see lofty egos brought low, humbled by their own need (Sylvester, this one is especially for you); and we see emotional honesty, on both sides, as the veneer of civilization is stripped away through anger, and resentment and fear, and all of that general discourtesy turns into empathy, and comfort with one another, and love. In many ways, being rude can be accounted the same thing as telling the truth (or, as *Buffy*'s Cordelia once put it, "Tact is just not saying true stuff"), and while sometimes the truth can hurt, wound and even scar, other times it can lead to deep understanding.

Which is a truth about humanity that Georgette Heyer understood very well indeed.

– Rachel Hyland, Patroness, International Heyer Society

~ | ~

#36 – THE GEORGETTE HEYER UNCONFERENCE BY KIM WILKINS

Friday, September 10, 2021

Georgette Heyer: A Century Spent Having a Ball. An Unconference, February 25, 2021

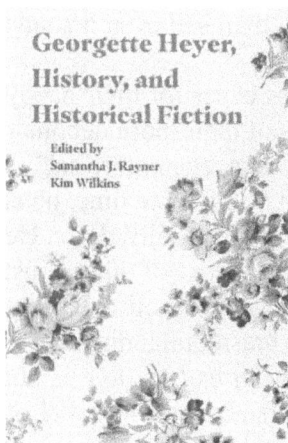

This is a story about two friends who met at a conference about medievalism, discovered they both loved Georgette Heyer, and had a crazy dream of running a series of events in London based around Heyer's work. This was in 2015. Fast forward to 2018, and that dream became reality in a creative writing workshop on Regency romance, an academic conference on Heyer, and a wonderful Regency-themed social evening.

The catalyst in all this was Jacks Thomas, then Director of the London Book Fair, and also great fan of Heyer's novels. With her enthusiasm and talent for Making Things Happen, everyone had a wonderful time, and some fascinating papers were produced, which eventually became *Georgette Heyer, History and Historical Fiction,* published earlier this year by UCL Press.

By this stage, it was clear that there were lots more Heyer readers out there – academics, writers, and general readers – and so, inspired again by the enthusiasm and support of Jacks, an "unconference" of online events was put together to celebrate the book's publication. Panels with writers from the book, and with other key authors (Cathy Rentzenbrink, Harriet Evans, Lois McMaster Bujold, Katie Fforde and Philippa Gregory) drew audiences from around the world; Stephen Fry did a short recording on Heyer for it, and the foremost academic expert on Heyer, Jennifer Kloester, gave a keynote on '*The Black Moth* and Beyond.' There was a panel focussing on historical novel writing, with authors Alison Goodman and Kate Forsyth, and even a podcast which explored Heyer's use of horses and carriages in her novels, which you can listen to here!

Given that this Unconference was held during the Covid-19 pandemic, when there was a great deal to feel anxious about, and plenty of personal and professional challenges to deal with, it was truly wonderful to connect to so many other Heyer enthusiasts and discuss what makes her such an effective comfort read during times of stress. Collaborating on all these Heyer events together has not felt like work, and we've been extremely lucky to "have a ball" of our own in producing them!

And now, in a year which also sees the hundredth anniversary of the publication of Heyer's first novel, *The Black Moth*, we're thrilled to be able to take part in the International Heyer Society's first HeyerCon, and continue to expand our Heyer knowledge and networks!

– Kim Wilkins, Guest Contributor

~ | ~

#37 – ON THE FOLIO SOCIETY, AND GEORGETTE HEYER BY RACHEL HYLAND

Friday, September 17, 2021

In 1947, three idealistic and/or enterprising English publishers got together to found the Folio Society, a mission steeped in bibliomania. The Second World War had just ended, and following the austerity and deprivation of those years and their immediate aftermath, what these visionaries wanted was to showcase how *beautiful* the printed word could be. The books were to be hardcover and gilded and lusciously illustrated; eventually they came to be picked out in silver and in gold, and would often arrive housed in elegant slip covers.

These were books for people who love books.

Folio's stated aim was "To produce editions of the world's great literature, in a format worthy of the contents, at a price within the reach of everyman." Despite rationing still being in effect – paper was in particularly short supply at the time – and the skepticism of booksellers who doubted that luxury editions of classic titles would indeed be attractive to the "everyman", the Folio Society nevertheless launched in October of that year, enticing subscribers from around the world with their gorgeous editions of classic works, both famous and near-forgotten.

The first outing was *Tales by Tolstoy*, a collection of short stories by the Russian master, now a rare collector's item ardently sought by bibliophiles everywhere. Each month a new, specially selected, title followed – November 1947 saw *Trilby* by George du Maurier; December 1947 saw a translation of the anonymous c.12th-Century French romance, *Aucassin et Nicolette*. And as the decades passed, the luminous line-up of monthly offerings brought forth names like Voltaire, Trollope, Melville, Brontë, Thackeray, Austen, Dickens, Wilde, Defoe, Collins, Chaucer, and more than a little Shakespeare, of course. The list goes on, and on, and on.

The list, however, does not include the name of Georgette Heyer. At no point in Folio's more than sixty-year history has a Heyer title found its way into their library.

Until now.

The book they have chosen to honour (first, we can only hope) is *Venetia*, and, in a sneak peek so sneaky that the website address listed here isn't even live yet – because their publication of *Venetia* hasn't hit Folio's website, as of this writing – *we* get to see what it will look like.

And, frankly, it is *stunning*.

Look at it! Over there to the right! Isn't it incredible?

I want it so badly!

Who are the people in the illustration, you may wonder? From left we have: Aubrey Lanyon; Venetia Lanyon; Charlotte, Lady Lanyon; and, on the stairs, what is most likely her ambitious mother, Mrs. Scorrier. The art is as pretty and as thoughtful as the book

FOLIOSOCIETY.COM/VENETIA   The Folio Society

153

itself, and this is just one of several that grace its pages.

It is, indeed, "a format worthy of the contents."

Of course, many readers of Georgette Heyer will wonder at the long delay in suitably recognising her work in this way. Our own Jennifer Kloester, arguably the world's strongest advocate for the enduring literary value of Heyer, has been campaigning Folio to release a special edition of one of her novels – one of her suggestions: *An Infamous Army*, in honour of the 200th anniversary of Waterloo back in 2015 – for more than a decade. But a few factors have to be considered before we cry foul at this seemingly long overdue tribute.

First, copyright. A quick look through Folio's extensive back catalogue shows that no royalties were payable for any of their titles for many, many decades. (And they still publish a lot that is out of copyright, of course.) Second, throughout most of the 20th-century they published no more than twenty titles in a twelvemonth. Moreover, for a quarter century of the company's existence, Georgette Heyer was still releasing new titles. Even after her death in 1974, at the age of 71, she would still have been considered a recent author for many years to come. Then – and this may be the main reason that seeing her name on a Folio edition has taken so inordinately long – the name Georgette Heyer started to become synonymous with "pulp" Romance, her comedies of manners and social satires and serious historical fiction all somehow conflated with the works of her imitators, the covers chosen by the likes of US publishers Bantam, Berkley and Signet not exactly helping.

Indeed, the effect was basically the opposite of a Folio Society publication.

Now, as an avid reader of Romance, I don't personally consider it a problem to see such works being enshrined in pretty hardcover editions, illustrated and picked out in silver and gold and housed in elegant slipcovers. It is fiction (mostly) by women (mostly) for women, and as such has just as much right as any other genre to be considered worthy of notice and acclaim. But not everyone agrees, and the *literati* of decades past definitely had strong opinions on Great Literature vs. Popular Literature, a dismissive attitude that we who love Heyer know all too well. Meanwhile, it should be noted that there is not much in the way of Western or Science Fiction in the formative annals of Folio, either. (Those other popular "pulp" classes that have nevertheless found respectability earlier than Romance – because more men traditionally write and read them, no doubt.)

All of that has now changed, however. In these twenty-first century days, the Folio Society has found a new *raison d'être* – producing heart-stopping versions of worldwide favourites, like *Game of Thrones* and *Jurassic Park* and the books of Roald Dahl, in addition to their signature "great literature" vocation, with both *The Divine Comedy* and *The Great Gatsby* part of their current booklist. And in an era unimagined by Folio's founders, when the "everyman" – read: everyone – has ready access to ALL THE BOOKS all the time, these premium editions are still very much sought after, even if the price is, perhaps, no longer exactly within the reach of all.

But, no matter what the cost, I know I am only one of many who cannot wait to get my hands on a copy of this new, glorious printing of *Venetia*. I know I am only one of many who is delighted to see Georgette Heyer properly acknowledged – at last! – by this prestigious and well-deserved mark of favour.

If only we hadn't had to wait so long.

– Rachel Hyland, Patroness, International Heyer Society

~ | ~

#38 – DISPATCHES FROM HEYERCON – DAY 1 BY JENNIFER KLOESTER

Friday, September 24, 2021

A wonderful time was had by all who attended last Sunday's online HeyerCon I: *Soirée*. For those fortunate enough to have attained a voucher admitting them into the hallowed precincts of the Zoom webinar, wondrous entertainments awaited. New arrivals were asked about their favourite Heyer novel and – unsurprisingly – the answers were many and varied, ranging from the adored *Devil's Cub* and *These Old Shades* to *Cotillion*, *Friday's Child*, *Sylvester*, *The Talisman Ring* and *Frederica* among others. *April Lady* was a surprise inclusion, with an affectionate account given by a long-time Heyer fan.

A warm welcome from Patroness Susannah Fullerton and the *Soirée* was underway. Sarah Golding, the acclaimed voice actor and owner of *Quirky Voices*, read three of Georgette Heyer's letters aloud, acting the part of our Miss Heyer with a perfect plummy English accent (Sarah is English), pearls and many appropriate gestures. It was a rare treat to hear "Georgette" read her letters, especially given her habit, when writing to her agent, L.P. Moore, and her publisher, Frere, of expressing herself in a sort of stream-of-consciousness style that cannot help but give the reader – or in the case of our *Soirée*, the listener – a glorious sense of the woman and her wit. Two international bestselling authors of Regency fiction, Anne Gracie and Alison Goodman, also graced us with their presence and a reading from their works. They each acknowledged the importance of Georgette Heyer on their writing and were lavish in their praise of the iconic author. (A slight controversy over *Venetia* and Alison's response to the kittens proved highly entertaining!)

As many Heyer fans know, to date only two of her novels have made it to the cinema screen and of those the 1959 German film version of *Arabella* has rarely, if ever, been seen by her readers. Thanks to the extraordinary efforts of our Rachel Hyland, who went above and beyond to secure a copy of the elusive film *and* help in translating it, we were able to watch the first twenty-five minutes of *Bezaubernde Arabella*. This experience was hugely enriched by the subtitles so painstakingly created by Rachel and a German member of our Society, Jacqueline—without them, I doubt few of those watching would have known what was going on or understood the connection between this film and the novel we all know and love! Jacqueline's introduction was fascinating and knowing about the director, the stars and the context in which the film was made in 1959 Germany definitely enhanced the audience's experience.

After the film, several people took part in a lively "Show & Tell" where they were able to reveal special Heyer collectibles, book covers, much-loved editions and those stunning Franklin Mint statuettes of Arabella and the Grand Sophy. From eager conversation about the joys of reading Heyer, we moved to a pre-recorded film on the "Business of Heyer". Jacks Thomas, former director of the London Book Fair and current guest director of Bologna Books, engaged in a fascinating conversation about Georgette with Heyer's publishers, including Dominique Raccah from Sourcebooks and Joanna Reynolds, CEO of the Folio Society. Next month the Folio Society will release their first-ever Heyer novel with a stunning edition of *Venetia*. Jacks also spoke with

Lara Speicher, head of publishing at University College London Press, and with Sam Rayner, who spoke about their excellent academic book, *Georgette Heyer, History and Historical Fiction*, which is out now in both hard and softcover and is also available as a free digital download.

The final event of this engaging and inspiring day was a pre-filmed conversation led by Professor Kim Wilkins, who spoke with bestselling Regency authors Eloisa James and Stephanie Laurens, as well as with yours truly. It was a pleasure and a privilege to be able to talk about Heyer with these experienced, intelligent writers and to hear their take on why Heyer continues to be read one hundred years after publishing her first novel. We ended our fabulous *Soirée* with a quiz and giveaways.

At the close of a day of entrancing entertainment, I called for my carriage, bade farewell to my fellow Heyerites, and retired to ponder on the pleasures of time spent in such excellent company. Thank you to everyone who attended the festivities and to those who made the event possible, and in particular to Rachel, whose incredible hard work, vision and enthusiasm made the day such a success. I look forward to Day 2 of our Heyer Convention and hope that you will all join us to continue celebrating the Georgette Heyer Centenary.

– Jennifer Kloester, Patroness, International Heyer Society

~ | ~

#39 – HEYER BY THE NUMBERS #1 - YEARS BY RACHEL HYLAND

Friday, October 1, 2021

The time has come for us to see the work of Georgette Heyer represented in graphs, for both the common interest and for ease of reference. Let us begin with the years in which her historical novels are set... NOTE: If there is some question over the exact year, the earliest possible date has been used, and the year given is when the story commences.

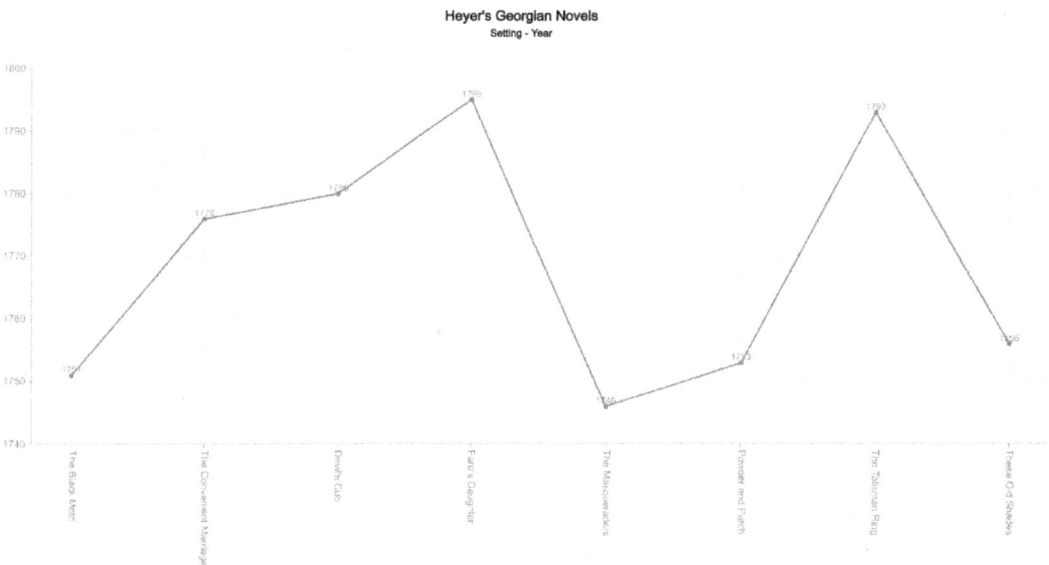

Heyer's Georgian Novels
Setting - Year

Heyer's Regency Novels
Setting - Year

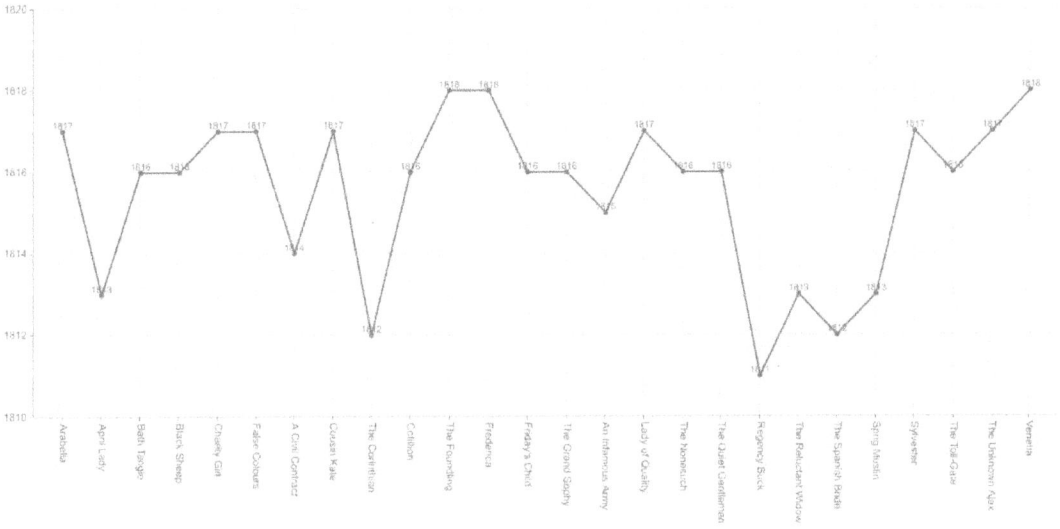

Heyer's Other Historical Novels
Setting - Year

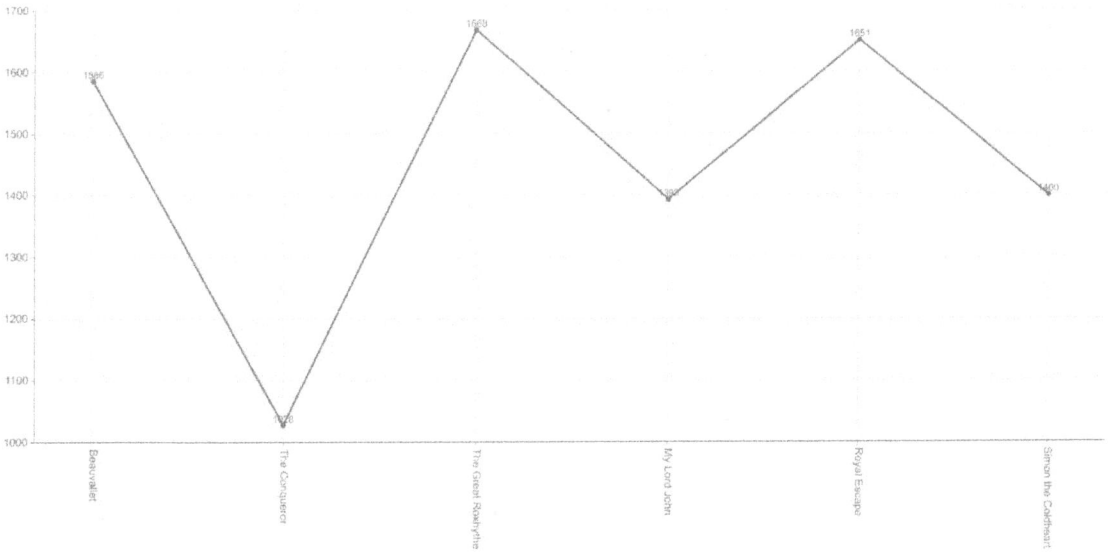

NOTE: For Georgette Heyer's contemporary novels and contemporary detective outings (with the exception of *Helen*, which begins with our heroine's birth), the novel's settings are very similar to their publication dates.

Speaking of which...

All Heyer Novels
Year Published - Alphabetical

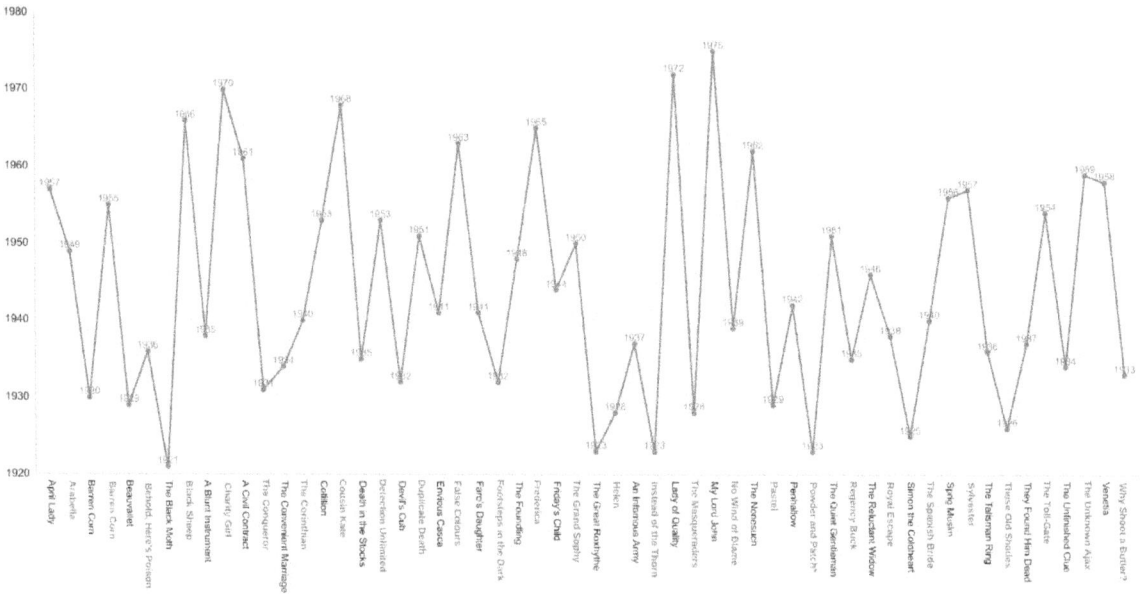

*Originally published as *The Transformation of Philip Jettan*; republished without the final chapter in 1930, and retitled *Powder and Patch*.

And here are Georgette Heyer's many novels again, this time listed in publication order...

All Heyer Novels
Year Published - Chronological

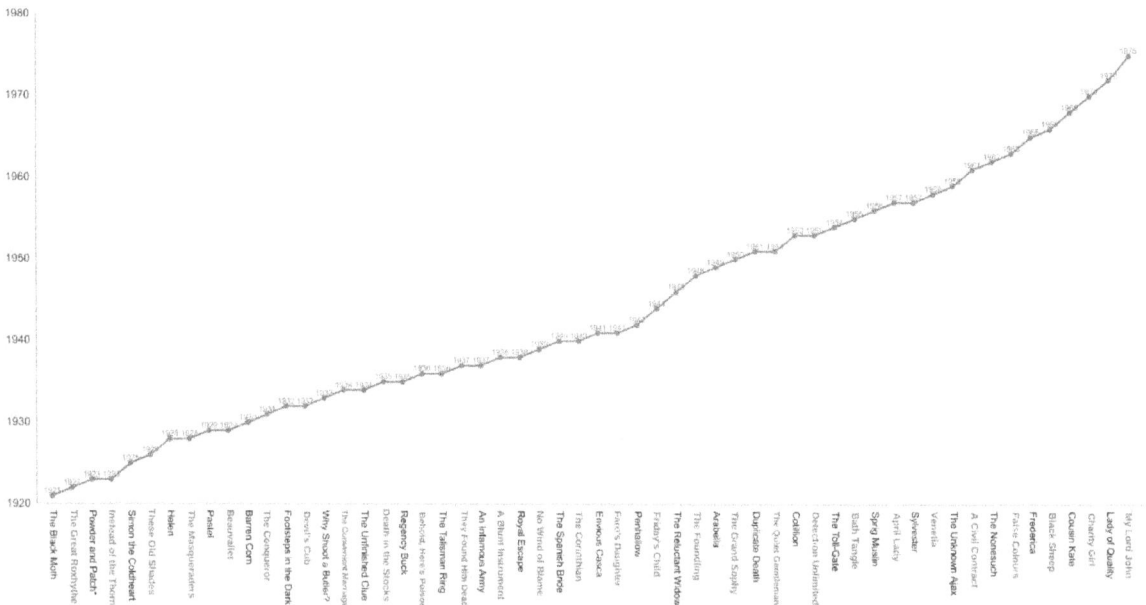

We often talk about Georgette's extraordinary output, but when you see it in a bar graph, you can really appreciate her diligence...

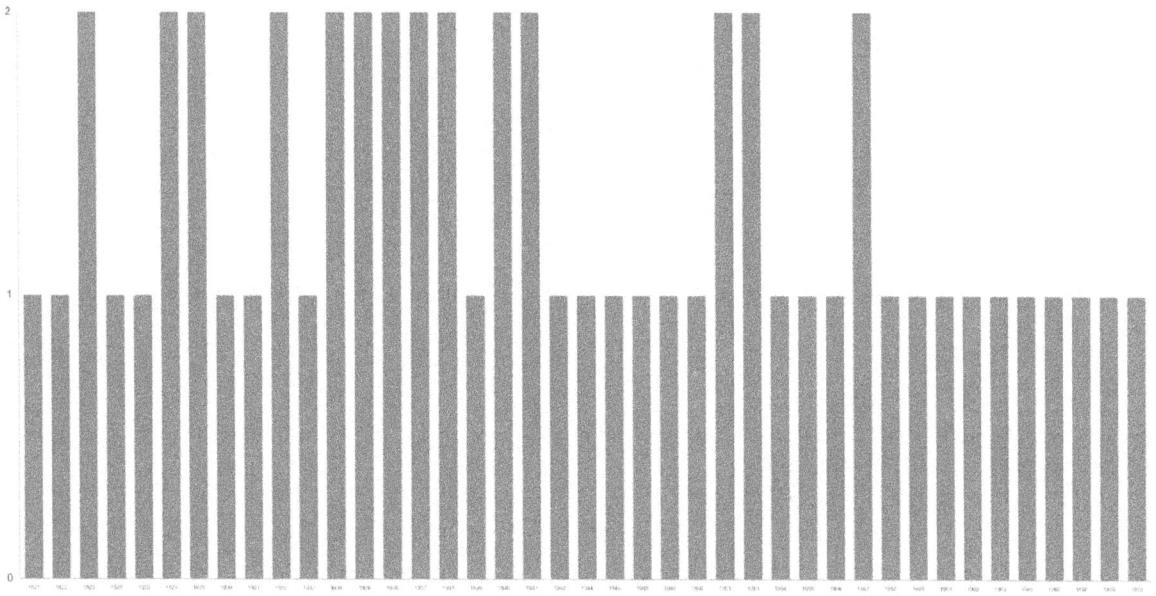

In the 51 years that she was active, there were only 11 years in which a new Georgette Heyer novel did not appear: 1924, 1927, 1943, 1945, 1947, 1952, 1960, 1964, 1967, 1969 and 1971.

Speaking of which...

Here is a graph of the publication years of her (known) short stories, in alphabetical order:

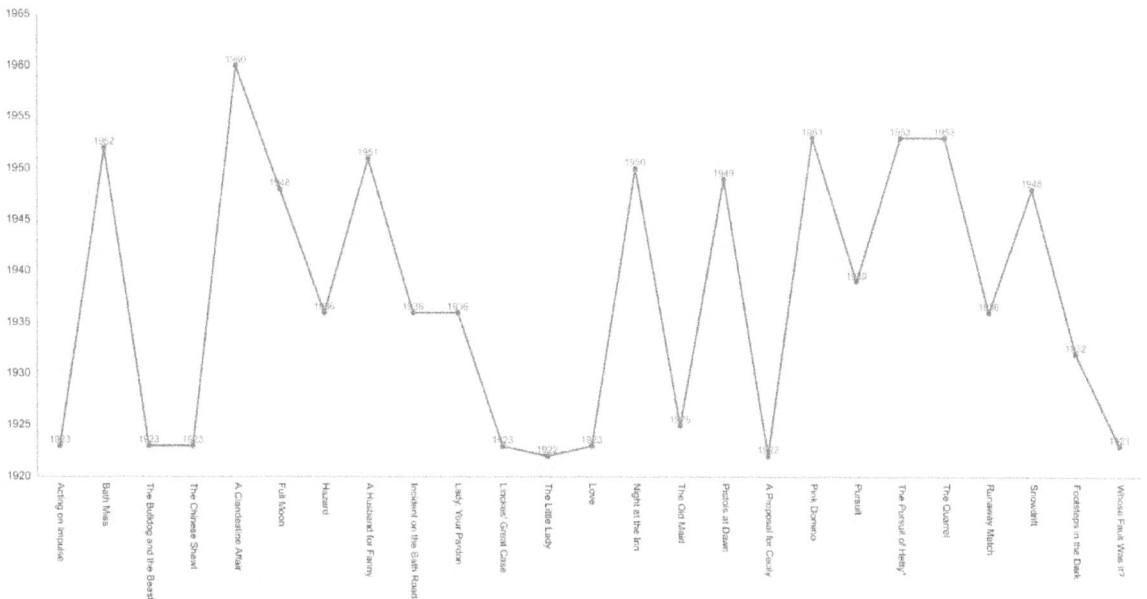

All Heyer Short Stories
Year Published - Alphabetical

But it is really when the short story data is represented in publication order that a fascinating pattern emerges...

All Heyer Short Stories
Year Published - Chronological

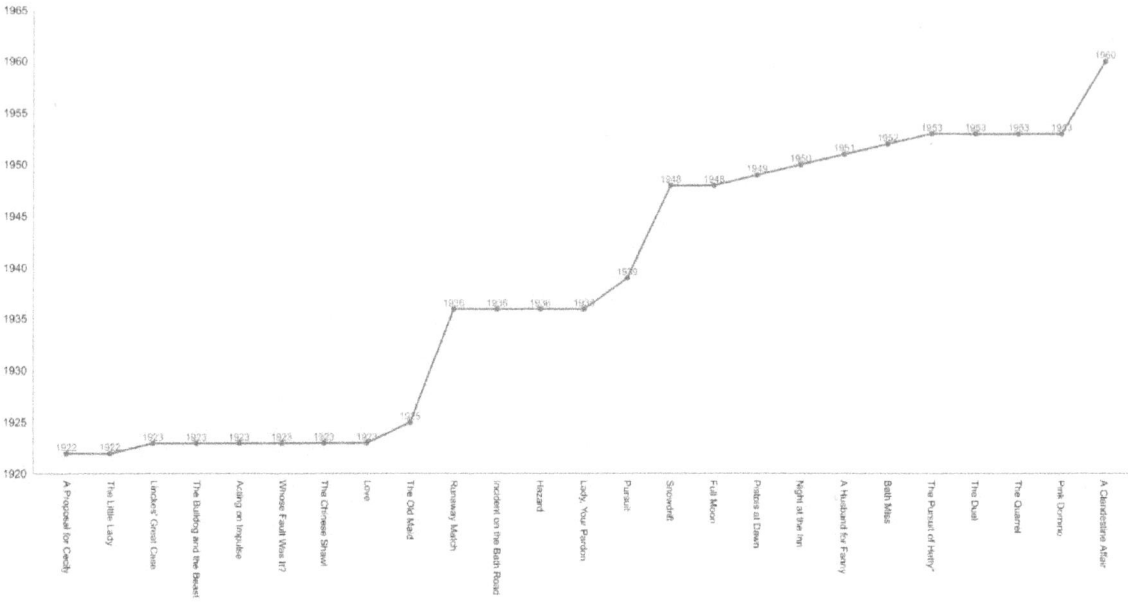

Just as interesting is the data for the stories when broken down into genres...

All Heyer Short Stories
Year Published - By Genre

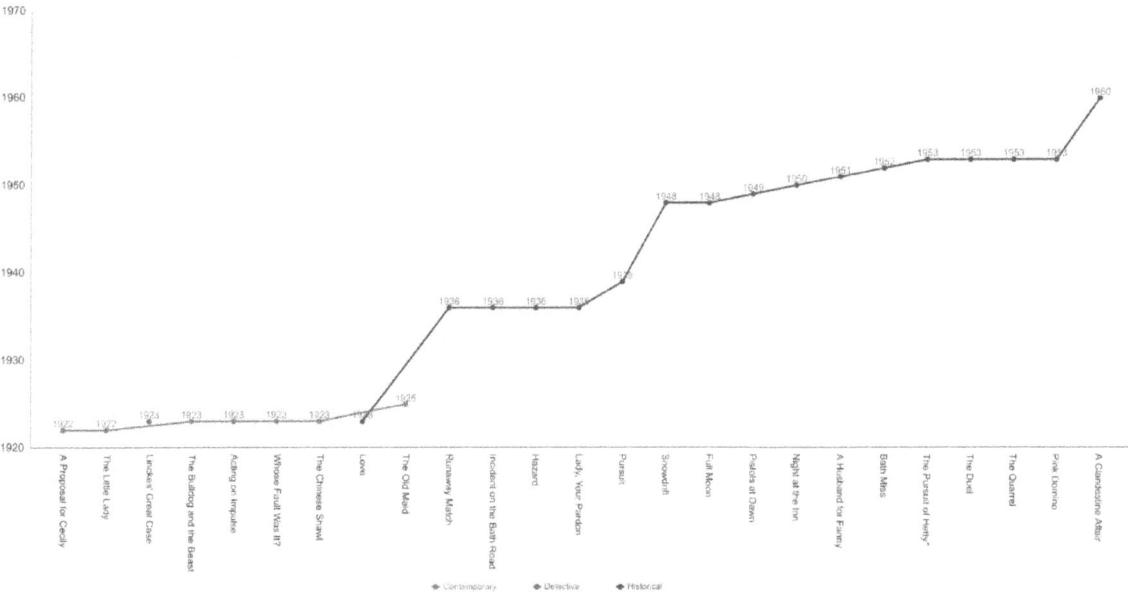

And finally, let's take a look at Heyer's novels, also broken down by publication year and genre:

All Heyer Novels
Year Published - By Genre

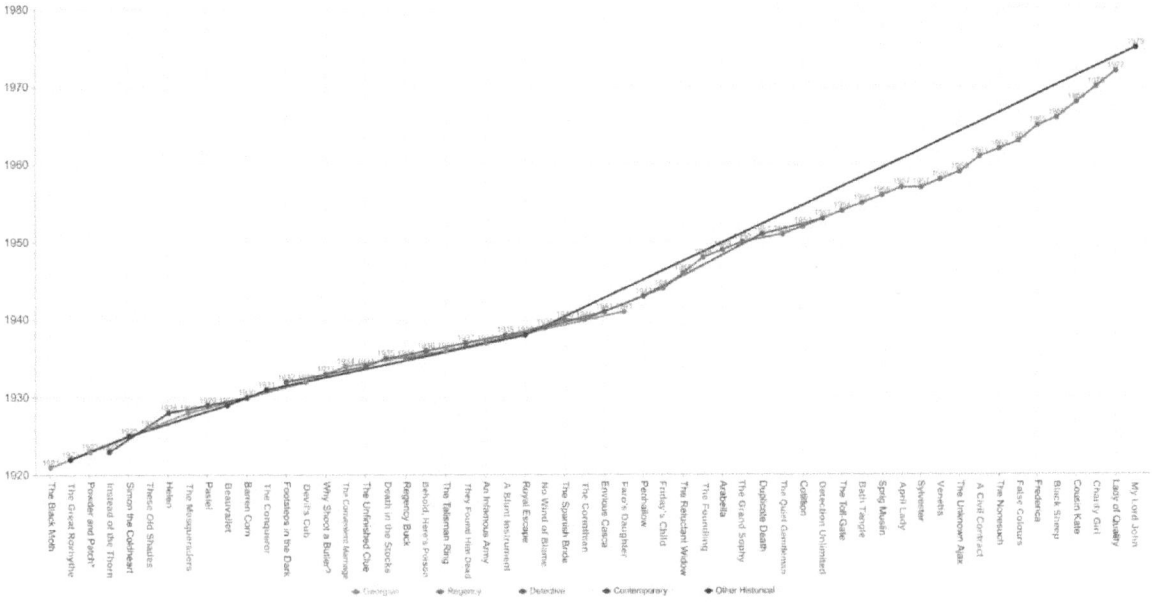

Truly remarkable! Especially that steep incline between her penultimate and final historical novels.

Next week, we will take a look at some character statistics in more Heyer by the Numbers. Brace yourselves.

– *Rachel Hyland, Patroness, International Heyer Society*

~ | ~

#40 – HEYER BY THE NUMBERS #2 - AGES BY RACHEL HYLAND

Friday, October 8, 2021

When thinking of Georgette Heyer's novels, it is hard not to think of her protagonists. The heroes and heroines around which the stories revolve are simply unforgettable, and their ages are fascinating...

Heyer Historical Romance Novels
Hero Age - Alphabetical by Novel

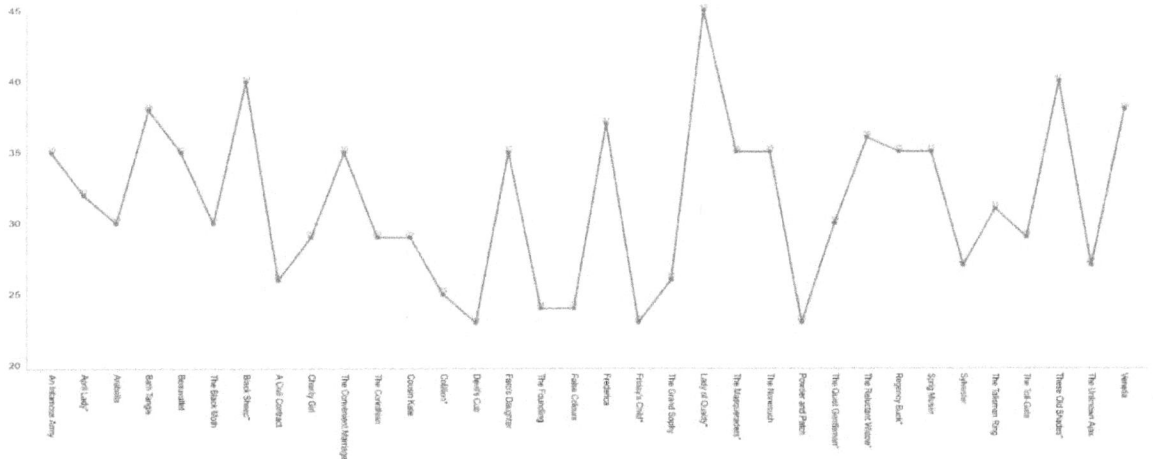

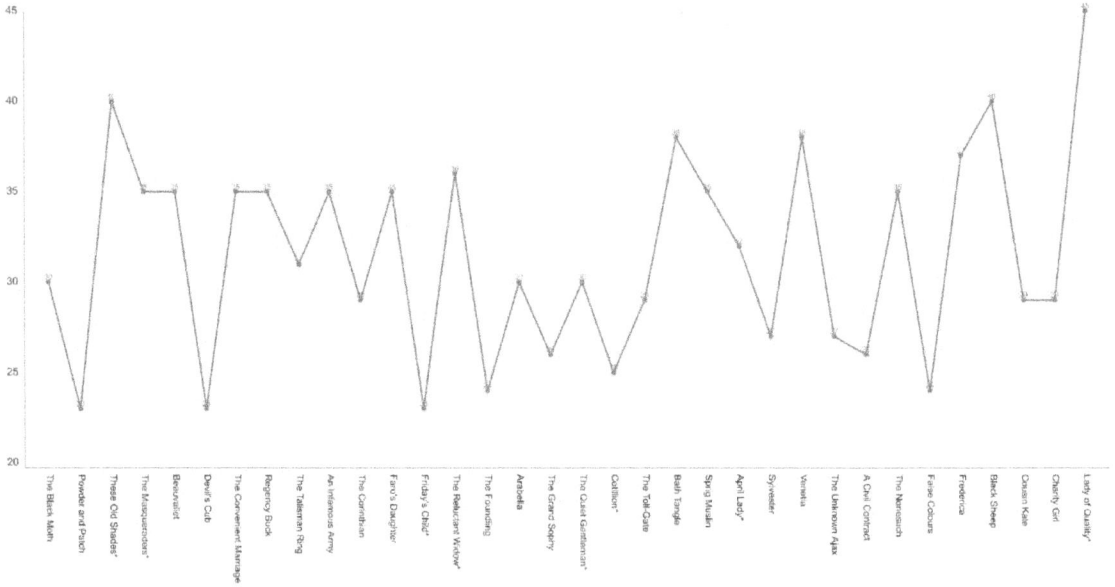

Heyer Historical Romance Novels
Hero Age - Chronological

*Age not explicitly given in the text and is worked out from context clues or characters' guesses

NOTE: If there is some question over the exact age, the earliest possible date has been used, and the age given is when the story commences.

.

No very clear pattern emerges from her heroes' ages, except we can see clearly that none of her romantic heroes is less than 20 years of age. In stark contrast to her heroines...

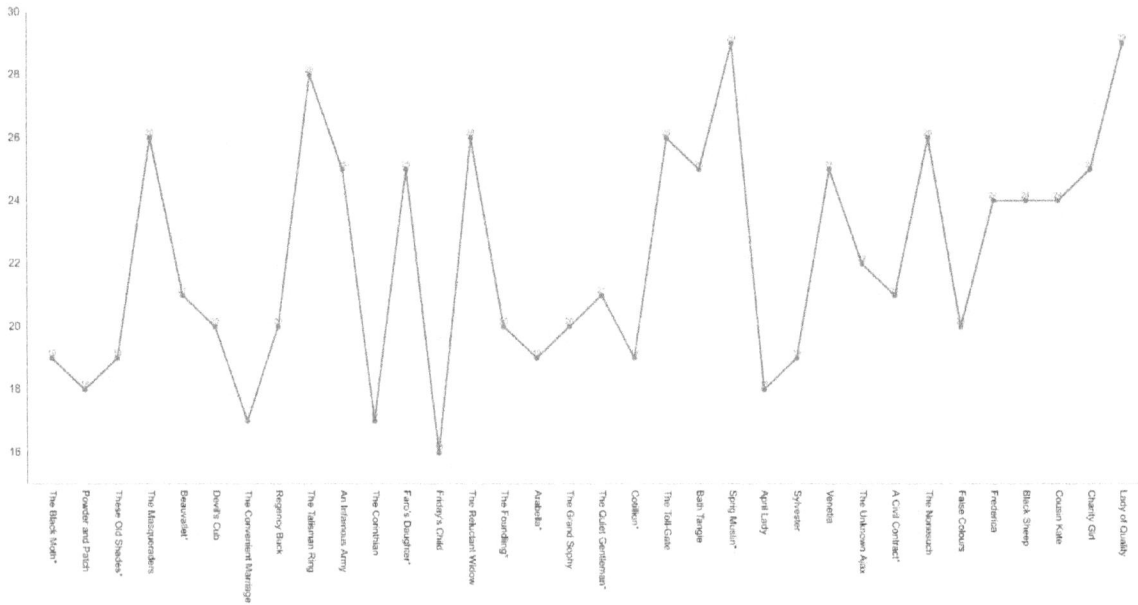

Heyer Historical Romance Novels
Year Published - Chronological

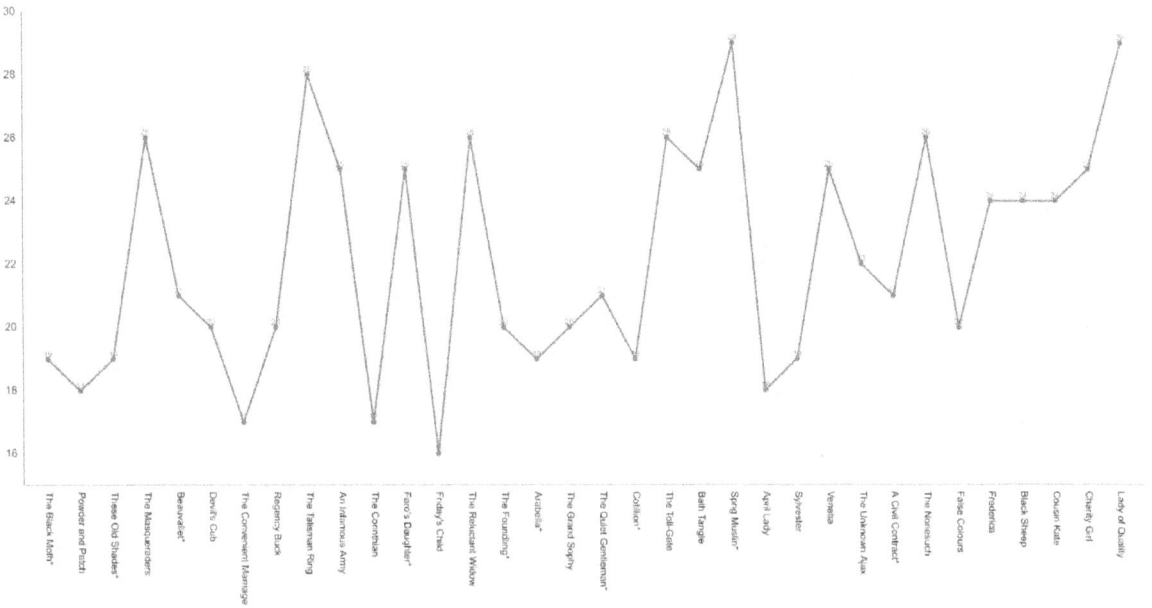

Heyer Historical Romance Novels
Year Published - Chronological

*Age not explicitly given in the text and is worked out from context clues or characters' guesses.

Rather more of a pattern emerges here, when we look at the ages of Heyer's heroines. The number of young ladies below the age of 20 is notable, as is the decided upward trend in heroine's ages when the novels are looked at in publication order. That said, there are rather more incidences of older heroines in Heyer's earlier novels than might have been otherwise suspected until the information is presented so clearly.

But how many of heroes and heroines did she have at each age? First, her heroes:

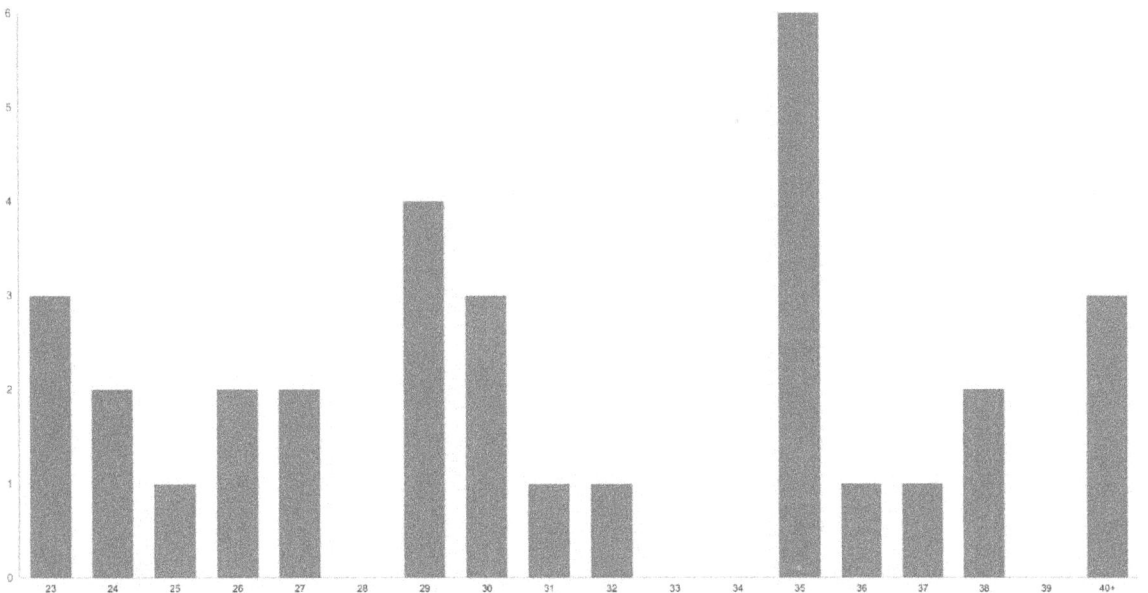

Heyer Historical Romance Novels
Hero Ages

Looking at this data, we can see that she had a clear preference for 35-year-old men...

Heyer Historical Romance Novels
Heroine Ages

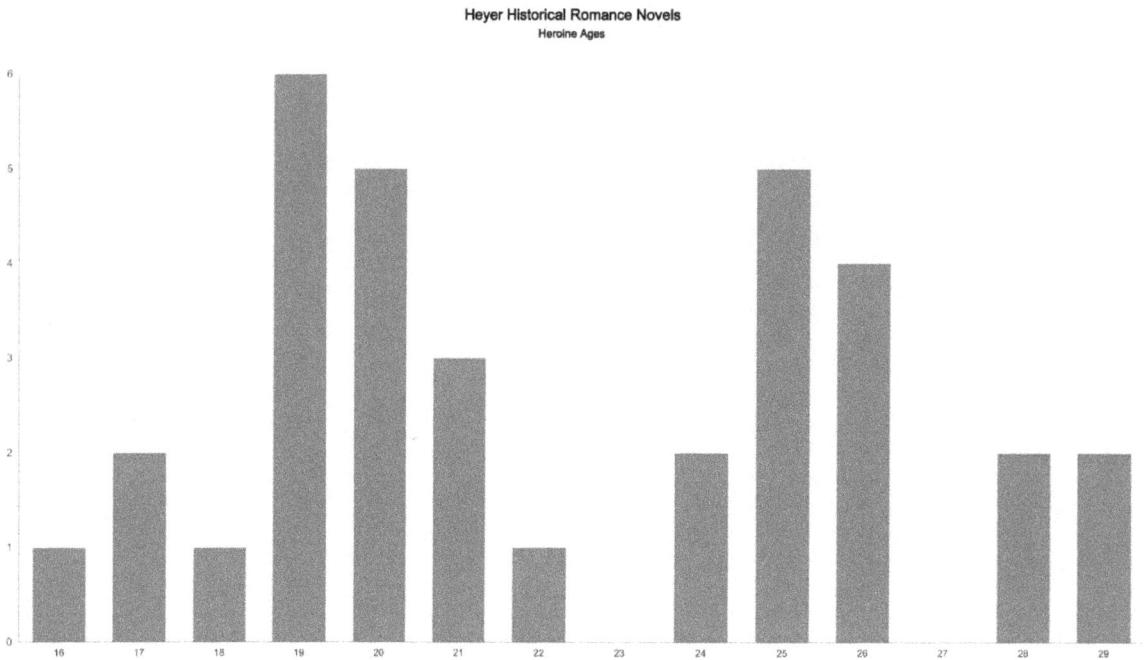

... and it seems she tended to favour 19- and 20-year-old women.

However, this exact combination is only seen in *Regency Buck* and *Beauvallet* (and even then we're only speculating, as Lord Worth's age is worked out through context and Dominica y Rada de Sylva's age is total guesswork.) And there are only a couple of other pairings with a specifically 15- or 16-year age gap.

Let's look at those age gaps now. Couple age gaps by novel, alphabetically...

Heyer Historical Romance Novels
Couple Age Difference - Alphabetical

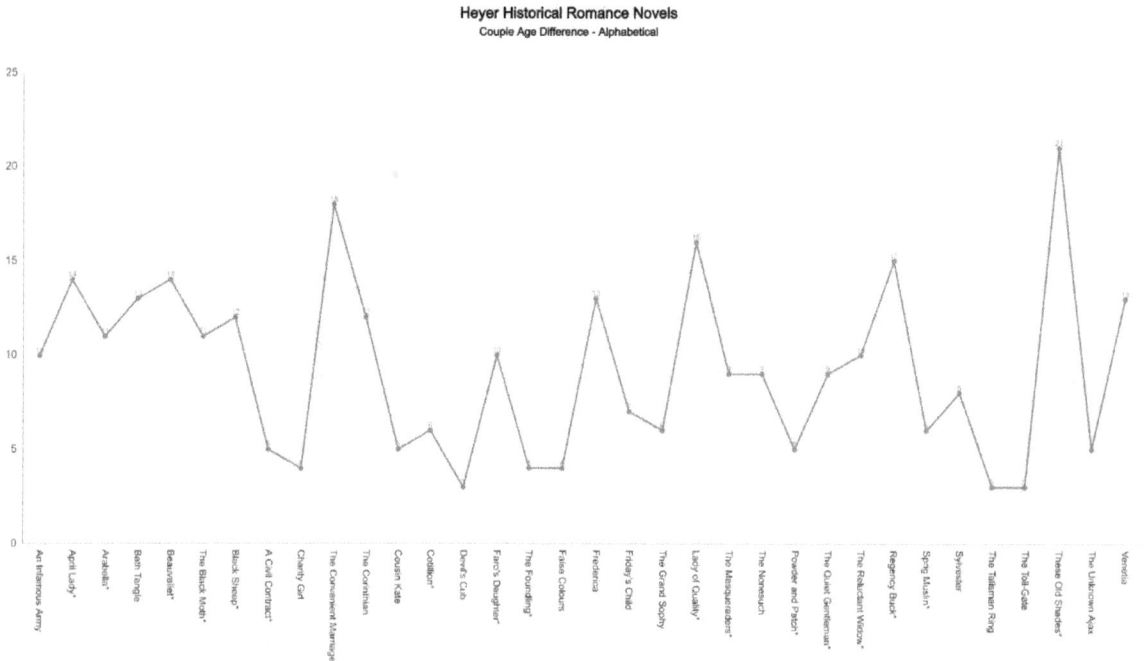

And couple age gaps by publication order of novel...

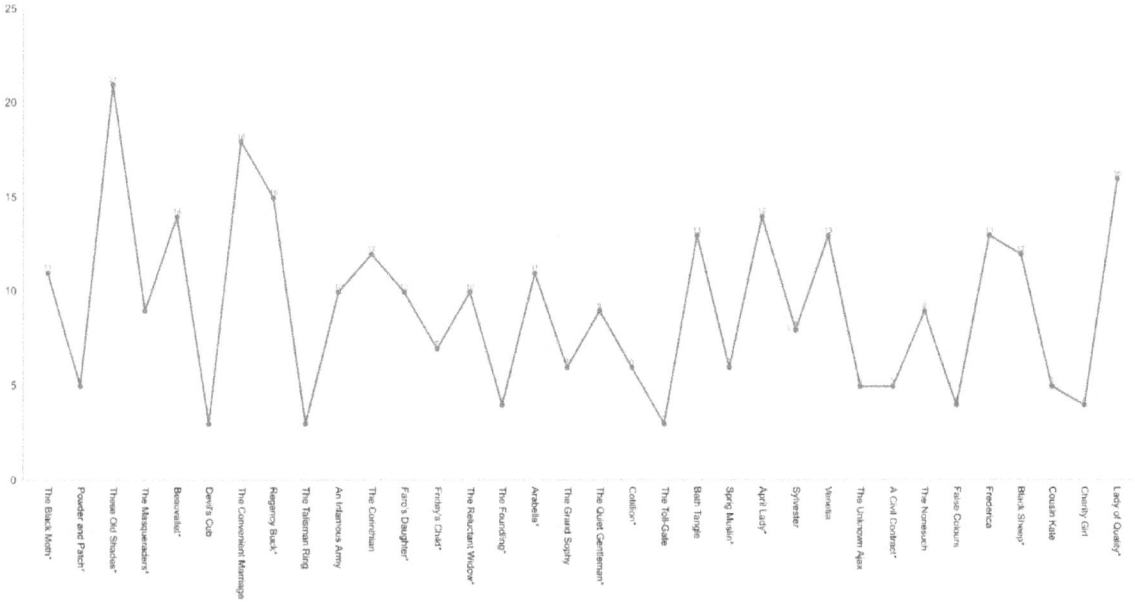

Heyer Historical Couples
Age Difference - Chronological

*Age difference is approximate, as age of either one or both characters is not explicitly given in the text and is worked out from context clues or characters' guesses.

An interesting pattern emerges when you look at the age gaps in the novels chronologically by publication order. Heyer clearly preferred to alternate between couples close in age and couples with more significant age gaps, as these many peaks and valleys prove.

But what was her preferred age gap between her couples? If you had to speculate, without looking at the data, you'd assume she gave most of her couples a pretty big age difference, right?

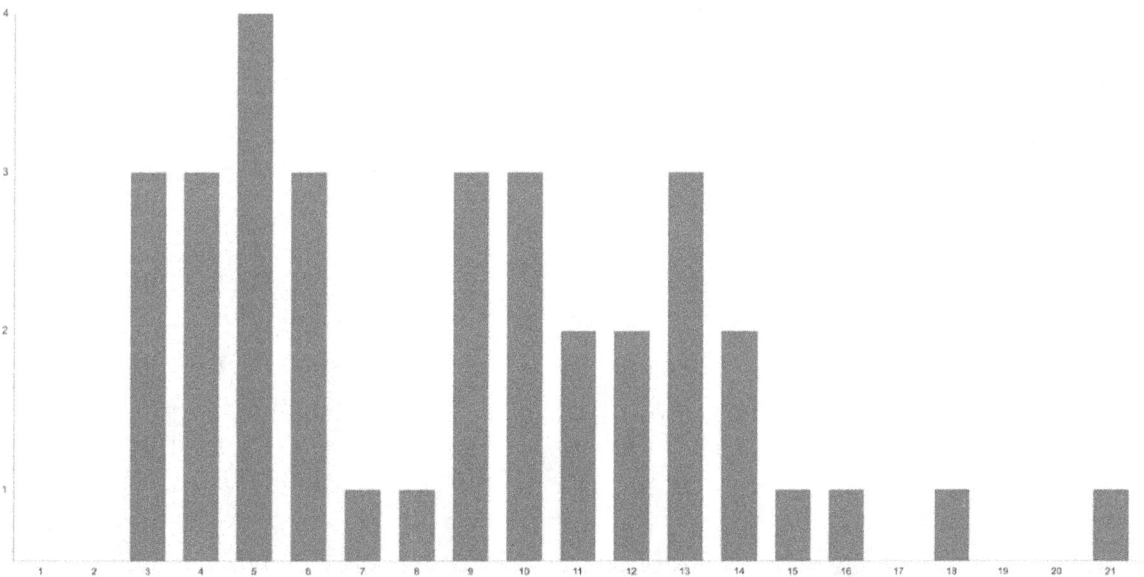

Heyer Historical Couples
Age Difference - Per Novel

However, this graph shows that a significant number of her couples are placed relatively close in age to each other, far more than some might have thought. This simplified version of the graph makes this even more apparent:

Heyer Historical Romance Novels
Couple Age Difference in Years

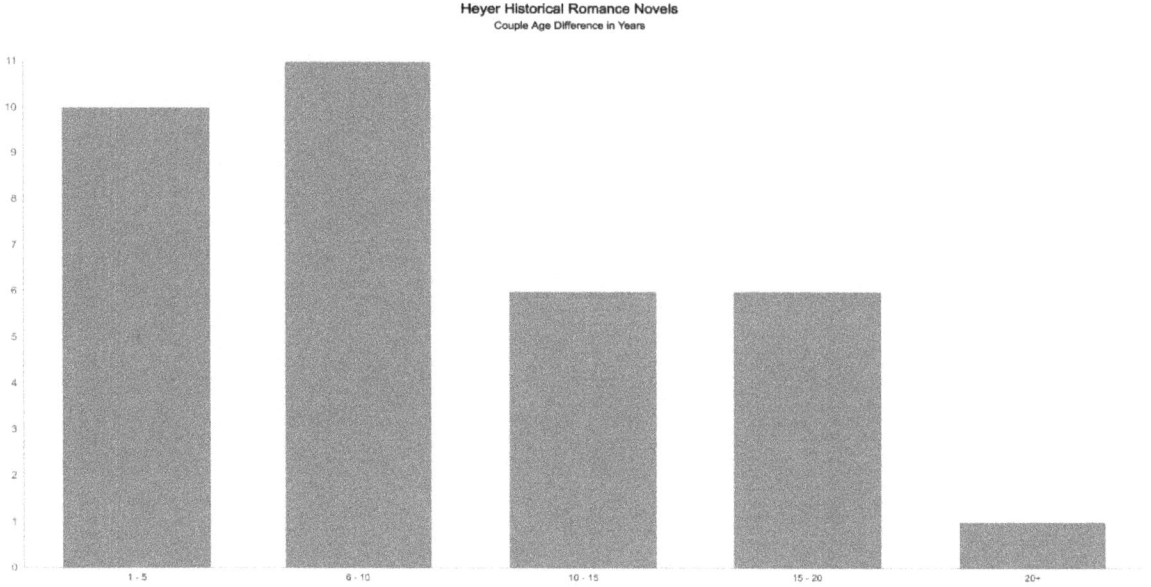

Amazing, the power of numbers to get you too look at familiar things in new ways.
— Rachel Hyland, Patroness, International Heyer Society

~ | ~

#41 – HEYER BY THE NUMBERS #3 – TITLES AND FAMILIES BY RACHEL HYLAND

Friday, October 15, 2021

It is nigh on impossible to think of Georgette Heyer's historical romances without thinking of the rarefied world of titled – not to mention entitled – privilege in which most of them are set. So many of her heroes bear hereditary or courtesy titles, as do some of her heroines. Let's take a look at them:

Heyer Historical Romance Novels
Hero Titles - By Novel

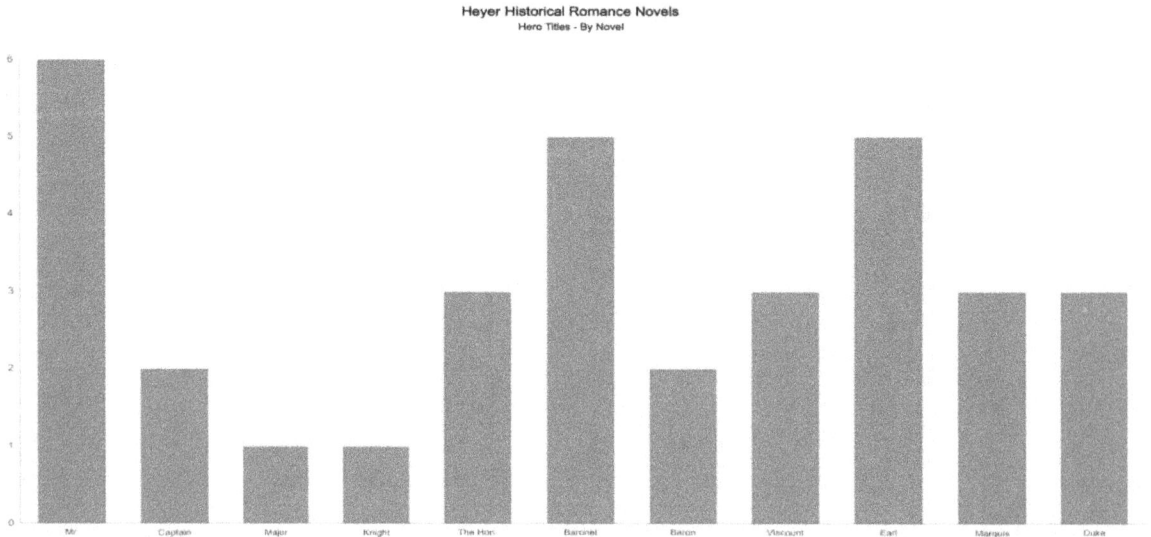

Of course, several of these gentlemen are heirs to assorted dignities, so these rankings are very much in a state of flux. The Hon. Kit Fancot is heir presumptive to his brother, the Earl of Denville; Sir Nicholas Beauvallet is heir presumptive to his brother, Baron Beauvallet; Captain John Staple is heir presumptive to his cousin, the Earl of Saltash; both of Heyer's heroes named Philip – Jettan and Broome – are heirs to baronetcies; the Hon. Freddy Standen is heir to his father, Viscount Legerwood, while the Hon. Charles Rivenhall is heir to his father, who we can only assume to be Viscount Ombersley (as barons most often have a family name that is the same as their title). Additionally, the Marquis of Vidal is heir to his father, the Duke of Avon.

It should also be noted that where a gentleman is both a "Mr." or an "Honourable" and also holds a soldier's rank, the soldier's rank applies, but soldier's ranks are superseded here by hereditary titles, as in real life.

Now let us take a look at Heyer's heroines... The number of titled leading ladies is vastly different to the amount of titled gentlemen in Heyer novels, as the following graph clearly shows:

Heyer Historical Romance Novels
Heroine Titles - By Novel

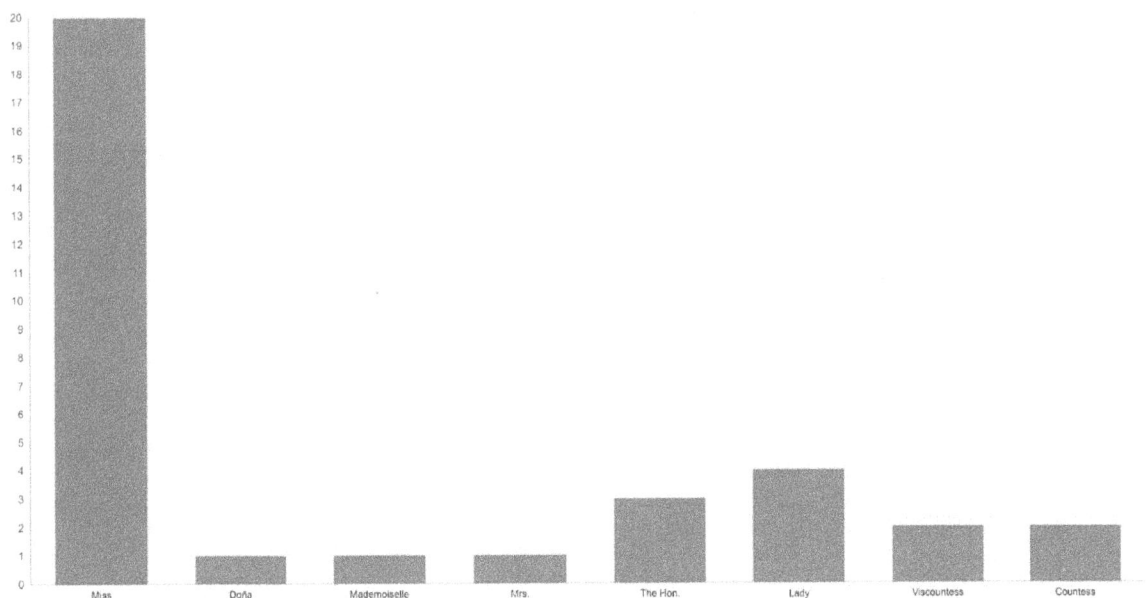

Miss	Doña	Mademoiselle	Mrs.	The Hon.	Lady	Viscountess	Countess
20	1	1	1	3	4	2	2

As can be seen, the overwhelming majority of Heyer's heroines are addressed as "Miss" (or their foreign language equivalent). There are a few Honourables in the mix, but not many, comparatively. Of those women whose marriage granted them the rank of Lady in Heyer's novels, just one – Nell Cardross of *April Lady* – was already known as such, as she is the daughter of an earl, while the former Horry Winwood of *The Convenient Marriage* was an Honourable before becoming the Countess of Rule. Both Jenny Chawleigh and Hero Wantage were simple Misses before their marriages to their respective viscounts.

Of course, after the conclusion of each book, when our heroines settle down into hopefully happy marriage with their heroes, their fortunes change rather dramatically. Only Lady Hester Theale – in marrying Sir Gareth Ludlow – and the Hon. Cressida Stavely – in marrying the Hon. Kit Fancot – can be said not to gain too much, in terms of titles, through their change in circumstances.

Speaking of all these inherited titles, however, let's now take a look at the makeup of the families from which our heroes and heroines received them...

Let's start with Heyer's heroes.

Heyer Historical Romance Novels
Hero Parents - By Novel

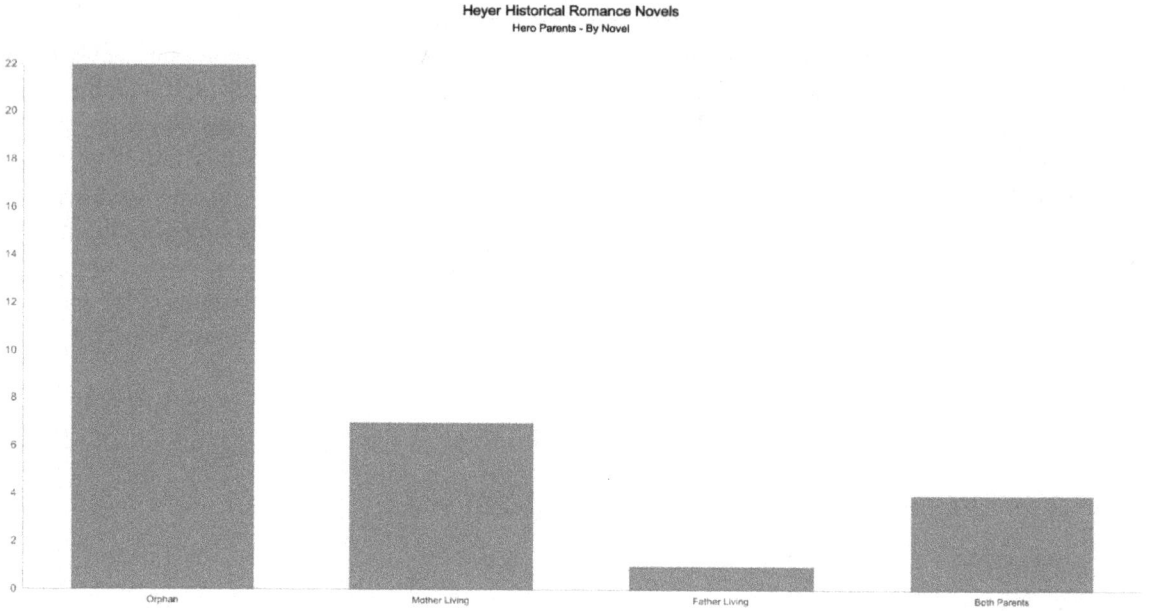

An overwhelming number of orphans here, don't you think? A very small number of her heroes have both parents still living, and only one is left in the care of a single father. (One can only wonder if Philip Jettan's mother would have been as anxious to change him.)

Of course, it makes sense for so many of Heyer's heroes to have lost their fathers, if not both parents. After all, how could they have succeeded to their titles otherwise? But what of Heyer's heroines? Surely they aren't quite so bereft?

Heyer Historical Romance Novels
Heroine Parents - By Novel

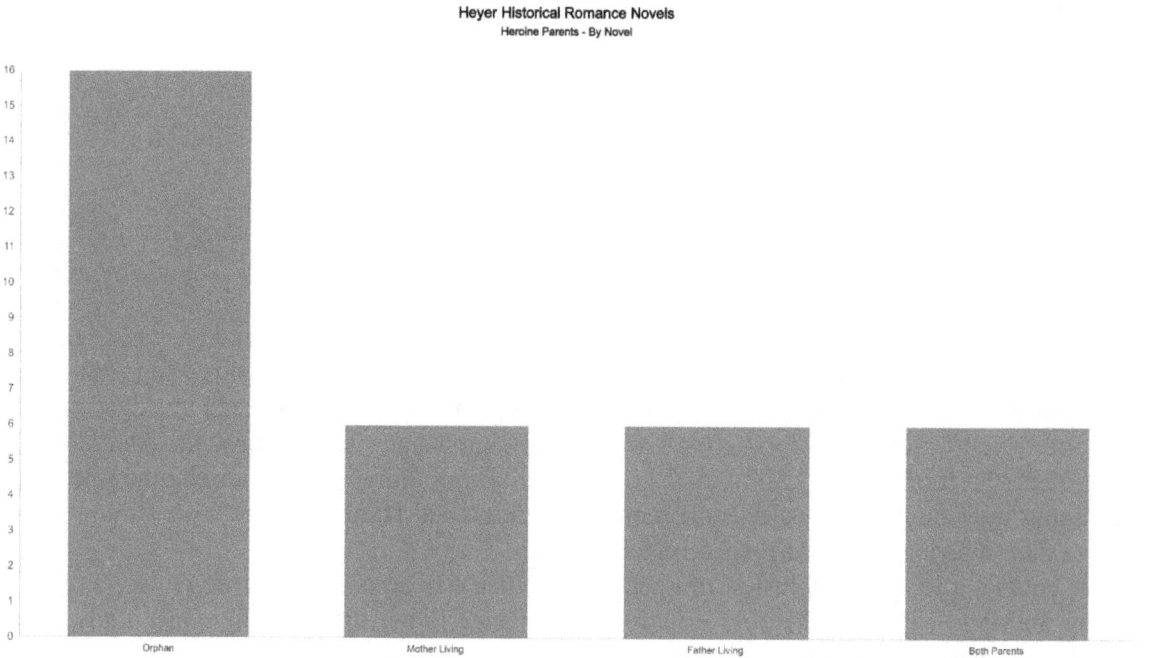

Actually, it turns out the case isn't so different for Heyer's heroines. They are not quite so unlucky in their losses, but a significant proportion of them are very much all alone in the world. Well, all alone except, sometimes, for siblings, that is...

First, let's see how many of Heyer's heroes have siblings:

Heyer Historical Romance Novels
Hero Siblings - By Novel

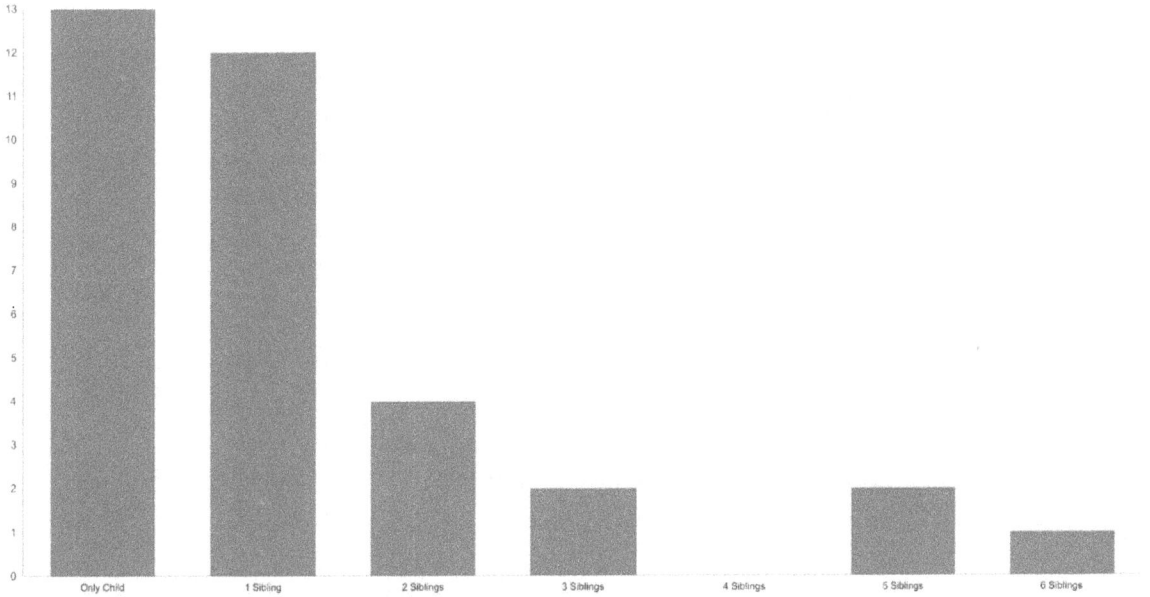

Compared to how many of her heroines have siblings...

Heyer Historical Romance Novels
Heroine Siblings - By Novel

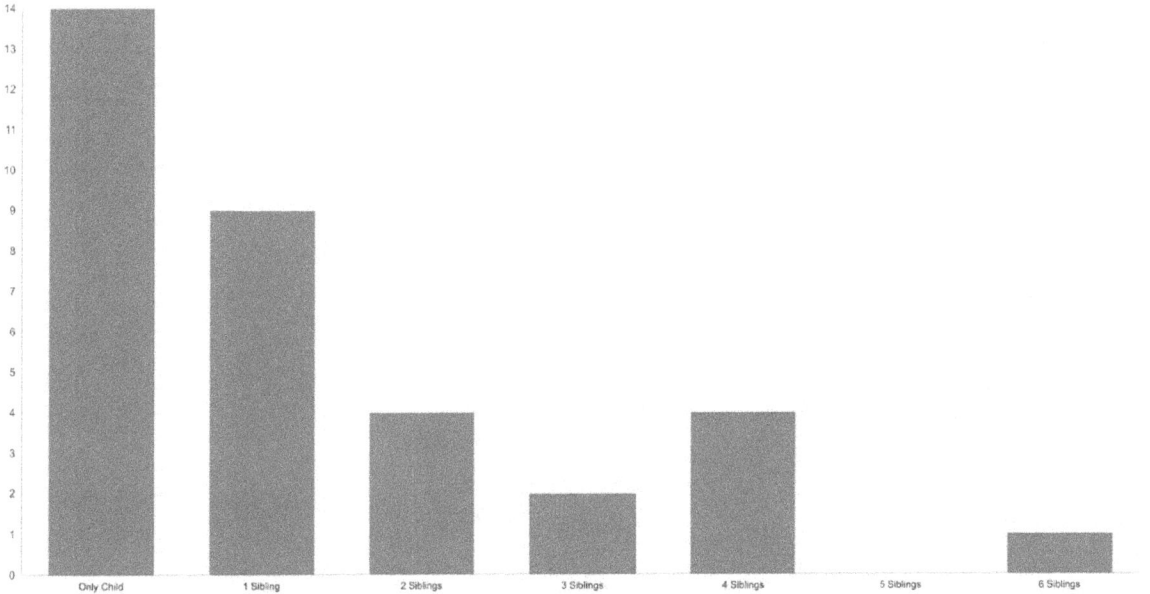

Some few of Heyer's heroes even have charge of their younger siblings – Cardross, Edward Carlyon, Gervase Frant, to an extent. Frederica and Venetia might also be said to have taken (if not given) charge of younger siblings, too. Moreover, most of Heyer's main characters are the eldest children in their families, with only few exceptions.

An overwhelming number of Heyer's heroes are eldest children, and even when they have older siblings, they are usually the eldest son. Only Sir Nicholas Beauvallet, Kit Fancot and Charles Audley are the exceptions to what appears to have been a fixation of Heyer's.

Heyer Historical Romance Novels
Hero Eldest/Younger - By Novel

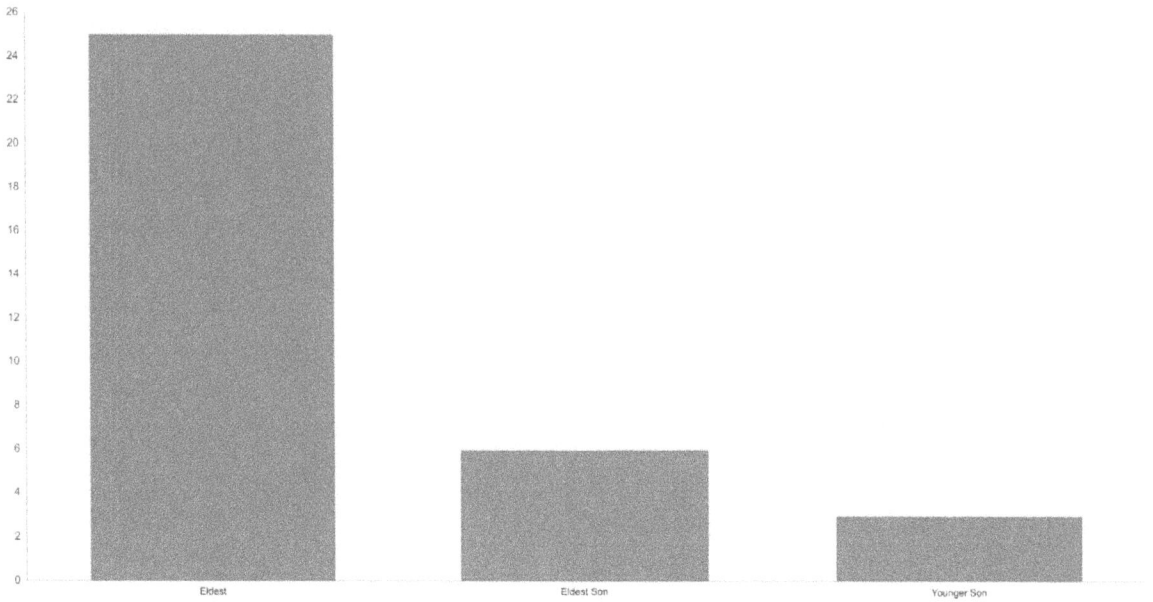

Nor is this fixation limited to the gentlemen, as this graph demonstrates...

Heyer Historical Romance Novels
Heroine Eldest/Younger - By Novel

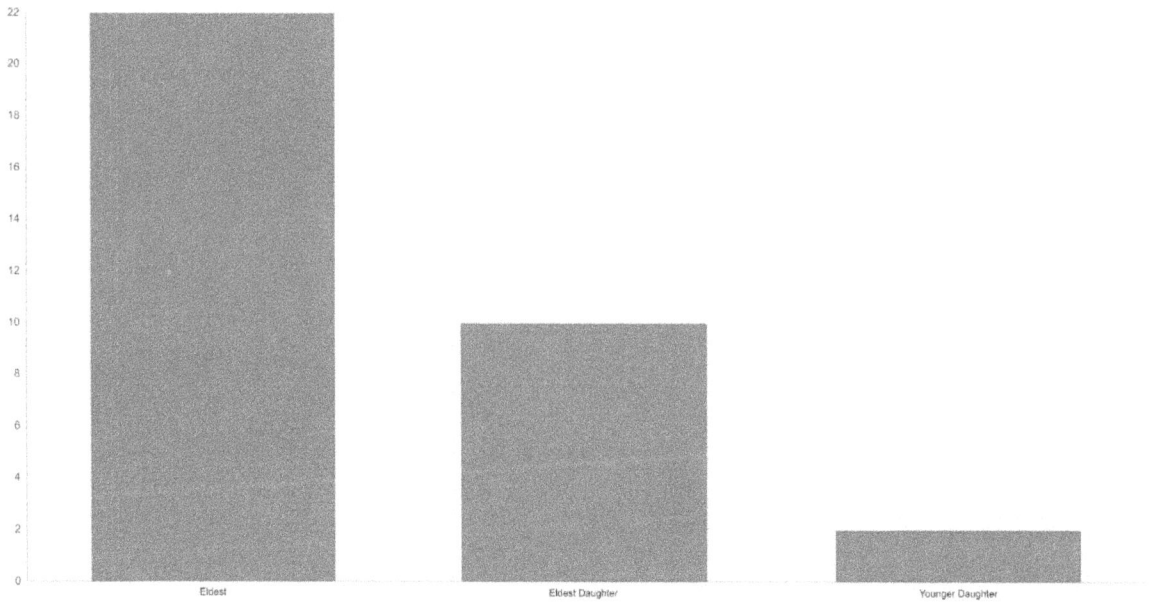

Only Horry Winwood of *The Convenient Marriage* and Abigail Wendover of *Black Sheep* are younger daughters, out of all of the heroines of Heyer's novels. It is very interesting, and yet might not have been considered before, how much emphasis is placed on the eldest (or, more often than not, only) child in these stories, whether there is a title in question or not.

– Rachel Hyland, Patroness, International Heyer Society

~ | ~

#42 – HEYER BY THE NUMBERS #4 – HISTORIC PERSONAGES BY RACHEL HYLAND

Friday, October 22, 2021

One of the most impressive and well-researched devices Georgette Heyer uses to get us absorbed into her historical eras is to namecheck assorted real-life personages alive and holding influence at the time. Indeed, sometimes it feels like all of the same people are constantly showing up in cameo appearances in her books -- but is this really true?

First, let's look at some popular Georgian-era inclusions:

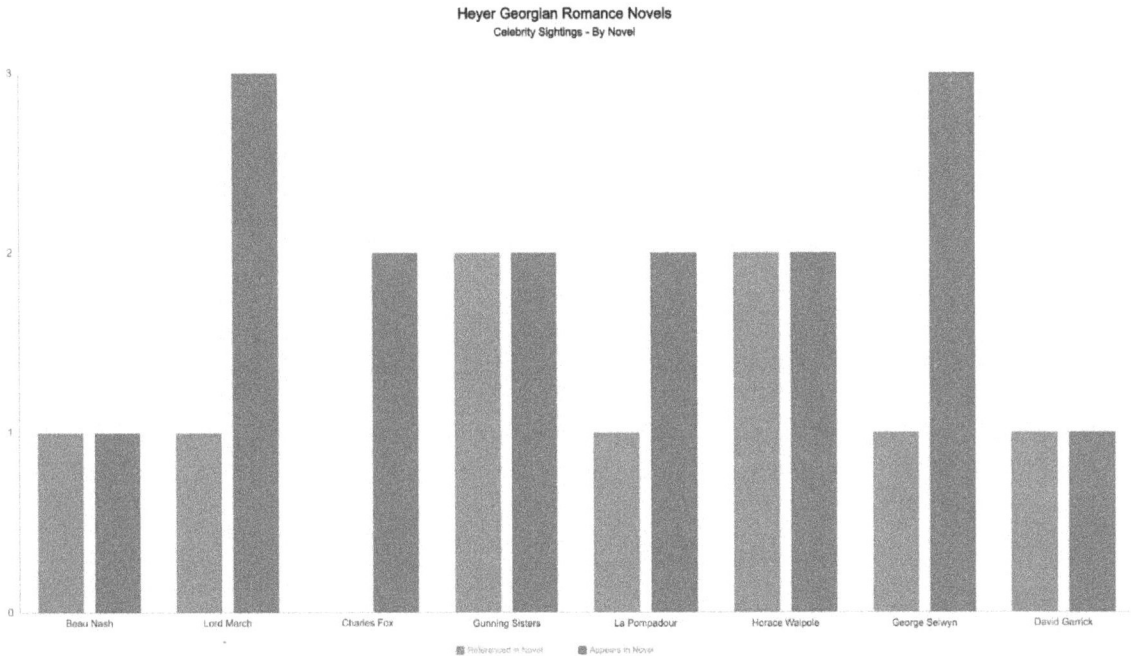

Heyer Georgian Romance Novels
Celebrity Sightings - By Novel

Heyer wrote eight novels set in the mid to late part of what we now call the Georgian era (1714 - 1811), and while she did, of course, use notables of the time to set the scene, she by no means overused any of them, as this graph shows. Those famous penniless Irish beauties, sisters Elizabeth and Maria Gunnning, are seen or heard about in a total of six out of the eight, with only prolific epistolorian (and source of much of the minutia was have of the era, and certainly a source of much of Heyer's knowledge), Horace Walpole, matching them. On the other hand, he is Horry Winwood's godfather in *The Convenient Marriage*, so it can be argued that he has rather more importance than even those diamonds of the first water.

Still, it comes as rather a surprise that Beau Nash, for example, or Charles Fox doesn't appear more, because it just feels like they do, somehow.

But what about in Heyer's Regency novels? Does this trend hold true there? In her 26 Regency novels, we see and hear about these following personages:

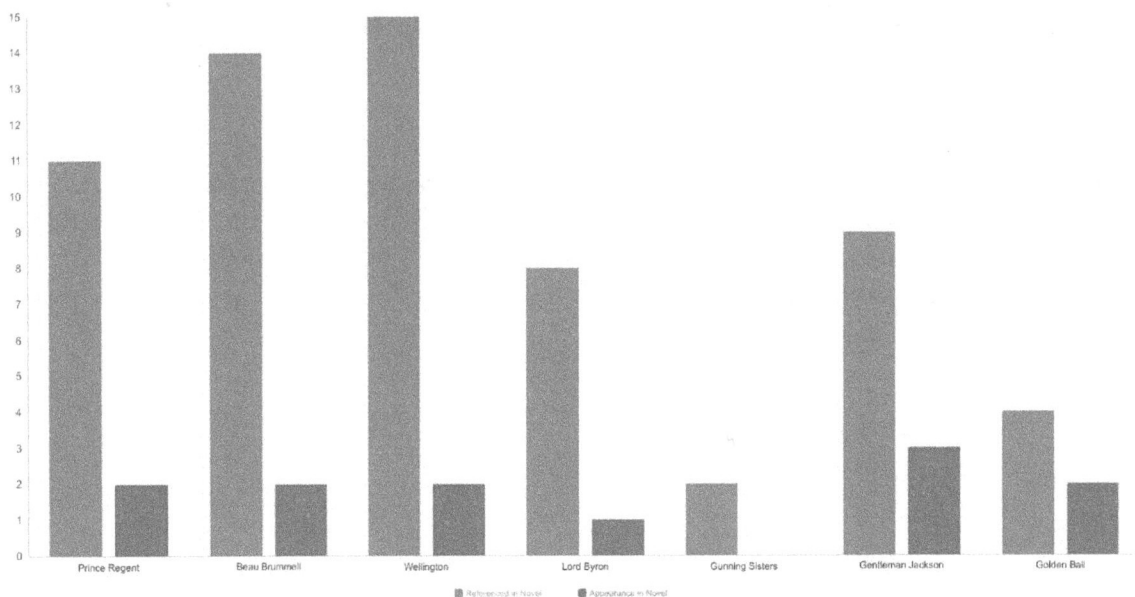

The fact that Beau Brummell is second only to Wellington in references here is, of course, not at all surprising, but the fact that he only actually appears in two novels (those being *Regency Buck* and *A Civil Contract*) might not be quite as expected.

But some very notable Regency ladies are missing from this graph: the Patronesses of Almack's, of course! It does seem as though they appear in every Heyer Regency, especially those set primarily in London, but is this so?

Heyer Regency Romance Novels
Celebrity Sightings: Almack's Patronesses - By Novel

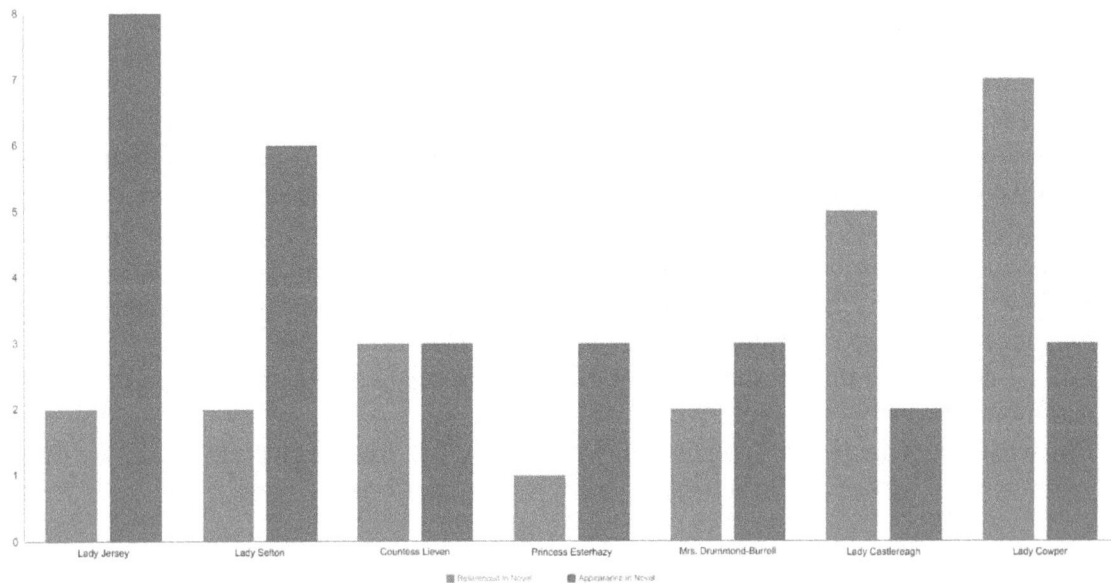

It turns out, not only is that not so, but who knew Lady Cowper was mentioned – and, indeed, appeared – so many times?

But what of royalty? Throughout Heyer's historical fiction and romances, various kings (and the occasional queen) show up in the narrative, or even as main characters, quite often.

Heyer Historical Novels
Royal Appearances - By Novel

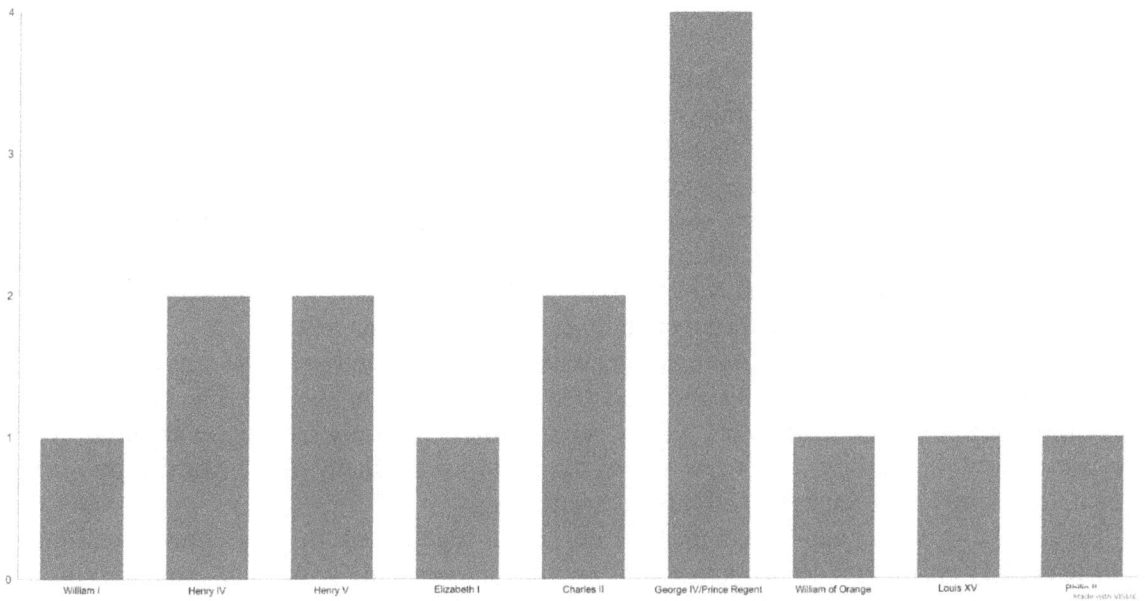

Of course, there are many other mentions of the royalty of various countries throughout Heyer's works – from France's doomed Marie Antoinette to England's own Henry VIII and his many brides (Miss Fishguard is particularly fond of his surviving queen Katherine Parr, as fans of *Cotillion* will surely recall) and beyond. And this is far from a complete listing even from the historical novels, which, given the scope of *The Conqueror, Royal Escape, The Great Roxhythe, My Lord John* and *The Spanish Bride*, is surely understandable. But as a snapshot of the thoroughness with which Heyer approached her time period, the facility she had with creating, even inhabiting, a character out of mere historical record, and the fascination she clearly held with certain royal personages of the past (she seems to have been particularly fond of Charles II, for example; certainly, she considered him to be a gentleman of wit and attraction, despite his notoriety), this graph tells us all we need to know.

And, for now, that's a wrap on Heyer by the Numbers. But there is much more to be mapped from the books, so look for more math-filled instalments in the future.

– Rachel Hyland, Patroness, International Heyer Society

~ | ~

#43 – FINDING SOPHY, LÉONIE AND ARABELLA BY RACHEL HYLAND

Friday, October 29, 2021

Established in 1964 in Wawa, Pennsylvania, the Franklin Mint was initially a manufacturer of commemorative coins, but within a decade had expanded into other memorabilia, and by the 1980s had become a world leader in high-end collectibles, soon offering exclusive media tie-in merch like diecast James Bond luxury cars, movie-inspired dolls and a gold-and-silver *Star Trek* 3-

Dimensional Chess Set. In the 1990s, the Franklin Mint also brought out three figurines based on the work of Georgette Heyer. To this end the company engaged the services of James Moore, an accomplished porcelain artist, to create three iconic heroines: Sophy, Léonie and finally Arabella, who was released in 1996 as a "75th Anniversary" tribute to the publication of *The Black Moth*. (Why, then did they not release a version of Diana? Probably because she just wasn't – and isn't – iconic enough. Sorry, Di!)

I still remember the first time I learned about these gorgeous creations. It was in a copy of *Reader's Digest* magazine, a monthly staple in the Hyland home, in which ran an advertisement for Sophy. One could tear out the Franklin Mint card, write one's name and address and enclose a money order for a crazy amount of money far in excess of a teenager's meagre allowance (even if said teenager knew what a money order was, which I don't believe she did), and within four to six weeks Miss Stanton-Lacy would arrive, in all her pinstriped glory. I wanted her so badly. So, so badly. But to my teenage self she was as far out of my reach as that elaborate gold-and-silver 3-D Chess Set. (Which I also really coveted, though perhaps not as much.)

In the decades since I have sporadically searched for Sophy, and her two companions, first in second-hand shops and garage sales and classified ads, and later online, as eBay and a variety of its marketplace cousins became more widely spread. But it was only recently, with the arrival of the vanishingly rare Léonie a few weeks ago, that I was finally able to fulfill my teenage dream, to not only own Sophy but all three Heyer ladies.

They now sit very happily together on my shelf, and I look at them often in immense satisfaction. They are just so *beautiful*. And, moreover, are made with such exquisite care and attention to detail that they can only gladden any Heyerite heart.

Let's start with Miss Sophia Stanton-Lacy, of *The Grand Sophy* fame. The elegant sweep of her dress, the regal carriage of her bearing, the gold detail of her riding crop… she is stunning. Here is the passage in the book from which this look was taken:

When Miss Wraxton's invitation was conveyed to Sophy she professed herself happy to accept it, and at once desired Miss Jane Storridge to press out her riding-dress. This garment, when she appeared in it on the following afternoon, filled Cecilia with envy, but slightly staggered her brother, who could not feel that a habit made of pale blue cloth, with epaulettes and frogs, à la Hussar, and sleeves braided half-way up the arm, would win approval from Miss Wraxton. Blue kid gloves and half-boots, a high-standing collar trimmed with lace, a muslin cravat, narrow lace ruffles at the wrists, and a tall-crowned hat, like a shako, with a peak over the eyes, and a plume of curled ostrich feathers completed this dashing toilette. The tightly fitting habit set off Sophy's magnificent figure to admiration; and from under the brim of her hat her brown locks curled quite charmingly; but Mr Rivenhall, appealed to by his sister to subscribe to her conviction that Sophy looked beautiful, merely bowed, and said that he was no judge of such matters.

The lace! The epaulettes! The ostrich feather! Perfection.

Then, there's Mademoiselle Léonie de St. Vire, of *These Old Shades*. Surely the reason she has been so elusive all of these years is how very delicate she is, and how difficult it must have been for many collectors to have kept her in pristine condition. The detail on her dress, the dainty golden fan she holds – just magnificent. I think we all know where this look comes from in the novel, but here is the exact passage:

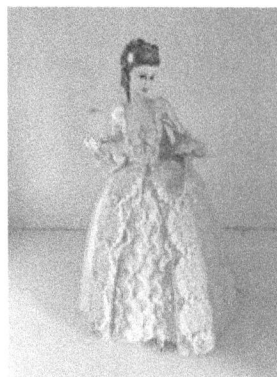

Léonie paused half-way down the stairs and unfurled her fan.
'But look at me!' she said reprovingly.
They turned quickly at the sound of her voice, and saw her with candles on either side, a little figure, all white, from the ordered curls to the jewelled heels: white brocade cut low across the shoulders, white lace to form a petticoat, white roses at her breast and in her hand. Only her eyes were deep, sparkling blue, and her parted lips like cherries, her cheeks faintly flushed.

The only wrong note here is that Leonie's hair is unpowdered, where in the novel she was *en poudrée* while wearing this white ballgown for her debut into Parisian society, and it was at her second ball – where she was dressed in gold and emeralds – that her red hair was allowed to be seen. But the red hair is so distinctly Léonie that even such a stickler as I cannot cavil at this liberty.

And finally, Miss Arabella Tallant, the eponymous heroine of *Arabella*. Here she is, dressed for her official bow into the London ton, at Lady Bridlington's evening party:

> Lady Bridlington, presently setting eyes on Arabella just before dinner was announced, was delighted, and reflected that Sophia Theale had always had exquisite taste. Nothing could have set Arabella off to greater advantage than that delicate yellow robe, open down the front over a slip of white satin, and ornamented with clasps of tiny roses to match those in her hair. The only jewelry she wore was the ring Papa had had made for her, and Grandmama's necklet of pearls. Lady Bridlington was half inclined to ring for Clara to fetch down from her own jewel-case two bracelets of gold and pearls, and then decided that Arabella's pretty arms needed no embellishment. Besides, she would be wearing long gloves, so that the bracelets would be wasted.

Her robe is not the yellow it should be – "jonquil crape" as it is described; perhaps the pigment was too hard to perfect? – but aside from that, from the way her hair is shown to be a "simple arrangement of those dark curls, twisted into a high knot on the top of her head" to the "spangled scarf hanging over her arms," this Arabella is near flawless.

As is the loving, respectful consideration lavished on all three pieces.

The very fact that they were made at all is something of a coup, since the Franklin Mint's other author-based collectibles honour the works of luminaries like Jane Austen, Charles Dickens, assorted Brontës and, of course, Shakespeare. We, of course, don't need confirmation that Georgette Heyer naturally belongs amid such illustrious company, but it's still nice to come across this kind of objective validation once in a while.

I, for one, continue to be amazed by the figurines' existence, as well as their beauty, and am beyond delighted to have been able to gather all three of these young ladies together, at long last, in my home. I hope that my fellow Heyer collectors out there have also found the Sophy, Arabella and ever-elusive Léonie of their dreams; but if not yet, there is still hope.

After all, it took me a quarter-century to make this happen:

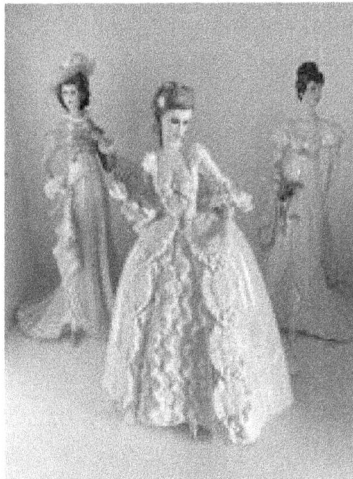

– Rachel Hyland, Patroness, International Heyer Society

#44 – RECONQUERING *THE CONQUEROR* BY CLARA SHIPMAN

Friday, November 5, 2021

Following the *Nonpareil* on the subject several months ago, I decided to reread *The Conqueror*. It had been years and years since I had even looked at this enormous, dense and, honestly, most depressing of Heyer's novels, but just a quick glance at the Celebrity Sightings, and seeing the enormous list of real people who are mentioned in the book, showed me that if I wanted to take my Learning! with Georgette Heyer to the next level (see: my essay "Learning! with Georgette Heyer" in *Heyer Society – Essays on the Literary Genius of Georgette Heyer*), I should really attempt to grapple once more with this book about the difficult-to-like William, Duke of Normandy, best remembered for conquering stuff.

These days, conquering stuff isn't considered a particularly socially acceptable pastime (unless you're the US Army, of course), but in the age of the novel's anti-hero, it was very much the height of fashion. All the cool kids were doing it, and they were pretty damned brutal kids as well. England's record of being conquered over the centuries is probably only outstripped by attractive strategic outposts like Malaysia and Malta, and when little baby Billy was born "on the wrong side of the blanket" in the north of France (then the Duchy of Normandy) somewhere around 1028, his future kingdom was changing hands on what seems like a yearly basis, whether because of outside invasion or assassination from within—which is just another way to conquer a country, really. (Plus, illness. People died young all the time in history, even when they were the richest people in the land. Bet they wish they could have gotten vaccinated against preventable diseases back then.)

Reading *The Conqueror* you learn exactly why William decided that he should get in on the fun of conquering England, too, and more than that, you learn about the HUNDREDS of people who have somehow been remembered all this time later, even though it had been more than 900 years since they had lived when this book was written (and it's closing in on a century since it was written now). Admittedly, most of the real people we learn about in *The Conqueror* were of the nobility, and so of course they were the kind of people who would leave behind a record of their existence, if only in the particulars of their births, deaths and marriages. But Georgette Heyer infuses these potential ciphers with so much personality and backstory, even expertly sketching out pictures of some of their homelives and their children and complicated relationships with their parents, that it's hard to believe she didn't have access to some secret cache of journals penned by 11th-century Norman aristocrats ("Dear Diary, Today I jousted, ravished a wench and betrayed my liege lord…").

I can't lie, rereading this book was an epic challenge. So much so that I only just completed it, and I began reading it five months ago. Of course, I have taken many a break and have read a lot of books in between (*Arabella* got me through William torturing prisoners; *Faro's Daughter* saw me through William literally whipping his future wife; *The Talisman Ring* got me through William tricking Harold Godwinsson into renouncing his father's throne), but I have to admit that this book took *work*. I have done whole college courses that took less out of me, hand to God.

Which is probably the biggest compliment I can give to *The Conqueror*. Reading it feels like studying, but the kind where you have the enlightened and inspirational teacher who uses rap or whatever to connect with a ragtag bunch of reluctant leanerrs, like *Dangerous Minds* but for 11th-century European History instead of high school English. As she does so often and so well, Georgette Heyer makes learning fun – or, as fun as such cruel (and, as I said, mostly depressing) history can be. Sure, I could probably just have read the Wikipedia page on William, followed a series of links to learn more about his subordinates, enemies and allies, and have found myself in a Google spiral in attempting to absorb all of this knowledge. I could have read learned essays about the Bayeux Tapestry, which artwork is also our source for a lot of the certainty we have about the period (a fascinating fact in its own right) and I could also have studied the hundreds of histories that have been written about the eventful life of William the Conqueror over the years. But why would I do any of that, when I have Georgette Heyer to give me the full picture – or as full as she could at the time, without ready access to today's vast collection of collective knowledge, aka the internet? Having read this book twice now – but only once as an adult – I feel certain that I now know all that I need to know about this turbulent period of French and English (and even Flemish and Danish) history, and for all that it was hard going at times, for all that I was often furious at William and his actions, Heyer's unflinching portrayal of the man and his time will forever be the impression of both that I carry in my head.

Also there's my man Raoul, Heyer's original creation and William's BFF. Loved Raoul so much on this reread. Boy can get it. (And does!)

I really do feel that I have conquered – nay, *reconquered* – this novel this second time around, understanding so much more of it than I did when I attempted, and mostly failed, to get through it as a teen. I highly recommend anyone who has yet to read it either once or for a second time (I'm assuming no one has read this book three or more times, but I could be wrong) to give it a shot. I doubt I'll ever feel the need to do it again, but then I don't feel the need to retake most of my college courses either, and yet I'm still glad I did them. *The Conqueror* taught me at least as much as any of them did, and didn't cost me a cent.

The emotional cost, though? That is immeasurable.

But, if nothing else, at least the patriarchal warmongering horrors of the past make the comparatively fewer such horrors of today seem a little more bearable, right?

– Clara Shipman, Guest Contributor

~ | ~

#45 – THE VERY BEST OF HEYER BY MAURA TAN

Friday, November 12, 2021

Today, I finished rereading all of Georgette Heyer's mysteries, and as a result I am happy to report that I have already made it to my ultimate goal for this year, which was to read all of Georgette Heyer's novels before the end of 2021. Not having ever been a reader, admirer or adherent of historical fiction, my conversion to Heyer was first enacted back in 2018, for *Heyer Society – Essays on the Literary Genius of Georgette Heyer* (and is further chronicled in my memoir *Heyer for Beginners*), and this is the first time I have completed a full reread of her works. In January, I started with the four contemporaries – which were my introduction to Heyer, through Society Patroness, Rachel Hyland – and then went on through the historical novels, the Georgian romances, the Regency romances, and then finished up with the mysteries. Along the way, I have discovered (or rediscovered) many new words, many new historical facts and, of course, many new favourites.

But then there are those that I, with a scholarly eye, look upon as the *best* of Heyer's many genres, and I wanted to share my thoughts on those with you now.

BEST CONTEMPORARY NOVEL

Barren Corn. This 1930 work was Heyer's last attempt in the genre, and we are all the poorer for her having given up. *Barren Corn* is an unforgettable tragedy of class distinction, insecurity and the perils of jumping into marriage too early, and it is as gripping and heartbreaking on subsequent reads as it is on the first. If you haven't read this yet, I highly recommend it. It's not the Heyer you know and love, but it is a worthy entry into the literary canon of its period and stands as a modern-day masterpiece wholly in its own right.

BEST HISTORICAL NOVEL

The Conqueror. This sweeping epic is just so perfectly researched that it is impossible not to be impressed with the scope and precision with which it is presented. Heyer looks upon the anti-hero at the novel's centre – the William the Conqueror of the title – with an unbiased eye, and even though no one wants to read about his villainy most of the time, especially when he beats his reluctant bride or when he tortures enemies because they taunt him, it is historical fact (or, at least as close as we have to that, when the events took place so very long ago) that cannot be denied, and which Heyer deals with in masterly fashion. It is not my favourite of her historical novels – that being *Simon the Coldheart*, of course – but it is the best of them, no question.

BEST GEORGIAN ROMANCE

Faro's Daughter. There is a lot of fun to be had in the others, but *Faro's Daughter* brings something wholly different into Heyer's writing: sexiness. Without being at all explicit or salacious (because she would never), she manages to bring an aura of imminent physicality to the contentious relationship between Max Ravenscar and Deb Grantham in such a way that, even on rereading, you wonder if this is suddenly going to turn into one of *those books* at any moment. Giving the whole the backdrop of a gaming house, and making the wise choice of having Deb remain a rather unsuitable bride (unlike with Prudence in *The Masqueraders*, my favourite of the Georgians) simply add to the book's supremacy over the others.

BEST REGENCY ROMANCE

A Civil Contract. Again, doing something very different makes for true genius. Again, the heroine is unsuitable, though this time it is her birth and not her relative wealth and occupation that make her so. But as heiress Jenny becomes necessary to the existence of viscount Adam, who married her solely out of duty in order to save his ancestral home, we see love bloom through shared joys and sorrows rather than due to beauty or wit or outrageousness, and it is just so perfectly enacted that there really is no comparison to Heyer's other, often rather fluffy, Regency outings. If this had been the only book she ever released (or, her first), it would be studied in every university. A triumph.

BEST MYSTERY

Penhallow. In many ways, this book should go under the Contemporary section, since there is little actual mystery in here – you know who dunnit, and even why, from pretty much the outset. But, despite this, *boy* is this book good. There is barely a likeable character, and that is mainly because Heyer depicts them all with such deadly satirical accuracy that one might think this more like Phoebe Marlow's *roman á clef* about Regency society than a fictional detective novel. (I wonder if any of Heyer's acquaintances saw themselves in here?) And that is more what this is – a novel of detection, rather than mystery, as the murderer is slowly discovered by circuitous but highly entertaining means. It's a dense book, and one filled with a terrible feeling of dread for much of it, but that only adds to its excellence. An under-appreciated gem.

And there you have it. The very best of Heyer – in my humble estimation.

What do you think?

– Maura Tan, Guest Contributor

~ | ~

#46 – MY POOR DEVIL: THE CONFERENCE BY SAM HIRST

Friday, November 19, 2021

Georgette Heyer's books have been a part of my life since I was a pre-teen. I come from a Heyer reading family and was handed *These Old Shades* when I was about twelve. I'd like to say that it was love at first sight but it was the wrong book at the wrong age and (shocking, I know) I put it to one side without finishing it. It wasn't until a year of so later when I picked up *Arabella* under my own steam that I fell in love and never looked back. That's not to say my relationship with Heyer hasn't undergone changes. Favourites have fallen out of favour (Freddy has always and will always be my favourite hero though). Books I once put to one side have risen to the top of my pile (I will die on the hill of *The Great Roxhythe* and *Penhallow* being some of her most interesting books). I've also come to approach the books from different perspectives, noticing things that I hadn't before: historical curiosities; things that make me deeply uncomfortable; aspects of her craft which were hardly discernible to an eleven-year-old but delightfully clear to older eyes; the edges of her Regency world, its eccentricities and its elisions.

I've had quite a few jobs in my time but I've ended up as a scholar of the eighteenth and early nineteenth centuries. I'm fairly sure that Heyer has a lot to answer for in my choice of career though it took me a long to get here through a variety of subjects and career paths (to be fair, Bernard Cornwell and his Sharpe series also have a lot to answer for). I specialised in an area of scholarship which doesn't seem to have much to do with Heyer – theology and literature. However, I primarily study the Gothic and when I did my Masters and had the opportunity to write on anything at all even vaguely connected to the Gothic, I knew exactly where my research was going. Scholarship around romance, and around Heyer particularly, is becoming increasingly prevalent but the academy still spends a lot of time ignoring romance and ignoring Heyer despite her notable impact. I wanted my scholarly work at that level to redress the balance a bit (quite grandiose, but you'll have to excuse the Masters student version of me with all their delusions of grandeur). While my PhD took me in *very* different directions, I've always maintained an interest in Heyer and published on her as often as I could. The intersections between her work, the periods which she writes about and the literature produced in those periods is endlessly fascinating to me.

All of which takes me to this weekend's conference 'My Poor Devil: 100 Years of Georgette Heyer's *The Black Moth.'*

During the pandemic, I began an online education project *Romancing the Gothic* offering free classes on anything and everything to do with the Gothic (including a class on Georgette Heyer). It started off as me giving a few free classes and it ended up being a project with hundreds of participants from 5 continents. I knew this was my chance to bring a dream to life. I have always wanted to run a conference on Heyer (and have very much enjoyed the ones I have attended) but it is difficult to find support for a conference on a subject which you're not even meant to be working on! *Romancing the Gothic* offered the opportunity to put together an event online, available to everyone, with participation from scholars and fans from any country in the world and any specialism. The fact that this was the centenary year of Heyer's first book sealed the deal! I wanted to make an event which would be appealing to scholars, experts and fans of all type so we have a range of events.

We've got panels on everything from food in Heyer, to the colonial realities which appear throughout her books, to the figure of the Highwaymen in folklore and on screen. We've got a keynote from Heyer scholar Jennifer Kloester, workshops on eighteenth century fashion (Kelly Mann) and dance (Helen Davidge) with the opportunity to participate. We've even got a quiz to test your Heyer knowledge. We finish the main part of the day with an author panel on queering Heyer from renowned authors KJ Charles, Olivia Waite, Cat Sebastian and Rose Lerner who all have a long-standing relationship with Heyer and write a Regency which builds on Heyer and expands her worlds to include marginalised groups. This conference is for everyone and seeks to recognise the broad range of people reading, enjoying, and critically engaging with Heyer.

Welcome and please join us!   – *Sam Hirst, Guest Contributor*

~ | ~

#47 – THE CONVENTIONS OF GEORGETTE HEYER BY RACHEL HYLAND

Friday, November 26, 2021

As anticipation grows for the in-person portion of our 2021 Heyer Convention next Saturday, let us take a look back at the previous conventions – more academic conferences, for the most part, but the idea is the same – dedicated to honouring our beloved Georgette.

The first Heyer conference held anywhere in the world, as far as we know, was the "Re-reading Georgette Heyer" colloquium held at Lucy Cavendish College, Cambridge in November of 2009. It was arranged by Professor Sarah Annes Brown, who said of the conference:

> "I've organised quite a few conferences now - but none have received quite so much enthusiastic attention as 'Re-reading Georgette Heyer'. But perhaps that's because I've never organised a conference about a writer who generates so much pure pleasure and enthusiasm in her readers."

Our very own Jennifer Kloester was in attendance, presenting a paper entitled "The Life of Georgette Heyer"; other notable presentations included jay Dixon's "Heyer and Place"; Sam Rayner's "Publishing Heyer: Representing the Regency in Historical Romance," and Professor Brown's own, rather intriguingly titled, "*Lady of Quality* and Homosexual Panic."

The next Heyer conference came in 2012, when our Susannah Fullerton got together with Heyer aficionado (and now Society member), the excellent Amanda Jones, to hold the first Sydney conference, at which Jen spoke as well. Also in attendance was Judy, Lady Rougier, Georgette's daughter-in-law, who brought with her one of Georgette's very own notebooks to show to attendees.

A second Sydney conference was held in August of 2016, and was entitled "Georgette Heyer: Complete to a Shade." A gorgeous booklet of Heyer reminiscences and reflections was produced for the conference, featuring contributions from authors, scholars and fans – including one of Heyer's biggest celebrity advocates, Stephen Fry. (You can find it on Susannah's website.)

Then in June of 2018 came "The Nonesuch? Georgette Heyer and Her Historical Fiction Contemporaries," held at University College London. Most of the papers presented at that conference – along with some new additions – have been published in *Georgette Heyer, History and Historical Fiction*. (See below.) Notable topics included "Heyer... in Space! The Influence of Georgette Heyer on Science Fiction" by Kathleen Jennings, "Georgette Heyer and the Language of the Historical Novel" by Tom Zille and "Georgette Heyer and Redefining the Gothic Romance" by Holly – aka Sam – Hirst. (Also see below.)

March of 2019 saw a third Sydney conference, this one called "Georgette Heyer: A Perpetual Delight." All three of your Patronesses were present for that one (though the International Heyer Society was not yet in existence), and it is where we launched *Heyer Society – Essays on the Literary Genius of Georgette Heyer*. A highlight of the day was Amanda's humorous and loving look at the dogs in Heyer – a lowlight was that one of your Patronesses (full disclosure: me) had to leave the stage in rather a hurry mid-talk, due to dizziness brought on by an undiagnosed case of pneumonia. (And if you were there and were one of those kind souls who offered to find me hartshorn, or a vinaigrette, trust me, I was much more amused by your clever jokes than I may have seemed at the time.)

And now we come to 2021.

February saw "Georgette Heyer: A Century Spent Having a Ball – An Unconference," an online event featuring pre-taped discussions on Heyer from leading authors, academics and avid readers, held in celebration of the release of *Georgette Heyer, History and Historical Fiction*, edited by Sam Rayner and Kim Wilkins. A highlight of that event was the discussion called "Heyer: The Nonesuch of her Time and the Original Influencer," featuring Harriet Evans, Katie Fforde, Lois McMaster Bujold and Cathy Rentzenbrink.

September saw our very own Heyer convention – or, the start of it, at any rate – as we held an online "Day 1" instalment of HeyerCon I: *Soirée*. Highlights included scenes from the 1959 German movie version of *Arabella*, wonderfully introduced (not to mention subtitled) by Society member Jacqueline Meintzinger, and a fascinating panel discussion on Heyer's legacy, featuring Jen and acclaimed Regency authors Stephanie Laurens and Eloisa James.

Then just last week saw Sam Hirst – who appeared at the "Nonesuch" conference – returning to Heyer, with a huge day of papers presented in Romancing the Gothic's fantastic UK-based online event, "My Poor Devil: Georgette Heyer's *The Black Moth* at 100." Both Jen and I spoke, and program highlights included talks on highwaymen – because, Jack, you know – an historical dancing tutorial, and much more.

And now! Saturday, December 4 will give us the final Heyer conclave of the year, as the long-awaited in-person Day 2 of HeyerCon I: *Soirée* will take place in Melbourne. It is shaping up to be a day packed with Heyer goodness, and we are looking forward to seeing a number of you there! For those who can't attend in person – due to time zones/border restrictions/vaccination status etc. – we are so pleased that you can be included, regardless, via our livestream, or simply view the recording after the event.

We can't wait! And, even more, we can't wait to see what 2022 will bring, as appreciation of the treasure that is Georgette Heyer continues to grow.

– Rachel Hyland, Patroness, International Heyer Society

~ | ~

#48 – THE FORGOTTEN PATRONESS BY RACHEL HYLAND

Friday, December 3, 2021

It is always disconcerting to discover that something which you have always held to be true just isn't true at all. Like learning that Mozart did not compose the music for "Twinkle, Twinkle, Little Star," or that Jesus was not born in December, or that Napoleon Bonaparte was actually a perfectly respectable height, these small but indisputable paradigm shifts in what you thought was certain knowledge always occasion surprise, and often a disbelieving "What, really? *Really?!?*"

Such it is with the Patronesses of Almack's.

I knew – *knew* – that there were seven of these ladies, the arbiters of all that was seemly and fashionable in Regency London. I knew – *knew* – that these women were Lady Jersey, Lady Sefton, Lady Castlereagh, Lady Cowper, Countess Lieven, Princess Esterhazy, and the biggest stickler of them all, Mrs. Drummond-Burrell.

But I was mistaken.

I was led astray.

By Georgette Heyer, no less.

I feel so betrayed.

There was at least one additional Patroness of that most holy of subscription balls, the weekly assemblies at Almack's, during the Regency.

Her name was Mary Hill, Marchioness of Downshire.

Heard of her?

No. Me either.

It turns out, upon further analysis, however, that Lady Downshire does rate a few mentions in *Regency Buck*.

The first is when Charles Audley is discussing London notables that she might have met with Judith Taverner:

> "Oh, Colonel Hanger! Yes, I have met him, of course."
>
> "And disliked him very thoroughly," said the Captain, with a twinkle. "He is not such a bad fellow, but to tell you the truth, the Regent's intimates are never excessively well-liked by the rest of the world. Here is one of them tittuping up the parade now. You must go far before you will find McMahon's equal. There, the little man in the blue and buff uniform, bowing and scraping before Lady Downshire."

Lady Downshire shows up again later, when she is brought up by the fluttering Mrs. Scattergood:

> "Judith, my love," she said, very busy with the yards of fringe she was making, "did I tell you that I met Lady Downshire in East Street this morning? You must know that I walked back to Westfield Lodge with her."
>
> "No, you did not tell me," replied Miss Taverner, laying down her book. "Was there any reason why you should?"
>
> "Oh, none in the world! But I must own I was rather taken aback by her asking me when your engagement to Charles Audley was to be made known. I did not know what to say."

And then, in all of Heyer's novels, she is never heard from again!

But, in fact, there is ample evidence to suggest that she was definitely a Patroness of Almack's during the Regency. In his 2020 paper, "Mary Marchioness of Downshire and Baroness Sandys part 2," Martin Hill (yes relation) writes, quoting liberally from the Journal jointly kept by her daughters, Ladies Charlotte and Mary Hill:

> As seen already, MDS* and her family formed part of a wide circle of friendship. But prominent among those not it seems counted as friends are some of MDS' fellow Lady Patronesses of Almack's: it is early in 1816 that she joins this elite group of female fair arbiters, controlling the exclusive balls held at James Willis' Assembly Rooms in King Street, St James's. Mrs Drummond-Burrell, for example (as reported in the Journal), spoke *so ill naturedly about people... had acted most unjustifiably* – and the Countess of Sefton was *fine & disagreeable*.
>
> Altogether, the responsibility of being a Patroness told upon MDS: *Attended the Committee at Almacks. The Ladies were very disagreeable.* And again, *Drove to Almacks & Mr Willis was very angry and said he could do nothing with the Ladies, who all made separate decisions & were continually flying from one subject to another. So that the whole thing was in confusion.* Eventually, in February 1819, MDS resigns as a Patroness, *which is a considerable relief of trouble to us as well as to herself. Are very glad of it."*

So, from 1816 until 1819, Lady Downshire was definitely a Patroness of Almack's – as disagreeable a task as she (and her family) appear to have found it. Eighteen of Heyer's twenty-six Regency romances are set in 1816 or later, including the likes of *Arabella, The Grand Sophy* and *Frederica*, which take place largely in London during the Season... so why was Lady

Downshire, reputedly among the richest women in Britain at the time, excluded from her historical record, when she should absolutely have been there?

Perhaps it was simply that, as impeccable as Heyer's research always was, the particular pieces of proof that would have provided her with this knowledge (notably, the Hill girls' Journal, which is kept in trust by the family) just never came in her way. Or it might have been a conscious decision, keeping the topic of Almack's more manageable to both her and the reader—there were already seven different Patronesses mentioned, after all; did we really need another? Or maybe Heyer just didn't like her, or didn't feel she had enough of a sense of her as a person to create a believable simulacrum. (Although, I feel if Heyer had known about the acrimony in the ranks of the Patronesses during Lady Downshire's tenure, she would surely have used it as a throwaway piece of gossip somewhere or other.)

The possibilities are endless.

Nevertheless, it turns out that there were eight Patronesses of Almack's during the Regency. AT LEAST. There may yet be more to be uncovered (I hear whispers that Lady Bathurst may have been one… more research is called for), and certainly there were several notable ladies who took charge of the sacred Marriage Mart in earlier times: the Duchess of Devonshire in 1801, for example.

We will never know why Heyer chose not to include this information in her novels, or even whether she knew about it at all, but what we do now know is that, as much faith as we have in Heyer's historical accuracy, sometimes the things we think *we* know because *she* knew them are not all there is to know.

You know?   – *Rachel Hyland, Patroness, International Heyer Society*

* Mary Hill, Marchioness of Downshire, signed herself as both "MD" (Mary Downshire) and "MDS" (Mary Downshire Sandys), as she became Baroness Sandys in her own right in 1802.

~ | ~

#49 – *VENETIA* AND THE THEME OF SELFISHNESS BY SUSANNAH FULLERTON

Friday, December 10, 2021

I have always felt that *Venetia* is one of Georgette Heyer's best novels. It appeared after *Sylvester* and before *The Unknown Ajax* – she was obviously on a writing 'high' at this period of her life. I recently listened to *Venetia* on the excellent audio version read by Phyllida Nash, and was this time struck by its theme – selfishness. Almost every character in the story is incredibly selfish. Most of them are busy castigating Lord Damerel for his wicked and rakish behaviour, but none of them look realistically at themselves and see the huge range of faults they display. Probably it would make them too uncomfortable – far easier to criticise others – and of course it wouldn't be such a fine story without these demanding, inconsiderate characters. The lovely, intelligent and witty heroine of the book is simply surrounded by those who always consider themselves before others.

So, I decided to prepare a little talk on this theme, and this was part of the HeyerCon event held earlier this month in Melbourne, which I was unable to attend in person. But I'd like to share my talk as a little Christmas gift with all my fellow members of the International Heyer Society. Please just search "Georgette Heyer – Venetia" in YouTube, sit back and listen (it takes about 30 minutes). I do hope you enjoy it and would love to hear who you think is the most selfish character in the book.

Can I also challenge you all? Are there decisive themes to other Heyer novels? How about we all try and make a list, and perhaps someday I'll do more video talks on the books and themes you suggest. We all know that there is so much in any Heyer novel – humour, marvellous character portrayal, travel, family life, illness, growing up and learning, etc. But perhaps some novels stand out more in the way they focus on one particular theme. Here are some suggestions to get us all started (and feel free to disagree with me):

Sylvester – the theme of pride and prejudice
The Grand Sophy - the theme of family relationships
Cotillion – the theme of escape and going out into the world to learn
Friday's Child – ditto
Cousin Kate – the theme of madness
The Talisman Ring – the theme of mystery and mayhem

Now that we've made a start, do send in your comments and ideas. I'd love to hear from you.

May Christmas be (in the words of Jane Austen) "the season indeed for friendly meetings", and may 2022 bring us all travel, some Heyer events where we can meet in person, and of course lots of fabulous re-readings of our favourite novels.

– Susannah Fullerton, Patroness, International Heyer Society

~ | ~

#50 – THE GIFT OF HEYER BY COLLEEN REID

Friday, December 10, 2021

It was only when I recently joined this Society – and thank you for having me, dear Patronesses and my fellow members! It is a pleasure to be here – that I learned of the existence of the 2021 Folio Society edition of *Venetia*. *Venetia* is one of my favorite Heyer novels, the others being *The Grand Sophy*, *Faro's Daughter* and *Bath Tangle*, so learning that it had been chosen out of all of Heyer's works to be so honored really touched my heart.

And then it touched my wallet.

The book arrived one day, and I took it out of its package with my husband in the room. As I stood admiring it, turning it over and over in my hands, slipping it in and out of its slip cover and leafing through to pages to the illustrations, he stood there in disbelief, he looked at me in what I could only consider was disbelief, shaking his head.

Why, he quite suddenly demanded of me in what I can only call a censorious tone, had I felt the need to spend $89.95 in good American money, plus postage, for a book that I already owned in both hardcover and paperback?

"I also own it as an ebook," I told him, to be completely honest about it.

He just stared at me in what I took as silent condemnation.

I should mention, here, that my husband is not a Reader. Of the newspaper, yes. Of magazines dedicated to angling after many different kinds of fish, most of which are endemic to lakes and rivers far distant from those close to us in the American Midwest, and to which he will never travel, of course. But he has no love of books, and so the idea of having multiple copies of any one book, and spending what he considered a quite exorbitant sum for one of those copies, seemed to him outrageous.

He is not a pinchpenny, or a nipcheese, or a tight squeeze or any other Georgette Heyer word for what we would more commonly call a cheapskate nowadays. He just Does Not Get It.

Even though he still buys physical copies of the newspaper to read each day rather than just finding it all online, because having the paper between his fingers just *feels* right, according to him.

I attempted to explain it to him.

"But it is one of my *favorite* Heyers," I said earnestly. "And it is the only one that the Folio Society have ever published!"

"So?"

"So? So? So, the Folio Society is… it's an honor for a book to be published by them, don't you know that? It is a mark of a book, or an author's, importance. Their cultural significance. It is…"

He held up the catalog that arrived in the mail alongside my copy of *Venetia*.

"They also publish those *Game of Thrones* books," he said, his tone dismissive. "And *Spider-Man* comics, by the looks of things."

"Yes, and those are *culturally important*," I bit out, getting really very annoyed by now.

 I am married to a Philistine!

Smart man that he is, he took notice of my tone and began to backpedal quickly.

"Well… I guess… if you're happy with it… it's your money, after all…"

Damn right it is. I work hard for that money. If I want to spend some of it – all of it! – on books that are important to me, then I can and will.

"And I suppose… it's an attractive book, isn't it… the purple…"

Yes! And the illustrations are lovely! It's really very pretty indeed.

My continued silence hastened the end of this particular *tete-a-tete*.

"Well… I'll leave you to read it then, dear… take your time…"

"I wouldn't dream of reading it," I told him icily, and returned to admiring its many beauties.

But a thought occurred to me then. How had my husband known that the book cost $89.95 plus postage in good American money? I looked around for the bill of lading. Had it fallen out, had he seen it? No, it was still in the box. Then what on earth—?

I went in search of him. He was in his study, and in his hands he held a very familiarly shaped box, a slightly dejected look on his face.

Oh, I realized. *Oh!*

"Oh, sweetheart!" I exclaimed, and threw myself across the room and into his startled arms. "Is that… was that for me?"

"Yes. For Christmas," he said, his voice dejected.

I was overjoyed.

"Oh, I love it! I love it!" I cried, kissing him all over his face.

"But you already own it," he protested, but accepting the kisses.

"Yes, and now I own *two* copies!"

He, the poor dear, will never understand it. But I now own two copies of the Folio Society edition of *Venetia*, one of which was given to me by my husband, who is not a Reader and who does not at all understand how much this means to me.

And that is the best gift of all.

— *Colleen Reid, Guest Contributor*

~ | ~

#51 – CHRISTMAS WITH THE LANCASTERS BY RACHEL HYLAND

Friday, December 17, 2021

It should come as no surprise that there are many Christmases celebrated in the course of Georgette Heyer's incomplete epic *My Lord John*. A biography of John of Lancaster, 1st Duke of Bedford and third son of King Henry IV, from the age of four until the age of 22 (at which point the already lengthy work cuts off abruptly), the story deals in some detail with this somewhat obscure historical figure's often tumultuous early years.

We are not given the specifics of every Christmas time – or, in Medieval parlance, Christmas-tide – spent by our titular hero in the novel's timespan, but almost. And while sometimes the holiday is merely mentioned to mark the passing of the years, there are several passages in which we are given some insight into just how the King's household (and, perhaps by extension, 1400s England at large) tended to celebrate the occasion.

In Part I of the novel, when John and his siblings are mere children, they celebrate the season at Eltham Palace. (Henry IV spent ten of his thirteen Christmases as King at that residence, but his children were not always there with him, which seems a terrible oversight.)

> "There had been Christmas-tide, with mumming in the Great Hall, sweet music provided by Spanish Grandmother's foreign musicians, and a joculator who created illusions so astonishing that Johanna Waring signed herself, and muttered that it was sorcery. Father had visited the castle then; probably he had brought gifts for his sons, but they were forgotten too.
>
> All the King's children were at Eltham Palace that Christmas-tide, and there were tournaments held in honour of a distinguished visitor to England. This was none other than Manuel Paleologus, Emperor of Constantinople, who was making a tour of Western Europe in the endeavour to interest even-Christians in the fate of his capital.

(Placing this particular Christmas as that of 1400, when the Byzantine Emperor visited.)

So, there was music, and a "joculator" – a catch-all term for a wandering minstrel of varied talents and skills, from storytelling to juggling to, as in this case, magic. Also, there was mumming.

What, you may well ask, was mumming? If you're anything like me, you have a vague feeling of it being some kind of playacting, and then you never really enquired any more deeply into it.

And, yes, we were right, it is a kind of playacting, but there is more to it than that.

A "mummers' play," it turns out, is a rather specific form of entertainment, in that the story is always about two characters getting into a fight and one of them being saved by a doctor, often through the use of an unlikely potion of some sort. The combatants change (though St. George is a favourite hero in such plays), as does the skill of the Doctor, but that is the essential plot, as far as we know. Sadly, no scripts from the era survive, and – of course, as the way of the times; and, it must be said, now – the term mummers' play, and troupe of mummers (also known as guisers, given their often clever disguises), has been conflated with other forms of dramatic entertainment over the centuries. The earliest textual evidence of the content of a mummers' play comes from the 1700s, but we have anecdotal evidence going back to the late 13th century, and probably even further back than that.

What we do know is that troupes of mummers would roam the Medieval countryside, especially at holiday time, and make their living through presenting these plays in both the great houses and the lowliest of village taverns.

Another of our Lord John's Christmases spoken of in the novel, taking place when he is in his teens, sees him at Raby Castle in the north-east of England (which still stands and can be visited).

> He was at Raby for the twelve days of Christmas, bringing the Umfravilles in his train, and arriving at the dinner-hour, and to the sound of carols. My lord's own minstrels were singing "Of a rose, a lovely rose," but when my lord brought the Warden and his company into the Great Hall they struck up a fresh tune. The Lord John, recognising it, chuckled, and trod up the hall to the dais where the family sat. He kissed his aunt's hand, and told her that he knew very well who had bade the minstrels sing "For now is the time of Christmas." He sat down beside her, and while he dipped his hands in the bowl of water presented to him by the ewerer, and dried them with the napkin offered by one of my lord's pages, the minstrels sang the carol of my lady's mischievous choosing.
>
> *"... Let no man come into this hall*
> *Groom, page, nor yet marshal,*

But that some sport he bring withal!
For now is the time of Christmas!
If that he say he cannot sing,
Some other sport then let him bring!
That it may please at this feasting!
For now is the time of Christmas!
If he say he can naught do,
Then for my love ask him no mo',
But to the stocks then let him go!
For now is the time of Christmas!"

The Lord John, sending a gold noble spinning into the hands of the chief minstrel, said that he would be set in the stocks without more ado; and when my lady insisted that at least he could sing, proved her wrong by venturing his breaking voice in the refrain of "All this time this song is best: *Verbum caro factum est!*"

It was the merriest Christmas he could remember, the only thing to spoil it being the absence of his brothers.   *– My Lord John*, Part III, Two, 4

So much to unpack here! Firstly, let's take a look at the twelve days of Christmas. Many of us know of this tradition from the Christmas carol about far too many birds to receive as gifts, but what, actually, are the twelve days of Christmas? Well, in some sects of Christianity, Christmas Day is considered the first day, and the last on January 5, while with others the "twelfth night" occurs on January 6, making December 26 the first. Why, though, are twelve days of Christmas celebrated and not, say, fifteen days, or seven?

Because of the Wise Men.

They, we are told, took twelve days to travel to Bethlehem when they recognized Jesus as the son of God. The Epiphany – most often celebrated on January 6 – marks the day of their arrival, and the presentation of their gifts of gold, frankincense and myrrh (better than birds, certainly) to the infant messiah.

In some traditions, each of the twelve days celebrates a different saint; elsewhere, various festivals are held throughout the 12-day period marking the nativity, the miracle of the shepherds, and other such myths. In a more secular vein, it is believed that the twelve days of Christmas were instituted in 567 by the Roman Empire to allow for the differences among the various calendars used in Rome and in their far-flung conquered regions.

And how about that Christmas song? Variously attributed nowadays to an anonymous songster from the 15th, 16th or even 17th century, we have no information about how Heyer might have come upon it, but it is certainly evocative of the kinds of festive singing one might expect in the time of Henry IV, isn't it?

This particular Christmas is the most exhaustively covered throughout the whole novel, and more details of the festivities followed:

All Ralph's sons and daughters were at Raby that Christmas-tide, and the castle teemed with visitors. Supper for the Earl and Countess, for the Lord John, and for the noblest guests, was served in one of the solars, but the mumming and the minstrelsy took place in the Great Hall. This was warmed by an immense fire of logs, and lit by so many rushlights and candles that it was as light as day. There was certainly no chinchery about the entertainment offered to the King's third son. Every day a new diversion was presented to him. There were mimings, and tumblers; a troupe of sword and rope dancers; and a tregetour who snatched objects out of the air, and even caused a grimly lion to appear suddenly in the Hall. This made all the ladies shriek with fright, and shattered the stolidity of my lord's eldest son by his second marriage, a three-year-old bachelor who shamed his manhood by casting himself upon his nurse's bosom, and bawling much louder than any of the ladies. But just as the entertainment seemed to be fated to end in disaster the lion vanished, and where it had stood a vine shot up from amongst the rushes, and was seen to bear bunches of red and white grapes. Everyone agreed that the tregetour was the most cunning one ever to visit Raby;

and my lord's confessor, a very holy, sely man, misdoubted him that he used sorcery. He tried to discuss the matter with Friar Matthew, but the more worldly Dominican was applauding the dexterity of a joculator balancing timbrels, and paid him scant heed. His demeanour quite shocked Father Peter, and he could not, when the dancing began, forbear the thought that Father Matthew would have been glad to have taken a place in the ring of the traditional carole. He certainly hummed the tune which the dancers sang, and pointed out to his disapproving brother in Christ the nimblest dancers in the round.
– My Lord John, Part III, Two, 4

It may be supposed that, as they are entertaining the son the King this Christmas, the Umfravilles have gone to some trouble and expense to lay on all the entertainments they could muster, but there is definitely a suggestion that such glories were very much the norm during a Medieval festive season in a noble keep. A tregetour, by the way, is another name of a conjurer (but you got that from context, didn't you?). Timbrels, should you be unaware, are instruments like tambourines but with a cover on one side. And the "traditional carole" is a round dance set to a festive tune, usually sung by all, as well.

Our Lord John's Christmas of 1403 was filled with revels, usually under the auspices of his brother Harry – later, Henry V – who was a great one for night-time debauchery.

The usual Christmas jousts were being held at Smithfield, and more than one foreign knight was coming to England under safe-conduct to break a lance with him. Richard [Beauchamp] seemed to be determined to make his name as famous in the lists as ever the King's had been, and nothing, he austerely informed Harry, could more surely impair judgment of eye than night roistering.
– My Lord John, Part III, Three, 2

Most noteworthy here is the phrase "usual Christmas jousts." Because, yes, how jolly!

A few other Christmases are mentioned in passing over the remainder of the extant book, but none give us much more insight into how the occasion was celebrated amongst the Medieval elite (and, perhaps, among the yeomanry and peasantry, as well). Essentially, we learn of entertainments like mummings and tregetours, annual jousting competitions and Christmas carols sung and danced to. More than anything, we get the impression that the Medieval Christmas-tide was an excuse for everyone to enjoy themselves hugely, and that has not changed a whit, in the centuries since, for those of us who still celebrate this particular holiday. If anything, today's Christmas indulgences probably have more in common with the extremes of the early 15th century royal court as they do to the Regency elegance or Victorian conservatism that are nearer to us in years, but far from us in terms of our appetite for sheer decadence.

So, a Merry Medieval Christmas to all who wish for it! May your joculators be bewitching and all your jousts victorious.
– Rachel Hyland, Patroness, International Heyer Society

~ | ~

#52 – A VERY HEYER CHRISTMAS BY CLARA SHIPMAN

Friday, December 24, 2021

Long-time Society members may recall that last year at around this time, our Patroness Rachel Hyland sent out a *Weekly Post* detailing the Christmas traditions prevalent in the Regency period, as shown to us through Heyer's works. Until that time, I hadn't realized how often the season had been mentioned in Heyer, since often it is used merely as a marker of time passing and not really as a major plot point.

My personal history with Christmas is a bit of an weird one. My father is Jewish, but my mother is of good Protestant stock, so we tend to alternate holidays, one year lighting the candles for Hannukah and the next year lighting up the Christmas tree (and half the house). I know many people could make this claim, but I feel that there is no bigger fan of Christmas than my mom.

Perhaps because she only gets to go all out biennially, she enthusiastically turns our house into a holiday-themed wonderland the day after Thanksgiving, the Santas and the angels and the mistletoe and the nativity sets taking over even my childhood bedroom, not to be packed away again until mid-January.

If you ever wondered if the tinsel-strewn women in those Hallmark Christmas movies are real, then I can assure you, they exist and I am related to at least one of them.

2021 is a Shipman family Christmas year, and, inspired by Rachel's Heyer Christmas piece from last year, I have decided that from now on, I will insert my own tradition into the already pretty packed calendar of family events that my mom lines up for us every second December. (Caroling, cranberry and popcorn stringing, puzzling and a themed neighborhood scavenger hunt are just a few of these.)

I will read Heyer – particularly, I will read the Heyer novels that deal with Christmas. Oh, not the ones in which the holiday is merely mentioned in passing, like in *Arabella* or *The Nonesuch* or *Cousin Kate*. But the novels that are actually set, at least partially, at Christmas time.

These novels are *Simon the Coldheart, Sylvester, A Civil Contract, Bath Tangle, Friday's Child* and *Regency Buck.**

In *Simon the Coldheart*, the determined military commander of the title promises that he and his men will dine inside the walls of the besieged Belrémy Castle at Christmas. And Simon is a man of his word.

In *Sylvester*, our hero spends the holiday with his extended family at his country estate, and it is during this occasion that his fond mama becomes increasingly concerned about her son's aloof arrogance.

In *A Civil Contract*, the newly wed Adam and Jenny have their first holiday together, and dispense good will amongst all their tenants. And Mr. Chawleigh is there, who is always a blast, whenever he is on the page.

At Christmas time in *Bath Tangle*, Lady Serena is astonished to learn that her former fiancée Lord Rotherham is making himself agreeable to one Miss Emily Laleham, and she isn't quite sure how she feels about it.

In *Friday's Child*, newlyweds Lord and Lady Sheringham enjoy a jolly visit with friends (and give the theft-prone Jason a watch of his very own), while the beautiful Isobelle Milborne frets over whether to commit to the Duke of Severn by spending the holiday with him.

And in *Regency Buck*, an annoyed Judith Taverner is told in no uncertain terms by her guardian Lord Worth that she *will* celebrate Christmas at his country estate—but this might be just to ward off the royal duke who wanted to take her away to his royal residence, instead.

I cannot tell you how overjoyed I am at spending the holidays in such excellent company! And I highly recommend that you all do the same. Some time spent with Heyer is the best gift we can give ourselves, after all.

A Merry Christmas to everyone! And/or a Happy Hannukah, and/or a very joyous whatever it is you celebrate. (Or just have a great day, if you don't celebrate anything this time of year.)

And on a (or, on another) personal note, I just want to thank the Patronesses for all they have done for us this year, and for so kindly allowing me to continue to contribute to both *Nonpareil* and the *Weekly Post* throughout 2021, which has been a real honor. I look forward to sharing more of the joy of Heyer with the Society members in 2022!   *– Clara Shipman, Guest Contributor*

* Two other Heyer novels do, very notably, feature a Christmas theme: the mystery *Envious Casca* (or, as it was recently retitled and rereleased, *A Christmas Party*) and, as Rachel detailed in the last *Weekly Post*, the unfinished *My Lord John*… but I think I will skip both of those, this time around. I might be ready to reread them by Christmas, 2023, however.

AFTER GEORGETTE

Recommended Reading for the Heyer Fan

1066 AND ALL THAT BY W. C. SELLAR & R. J. YEATMAN (1930)

The funniest, yet silliest, history of England since Jane Austen's juvenile work, this short account takes the reader on that small isle's quest to become "top nation" through the reigns of successive monarchs and ever-increasing imperialism. A touch out of date, but still a whole lot of satirical, often nonsensical, fun for the Anglophile. (The sequel, *And Now All This*, may sound like it is a more recent stab at history, but is in fact a miscellany of pop psychology, geography, and mythology for some reason. Still fun, though.) – *Rachel Hyland*

A IS FOR ARSENIC: THE POISONS OF AGATHA CHRISTIE BY KATHRYN HARKUP

If you enjoy reading the crime novels of Georgette Heyer, you might well enjoy this. It goes into 14 different poisons that the other Queen of Crime uses to kill characters in her books, shows what her knowledge of them is, and explains how they work. I knew that Christie had worked with poisons in a dispensary, but had no idea that her knowledge of them was so extensive. – *Susannah Fullerton*

A CHRISTMAS CAROL BY CHARLES DICKENS (1843)

This famous novella was a hit from its first appearance nearly 200 years ago. This short but delightful book sold out within five days of publication – and no wonder! Its iconic old miser, Mr Scrooge, is a legendary literary figure whose very name has become a synonym for the meanest kind of person, and his story is about second chances and redemption and kindness. Full of wisdom, it is never preachy but, rather like a Christmas feast, is delicious and satisfying. So read it and enjoy. Merry Christmas and, as Tiny Tim would say: "God bless us, Every One!" – *Jennifer Kloester*

COLD COMFORT FARM BY STELLA GIBBONS (1932)

Georgette Heyer loved this book and so do I. Stella Gibbons' best-known novel is a very funny parody of the rural novels popular in the 1920s and 30s. It features the pragmatic town-dweller, Flora Poste, who descends upon the Starkadder family at their farm and proceeds to sort out their lives. Heyer said of her novel *Penhallow* that it was "getting hourly more Cold Comfort Farmish". Another reason to read both books. – *Jennifer Kloester*

CONTINENTAL DRIFTER BY TIM MOORE (2001)

King of the quirky travel narrative, in this outing Moore follows the footsteps taken by history's very first Grand Tourist, back in 1608. Moore does the trip, moreover, dressed in a 17th-century velvet suit, and driving a vintage Rolls Royce (in lieu of a carriage). Hilarious, educational, intriguing and inspiring. Not to mention leading to a good deal of travel envy, as do all of Moore's books, each one a real treat! – *Rachel Hyland*

THE DIARY OF A PROVINCIAL LADY BY E. M. DELAFIELD (1930)

From her often difficult neighbours to her always unsympathetic husband, her rambunctious children, and the household staff she in no way rules, this anonymous diarist shares the minutia of her life in an often wry and witty, but charmingly, adorably self-effacing, manner that is sure to delight any Heyer fan. The series continues as our lady leaves the provinces, and all are delightful, but the first is the best. – *Rachel Hyland*

THE DICTIONARY OF LOST WORDS BY PIP WILLIAMS (2020)

A novel born from the discovery of a missing word. Pip Williams picks up where Simon Winchester left off in his Surgeon of Crowthorne (another great read). This fictional tale tells the story of young Esme Nicholl and how the making of the *Oxford English Dictionary* became intertwined with her life. Clever, well-written and thought-provoking. – *Jennifer Kloester*

DOCTOR THORNE BY ANTHONY TROLLOPE (1858)

This is my favourite Trollope novel. It has so much to delight Georgette Heyer and Jane Austen enthusiasts – a spirited heroine, tangles over money, a ferocious matriarch, and a moving love story. Trollope is an addiction and once you get hooked, you have forty-seven of his novels with which to feed your addiction. – *Susannah Fullerton*

THE ENCHANTED APRIL BY ELIZABETH VON ARNIM (1922)

Four women rent a castle in Italy for a month and during that time they solve many of their problems, as Italy works its magic on them in different ways. Do listen to the superb audio reading by Eleanor Bron, and once you have read the book, you can also watch the movie version, which was filmed at the actual castle where the author herself stayed and where she set her novel. – *Susannah Fullerton*

EX LIBRIS BY ANNE FADIMAN (1998)

Those of us who love books tend to enjoy books about books. My favourite is *Ex Libris: Confessions of a Common Reader*. It's a collection of witty, delightful essays about loving books – arranging them, marrying someone whose book collection needs to be merged with one's own, literary gluttony, playing with books as a child (her father's 22 volumes of Trollope), and so much more. I simply adore these elegant essays (and you have to love a woman who names her dog Typo). – *Susannah Fullerton*

EXCELLENT WOMEN BY BARBARA PYM (1930)

Miss Mildred Lathbury is an unmarried woman in her thirties in 1950s London, in a world that is still recovering from the ravages of war. She is eminently respectable in every way, a stalwart in her church and kind friend to all. Into her small life come new neighbours, and into whose tempestuous relationship she becomes entangled, even as she is charmed by the smooth, careless Rocky. The story unfolds with warmth and wit, Mildred's often caustic inner-monologue often causing laughter, at other times cringe, at other times total empathy. Just lovely. A very excellent woman, indeed. – *Rachel Hyland*

THE GUERNSEY LITERARY AND POTATO PEEL PIE SOCIETY BY MARY ANN SHAFFER AND ANNIE BURROWS (2009)

If you haven't read it, I highly recommend you set aside and afternoon and curl up with Juliet Ashton and her letters to the people of Guernsey. The characters come to life and it will make you want to go to this Channel Island. A surprising novel, but such a compelling one. Delightful! – *Jennifer Kloester*

THE HELP BY KATHRYN STOCKETT (2009)

Highly entertaining and very moving, I loved *The Help*. A controversial novel because it was written by a white woman about the African-American experience, especially about the endemic racism endured in 1960s Mississippi, I admire its cleverness and insight. Written from the heart, the author grew up with women like those that the novel honours and esteems. – *Jennifer Kloester*

IMAGES AND SHADOWS: PART OF A LIFE BY IRIS ORIGO (1970)

A memoir by an English-Italian writer, it is simply fabulous. She grew up in the Villa Medici in Fiesole, married an Italian and created a wonderful house and garden in the Val d'Orcia, which I have been lucky enough to visit. I met her charming daughter Benedetta. The memoir is elegiac, packed with fascinating information and so beautifully written. – *Susannah Fullerton*

I SHALL BE NEAR TO YOU BY ERIN LINDSAY MCCABE (2014)

In this breath-taking novel our main couple, Rosetta and Jeremiah, are newly married, but that does not make their story any less romantic. Indeed, the opposite is true – the fact that Rosetta is so concerned for her husband off fighting the Confederacy that she Mulans herself into the Union Army to fight alongside him is the most remarkable of grand romantic gestures. Inspired by hundreds of true stories, this is an epic, moving tale that you won't soon forget. – *Rachel Hyland*

THE LADIES OF MISSALONGHI BY COLLEEN MCCULLOCH (1987)

If you've read the fabulous novel *The Blue Castle* by L. M. Montgomery you're bound to be intrigued by Colleen McCullough's *The Ladies of Missalonghi*. There are some decided similarities between the two novels, though one is set in Canada and the other in Australia. McCullough was accused of plagiarism, which makes the book even more interesting. – *Jennifer Kloester*

LEAVE IT TO PSMITH BY P. G. WODEHOUSE (1923)

Of all the genius comic creations of P, G. Wodehouse, my absolute favourite is the elegant, intelligent and sardonic Psmith. (Pronounced, of course, Smith.) Beginning in his school days, we get to see the carefree Psmith blossom, but it is in this fourth outing that he becomes an unlikely romantic figure, as he falls in love and is instantly made into a compelling leading man. If you have yet to make Psmith's acquaintance, do so right now! – *Rachel Hyland*

THE LIGHT YEARS BY ELIZABETH JANE HOWARD (1990)

I have recently adored this novel and its sequels, set just before and during WWII. Howard writes so evocatively of the lives of women and I know I'll feel bereft when I've finished the whole series, though there is the TV adaptation to then look forward to. The books in the series are: *The Light Years, Marking Time, Confusion, Casting Off* and *All Change*. – *Susannah Fullerton*

LORNA DOONE BY R. D. BLACKMORE (1869)

R.D. Blackmore's *Lorna Doone* was not an instant success. Only when it came out in a cheaper edition in 1870 did the novel suddenly take off. Thousands of little girls have been named Lorna as a result of it. It is a story of murder, revenge and passion, but I really love its wonderful descriptions of Exmoor, a very beautiful part of the world. Blackmore's prose makes you really see and feel the landscape. – *Susanna Fullerton*

MYTHOS BY STEPHEN FRY (2017)

The beloved actor, writer, host, wit, raconteur and Heyer fan takes on the myths of Ancient Greece with typical aplomb in this eminently readable, often very humorous and always entertaining retelling of some of the more compelling stories to come out of the Age of Heroes. Appropriately, the rest of Fry's *Mythos Trilogy* is rounded out with *Heroes* and *Troy*, and all three are positively sparkling with the kind of informative yet amusing historical detail of which Heyer must surely have approved. – *Rachel Hyland*

NEWT'S EMERALD BY GARTH NIX (2016)

I happened upon Garth Nix's work after discovering he was an avid Heyer fan. There is no better recommendation and so I devoured his Regency-with-magic novel *Newt's Emerald*. Full of hints of Heyer and homages to her many iconic moments, this is a fun fantasy with a stolen emerald, a cross-dressing heroine and plenty of action. Lots is familiar here, but this new take on the Regency novel is still a lovely book to curl up with. – *Jennifer Kloester*

THE PARIS LIBRARY BY JANET SKESLIEN CHARLES (2021)

A delightful read set in two time periods: one, based on the true story of the American Library in Paris and how it survived when the Nazis arrived in WWII, with a young, book-loving heroine named Odile; and the second set in the USA of the 1980s and 90s, with a young girl named Lily, grieving for her dead mother, who meets her mysterious neighbour Odile and starts learning French from her. This is a novel for those who love books and the city of Paris. – *Susannah Fullerton*

A POOR RELATION BY CAROLA DUNN (1990)

The indominable Rowena Caxton loses her home and fortune all on one terrible day, and is forced to take refuge with her (mostly abominable) relatives. Enter the Earl of Farleigh, newly come into his title and a kindred spirit the likes of which Rowena has never met. But will money keep these two apart? Ignore the lacklustre cover of the reissued digital edition – the novel was first published as a Harlequin Regency Romance, back when there were such things – as this is nonetheless an accomplished, thoroughly pleasant example of this ever-vanishing subgenre. – *Rachel Hyland*

POSSESSION BY A. S. BYATT (1990)

After reading *Possession* I was so impressed that I wrote to the author to congratulate her on it! From the moment of discovery by academic Roland Mitchell of hidden letters in a book in the London Library I was hooked! Part mystery, part romance, part literary adventure, this is a novel for any Heyer fan. – *Jennifer Kloester*

THE PURSUIT OF LOVE BY NANCY MITFORD (1945)

This book and its sequel *Love in a Cold Climate* were published in the 1940s and were instant bestsellers. I love her waspish style and ironic wit, the madly eccentric Radlett family and their friends, and the English settings. Mitford's shrewd understanding of the English class system, so well captured in her book *Noblesse Oblige* about the speech patterns of the different classes, is sure to delight readers of Heyer's novels. A new film version of *The Pursuit of Love* is due out soon. – *Susannah Fullerton*

A QUIET LIFE IN THE COUNTRY BY T. E. KINSEY (2015)

Elderly but far from frail, the widowed Lady Hardcastle takes up residence in a quaint town in pre-War England, putting her much-mentioned world adventuring behind her, determined to settle into a gentle retirement. But she and her devoted ladies' maid, Flo, are soon drawn into a local mystery, sending them to seek both below and above stairs for answers. Sparkling with humour and enchantingly depicting the friendship between my lady and her maid, this is the first in a very enjoyable series indeed. – *Rachel Hyland*

REBECCA BY DAPHNE DU MAURIER (1938)

One of my favourite novels with one of the most famous opening lines in English literature, Rebecca will take hold of you and not let go until the last page is turned. There's a great Hitchcock film and a new Netflix adaptation to enjoy but nothing beats this remarkable book. – *Jennifer Kloester*

THE REMAINS OF THE DAY BY KAZUO ISHIGURO (1989)

The life of Stevens, the very correct butler at Darlington Hall, is revealed with exquisite sympathy and pathos in this cleverly restrained work. Told by the dignified Stevens as he drives through an England of fading grandeur, he looks back on his life, his decisions, and his employer, with the unspoken suspicion that he might have gotten things very wrong. His clashes with Miss Kenton, the Hall's feisty onetime housekeeper, are a highlight. Masterful, subtle and thought-provoking. – *Rachel Hyland*

RULES FOR DATING A ROMANTIC HERO BY HARRIET EVANS (2014)

Harriet Evans is an avid reader and admirer of Georgette Heyer, and it shows. Her prose sparkles and her character building is deft, and though her stories are set in modern times, they still feel like they could easily be transported into any era. Especially this short, delightful novella, in which a "normal" young woman dates a marquis, and is forced to deal with all of the craziness that surrounds his ancestry, fame and family estate. Lovely, funny and romantic. – *Rachel Hyland*

THE STRANGE CASE OF THE ALCHEMIST'S DAUGHTER BY THEODORA GOSS (2017)

Told in rather scattershot fashion, in which the characters of the story oversee its construction (it makes sense when you read it), this is a book for avid readers. The alchemist's daughter is one Miss Mary Jekyll, who checks into her secretive father's mysterious death and soon meets the fractious Diana Hyde, along with Catherine Moreau, Beatrice Rappacini and Justine Frankenstein, while also uncovering a sinister plot by Victoria-era pseudo-scientists to rule the world. Throw in a suave appearance by ace detective Sherlock Holmes (whom Mary finds strangely attractive...), and this book becomes a thoroughly amusing experiment of fantastical imagining — and reimagining — that is a pure delight. – *Rachel Hyland*

A SUITABLE BOY BY VIKRAM SETH (1993)

What a joy to recently re-read this magisterial, panoramic and moving novel, packed with literary allusions and quotes. In so many ways, this is a 20thC Indian version of *Pride and Prejudice*. In spite of its weight, I just didn't want to put it down! – *Susanna Fullerton*

THE UNCOMMON READER BY ALAN BENNETT (2007)

In this wickedly funny and very clever novella, the Queen has a chance encounter with a mobile library outside Buckingham Palace. She feels obliged to borrow a book, and soon becomes addicted. I think it would have appealed to Georgette. Evidently, the Queen in real, not fictional, life, did enjoy Georgette's novels, but sadly Alan Bennett makes no mention of her. But I do so love this gem of a book! – *Susannah Fullerton*

THE VICAR OF WAKEFIELD BY OLIVER GOLDSMITH (1766)

I love this classic novel. It tells the story of Doctor Primrose and his family and is poignant, funny, surprising and very entertaining. This was a novel that Georgette Heyer also read and there are lots of Heyer-like moments in the book. Plenty of ups and downs long along the way but a guaranteed happy ending! – *Jennifer Kloester*

WEATHERLAND BY ALEXANDRA HARRIS (2016)

In most of Heyer's novels the weather is fine and characters are rarely stopped from driving in the park or doing some shopping. But in *Sylvester* the weather at the start is cold and miserable, Keighley gets a bad cold and Sylvester has to do more than he bargained for. Alexandra Harris's excellent book *Weatherland: Writers and Artists under English Skies* is a fabulous look at changing English attitudes to the weather and how it is reflected in books, poems and paintings. – *Susannah Fullerton*

WHITETHORN WOODS BY MAEVE BINCHY (2006)

My first Maeve Binchy book and still my favourite. She is a great storyteller and her characters leap off the page. I love the Irishness of her novels and the pictures she draws of life in Ireland a few decades ago. There's a miraculous well in Whitethorn Woods that inspires the local people and frustrates the village priest. Delicious! – *Jennifer Kloester*

THE WIND IN THE WILLOWS BY KENNETH GRAHAME (1922)

One of my all-time favourite novels, I first read about the adventures of Ratty, Mole, Toad and Badger when I was about eight. I was entranced. Toad was so naughty, Ratty so wise and shy Mole was a darling! It's a wonderful read-aloud and the audiobook with Sir Michael Hordern as badger is wonderful. It's also worth reading the play, *Toad of Toad Hall*, by A.A. Milne. – *Jennifer Kloester*

THE READING ROOM

Books about Georgette Heyer, and her work

ACTING ON IMPULSE - CONTEMPORARY SHORT STORIES BY GEORGETTE HEYER
(2019) Eight contemporary shorts, and one historical tragedy, with commentary from experts collected for the first time.

COMPLETE TO A SHADE - A CELEBRATION OF GEORGETTE HEYER
(2016) Discover the enormous pleasure of Georgette Heyer in this collection of reminiscences from some of her most ardent admirers.

GEORGETTE HEYER: A CRITICAL RETROSPECTIVE
(2001) Fully indexed collection of articles on the popular author's works, addressing such subjects as "Georgette Heyer and the Uses of Regency" and the like.

GEORGETTE HEYER: BIOGRAPHY OF A BEST-SELLER BY JENNIFER KLOESTER
(2011) The ground-breaking biography of one of the world's best-loved and bestselling authors. Who was the real Georgette Heyer?

GEORGETTE HEYER: HISTORY AND HISTORICAL FICTION
(2021) This intriguing collection brings together an eclectic range of chapters from scholars all over the world to explore the contexts of Heyer's career.

GEORGETTE HEYER'S REGENCY ENGLAND BY TERESA CHRIS
(1989) Join Judith Taverner, Annis Wychwood, the Prince Regent and more on a nostalgic, visual tour of Georgette Heyer's Regency England.

GEORGETTE HEYER'S REGENCY WORLD BY JENNIFER KLOESTER
(2005) The definitive guide for all fans of Georgette Heyer, Jane Austen, and the glittering Regency period.

THE GRAND TOUR - A TRAVEL GUIDE TO GEORGETTE HEYER'S LONDON
(2020) Visit important London landmarks, then and now, from hotels to gardens to the shops, homes and famous thoroughfares that were the playgrounds of the ton.

HEYER FOR BEGINNERS BY MAURA TAN
(2020) Contemporary fiction scholar and historical fiction naysayer Maura Tan takes a journey through Georgette Heyer, soon becoming a convert...

HEYER SOCIETY - ESSAYS ON THE LITERARY GENIUS OF GEORGETTE HEYER
(2018) Scholars, authors, bloggers and fans come together in a celebration of the works and worlds of Georgette Heyer.

THE PRIVATE WORLD OF GEORGETTE HEYER BY JOAN AIKEN HODGE
(1984) Lavishly illustrated, with extracts from her correspondence and references to her work, The Private World reveals a formidable and energetic woman.

READING HEYER: THE BLACK MOTH BY RACHEL HYLAND
(2018) An exploration of the great Georgette Heyer's seminal masterwork *The Black Moth*, taking a chapter-by-chapter look at the book's genius...

READING HEYER: POWDER AND PATCH BY RACHEL HYLAND
(2019) Bright, lively and incredibly detailed, this analysis exults in the novel's wit and historical nuance while also deploring the novel's heroine...

READING HEYER: SIMON THE COLDHEART BY RACHEL HYLAND
(2022) Looking at this one-time "suppressed" novel with a critical eye and a view to history, here Reading Heyer takes a turn towards the Mediaeval, with joyous results…

GEORGETTE HEYER'S BIBLIOGRAPHY

GEORGIAN NOVELS
The Black Moth (Constable, 1921)
The Transformation of Philip Jettan, aka *Powder and Patch* (Mills & Boon, 1923)
These Old Shades (William Heinemann, 1926)
The Masqueraders (William Heinemann, 1928)
Devil's Cub (William Heinemann, 1932)
The Convenient Marriage (William Heinemann, 1934)
The Talisman Ring (William Heinemann, 1936)
Faro's Daughter (William Heinemann, 1941)
REGENCY NOVELS
Regency Buck (William Heinemann, 1935)
An Infamous Army (William Heinemann, 1937)
The Spanish Bride (William Heinemann, 1940)
The Corinthian (William Heinemann, 1940)
Friday's Child (William Heinemann, 1944)
The Reluctant Widow (William Heinemann, 1946)
The Foundling (William Heinemann, 1948)
Arabella (William Heinemann, 1949)
The Grand Sophy (William Heinemann, 1950)
The Quiet Gentleman (William Heinemann, 1951)
Cotillion (William Heinemann, 1953)
The Toll-Gate (William Heinemann, 1954)
Bath Tangle (William Heinemann, 1955)
Sprig Muslin (William Heinemann, 1956)
April Lady (William Heinemann, 1957)
Sylvester, or the Wicked Uncle (William Heinemann, 1957)
Venetia (William Heinemann, 1958)
The Unknown Ajax (William Heinemann, 1959)
A Civil Contract (William Heinemann, 1961)
The Nonesuch (William Heinemann, 1962)
False Colours (The Bodley Head, 1963)
Frederica (The Bodley Head, 1965)
Black Sheep (The Bodley Head, 1966)
Cousin Kate (The Bodley Head, 1968)
Charity Girl (The Bodley Head, 1970)
Lady of Quality (The Bodley Head, 1972)
HISTORICAL NOVELS
The Great Roxhythe (Hutchinson, 1922)
Simon the Coldheart (William Heinemann, 1925)
Beauvallet (William Heinemann, 1929)
The Conqueror (William Heinemann, 1931)
Royal Escape (William Heinemann, 1938)
My Lord John (The Bodley Head, 1975)
CONTEMPORARY NOVELS
Instead of the Thorn (Hutchinson, 1923)
Helen (Longmans and Co., 1928)
Pastel (Longmans and Co., 1929)
Barren Corn (Longmans and Co., 1930)
DETECTIVE NOVELS
Footsteps in the Dark (Longmans and Co., 1932)
Why Shoot a Butler? (Longmans and Co., 1933)
The Unfinished Clue (Longmans and Co., 1934)
Death in the Stocks (Longmans and Co., 1935)
Behold, Here's Poison (Hodder & Stoughton, 1936)
They Found Him Dead (Hodder & Stoughton, 1937)
A Blunt Instrument (Hodder & Stoughton, 1938)
No Wind of Blame (Hodder & Stoughton, 1939)
Envious Casca (Hodder & Stoughton, 1941)
Penhallow (William Heinemann, 1942)
Duplicate Death (William Heinemann, 1951)
Detection Unlimited (William Heinemann, 1953)
SHORT STORY COLLECTIONS
Pistols for Two (William Heinemann, 1960)
Snowdrift and Other Stories (William Heinemann, 2016)
Acting on Impulse – Contemporary Short Stories by Georgette Heyer (Overlord, 2019)

GETTING TO KNOW YOU...

How old were you when you read your first Georgette Heyer novel?

What was it?

How did you discover her work?

Did Heyer lead you to read other authors in similar genres?

Which of her books have you read the most often?

Which, if any, would you never read again?

If you could be a Heyer heroine or hero, which would you choose?

Which Heyer hero or heroine would make the best husband/wife/partner?

How has Georgette Heyer influenced your life?

Send your responses to patronesses@heyersociety.com.
We'd love to hear from you!

JOIN THE INTERNATIONAL HEYER SOCIETY
AT
HEYERSOCIETY.COM

www.ingramcontent.com/pod-product-compliance
Lightning Source LLC
Chambersburg PA
CBHW081425090426
42740CB00017B/3180